FAITHI

MW01193340

ESSAYS ON WRITING MORMON HISTORY

FAITHFUL HISTORY

ESSAYS ON WRITING MORMON HISTORY

Edited By

George D. Smith

Signature Books   Salt Lake City   1992

To inquiring readers who confront their own biases of language and opinion with ambiguities from another age

COVER ILLUSTRATION: *ODESSA*, BY NEIL HADLOCK, 1987, LAQUER ON METAL, COURTESY JOHN KEAHEY

COVER DESIGN: JULIE EASTON

Printed on acid free paper.

96   95   94   93   92   6   5   4   3   2   1

Library of Congress Cataloging-in-Publication Data

Faithful History : essays on writing Mormon history / edited by George
    D. Smith.
        p.   cm.
        ISBN 1-56085-007-8
        1. Mormon Church—Historiography. 2. Church of Jesus Christ of
    Latter-day Saints—Historiography.   I. Smith, George D. (George
    Dempster)
    BX8611.F35   1992
289.3'072—dc20   91-21222
                                                         CIP

CONTENTS

EDITOR'S INTRODUCTION

THE TERM "FAITHFUL HISTORY" HAS AT LEAST TWO MEANINGS: HISTORY written to express and support religious faith, and history that attempts to be faithful to the past. In the Mormon community these two perspectives are usually labeled "traditional" and "new," and between them lies an on-going dialogue about the appropriate way to portray the Mormon past.

Recorded European history dates back to the Greeks. Herodotus (485-425 B.C.) was one of the first to write systematic history, but his record of Greece's war with Persia was influenced by national pride. Roman historian Livy (59 B.C.-17 A.D.) similarly extolled the heroism of his people. After the triumph of Christianity in the West, medieval historians, often members of the clergy, described past events from within a framework of Christian assumptions. Composing devout narratives, they presented history as God's plan that began with Genesis and ended with a vision of the Millennium and Judgment Day. Alternative views were not only unacceptable but heretical.

The recovery of Greek manuscripts during the Renaissance gave birth to a new historical tradition. As they studied multiple versions of the same event, Renaissance humanists asserted that history could be interpreted from more than one point of view. To separate factual information from legends, they began to evaluate, correct, and organize the material they collected. The rewriting of previously accepted historical and religious truths continued through the Protestant Reformation of the 1600s and into the Enlightenment with its emphasis on science and human progress.

Historical writing flourished in the Age of Romanticism when, for the first time, history was taught in schools throughout Europe. Nineteenth-century Romantics sought evidence of the human story in diaries, letters, and legal documents, and historiography developed into a social science.

By the early twentieth century, most accounts had abandoned God or any other organizing principle of human history. The focus of writing history shifted to the retrieval of verifiable facts and meaningful context. Context, however, has become elusive as linguistic theory has declared that language itself shapes human experience. If the nature of an event is defined by the language and mindset of the individual experiencing it, the story of the past necessarily varies with the narrator. Such relativist methodologies have placed modern religious historians in a milieu which no longer affirms God's authoritative presence or the possibility of a "true" account; therefore some traditionalists have added religious presuppositions to the terms of inquiry.

Religious traditionalists have generally resisted the secular redefinition of history. Nineteenth-century German theologian Friedrich Schleiermacher, commonly acknowledged as the father of modern Protestant theology, contended that historians cannot understand the spiritual side of faith unless they themselves have faith. Protestant churches split over the 1898 Fundamentalist Manifesto which opposed historical criticism and maintained that the Bible is inerrant, plenary, and literally true. But by the 1960s the Second Vatican Council began to encourage Roman Catholic scholars to use the tools of modern historiography to examine scriptural and ecclesiastical history. The resulting *Jerome Biblical Commentary* aroused concern among conservative Catholics when it endorsed critical evaluation of the Bible by affirming, for example, that several Hebrew writers, not Moses, wrote the first five books of the Old Testament.

At approximately the same time and using similar tools, the New Mormon History ignited similar controversy. Within the LDS community, traditional narratives of the supernatural have usually been taught as factual events. Beginning in the 1950s, however, professional Mormon historians with greater access to important primary documents have begun to present a more inclusive past. Historical inquiry has reexamined traditional accounts in the context of contemporary American culture and has challenged some of the sources. Thus Latter-day Saints have discovered that most early Mormons were probably unaware of Joseph Smith's "first vision," and that the accounts were retrospective and self-contradictory. Church members have also learned that the Word of Wisdom's dietary proscriptions coincided with a national temperance movement. And similarities have been found between Joseph Smith's revelation of the three degrees of afterlife glory and the contemporary writings of Thomas Dick and Emanuel Swedenborg. The new historiography has not attempted to argue whether Joseph Smith was a prophet or a fraud, but essentially to understand Mormonism as part of American religious experience.

Traditional Mormon historians, however, deny that the New Mormon History represents progress. They also typically reject compromises, such as the view that a mythical Book of Mormon can evince religious authenticity as "inspired redaction." Everything in the Book of Mormon, they say, must be accepted as historical fact. They also take issue with the methodology of New Mormon historians.

In support of their views, traditionalists incorporate theories from modern linguistics. They declare that objective truth cannot exist free of human interpretation. If all knowledge is bound by pre-knowledge, they say, no historian can be completely neutral; no "objective" record can exist; so-called "facts" demand interpretation. Thus in a world where knowledge is relative to point of view, traditionalists declare that their faithful interpretation is just as valid as that of the new school of history. Furthermore, they argue, the language of modern historiography is flawed because it is secular and excludes spiritual experiences which are essential to religious tradition. Historians who strive for objectivity have their own unconscious secular agendas based on presuppositions they cannot overcome. Only true believers can understand and write faithful history.

This discussion about alternative directions in LDS history continues. Current New Mormon Historians claim that they allow for the supernatural by recounting past religious experiences in the words of the people having them. Thus Joseph Smith's ideas deserve examination even though their inspiration cannot be verified; the words of the three witnesses express their beliefs but they cannot prove the authenticity of the Book of Mormon. From this perspective Mormon history addresses narratives of spiritual events without trying to authenticate them. Historian Malcolm R. Thorp comments, "It is not for historians to assign divine significance to those [human] events." Traditionalists counter that historians begin their search from a position of either faith or disbelief; if they challenge the validity of spiritual narratives it is because they lack faith.

The essays chosen for this compilation explore, in their own words, the perceptions of traditional and New Mormon Historians. History, myth, and legend are not always distinguishable, but there are some things we can know. The authors of these essays attempt to define the boundaries between objectivity and biases of belief and unbelief which may color what is written about the past. Readers should understand that different positions and perspectives are to be expected, that neither the authors nor the editor necessarily agrees with the views, criticisms, and conclusions reached in each of these essays.

Appreciation is extended to the following authors, publications, and publishers for permission to reproduce, sometimes under a different title, many of the essays appearing in this collection: to *Sunstone* for essays by Richard Sherlock, Edwin S. Gaustad, Lawrence Foster, C. Robert Mesle, Neal W. Kramer, David Earl Bohn, Malcolm R. Thorp, and Leonard J. Arrington; to *Dialogue: A Journal of Mormon Thought* for essays by Richard L. Bushman, Robert B. Flanders, and Kent E. Robson; to the *Journal of Mormon History* for the essay by Martin E. Marty; to the *John Whitmer Historical Association Journal* for the essay by Melvin T. Smith; to the *Utah Historical Quarterly* for the essay by Paul M. Edwards; and to Deseret Book and the Foundation for Ancient Research and Mormon Studies for the essay by Louis Midgley. Published here for the first time are "On Being a Mormon Historian (and Its Aftermath)," by D. Michael Quinn, and "Historicity of the Canon," by Edward H. Ashment.

1.
Faithful History

Richard L. Bushman

WRITTEN HISTORY RARELY SURVIVES THE THREE SCORE AND TEN YEARS allotted to the men who write it. Countless histories of the French Revolution have moved from bookstore shelves to library stacks since 1789. The same is true of any subject one could choose—the life of George Washington, the medieval papacy, or Egyptian burial rites. Historians constantly duplicate the work of their predecessors, and for reasons that are not always clear. The discovery of new materials does not sufficiently account for the endless parade of books on the same subject. It seems that volumes written even thirty or forty years before fail to persuade the next generation. The same materials must constantly be recast to be relevant, the past forever reinterpreted for the present.

Books on the framing of the Constitution written over the past hundred years illustrate the point. Through most of the nineteenth century, Americans conceived of the framers as distinguished statesmen, if not demi-gods, who formulated a plan of government which embodied the highest political wisdom and assured freedom to Americans so long as they remained true to constitutional principles. Near the end of the century, however, when certain provisions of the Constitution were invoked to prevent government regulation of economic excesses, reformers began to think of the Constitution less as a safeguard of absolute liberty than as a shield for greed and economic domination. Proposals for drastic revision began to circulate. Among advocates of reform was a young historian, Charles Beard, who set out to rewrite the story of the Constitution. As reported in *An Economic Interpretation of the Constitution,* Beard dis-

1

covered that most of the framers were wealthy men who feared popular attempts to encroach on property rights.[1] Naturally they introduced provisions which would forestall regulation of business by the democratic masses. The deployment of the Constitution in defense of business interests in the late nineteenth century was to be expected. The framers themselves were businessmen who had foreseen the tendency to attack property and had written a document that could be brought to the defense of business. Far from creating a government for all the people, they constituted the power of the republic so as to protect property. Their interests were narrow and by implication selfish.[2]

That interpretation caught on in the early twentieth century when the thrust of reform was to regulate business. For nearly twenty years historians found Beard's interpretation true to life as they knew it and faithfully taught his views to their students. Shortly after World War II, however, the temper of the times changed again. Business interests no longer appeared so malevolent; the Supreme Court had taken a brighter view of government regulation; and constitutional principles were invoked on behalf of civil rights and other libertarian causes. All told, the provisions protecting property no longer stood out so prominently, and people began to see once again the broader import of the document. A number of historians then began to attack Beard. They argued that all political leaders of the eighteenth century were men of property and that wealth did not distinguish those who favored the Constitution from those who opposed it. Rather than being protectors of class interests, the framers were seeking a balance in government that would keep order while preserving liberty, and they generally succeeded. Now the consensus of opinion has swung around once more to honor the framers as distinguished statesmen of unusual political wisdom who framed a constitution for which we can be thankful.

Presumably we are closer to the truth now than sixty years ago when Beard's views held sway. And yet for some it is disconcerting to observe the oscillations in historical fashion and to recognize how one's times affect the view of the past. Anyone unfamiliar with the writing of history may wonder why historians are such vacillating creatures. Are not the facts the facts and is not the historian's task no more than to lay them out in clear order? Why the continual variations in opinion? It seems reasonable that once told the story need only be amended as new facts come to light.

The reason for variation is that history is made by historians. Facts are not fixed in predetermined form merely awaiting discovery and description. They do not force themselves on the historian; we select and mold them. We cannot avoid sculpting the past because the record contains so many facts, all heaped together without recognizable shape. We must select certain ones and form them into a convincing story. Inevitably we come up with differing accounts of the same event. Take the following vignette, the individual components of which we will assume are factual: "Having come from a broken home, Jack yearned for a warm and stable family life. For many years he went out with different women without finding one he could love. At age thirty-four he finally met a woman who won his heart, and in his happiness he dreamed of creating the home he had missed in his childhood. In the fall of 1964, one month before their wedding, the woman withdrew from the engagement. Jack was heartbroken and deeply distressed. Two months later he entered the hospital and in three months was dead."

No explicit causes for the death are given, but we surmise a tangled psychic existence connected with Jack's ambivalence about marriage. He yearned for a wife and happy home life, and yet his experience as a boy prevented him from risking it until long after most men are married. When he finally found the right woman, the long pent-up desires were promised fruition. Her withdrawal shocked his nervous system and induced an ailment serious enough to kill him. Admittedly we have to read a lot into the story to reach that conclusion, but it is not implausible. If the historian only gave us those facts and we were of a psychological bent, we would probably believe the account.

But listen to a briefer narration from the same life: "Beginning in his last year in high school, Jack smoked two packs of cigarettes a day. In the winter of 1965, his doctor diagnosed lung cancer, and three months later he was dead." Aha, we say, now we have the truth. We do not have to resort to psychological theories to explain what happened. We all know what cigarettes can do.

But as careful historians we cannot yet close the case. The most obvious diagnosis is not necessarily the true one. Only a small fraction of those who smoke two packs of cigarettes a day contract lung cancer at age thirty-four. Smoking alone does not explain why

Jack was one of them. Can we rule out the possibility that psychic conflict broke his resistance and made him susceptible? I do not think we can, though most people prefer a more straightforward explanation. The point is that given the multitude of facts, historians, by picking and choosing, can make different but equally plausible stories, and it is difficult to demonstrate that only one of them is true. There is room for debate about the cause of Jack's death even when all the facts are in, including a medical autopsy. When so simple a case refuses to yield an indubitable result, think how interpretations of broad, complex events can vary: the motives of a presidential candidate, the causes of a war, or the origins of the Book of Mormon?

Notice also that neither of these explanations would have convinced reasonable people thirty or forty years ago. After the demise of romantic notions of broken-hearted lovers and before the currency of psychological ideas about psychosomatic disease, a death by a broken engagement would have sounded outlandish indeed. In the same period the connection between smoking and cancer was not yet established. The juxtaposition of two packs a day and a doctor's diagnosis would have been irrelevant, like linking the ownership of cats or a taste for bright neckties to tuberculosis. Nowadays, however, both theories make sense. New outlooks demand that past events be surveyed anew in search of relationships overlooked by earlier scholars. Reasonableness and plausibility, the *sine qua non* of good history, take on new meanings in each generation.

I doubt if any historian today thinks of history as a series of bead-like facts fixed in unchangeable order along the strings of time. The facts are more like blocks which each historian piles up as he or she chooses, which is why written history always assumes new shapes. I do not mean to say that historical materials are completely plastic. The facts cannot be forced into any form at all. Some statements can be proven wrong. But historians have much more leeway than a casual reading of history discloses. Our sense of relevance, our assumptions about human motivation and social causation, and the moral we wish readers to draw from the story—what we think is good and bad for society—all influence the outcome.

Perhaps the most important influence is the sense of relevance—what historians think is worth writing about. For that sense determines what part of the array of facts we will work with. When you consider all that has happened in the world's history—children reared, speeches given, gardens planted, armies annihilated, goods traded, men and women married, and so on, more important than how you answer a question is what question you ask in the first place. Not until you decide that you want to know the history of child-rearing, or oratory, or gardening do you even bother to look at all the facts on those subjects stored away in archives. A large part of creativity in writing history is the capacity to ask new questions that draw out previously neglected facts.

Fashions in historical questions come and go like other fashions, and these changes in the sense of relevance require that old stories be told anew. Beard's generation took great interest in economic forces. They wished to know (and we still do today) the wealth and sources of income of historical figures, the distribution of wealth through society, price levels, and the volume of trade and production. Earlier generations, particularly those before 1800, did not even think such facts important enough to record them properly. Economic historians today are hard pressed to answer the questions which interest them most. The same is true of demographers who bewail the failure of colonial Americans to take even a crude census before 1754. The present generation would also love to know the opinions and feelings of the poor and enslaved. One hundred and eighty years ago hardly anyone thought it worth the effort to record their thoughts. Now we must laboriously collect materials from scattered sources, speculate on the implications of the skimpy materials we have, and try to answer questions our generation is asking in order to make the past relevant for us.

To sum up, written history changes simply because history itself brings change. Were we exactly like our ancestors, their history would satisfy us just as their houses and clothes would. But time has altered our concerns, our beliefs, our values, just as it has changed our taste and technological skill. We need new histories that appeal to our views of causation, our sense of significance, and our moral concerns. Since the materials out of which histories are made are so vast and flexible, historians are forever rearranging old facts and assimilating new ones into accounts that will help men and women of the present understand the past.[3]

Historians nowadays are philosophical about the frailty of their work. Most of my contemporaries realize the next generation's books will supersede their own and are content to write for their own times. They know their work will pass into obsolescence just as architects build knowing their structures will come down. Looking at the matter realistically, we can probably hope for nothing more. So long as people change, their understanding of the past must also change. Even from a religious perspective, at least from a Mormon point of view, there can be no lasting history for mortals. So long as we progress, we will enjoy ever broader horizons, and these must inevitably reflect on our understanding of what went before. As our wisdom enlarges, we will see more deeply into all of our experiences. Only when we come to the limits of knowledge and intelligence will we reach the final truth about history.

Recognizing the contingency of written history does not mean we can dismiss it as trivial. No human activity, including the physical sciences, escapes these limitations. We must try to speak the truth about the past as earnestly as we try to tell the truth about anything. Accepting the inevitable role of beliefs and values in history simply compels us to examine more closely the concerns which influence us and to make sure that we write history with our truest and best values uppermost.

It seems to me that given these premises, Mormon historians, if they are given to philosophizing about their work, must ask themselves what values govern their scholarship. What determines their views of causation, their sense of significance, and their moral concerns? One might think that their religious convictions, their deepest personal commitments, would pervade their writing. But in my experience, religious faith has little influence on Mormon historians for an obvious reason: we are not simply Mormons but also middle-class Americans trained for the most part in secular institutions.

It is perfectly clear that all Mormons live by varying values and outlooks, not all of them religious. When we sell cars, we act like most car salespeople. When we preside over a ward or teach a gospel lesson, we act in another frame of mind. The two are not entirely separable, but we all sense the different spirit of business and church settings. Obviously different ideas and assumptions about life prevail in each place. Similarly, historians who are Mormons write history as they were taught in graduate school. The secular, decent, tolerant values of the university govern us. Indeed the liberal, scholarly outlook is the one we instinctively think of as objective, obvious, and natural, even though when we stop to think about it we know it is as much a set of biases as any other outlook.

That said, if given a choice would not most Latter-day Saints agree that their religious faith represents their best selves and their highest values? Is it not the perpetual quest of the religious person to have religious principles regulate all conduct, the selling of automobiles and the writing of history as well as Sunday preachments—in short, to do all things in faith? Abandoning the hope that we can write objective history, I think Mormon historians should at least ask how we might replace our conventional, secular American presuppositions with more of the penetrating insights of our faith.

I am not contending for orthodox history in the sense of adherence to one opinion. Gospel principles do not point toward one superior way of describing the past any more than they specify one kind of human personality. I doubt that God intends that we all be exactly alike. The possible styles of Mormon history are as varied as the people who write it. The authentic forms of Mormon-style history can emerge in the various works of only Mormon historians. They cannot be deduced from theological doctrines. All we can do in a theoretical vein is to speculate on some of the directions which Mormon historians might take, apart from those their secular colleagues choose to pursue. And that is what I intend to do in the remainder of this essay.

The Book of Mormon is a source of insight about the nature of history. Since Latter-day Saints believe it was written by prophets, we can assume that the extraneous cultural influences were largely subordinated to faith in its composition. What clues does the Book of Mormon offer about appropriate concerns for a Mormon historian?

As I read the book one pervasive theme is the tension between humanity and God. Class struggles, dynastic adventures, technological change, economic forces are all subordinated to this one overriding concern. Human obedience and divine intervention preoccupied the prophets who told the story. Where is God leading the Nephites? Will he help Nephi get the plates of Laban? Will Laman and Lemuel repent? Will God protect the Nephites on the voyage? Will they serve him in the new land? The prophets are most interested in what God does for people and their willingness in turn to serve him. All events take on meaning as they show God's power or as they depict people coming to him or falling away. The excitement of the story often lies in finding out what God will do next or how the people will respond. As would be expected of prophet-historians who had experienced God's glory, the fundamental axis of every story stretches between earth and heaven.

Presumably Mormon historians today might concentrate on the same relationship. Just as the concerns of the Progressive Era led historians to focus on economic forces, our concerns center on the hand of God in history. Nothing could be of more lasting importance. As we examine our best selves in moments of faith, God's presence seems to fill our consciousness as the ultimate source of meaning in life. Inevitably, we must ask how God has shaped human experience generally, just as historians overawed by industrialization and business power asked how economic forces affected the past.

Admittedly, we are not as gifted as prophets in discerning the hand of God or even the consequences of sin. Who can say where God intervened in the lives of Charlemagne or Napoleon or even in the formation of the Constitution? Belief in God is not a simple guide to relevant history. But our faith certainly compels us to search for him as best we can, and the scriptures suggest some avenues to follow. We know from our doctrine that God enters history in various ways: revelation, providential direction, and inspiration. Each of these offers an interpretive structure that puts God to the fore and suggests a strategy for Mormon historians. Someone someday may work out more systematically the implications of each of these perspectives and perhaps even approach a Mormon philosophy of history. But even on first inspection some of the possibilities—and problems—can be seen.

1. *Revelation.* We are most certain of divine intervention when prophets, whose judgment we trust, tell us God has spoken or acted. The most obvious subject for Mormon historians is the history of the church, the story of God's revelation to his people and the implementation of his will in the earth. Mormons are drawn to their past not merely out of ethnocentrism but because they see it as part of a divine work.

Faith in the revelations does not, however, determine how the story is told, not even its basic structure. The fundamental dramatic tension can be between the church and the world or between God and the church. In the first God establishes his kingdom and the Saints struggle to perform his work against the opposition of a wicked world. Joseph Fielding Smith's *Essentials in Church History* rests on this structure.[4] In the second, God tries to establish his kingdom, but the stubborn people whom he favors with revelation ignore him and must be brought up short. I know of no modern Mormon who has written in this vein, but it is common in the Bible and the Book of Mormon. Prophets mourn the declension of faith within the church more than they laud the righteousness of the Saints. In the first, the Saints are heroes and the world villains. In the second, the world is wicked, but so are the Saints. What we need are historians who will mourn the failings of the Saints out of honor for God instead of worshipping achievement because it proves God's favor, or relishing warts because they show the church was earthbound after all.

However we write our story, we cannot, of course, content ourselves with the history of the church, for statistically speaking it is a small part of world history. We must find some way of bringing a larger portion of humanity within our field of vision. The most common device among Mormons for comprehending the whole of world history within the scope of revelation has been the concept of a pattern—or dispensation—repeated through history to various people in many places. Usually an apostasy follows each dispensation so that history follows the path of an undulating curve. Each dispensation raises people toward God, who fall away, only to be lifted by a succeeding dispensation.

The archetype of this pattern was the "Great Apostasy," the period of time intervening from the dispensation of Jesus Christ to the restoration of the church through Joseph Smith. B. H. Roberts and James Talmage have most vividly explicated this period of history for Mormons with the liberal assistance of Protestant scholars who were equally committed to belief in the apostasy of the Roman church. (Indeed Roberts, Talmage, and James Barker may not have added anything to the findings of Protestant scholars.[5]) On this framework Mormons have hung the course of western civilization since Jesus. Milton Backman in *American Religions and the Rise of Mormonism* has filled in the picture with a more detailed account of the Protestant Reformation and the growth of tolerance prior to the emergence of Mormonism.[6] Together these works tell of the church's glory under the original twelve apostles, declension under Roman influence, upward movement with Protestantism and religious liberty, and climax in Joseph Smith and the restoration.

Beyond this one period the dispensation pattern is more

difficult to apply because scriptural and historical materials are much thinner. Milton Hunter's *Gospel Through the Ages* briefly told the whole story from Adam to the present, relying almost entirely on the scriptures.[7] But clearly the most significant advances in this area are those of Hugh Nibley. Nibley's innovation is to argue that the influence of revelation in the dispensation cycle does not end with apostasy; revelation leaves its mark long after people cut themselves off from God. Gnostics yearn for revelation and even counterfeit it; medieval Christians envy the temple when temple ceremonies are forgotten. In short the structure and aspirations of declining religion are derived from the revealed religions from which they sprang.[8] The dispensation pattern thus does not restrict itself to the people who figure in the scriptures. Revelation to prophets more or less directly influenced vast portions of world civilization, perhaps all of it.

My only misgiving about this method is its limited sympathy. Nibley's gospel framework may illuminate some aspects of a people's culture. But it may also distort a culture's values and purposes. According to Nibley, LDS temple ceremonies may have shaped Roman liturgy or Icelandic sagas, but does not time alter a culture until it means something different to the people absorbed in it than was originally intended? Should we not be sensitive to what the mass means to Catholics today as well as to the ordinances from which it is believed it was derived? If nothing else, our love for all people as part of God's progeny should caution us against stuffing them into our own categories. At its best, Nibley's analysis would show the interplay of what a religious tradition was originally and what history made of it.

For the most part, all the history written with an identifiable Mormon twist falls into two categories: history of the church or history of the dispensation cycle. The reason for this concentration is obvious. In both cases prophets tell us where God intervened. We do not have to rely on our own insight to make this difficult judgment. The historian has only to work out the implications of this divine action. God's part in other forms of history is far more conjectural, and historians have understandably shied away from them. Until we develop more precise techniques, these categories will probably remain mere theoretical possibilities.

2. *Providential direction.* A still broader historical scheme encompasses three of the national histories in scripture. The record

of the Nephites in the Book of Mormon, the Book of Ether, and the Old Testament have the same dramatic structure: God and humans interacting. Events in these three histories are not a shapeless heap of successes and failures; they are given meaning by the effort of God to choose and guide a people with whom he has covenanted. The idea of providential direction enters into the day-by-day story, but in addition, that direction gives a shape to the whole course of the histories. There comes a time when God casts off these covenanted people, after repeated apostasies, and they are then subject to national humiliation and suffering. For a time God abandons them, though not forever. In two cases he ultimately restores them, giving the histories a happy ending.

This divinely supervised rise, fall, and restoration is related to the dispensation cycle but stands above it as a pattern of its own. The history of a nation forms the next larger historical unit after the dispensation. It tells the whole story of a people, following the curve of their history along its ups and downs of various dispensations and apostasies, charting the overall ascent and decline.

Could this scriptural structure guide the study of all nations? Does God have a plan for them as well? Does their history follow a providential pattern? It seems to be a fact that all civilizations rise and fall much as Israel did. Could it be for similar reasons? Nibley suggests that the dispensation cycle could be enlarged to include many cultures. Could providential history apply to their nations too?

The possibility of broadening the scope of providential governance leads us to examine more carefully the causes of Israel's ascent and decline. The Old Testament leads one to believe that God rejected the Jews because they rejected him. The tribes of Israel entered into a covenant at Sinai, and when they consistently refused to honor it, God's patience wore thin. Finally he cast them aside. If that is all there is to it, Israel's case would apply only to covenanted nations. Egyptian and Hellenic civilizations would be another matter entirely. Not having been chosen, they could not be rejected. Providence must govern them according to another plan, and the Old Testament does not tell us what it is.

Possibly the Book of Mormon does. Much less is said there of original covenant and more of righteousness. The impression one receives is that righteousness brings peace and prosperity, while war and misery come close on the heels of sin. The people of Lehi declined when they persistently broke the commandments. Their fate was less dependent on a personal quarrel with God than on refusal to comply with his laws. By extrapolation, righteous behavior and the well-being of a civilization may be linked to gentiles as well as among covenanted people. The historian who understood divine laws well enough could perhaps explain the course of a nation's development.

A simplistic form of such a history could model itself after David McClelland's study of the achievement motive.[9] McClelland worked out a measure of people's desire for concrete achievements and used it to assess the presence of this need in popular literature over the past two or three centuries. To his delight the production of iron and steel, a rough indicator of economic growth, followed the ups and downs of his need achievement curve. Presumably when people decided to get things done, that desire ultimately improved the overall economy. A need for righteousness or for religion might yield similar results. Could it be that when pride increases so does civil strife, or when a nation humbles itself it enjoys peace?

The difficulties of this approach are obvious. How does one measure righteousness, and what kind of righteousness is most critical? What are the historical consequences of goodness? Wealth? Peace? An artistic flowering? Military power? Imperial conquest? I doubt that the relationship will be the simple one which held for McClelland. However it would be a mistake to give up on the scriptures as a source of historical understanding. We still might be able to derive a religious sociology and psychology which would illuminate national histories. We sense that virtue affects the quality of social life. Prophets have expressed the same sentiment rather emphatically. Can that insight be worked out in concrete historical instances? We may not be able to plot the course of a people through all of their history as the scriptures do for Israel. But perhaps we can penetrate lesser events or epochs to show providence at work governing the world by divine law.

3. *Inspiration.* Mormons have long entertained the vague belief that God guides all good people everywhere to various triumphs in art, government, and science. In general we have attributed the appearance of "the finer things" to the activity of the spirit of Christ, thereby reconciling our Mormon convictions with our commitment to middle-class American culture. I have no objection to this comforting belief so long as we do not fall prey to secularization of

the worst sort, that is, to clothe worldly values in religion. But what I have in mind as a program of historical research has a different purpose than the sanctification of culture heroes.

My proposal rests on two doctrines: spiritual death at the fall of Adam and spiritual life through the light of Christ. The assumption is that our separation from God wounded us and we desire to be healed. The truest and only completely satisfying course is to yield to the spirit of Christ which God sends to the world in lieu of his own presence. Following that spirit brings us eventually to God where we enter once again into his rest. But en route most humans are waylaid or deceived. They accept counterfeit gods and fruitlessly seek fulfillment in them. Rarely are individuals entirely defeated, for the spirit continues to strive with them, and they, however badly misled for a time, will always back away from their false gods and start again on a more promising path. Thus the search is perpetual, driven by humanity's deepest need. All of human history in this sense can be thought of as *heilige geschichte,* a quest for salvation.

The model for this mode of history, I must confess, is not the scriptures but Reinhold Niebuhr's *The Nature and Destiny of Man.*[10] Niebuhr's categories were human finitude and divine infinitude. We are limited and contingent but because of a divine component yearn to be infinite and free. Our quest has taken two major forms, romantic and classical, which roughly correspond to emotion and reason, loss of self in the senses and exaltation through the mind. The romantics are Dionysians, giving themselves over to feeling and seeking union with the All through sense and emotion. Classical figures are Apollonians. They seek order and control. The scientist is a classical person who tries to reduce all of life to laws of which he or she is perfectly certain and which afford complete control. Both of these styles are idols, Niebuhr argued, false and misleading efforts to be God, that eventually lead to tyranny and death. The only true way to reach the infinite is through worship, which permits us to reach God without claiming to be God ourselves. I do not subscribe entirely to Niebuhr's categories, although they are useful, but his model of incomplete humanity striving for completion does accord with the scriptural view of the human situation.

Furthermore, I find that the model works in historical research. My own academic interests center on studying religious and political thought in America in the early eighteenth century. Without

forcing the issue, I see people in this period attempting two things in
their ideological discourse. The first is describing life as it should be.
This generation was vexed by its own greed and contentiousness. The
self was forever getting in the way, venting bitter and rancorous
emotions, or pursuing its private interests at the expense of the
whole. People yearned for peace and union, ways of keeping the self
in check or of giving themselves to noble causes that would make
them forget the self. Union, tranquility, peace, harmony were among
their most prominent values, and these, I think, represent in some
way a response to the desire for the "rest of the Lord."

The second quest is for moral justification. People yearn to
prove themselves right, that is, to reconcile what they are with what
they think they should be. I am willing to work on the assumption
that our consciences are somehow related to the spirit of Christ.
Warped as moral standards sometimes appear to be, usually we find
behind specific standards of behavior an intention which we can
recognize as admirable in our own terms. What I am arguing is that
conscience is not entirely relative, though in detail it varies immensely. When we find people justifying themselves or setting standards for others, we see them wrestling with the influence of heaven.
These eighteenth-century figures, living as they did in a rapidly
expanding society, were forever contending with one another and
following naked self-interest in contradiction to what they believed
ought to be. Their tortured efforts to justify their actions I think open
a window on an authentic religious struggle.

All of this becomes interesting historically when we see
various ideals, sometimes disparate ones, working against a reality
which drives people to fight with themselves. The ideals and the
actual situation create a dynamic interplay which goes far to explain
specific events and to account for changes in ideology. In eighteenth-
century America, the ideal of harmony and the reality of conflict
moved people toward a new view of the social order that envisioned
life as compartmentalized, each person secluded and safe within the
bounds of his or her own rights, in short, an order more like our
present pluralistic society. This minimized contention and unleashed
ambition, but it also separated people from each other and required
another ideal to give moral significance to life: the free individual
progressing toward his or her own destiny. Nineteenth-century
Americans sought their salvation by pursuing that ideal.

Again without forcing the issue, I am convinced that people require a moral setting for their lives. They want to measure themselves against some standard, however grotesque, inarticulate, or irrational it may be. Life has to have purpose and meaning, to operate within a structure which describes existence as it should be and permits people to justify their exertions by some standard outside themselves. In some respects these moral frameworks are godly, and rightly attributed to the spirit of Christ. They seem to be among the chief means by which people undertake to save themselves.

The advantage of the history of salvation over the history of revelation or the history of providence is that the first applies to all people and permits, even demands, full sympathy with them. There is no danger of narrowness, which is inherent in concentrating on the locus of revelation or on the vicissitudes of covenanted nations. Its disadvantage is that it may blend imperceptibly with secular history. I confess my indebtedness to Niebuhr and to Carl Schorske, two non-Mormon historians. If these men write history as I aspire to write it, can I still claim to be working out of a Mormon heritage in response to the self I encounter in moments of faith?

This query brings me to my final point. There is a paradox in discussing the subject of Mormons writing history. On the one hand I wish to encourage Mormon historians, like Mormon psychologists and Mormon physicians, to think about the relationship of their faith to their professional practice. On the other hand I do not wish my categories to be thought of as prescriptive. I think it would be a mistake to set out to prove that nations rise and fall according to principles of righteousness outlined in the Book of Mormon. The outcome would probably be no more convincing than books which try to show principles of psychoanalysis governing novels. Such works always seem stilted, forced, and artificial.

Scriptural principles guide us toward more powerful works of history only when those principles are fully and naturally incorporated into our ways of thinking; so that when we look at the world we see it in these categories without lying to ourselves or neglecting any of the evidence. We must believe in our framework as sincerely as Progressive historians believed in economic forces or as any of our secular contemporaries believe in their theories of motivation or social change. It must be part of us, so much so that we will not consciously write as Mormons but simply as people who love God and are coming to see the world as he does.

Thus my history of the eighteenth century as a quest for salvation may partake of secular strains of thought. But I also know that for me it is religious as well. It is faithful history. As I look at the world in my best moments, this is how I see it. I am not lying to any part of myself, neither the part that prays nor that which interprets documents. If I am still a victim of secularism, the recourse is not to a more obviously Mormon approach but to repentance. Merely altering technique or a few ideas will not make the difference. My entire character, all the things which shape my vision of the world, must change.

The trouble with wishing to write history as a Mormon is that you cannot improve as a historian without improving as a person. The enlargement of moral insight, spiritual commitment, and critical intelligence are all bound together. We gain knowledge no faster than we are saved.

NOTES

1. Charles A. Beard, *An Economic Interpretation of the Constitution of the United States* (New York: Macmillan Co., 1913).

2. For an analysis of Beard's work and its intellectual milieu, see Richard Hofstadter, *The Progressive Historians: Turner, Beard, Parrington* (New York: Alfred A. Knopf, 1968), chaps, 1, 5-8.

3. The questions I raise are explored more fully in E. H. Carr, *What Is History?* (New York: St. Martin's Press, 1961).

4. Joseph Fielding Smith, *Essentials in Church History: A History of the Church from the Birth of Joseph Smith to the Present Time* . . . (Salt Lake City: Church of Jesus Christ of Latter-day Saints, 1922).

5. B. H. Roberts, *The "Falling Away," or, The World's Loss of the Christian Religion and Church* . . . (Salt Lake City: Deseret Book Co., 1931); James E. Talmage, *The Great Apostasy Considered in the Light of Scriptural and Secular History* (Salt Lake City: Deseret News Press, 1909); James L. Barker, *Apostasy from the Divine Church* (Salt Lake City: K. M. Barker, 1960).

6. Milton V. Backman, Jr., *American Religions and the Rise of Mormonism* (Salt Lake City: Deseret Book Co., 1965).

7. Milton R. Hunter, *The Gospel Through the Ages* (Salt Lake City: Stevens and Wallis, Inc., 1945).

8. Nibley's articles in church and secular journals as well as his books through 1967 are listed in Louis Midgley, "Hugh Nibley: A Short Bibliographical Note," *Dialogue: A Journal of Mormon Thought* 2 (Spring 1967): 119-21.

9. David C. McClelland, *The Achieving Society* (Princeton, NJ: Van Nostrand, 1961).

10. Reinhold Niebuhr, *The Nature and Destiny of Man: A Christian Interpretation* (New York: Scribner's Sons, 1941).

2.
The Irony of Mormon History

Paul M. Edwards

AN EARLY ISSUE OF *DIALOGUE: A JOURNAL OF MORMON THOUGHT* carried a remarkable article by Richard L. Bushman entitled "Faithful History."[1] Too appropriate to be coincidental there appeared in the same issue—though separated by what the second author would have called the "divided payoff"—an article by Samuel W. Taylor entitled "How to Read a Mormon Scholar." The juxtaposition of these two essays and their content is characteristic of the topic I would like to address: the idea of faithful history and some of the complexities and ironies arising when Mormons and historians open Pandora's box of mixed loyalties.

Perhaps I should clarify two points in order to preclude unnecessary confusion and judgments. My concern is with the Mormon movement in its widest perspective and with that wide historical search within Mormonism. We share so much in common it seems unnecessary at this point to be alerted to theological and social differences be they real or imagined.

Another definition concerns the term irony. I use the word "irony" to refer to the incongruity between that which is expected and that which occurs. Adopting its dramatic usage, I also refer to the fact that an audience is often more aware of the incongruity than the characters who voice it. Unlike some who use this word, I am not implying any metaphysical character to the irony and do not consider the situation to be negative or necessarily hopeless.

First, I would like to consider the concept of the faithful

historian about which so much has been written and so little said. Leonard J. Arrington in his tribute to President Joseph Fielding Smith introduces the question. He reports President Smith saying: "The chronicler of important events should not be deprived of his individuality; but if he willfully disregards the truth no matter what his standing may be, or how greatly he may be respected, he should be avoided."[2] I agree wholeheartedly.

Arrington goes on to say that "'Objectivity' for President Smith meant seeing that the history of the Church was presented in a positive light, rejecting the extreme and irresponsible charges of the Church's enemies." This is less clear; for it suggests that either the church (the larger Mormon movement in our case) is always positive, that extremes are necessarily wrong, or that non-positive statements about the church are either extreme or irresponsible. These positions do not seem defensible. My concern is not with Smith or Arrington—far from it. What does concern me, however, are these questions: questions of integrity and the integrity of questions.

Bushman in "Faithful History" brings the issue further to a head by saying that when a professional historian is being a good historian, he is being religious.[3] I agree. I would also assert that when a professional plumber is being a good plumber he is being religious. The common term in both these cases is "good" not historian or plumber. To suggest that the religious conviction of the historian alters history is a fallacy. Such convictions may well change the shape of the future, but they only confuse the understanding of the present. History which depends on an individual's faith becomes a proclamation of convictions, not a statement of the conviction of his or her inquiry. If we are interested in the former rather than the latter, then we should be searching for a pastor—not a historian.

We might profit here from distinguishing between a fairy tale and historical interpretation. The fairy tale represents permanent longings and concerns itself with traditional and unchallengeable convictions which are true despite evidence to the contrary. History begins with a willingness to consider the evidence, to challenge the story, to question the values, and to deal with the end as direction rather than conclusion. These two are often confused, and the confusion creates fallacies which denigrate the value of each.

Let me construct a hypothetical case aimed at no one but threatening us all. Many of the best things being done in Mormon history are being done by professional historians who have made their mark on areas other than Mormon history. This is understandable for a variety of reasons, not the least of which is economic. These men and women built their reputations by abiding by the rules of the academic disciplines to which they were subject or to rules they had publicly offered as their own. They played, in either case, according to a defined system which was subject to criticism and was internally defined by others playing the same game. Then these professionals, taking their credentials with them, turned their attention to the Mormon movement. In their new role they have focussed on concerns arising from their religious backgrounds and have produced works in a variety of media, all labeled "historical."

Because of their reputations we listen and open our minds to their presentations, assuming that they will bring the same level of responsibility and respectability to Mormonism. Instead we often find that they use their faith as a club with which to beat their perceptions. They involve themselves in methodologies and interpretations that deny their training and reputation. They answer the questions of their inquiries with straw men and women who weep in the face of contradiction. They seem to believe what they wanted to know in order not to be forced to know otherwise. We find these historians have gone into history in search of a text for their sermons rather than for an understanding of the past.

I can understand this hypothetical problem. I think I have been guilty of it. But I deplore it; it cannot be justified. If the answer to historical contradiction is faith—if we believe regardless of the evidence at our disposal—then we do not need historians. In fact, we do not need theologians. We already know all we are willing to believe. If the justification for this selective methodology is that the questions being asked are beyond reasons, then readers have the same right of selectivity. There is no "reason" for asking a reasonable and/or responsible person to interpret an illogical world. If what we want are logs for the fires of our expectation, we who are still unsure need psychiatrists, not historians, in order that history might be constructed in the light of our needs.

Bushman states, "The facts are more like blocks which each historian piles up as he chooses, which is why written history is always assuming new shapes."[4] This adopts the attitude of English historian James A. Froude without his ironic pessimism; for his statement was,

"It often seems to me as if history was like a child's box of letters, with which we can spell any word we please. We have only to pick out such letters as we want, arrange them as we like, and say nothing about those which do not suit our purpose."[5] I have no quarrel with Bushman as far as he goes, but it is the second part of Froude's quote which is important. There are many Mormon historians who do not seem in the least chagrined when they discover that all the uncomfortably shaped blocks remain.

Bushman affirms that Mormon history cannot emerge from "theological doctrine." This interesting statement is followed later by, "The Book of Mormon is a source of insight about the nature of history which Mormons have only begun to mine. Since it was written by prophets, we can assume the extraneous cultural influences were largely subordinated to faith."[6] This is a rather interesting assumption—one which would be seen by anyone else as a theological doctrine. With such a statement Bushman applies as a philosophy of history a theological assumption which is, I believe, inconsistent in terms of his essay. The role of the historian is not to prove religion. It is not, I believe, even to record the history of religion. It is to interpret the duration of a people who are, in this case, religious. Joseph Smith's experience in the sacred grove is not to be proven. At this stage it can only be dealt with. The difference for the Mormon movement is often the difference between "sanctioned" and "suspicious" histories.

John Stuart Mill's essay *On Liberty*—still the greatest piece ever written on intellectual honesty—suggests that freedom of thought must include protection against "the tyranny of prevailing opinion." His argument for the necessity of freedom warns us that silencing an opinion puts us into the position of ignoring the partly true on the grounds that it might also be partly false. "True" histories, when the word means edited and accepted, add to the prevailing opinion of the age. In doing so they fail to challenge traditions or more important to challenge the age with the prospect of growth.

Remember Mill's warning, "All silencing of discussion is an assumption of infallibility." This is the danger of our "positiveness." The greatest harm in persecution, particularly in the written word, is not done to those who are themselves heretics. Instead, as Mill has suggested, it is to those who are *not* heretics, because the mental development of the latter is stifled by fear of the position of heresy.

The danger of manipulated history is not really the danger that this year's history is more myth than narrative but that this year's historians will come to accept this myth as history's only offering. For thinking people belief in the potential of their processes is their source of energy. It will die when they find that they can no longer follow the light of their inquiry, carrying with them the belief that it makes a difference. When thinking people discover that they have become simply the connection between yesterday's prevailing concept and today's popular acceptance, they have lost the source of their initial inquiry.

When it becomes necessary to adjust one's thinking to the "truth," there is no way to avoid the corollary consideration that "truth" is no longer subject to challenge, that it is infallible. The suggestion of infallibility is a strange and ironic position for a movement dedicated to the progressive nature not only of humanity's involvement but, for portions of the movement, to the progressive nature of God.

The faith of historians is not faith that history will prove their point or that they can select events and parade phenomena to evaluate their longings. Nor is it obedience to a creed or a dogma. The faith of the historians of faith is that they believe in the unity of the world in such a way that whatever they discover in humanity, or in gods, good or bad, in support or in criticism of institutional views, their discoveries cannot help but express the divine nature of things and bring security to the dreams that are within us.

The problem is, however, more than just a question of integrity. It also deals with the integrity of questions. Much of what is being written in Mormon history answers questions that are no longer being asked. The expanded contribution we can make lies in understanding the nature of the questions to be asked. The concerns are not necessarily sacred grove experiences or missionary activities in England or lines of succession but problems that face the churches—questions which appear to this generation to be suspended in time. If ever people were in need of understanding both the legality of their doubts and the eternal nature of their paradoxes, it is now.

The answer appears to be, as Elbert Smith, oldest son of David H. Smith, used to say, that we stop setting the sun by our watches. We start to write history honestly. This means using as our restraints not the dictates of a traditional institution or heritage but the character of our discipline that has grown and is growing through analysis and self-criticism. Be a faithful person, be a faithful historian, be a faithful creature of God, and it is hard, as the saying goes, "to be false to any man."

A reevaluation of the questions being asked would alter the trends in the writing of Mormon history. I do not intend here a critique of Mormon historiography. For such a critique I would suggest readers consult works such as those of Robert B. Flanders or Marvin Hill.[7] I wish, however, to make a brief observation about these trends.

The ironic aspect of these trends is that we have not related the lesson of our religion to the value of our discipline. We have not allowed the revolutionary nature of the movement from which we have sprung to make us revolutionaries. The one thing about which we might all agree concerning Joseph Smith is that he was not the usual sort of person. He did not approach life itself—or his religious commitment—in a usual way. Yet the character of our historical investigation of Joseph Smith and his times has been primarily traditional, unimaginative, and lacking in any effort to find or create an epistemological methodology revolutionary enough to deal with the paradox of our movement. The irony of our position is that many of our methods and interpretations have become so traditional that they can only reinforce the fears of yesterday rather than nurture the seeds of tomorrow's dreams.

Many historians are asking us as a matter of pure historical credence to deny historical credence. None of us knows anything but second- or third-generation interpretations, and the basis from which we operate is one of historical acceptability. Our very involvement is evidence of the credibility of learning from and interpreting through history. We cannot assume that our discipline is unchanged if we study that discipline or that we can be Mormons and Mormon historians and not be changed by the fact that we are altering our present as we investigate our past.

My observation is that a good portion of our efforts are polemical. These works begin with the assumption that some people and some ideas are valuable in and of themselves as "recognized" masters of thought and action. Our histories are discussions of the correctness of these ideas. They appear designed to challenge not the idea but any suspicions that might arise about the ideas. Many discuss developments of the institution from the view that each new thinker, each new idea, must be evaluated as being "good" or "bad" in relation to that initial record. Probably the best example of this is Inez Smith Davis's history of the Reorganized Church of Jesus Christ of Latter Day Saints, *The Story of the Church.*[8]

One reason for this trend is that we act as if there were no permanent problems in Mormonism. The lack of perennial problems leaves the historian with the tendency to exaggerate individual greatness and to exaggerate the necessary contemporariness of even the most archaic of ideas and positions. An example of this is Stanley P. Hirshson's biography of Brigham Young, *The Lion of the Lord.*[9] Partial challenges have been the social and cultural histories such as those by James Allen and Marvin Hill, and the writings of Davis Bitton, S. George Ellsworth, Juanita Brooks, and Charles Peterson, and to a lesser degree by the articles appearing in *The Restoration Movement: Essays in Mormon History.*[10]

Another trend consists of those works designed to tell us what "really happened." These seemingly popular presentations bubble with the effervescence of "good faith." Two varieties are obvious. The first is what I call doxographical history. One example will make my point—Pearson H. Corbett's biography *Hyrum Smith: Patriarch.*[11] This is the cut-and-paste method of writing, wherein all that has ever been said by or about some person or topic is collected, cut into pieces, and molded into a puzzle of the author's peculiar design. It reports only what others have said and often tries to repaint old pictures using stiff brushes. Works of this kind simply confuse the issues, for in them truth appears to depend on the number of scraps of materials that can be collected.

F. Mark McKiernan's biography of Sidney Rigdon is another example of this methodology.[12] It is a valuable collection of information but only rarely a history, for it offers little interpretation. One suspects that each bit of information was collected and given importance simply because Sidney Rigdon's name appears on it.

The second variety of this "really was" view is the retrospective. In these works, each period is seen as a contribution to the previous; thus the new cannot contradict the old, and all "growth" is seen as evolutionary rather than revolutionary. Each bit of information is "yet more light." The retrospective is too committed to determinism—often even to predeterminism—which is strangely ironic for an institution in which agency is the clue to humanity.

One variety of the retrospection is the "speedy interpreta-tion." In this the author, called a "skimmer," tends to run through the forests of facts making virgin pronouncements before really seeing the trees. An example of the "growth retrospection" is the seven-volume history of the RLDS church.[13] These volumes make important contributions, for "Reorganites" have never maintained day books or statements of duration. However, they are not histories in the sense we have discussed; they are less than the Reorganization needs and less than the author could contribute if freed from the institutional format he inherited. Many problematic questions are easily avoided in selective piecemeal accounts.[14]

At this point may I encourage as an alternative the break-throughs in problematic history of which Max Parkin, Leonard Arrington, Davis Bitton, Robert Flanders, Klaus Hansen, and Warren Jennings have been good examples. By this I mean the development of the historical investigation which arises from the fact that histori-ans are puzzled human beings who are aware of the confusion of being contemporary men or women with a memory. These are people who ask themselves, "What is it that we are trying to understand?" and search and interpret in the realization of this query. But it is not just a question of being puzzled. It is more than that. We are talking about what it means to have the feeling of puzzlement. It includes the willingness to seek from the past and from the present and to do so in the hope that the search, even with some error, is the key to tomorrow. These people face the irony of the fact that Mormonism, which is integrated in its complexity, has been studied in such a disjointed fashion.

Such people leave the antiquarianism of their colleagues behind. They no longer delight in facts for facts' sake or in artifacts for artifacts' sake. They leave behind also scholastic pretense and have deserted their love for distinction. And they expose themselves to be the test of doubt in a world of assumed answers. So many Mormons who would be historians expend their energies in scholastic antiquar-ianism.

My third observation deals with the philosophy of history. Every attempt to sum up the totals of the past, to comprehend the past as a whole, to decipher or impose upon the past some ultimate meaning is a philosophy of history. To wait for an official philosophy of history is itself a philosophy of history. Few historians write from any consistent philosophical system, but their investigations are influenced by implied metaphysical assumptions. This is not the time for an analysis of these implied philosophies, but I would like to make some general observations about Mormon histories, Mormon historians, and philosophies of history.

Let me begin with the obvious by distinguishing between the past and history. The past is yesterday. It is that series of events and reactions to events, as well as memories of the memory of the events, which cannot be retrieved. They belong to yesterdays; and, like yesterdays, they have no existence, not even their present, except through their relation to tomorrow.

History, however, is what has been done to the past by those to whom the past is meaningful enough to be interpreted. The historian is a person who does things to and with the past so that *they* (the past and the historian) develop significance in the present. The manipulation is not by historians but of historians.[15] The mere massiveness of the past requires the classification and lumping of events and ideas, all of which are invented (like the term "restoration") to simplify, codify, and classify. All of these activities are intuitive and being so are not in the same category as the events they are designed to classify and explain. Hence the irony: the more "subjective" the system must be, the more "objective" we are called to be with it.

Remember also that historians deal with human beings. They deal with those who have commanded the attention of an era and who have emerged as the leaders and the led. They deal with what people are supposed to have done, the thoughts they are supposed to have had, and the decisions they came to—or did not come to.

What historians really want to know—and what they often give the impressions that they do know—is forever gone, as is the past about which they abstract. The historians' search for realities is a futile search, for what they find instead are Platonic images dancing on the cave wall. And their trauma is extended, for they are writing not only about strangers but for strangers. These readers are as incomprehensible in their own time as those about which we write.

So to round out the obvious, when historians try to present things they think they can say about the past, they must say it to humans who are strange, incomprehensible, predetermined in part by their environment, and more than a little suspicious. Unless historians write only for other historians (a dangerous vocation at best), they must deal with the influences of history upon those for whom they write.

Richard D. Poll, at the time a professor of history at Brigham Young University, stated in his timely article, "God and Man in History," that the Latter-day Saint church had no official philosophy of history. It seems to me he was telling us this as if it were in some way tragic. I view it as an evidence of modern miracles. Poll explains that by a philosophy of history he means "a central conception of what history is about. What does the process add up to?"[16] Poll is correct in pointing out that any attempt to draw a philosophy of history from the "doctrine of the church" has never been done. He makes a beautiful case for the inconsistencies rampant in those doctrines and suggests that the LDS have a tendency to venerate rather than a commitment to a sense of history.[17]

One example that Poll did not mention is the utopian concept of history which plagues the discipline with self-doubts. This concept anticipates that historical inquiry will support the idea that the source of our end and the salvation of our times will in fact arrive outside of history. I do not want to debate the theological aspects. But I believe such an assumption is ironic if not unhistorical. This paradox asks us to discover from our history that in the long run, history has no effect. The role of the personally involved God dealing in history when he feels it necessary may well be true. That is not my question. But if it is true, then history can lay no credit to, nor draw information from, such mundane things as cause and effect, prescription, duration, and certainly not the assumption of historical indeterminism.

The problem is that for many historians not only is God working out his visions on the anvil iron of history but what is assumed to be God's "visions" are often recorded as official truth. The historian is forced into the role of either anticipating history or remaking history. There is always the temptation as well—succumbed to in such works as Pearl Wilcox's *With the Latter Day Saints on the Missouri Frontier*[18]—to assume that "God wouldn't do that" in evaluating evidence.

Linked with this utopian image is another related problem, for one of the dangers inherent in our movement is that many historians take themselves far more seriously than they do their subject. Fawn Brodie, who is open for criticism from a dozen directions, seems to be most suspect when, as Rodman Paul points out, she is being sarcastic. Samuel W. Taylor is not always appreciated for his humor though it seems to me he is laughing at historians, not history. Gordon Mesley's sarcasm in *Courage* received more criticism than articles which questioned the historicity of the Book of Mormon.[19] At this point the primary necessity is not a philosophy of history but a philosophy or a doctrine of humanity which, I trust, will include historians.

I believe that a doctrine of humanity must be understood prior to our ever assembling any very significant theories of history. In the meantime, we must deal with that approach which arises from our own training and which is expressed within an existing series of philosophical and theological contexts that most of us neither understand nor would accept if we did. History is a serious subject, but people are not necessarily serious or always dedicated or reverent. Thus the humor which speaks truth has much to say to us.

Still another related question concerns the scarcity of Mormon scholarship. Rodman Paul, reflecting surprise that so little first-rate work had been done in Mormonism, suggested that it might be due to lack of curiosity necessary to inspire students.[20] I think an earlier comment in the same article might have been more indicative of the problem. First, it is true, as he suggests, that social scientists have rushed in where historians failed to tread. The problem is that they deal with Mormonism as a movement and then call it history. Thus what is known about us is descriptive of past behavior and is often considered prescriptive for future behavior rather than indicative either of present conditions or future extension.

I think sometimes sociological assumptions are decreed to be historical laws and then in turn philosophies of history. Empirical data, coming as they do from experience and observation of events, are called historical but are not until they include interpretation. They are only past—empirical past. A philosophy of history is not empirical. It does not try to tie events together by some external connection of these past events. Instead it tries to deal with all that is known in connection with some larger assumptions. These assumptions are a part of the imaginative nature of historians, assumptions which they cannot ignore, for they work within them to find meaning from the chaos of their factual data. A philosophy of history does not postulate this unity of process.

Likewise the attempt to support any historical presentation by a philosophy of history which is "proclaimed" rather than emerging is in vain. At the root of most proclaimed philosophies of history is the attempt to collect an army of facts and information to proselytize an official view of the past—at least the past as is presently present. Poll suggests some paradoxical characteristics of Mormon theology which will make an "Official Philosophy of History" difficult if not impossible. I would go further to suggest that having once arrived at these truths the problem of an official philosophy becomes moot.

Poll does discuss how he as an LDS historian handles some of the questions of faith that stem from his vocation. He affirms that (1) God is present in history as organizer, definer of goals, director, and influencer to the extent he keeps us moving toward these goals; and (2) divine intervention is to be expected at those points where it can "be no other way."[21] While in no way disparaging Poll, might I suggest that this statement is a theology of history not a philosophy of history, the difference being that a theology of history is based on an ultimate commitment which one holds in such a way that it is the organizer of evidence not the result of evidence. Thus I agree with Poll there is no "official" Mormon philosophy of history.

Finally I would like to present a postulate for consideration. I recognize a good deal of German historicism in the writing of Mormon history. I mean that there appears to be little distinction between method, subject matter, and procedures of the natural and human sciences. I feel we have not found the epistemological method necessary to deal with our history honestly while providing the foundation for historical judgments. Wilhelm Dilthey, a nineteenth-century German philosopher, presented an epistemology that I think might well work for us, but few have recognized it and fewer still have paid any attention to it.[22] Examining its scope and narrowing it in complexity, I would like to comment briefly on it here.

It is impossible to view the past as it "actually was." Nevertheless, we feel some compulsion to deal with the now non-existent past with some sense of objectivity in order for there to be historical judgments rather than contemporary opinion. For both Dilthey and John Dewey this "empirical" judgment is made on the "inner or conscious side" of the no-longer-present. Leonard Arrington introduced British historian and philosopher R. G. Collingwood and this general idea in an early issue of *Dialogue*.[23] By "inner" they mean the objectivity available within our present experience when we are reliving to our fullest that which is no longer present. The empirical grounds for our past, says Dewey, must somehow continue to exist. And he found the clue to that in critiquing momentary experience on the basis of long, honest, and assimilated historical evidence.

Inasmuch as this is possible, the integrity of historical inquiry begins with the realization that momentary dropping into history—as is the case with our doxographical authors—prevents us from sensing, knowing, or understanding the consciousness of external events. Since there is no way to avoid the fact that judgments about the past are based on the contemporary *us*, it seems that objectivity must start with projecting our own subjective selves into those external objective events we must consider. It means thinking, feeling, fearing, questioning; it means inventive and imaginative interpretation; it means applying human, personal judgments to those feelings that arose from our study. This is one of the major justifications for Mormons writing Mormon history, because we can more easily arrive at the inner consciousness of our Mormon predecessors.

When I use the terms "inventive" and "imaginative," I am not suggesting mystical daydreaming or myth-making. I am talking of imaginative minds as historically informed and molded minds which feel and sense beyond that which they can touch. Mormon historians must by all means take advantage of every disciplined means of self-correction and judgment possible. But having done that, they must not rest on the assumption that they have now been historians. For their job is not one of simply collecting but of appraising within themselves the meaning. There is more to being a historian than ascribing information; historians are people in time and as such they give human significance and divine involvement in time.[24]

History, I maintain, is a liberal art; and its contribution is not what it can find out but what it does to those who study it and are involved in it. Certainly it must be faithful to its own rules of research and evidence; and it must be free from the multitude of pressures which could twist the evidence, or the historians, to prove some position not subject to the quest. Historians paint on the canvas of life, but they neither make the canvas nor sell it. If historians are people of concern, commitment, faith, they will contribute such; they do not need to write history according to policy. This commitment to involvement supports what we already know—that it is interest, love of the past, willingness to become half lost in the imagination of previous days that is the historian's first tool and the one which few graduate students learn to use.

Of this kind of history Leonard Arrington writes, "Interpretation history must by its very nature be private and not a Church venture." I must agree, but my agreement lies in the fact that the church must always be the collector rather than the interpreter of history. Arrington goes on to say, "The Church itself must not be burdened with the responsibility of weighing the worth of one interpretation against another. Contrariwise, the historian ought to be free to suggest interpretation without placing his faith and loyalty on the line."[25] Again I agree, but this seems to be only more evidence against any "official history," for institutional histories are written by one person under different names.

In history the act of analysis is the act of synthesis. It is like passing through the countryside. The view is both witnessed and synthesized while passing. The knowledge we seek is to be acquired by penetration into the events; by living in the times; by assuming the doubts, the questions, as well as the joys of those who came before us. It is not, therefore, the result of either general laws of history or official philosophies of history.

Having said this, there may well be some doubt as to my faith. But let me leave this comment. I am both sinner and believer. Suspended as I am between the evils I point out and the visions I see, I do criticize but give voice to my faith. I am a faithful historian. I have faith in history. I also have theological faith. As well I have faith in the intellectual process and in the investigative outcome of that process. I believe that history investigated with integrity, fearlessly questioned, honestly systemized, and fairly presented is a far more ethical and rewarding road to mutual understanding and significant appreciation than are unchallenged and uninvestigated beliefs. I am not so unfeeling that I cannot understand those who fear the consequences of such open investigation. Yet I must assume such fears really are—paradoxically—a lack of faith. It is not difficult to become confused between faith and truth; but if I may, I would like to close with a quote from Sir Basil Henry Liddell-Hart, the British military historian and strategist, that bears some consideration: "Faith matters so much in times of crisis. One must have gone deep into history before reaching the conviction that truth matters more."

NOTES

1. Richard L. Bushman, "Faithful History," *Dialogue: A Journal of Mormon Thought* 4 (Winter 1969): 11.
2. Leonard J. Arrington, "Joseph Fielding Smith: Faithful Historian," *Dialogue: A Journal of Mormon Thought* 7 (Spring 1972): 23.
3. Bushman, "Faithful History," 11-17.
4. Ibid., 14.
5. James Anthony Froude, *Short Stories* (London, 1888), 7.
6. Bushman, "Faithful History," 16, 17.
7. Robert B. Flanders, "Writing on the Mormon Past," *Dialogue: A Journal of Mormon Thought* 1 (Aug. 1966): 46-61; Marvin S. Hill, "The Historiography of Mormonism," *Church History* 28 (Dec. 1959): 418-26. These are only two of many good works done recently.
8. Inez Smith Davis, *The Story of the Church* (Independence, MO: Herald House, 1943).
9. Stanley P. Hirshson, *The Lion of the Lord* (New York, 1969).
10. To cite just a few works: James B. Allen and Marvin S. Hill, eds., *Mormonism and American Culture* (New York, 1972); Juanita Brooks, *John Doyle Lee: Zealot, Pioneer, Builder, Scapegoat* (Glendale, CA, 1972); and F. Mark McKiernan, Alma R. Blair, and Paul M. Edwards, eds., *The Restoration Movement: Essays in Mormon History* (Lawrence, KS: Coronado Press, 1973). Many others are making a like contribution.
11. Pearson H. Corbett, *Hyrum Smith: Patriarch* (Salt Lake City: Bookcraft, 1971).
12. F. Mark McKiernan, *The Voice of One Crying in the Wilderness* (Lawrence, KS: Coronado Press, 1971).
13. Joseph Smith, Heman C. Smith, and F. Henry Edwards, *History of the Reorganized Church of Jesus Christ of Latter Day Saints*, 7 vols. (Independence, MO: Herald House, 1897-73).
14. Topics of significance have been suggested by many concerned with the development of Mormon history. James B. Allen and Richard O. Cowan, "The Twentieth Century: Challenge for Mormon Historians," *Dialogue: A Journal of Mormon Thought* 7 (Spring 1972): 26-36, is one excellent source. Other suggestions can be found in the *Utah History Research Bulletin* published by the Utah State Historical Society.
15. Compare Fawn M. Brodie, *Can We Manipulate the Past?* (Salt Lake City, 1970); Marvin S. Hill, "The Manipulation of History," *Dialogue: A Journal of Mormon Thought* 5 (Autumn 1970).

16. Richard D. Poll, "God and Man in History," *Dialogue: A Journal of Mormon Thought* 7 (Spring 1972): 101.

17. Ibid.

18. Pearl Wilcox, *With the Latter Day Saints on the Missouri Frontier* (Independence, MO: Herald House, 1973).

19. Gordon Mesley, "An Apostle Trips," *Courage: A Journal of History, Thought, and Action* 3 (Winter-Spring 1973): 138.

20. Paul W. Rodman, "The Mormons as a Theme in Western Historical Writing," *Journal of American History* 54 (Dec. 1967): 511.

21. Poll, "God and Man in History," 105-107.

22. For the best discussion of the concepts suggested here, see Howard N. Tuttle, *Wilhelm Dilthey's Philosophy of Historical Understanding* (Leiden, Neth., 1969).

23. Leonard J. Arrington, "The Search for Truth and Meaning in Mormon History," *Dialogue: A Journal of Mormon Thought* 7 (Summer 1968): 56-65.

24. Such a person is Alma Blair, whose years of interest and study have made him friend, teacher, and the professor of the church. His contribution has been as reflector, thinker, and as expounder and interpreter but most of all as a man to whom history has been his mentor.

25. Arrington, "The Search for Truth," 59-60.

3.
Some Reflections on the New Mormon History

Robert B. Flanders

IN THE LAST FORTY TO FIFTY YEARS A SIGNIFICANTLY DIFFERENT UNDER-standing of the Latter-day Saint past has begun to emerge in a series of books, journal articles, oral addresses at various conferences, and more informally, in a dialogue that has continued among the devotees of the inquiry. This significantly different understanding has been called the "New Mormon History." It differs from the "Old Mormon History" principally in a shift of interest and emphasis from polemics, from attacking or defending assumptions of faith. It is a shift from an evangelical towards a humanistic interest. As Mormon historian Richard Bushman put it, it is "a quest for identity rather than a quest for authority."

Historical studies embrace the most extensive, intensive, and well-matured of scholarly endeavors which have Mormonism as their subject. The paucity of critical writings in the various fields of theology and philosophy is by comparison especially striking. The phenomenon is understandable however. Mormonism as a religious culture is and always has been based heavily on a complex of histories—the histories of biblical peoples and of subsequent Judeo-Christian histories; the histories of pre-Columbian Americans; and especially the religious and secular histories of the United States. Finally the histories of the Latter-day Saints themselves and of Joseph Smith, the most important Mormon, have been crucial to all Latter-day Saint self-perceptions and to the images which they have attempted to present to the world. Of all these pasts, the most accessible to writers are the most recent. The Great Revival of 1800, the world of Joseph Smith and his generation, the religious environment of the time, the first vision, the writing of the Book of Mormon, Kirtland, Nauvoo, Utah of 1857, 1869, and 1890, and so on, are not irretrievably lost in the mists of time and myth. Students are blessed (and sometimes cursed) with an abundance of written records carefully preserved. It has been and continues to be inevitable that almost everyone with an interest in the religion of the Latter-day Saints shall read—and sometimes write—Mormon history. The generalization may be reversed—historians of Mormonism have shared an interest in and often a dedication to religious concerns. So Mormon studies have tended to be historical studies of Mormons themselves. The New Mormon History is based in religious concerns but is at the same time different from and a necessary precursor to critical religious studies yet to be written.

Practitioners of the Old Mormon History usually had a clear-cut position on Mormonism, either for or against, and tended to divide into two types: Defenders of the Faith (whatever their faith might be) and Yellow Journalists. With few exceptions, nonMormon practitioners were anti-Mormon, and likewise with few exceptions, Mormons were pro-Mormon. Ex-Mormons often became anti–Mormon. The New Mormon History, on the other hand, exhibits different characteristics in both practice and practitioner. Most of the new historians are professionals whose work exhibits critical-analytical techniques. Many are Latter-day Saints in background or persuasion, but their work seems influenced by their literary or their historical training as much as or perhaps more than by their religious training. Their point of view might be described generally as interested, sympathetic detachment. One senses a shift in mood too from Victorian romantic sentimentality to a more realistic and tragic sense of the past. The fact that some New Mormon Historians are not Latter-day Saints is an exception which proves the rule. In sum the New Mormon History is a modern history, informed by modern trends of thought, not only in history but in other humanistic and scientific disciplines as well, including philosophy, social psychology, economics, and religious studies.

There is a temptation at this point to indulge a favorite pastime of historians and discuss the historiography of the New Mormon History—that is, the history of its development. For the sake of conciseness in my primary purpose, I will forego that exercise. Suffice it to say that the trend under discussion is one in which the 1945 publication of Fawn M. Brodie's *No Man Knows My History* was a landmark. Certainly not all of the work published earlier should be called "Old History," and neither is the reverse true. However, Brodie's famous and influential biography of Joseph Smith clearly exemplifies both Old and New, and so is a transitional work. A new era dawned with her book. All subsequent serious studies of early Mormonism have necessarily had Brodie as a referent point.[1]

A generation or two later it is useful to analyze some of the implications of the New Mormon History for Latter-day Saints whom it has already touched during that time, as well as some possible future implications. The following discussion of these implications is divided into three topics: 1. The New History as an existential history; 2. The New History as a political history; and 3. The New History as an ecumenical history.

1. *The New History as an existential history*: Although new historians are not necessarily existentialist in their philosophy, there does appear in the New Mormon History a tendency for which the word "existential" is the most descriptive. Existentialism, briefly, protests against policies of action in which individual human beings are regarded as the helpless playthings of historical forces, or as wholly at the mercy of the operation of natural processes. It emphasizes the dignity and uniqueness of the individual human personality against claims and demands of monolithic social systems such as church or state. So the existential situation of humanity is often described as a series of agonizing moral choices to be faced by people privately and alone. These choices appear as dilemmas where the possible consequences are hidden from view and may be equivocal at best.

By contrast in the Old Mormon History life is inclined to be depicted as a morality play, where moral choices are simply between good or evil, right or wrong. The choices divide the cast of characters into White Hats and Black Hats. The Old Historians are seldom comfortable until everyone in the cast has settled on one side or the other. Furthermore for pro-Mormon Old Historians, individuals win esteem not necessarily for the dignity and humanity with which they confront dilemmas of the Mormon experience, but for their piety, their orthodoxy, and the ardor of their fealty to church leaders. In

reality the first generation of Latter-day Saints included many followers whose hearts were melted by the prophet's evangel but whose
heads were skeptical of some of his policies. Their anguish, unless
finally resolved in favor of a "sure testimony," was likely to cause them
to be ignored by Old Historians who desired to marshall a panoply
of faithful witnesses and to consign doubters to the side of the enemy
or to oblivion. (A number of names spring to mind in this regard:
Oliver Cowdery, Warren Parrish, John Corrill, Thomas B. Marsh,
John and David Whitmer, and William Law.) A special terminology
exists in the Old History to describe their experience: they "break"
with the church and become "apostates," who cease to exist in the
history. As an RLDS, I was fascinated in my student days to learn of
this exercise, because in the Old Mormon History of the Utah church,
the Reorganized Church and its generations of people have no
existence and are not only unaccounted for but by definition cannot
be accounted for. The Reorganized Church developed its own version of the same phenomenon, in which the vast majority of Latter-
day Saints drop from serious consideration after 1844 and with their
arch-villainous leader, Brigham Young, become stereotypical scapegoats.

     In the old *anti*-Mormon history the church was a tyranny, and
individuals within it were of little interest (top leaders excepted) until
they "escaped" and "exposed" Mormonism. Ex-Mormons who escaped to the east, like ex-communists who escaped to the West a
century later, were expected to write books detailing the horrors of
their experience. They also were expected to reinforce rather than
to alter significantly the existing stereotypes about the tyranny from
which they fled.

     The New Mormon History by contrast is interested in more
than the narrowly sectarian experience of Latter-day Saints. More
aware of and sympathetic toward the ambivalences of the human
condition, it tends to be more patient with the "slow of heart." There
are fewer apostates, few Mormon dupes and villains, at least in the
traditional sense of these terms. A "break with the church" is just as
likely to be interpreted as a political, economic, psychological, or
cultural phenomenon as it is a moral or spiritual failure on the one
hand or as an escape on the other. The New History is rediscovering
the lost people of the Mormon past—the ubiquitous dissenters and
the "churches of the Mormon dispersion," as Dale Morgan called the

splinter groups. There is even new interest in "enemies" of the church, who instead of being simply explained as the devil's tools are now imputed with human characteristics, their actions described, and their motives analyzed. The New History senses the multiple influences which play upon individual and group decisions, and so it fashions a more humane, less doctrinaire history. The New History understands that the shortcomings of the Old History were not so much that the answers it gave were necessarily false but that the questions it asked were often incomplete.

In short the New Mormon History is an existential history because it perceives the Latter-day Saint experience as a species of history not unrelated to other species of human history—of people and groups acting and interacting in process, in time, in space, in culture. Latter-day Saint history in its early generations becomes an American history, a nineteenth-century history, a protestant-revivalist-restorationist history, a corporate history, a nationalistic history, a white, predominately middle-class history, a mid-west and far-west history. Therefore almost necessarily it becomes a political history. So to the second point.

2. *The New History as a political history:* At the outset Joseph Smith's movement was essentially a kind of special religious revival containing restorationist, associational, and millennarian elements. It was no ordinary revival to be sure nor was Smith an ordinary revivalist. I use such a description to emphasize the *religious* character of the movement and of Smith's religious role at the beginning. It was to this new *religion* that the majority of first generation Mormons was converted.

However as the policies of the kingdom of God began to unfold in practice and in doctrine, the movement and Smith's role in it gained a political dimension with consequences which were both unanticipated and objectionable to some Mormon converts. This new politico-religious mix was evident in Missouri almost from the beginning of settlement in 1831, in Ohio at least from the mid-1830s, and in Illinois from 1840. In each case the Mormon corporation sought to influence and if possible to dominate the local power structure in regions which it colonized and finally to enlarge the parameters of its political action to include the state. In the "imperial" phase after 1842, the parameters were raised to the national and international level.

The character of this political activity I call "utopian politics" or "apocalyptic politics."[2] The coining of such strange terms requires an explanation, for utopian or apocalyptic conditions imply the absence of politics or the struggle over power. It is just such a peculiar—one might even say bizarre—incongruity which marked Mormon politics. In practice the Mormon political process was characterized by a unique and potent blend of the following: a rapid increase in local or regional Mormon population densities through conversions and "the gathering," a superior corporate organization with the operation of a pyramidal authority structure, a superior group discipline, a high degree of cultural homogeneity, a superior quality of internal communications, and sometimes a more rapid rate of economic development based on greater talent, motivation, and pooling of capital. Underlying these was a set of powerfully held faith assumptions centering around the notion that God was actively engaged in the work and would bring it to pass in apocalyptic fashion if necessary. "Men have a form of Godliness," Mormons reminded themselves and others, "but deny the power thereof."

Nevertheless everywhere the early Mormon political enterprises ultimately failed. They failed in part because the leaders, especially Joseph Smith, exercised unwise judgment and because the methods and objectives of Mormon politics were so radical—even revolutionary—that defection by Mormons from the enterprise was endemic and disruptive. But the greatest cause for failure before the move west was due to the fact that locals would not suffer Mormons to succeed. Gentiles responded to what they defined as "Mormon insurrection" with brutal, crushing, lethal overkill in the same way that they responded to black or Indian insurrections.

I mentioned that the political dimension of Mormons was in effect an unpleasant surprise for many Mormons. I do not mean to imply that political Mormonism was a *sub rosa* or underground movement cloaked in the guise of a religion, although this was a charge frequently leveled both at Smith and at Brigham Young after him. The doctrine of the political kingdom of God, including the notion of the union of church and state under the hegemony of the Mormon priesthood, was explicit well before Smith's death. However, events moved so fast, and the many-faceted character of the Mormon experience was so engrossing—the very excitement and drama of the whole was so engaging—that the implications I have described might well have been missed by individual Mormons until they were deeply involved in the enterprise.

Furthermore most Mormons were so captivated by Smith as a charismatic personality that they found it difficult to make a calculated assessment of his policies. (It is difficult for adherents of any radical reform movement to know how literally they should interpret the rhetoric of leadership. They assume that rhetoric to be exaggerated; but how much and in what areas? In the end Smith demonstrated that he had not greatly exaggerated his intentions.)

In any event the successive failure of the various early Mormon corporate enterprises through internal division and through what amounts to counter-revolutionary gentile vigilante actions was a double shock to Mormons. First, they suffered real and personal losses through lootings, burnings, and drivings. Second, they suffered from the realization that some of their faith assumptions about an apocalyptic kingdom triumphant might be faulty. The different ways in which Mormons reacted to these twin shocks were crucial determinants of the peculiar character of all subsequent Latter-day Saint sects.

One reaction was dissent from the doctrines of the political kingdom. Some Mormons gradually began to reject the notion of a literal, political kingdom of God. The Reorganized Church was the first large-scale expression of that rejection; but descendants of Brigham Young's followers also abandoned the political kingdom ideal around the turn of the century. Finally all surviving Mormons have accepted some version of the standard American denominational settlement between church and state, which includes the understanding that churches abstain from politics. The common acceptance of this settlement by church managers and members alike is what tends to make American churches traditionally conservative in politics as well as in social and economic spheres. The Mormon movement, which began by rebelling against that settlement, finally joined it. For Latter-day Saints, "apocalyptic politics" changed to "survival politics," which meant in effect the politics of accommodation.

It is ironic that Latter-day Saints have not only rejected the political kingdom but by successive acts of group forgetfulness have erased the matter from the traditions that they understand to be their history. Many Latter-day Saints know little or nothing of the political kingdom idea and have not even heard of the Council of Fifty. In 1966 Klaus Hansen, writing of Nauvoo as prototypical of the Mormon political kingdom, said, "In many ways Nauvoo was less the prototype of the [Mormon] future than was the Mormonism of those who rejected all the city stood for. Today kingdom building is frowned upon not only in Independence but in Salt Lake City as well."[3]

The New Mormon History has rediscovered the political dimension of early Mormonism. That dimension is now a main subject of at least three books (Leonard Arrington's *Great Basin Kingdom*, my *Nauvoo: Kingdom on the Mississippi*, and Klaus Hansen's *Quest for Empire: The Political Kingdom of God and the Council of Fifty in Mormon History*) and numerous essays. Consequently Latter-day Saints might well re-examine the bases of their self-identity, inasmuch as it is now clear that Mormonism was shaped early in a crucible of political conflict, rather than one of religious persecution alone. Equally important is the task of re-examining the terminology and ideology of the doctrine of the kingdom, which was in the first generation both literal and political.

3. *The New History as an ecumenical history:* Joseph Smith intended that the moral and spiritual chaos of the world should be resolved and replaced by one faith, one God, one church-state, in preparation for the Second Coming. That intention embodied a radical ecumenism to match in breadth and scope the secular and profane vision of Smith's contemporary, Karl Marx. By another of the many ironies of Mormon history, Smith's movement was nevertheless characterized by the tendency of members to split off and go their own way, a tendency brought about by an antinomian disposition within Mormonism which was difficult to control. This centrifugal tendency was a constant embarrassment and a real weakness which Smith inveighed against with only partial success. He became almost paranoid about dissenters; and indeed it was the great schism of 1844 that led indirectly to his death. That tragic event precipitated a succession crisis which brought the greatest fragmentation of all, a fragmentation which has continued to the present. The Church of Jesus Christ of Latter-day Saints has done its best to ignore and even deny the existence of any devotees of Joseph Smith who are not in its own fellowship, while the Reorganized Church has achieved its traditional identity by the affirmation, "we are not Mormons." In short the modern self-identities of most Latter-day Saints are based

in part on discrete sectarian polarities growing out of an historical fragmentation.

But sectarian grounds alone are inadequate for religious and cultural self-identity. Indeed in the world of the late twentieth century, all narrow self-definitions, whether sectarian, ideological, national, racial, or whatever, need to be superceded by more humane, more ecumenical self-definitions. The New Mormon History suggests the possibility that the sectarian self-identities with which Latter-day Saints of whatever denomination have had to live may become less exclusive and more inclusive. The New History urges upon the Saints the fact that all people of the Restoration movement have had a common past despite themselves. Saints have survived and endured even if they have done so separately. If an LDS asks an RLDS (or vice versa), "Is your religious history legitimate?" the proper answer should be, "My religious history is authentic." Which is of course an answer to a different question. Like all peoples who have a rich heritage but suffer from cultural isolation or estrangement, Latter-day Saints need to discover authentic pasts other than their own. The New Mormon History is more diverse than the old but also more inclusive. All Mormons are there. So are non-Mormons and ex–Mormons. As a final generalization the New History attests that there is a common Mormon history that all Latter-day Saints share and that is indeed authentic.

Late one night several years ago, a new LDS friend asked me as a consequence of several hours of conversation about our common faith, "Do you think the two churches will ever unite?" My answer then was equivocal. But now with some additional understanding perhaps, I would answer that they will not and probably cannot given the fact that each rests upon the same institutional foundation of Joseph Smith's doctrine of an exclusive authority structure. The question, "Will the churches unite?" should be superseded now by a different question: "Will each accept the other's history, as well as the common history, and be informed by it?"

There is another dimension of the New History as an ecumenical history. Not only do Latter-day Saints have the framework within which to understand their past as existential history rather than as a branch of dogmatics and polemics, but interested people who are not Latter-day Saints and who do not share Mormon faith assumptions also have the opportunity to discover Mormon history as a legitimate rather than an aberrant phenomenon in American culture. As a result of these two developments, a kind of new middle ground has been created between those with and those without LDS faith assumptions, with the accompanying possibility of communication between them that does not have to struggle with the *a priori* issue of the legitimacy of faith assumptions. Such middle ground is created when mutual interest in the existential history of the Latter-day Saints replaces mutual anxiety over dogma. Additionally it has provided a new location where "marginal" Latter-day Saints, who hold some faith assumptions but reject others or who are attached to Mormon societies or social networks but not to the religion *per se*, can share in the dialogue about the significance of the Mormon experience. The New Mormon History may enable such people to discover a more comfortable and acceptable definition of their situation *vis a vis* both Mormons and non-Mormons.

There is no doubt that the most profound dialogue now occurring between LDS and RLDS people goes on among those who are readers and writers of the New Mormon History (including a few non-Mormons). The dialogue is about history, but it is also very importantly about religion. It is a discussion of religious experience. But the dialogue has become a religious experience of Christian fellowship in its own right. The spring 1974 meeting of the Mormon History Association in Nauvoo was a memorable experience of probing, of sharing, of fellowship, of love. It was for many people both a culmination and a commencement. At the closing fellowship service, one participant said simply, "I walked at dawn today with my friends in the streets of Nauvoo. I thank God for my friends, and I thank God for the streets of Nauvoo." So the dialogue proceeds in the classic manner of modern ecumenism. Viewed in the traditional sectarian frame, this New History dialogue is a threat to sectarian boundaries. The threat is real. At the same time the tendency is a conservative one—its ultimate purpose is to recover, to preserve, and to augment the faith of the fathers and the mothers. It lays the groundwork for a fourth history—a religious history.

History is one of civilization's most important service enterprises. The ends which it serves shift according to the values of people. The New Mormon History is a response to such shifting values. Latter-day Saints, like people of different faiths and persuasions, increasingly seek the services of a history that will aid them in ending their isolation; a history that will help dissolve arcane enmities and offer their children a tradition which is less parochial, less tribal, more humane, more universal. Here is the real meaning of the New History as an ecumenical history. It does not suggest that people of good will should not differ but rather that people of good will should seek a mature understanding of their differences and of their commonwealth.

NOTES

1. See Marvin S. Hill, "Secular or Sectarian History? A Critique of *No Man Knows My History*," *Church History* 43 (Mar. 1974): 78-96, for an important discussion not only of Brodie but of many large issues in Mormon religious history.

2. See my "The Kingdom of God in Illinois: Politics in Utopia," *Dialogue: A Journal of Mormon Thought* 5 (Spring 1970): 26-36.

3. "The World and the Prophet," *Dialogue: A Journal of Mormon Thought* 1 (Summer 1966): 107.

4.
The Gospel Beyond Time: Thoughts on the Relation of Faith and Historical Knowledge

Richard Sherlock

IN THE LAST QUARTER CENTURY WE HAVE WITNESSED A REMARKABLE renaissance in the scholarly study of the Mormon faith and experience. Several disciplines have contributed to this blossoming but none as profoundly as the study of history. Given the Mormon propensity for record keeping, for genealogy, and for family history, this emphasis is hardly surprising. But history potentially poses profound questions for a community of faith, and no other liberal arts study is as likely to necessitate reevaluation of our self-image as a people.

My thesis is simple: The study of history raises questions that we Mormons have yet to consider seriously. In this essay I will first discuss some of these questions and then offer some suggestions about how we might face the difficulties posed by the scholarly examination of our past.

Better than two decades ago James Allen published a pathbreaking essay on Joseph Smith's first vision as a historical event. Allen made two important points concerning the experience. He pointed out that the version we have in our Pearl of Great Price is not the only nor is it the earliest such account. It is a rather late version, and unlike some others, it was not written in Joseph Smith's own hand. Second, he called attention to the fact that in the earliest days of the church, the story was largely unknown and therefore not used for missionary purposes. When it did become known and widely quoted in the church, it was not used for the missionary or devotional purposes we use it for now.

Subsequent research has confirmed these conclusions. We now know that there are eight separate versions of the first vision. We know that the canonical version is one of the latest. Most significantly, we know that all eight versions differ in ways that are significant and sometimes theologically crucial. We also know that the early church was largely ignorant of these versions. It was not until publication of the canonical account that any attention was paid to the experience. Even after that time it was used to buttress Joseph Smith's prophetic authority and not to demonstrate the existence of God and Jesus Christ as separate material beings.

Given so many primary sources, historians do not of course throw up their hands in dismay. They analyze each document to see if it is spurious. They check handwriting. Is it Joseph Smith's or that of a known and trusted scribe or simply that of someone to whom Joseph Smith told the story? Are some versions more accurate in describing confirmable details than others? Are others less so?

The critical question, however, is where does such study lead? It leads finally to a probable conclusion about the precise character of the event. Historians give their best judgment that one of the versions is better than another, that there are irreconcilable differences among them, and so on. Their judgment is based on skill, training, and experience, but it is, nevertheless, a human judgment. No matter how certain they may be, they cannot declare one of these versions to be definitive in the life and faith of the church.

The potential problem lies in the tentative quality of the historian's conclusions. Historians operate on the basis of presuppositions (impartiality, evidentiary relevance, and persuasiveness) that may be incapable of leading them to the kinds of conclusions accepted by the church. Even the most certain conclusions of the researcher are probable, certain only in the most human of ways and justified only by the skill and diligence of the researcher and the availability of evidence.

The distance between historian and unquestioning believer is immense at this point. It cannot be swept away with the facile observation that historical study will eventually end up supporting the claims of the church. That may be true, but it is irrelevant. The issue is really one of method not conclusions. By their very methods historians are committed to a process of inquiry whose results are open-ended. Even the most scholarly dedicated defender of the faith is committed to a method of inquiry that could produce conclusions utterly worthless for apologetic purposes. As Hugh Nibley is fond of pointing out, there are enormous gaps in our knowledge of ancient times. The filling in of just one of these gaps could destroy an apologist's entire defense.

A true believer is not comfortable with this possibility. Men and women do not become faithful Saints for a tentative, probably true gospel. Tentative conclusions lead to tentative faith. To put it bluntly, religious men and women seek what no mortal can give them—a certainty that is beyond dispute. They long for the sure knowledge that their view of humanity, world, and cosmos is true beyond a shadow of a doubt, that they have grasped the iron rod and are justified in their religious life by a power beyond the flux of human history and knowledge.

The historian's knowledge cannot lead the religious man or woman to that certain path. To put it directly, the honest historian cannot say whether Joseph Smith saw—or even thought he saw—one being or two on a spring morning in 1820. Our canonical account speaks of two, as do most others, but the earliest account, the one closest in time to the event, speaks of only one being. Of course it may be argued that two is more likely: most of the accounts, including the one published by Joseph Smith, which he never repudiated, describe two beings. Unfortunately such reasoning misses the point. On historical grounds we cannot say with the certainty of the faithful apologist that one of these versions is the most truthful record of the past. To do so would be to forsake the pursuit of human truth, retreating into the comfortable irrationality that leads to an incoherent faith and an incomprehensible God. Mormons have always been wary of religious questioning that yields inscrutable mysteries.

But can we not believe in the canonical account without forsaking historical knowledge? Perhaps we cannot prove that this version is the best account, but then we cannot show that it is not the best account either. Another example will prove the shallowness of this response. Consider the book of Daniel in the Old Testament, supposedly a record of the experiences of an individual of considerable importance in the political affairs of one of the chief empires in the Near East during the first millennium B.C. The earliest texts we have are dated several hundred years after the events supposedly happened (copies of copies of copies), but this does not affect the fact that the text claims to record actual events. For the historian this claim poses both a problem and an opportunity. Because the Babylonian empire was so important, many decipherable archaeological records have survived. Thus we may check Daniel's history against records unquestionably dating from the precise period in question—a test that any good historian would apply. Unfortunately the book of Daniel comes off rather badly. It makes documentable errors which would be similar in magnitude to claiming that George McGovern won the 1972 presidential race. Now either Daniel is right and all the tablets, epigraphy, and king lists are wrong, or Daniel is wrong. And if he is wrong in these verifiable political details, why should we trust the historical truthfulness of the rest of the story?

To maintain that Daniel is right is to grasp at unconvincing straws and to give up rational demand for evidence—retreating to the nihilistic irrationality of the fundamentalist. It would require that we abandon the merging of reason and faith, which the church has supported through its higher education system and which many Saints have proclaimed in their pursuits of knowledge, for a know-nothing response, hiding our heads in the sands of faith.[1]

So far we Mormons have tended to assume that faith necessarily depends on history, or rather on a particular view of past events. But perhaps we have built our dilemma on a false set of presuppositions. Unless we assume that any particular view of the past is necessary for faith, the problem is itself non-existent. Do we really need to assume this? To do so simply buys into the world view of the Protestant fundamentalist concerned with preserving a most un-Mormon, errorless Bible.

We may further see the falsity of assuming that faith depends on history by considering what we call "testimony." The experience of "testimony" is one of the distinguishing marks, if not the distinguishing mark, of the Mormon church. In a testimony meeting we do not hear about events in the past but rather about the present acts of God and about our relationship with him (and that of the church with him through the prophet). We do not preach that the dead Jesus is the head of the church but rather that the living Jesus Christ now rules in heaven.

Observations about the primacy of current religious realities over historical ones lead to the following question: Is there any conceivable fact or set of facts that might be discovered about Joseph Smith that would cause one to lose one's faith in the church? If the answer to that question is yes, then I submit that you have placed your faith in hock to the historian, that you are willing to believe the church is true only to the extent that you have not found any human evidence to contradict it. It seems to me that this is an entirely un-Mormon way of looking at faith. If we have seen God at work in our lives and in the church, then any particular fact about the past will be irrelevant insofar as the commitment we have to Mormonism is concerned. Faith comes from the present reality of God not from remote events whose meaning is inevitably colored by the language and perceptions of those who recorded the events and those who present them to us today.

That a living faith is based on the experiences of living men and women with their God is, it seems to me, an incontrovertible point. But granting this premise still leaves many questions unanswered. We must still find a way to relate faith and history. The knowledge of history can no longer be decisive in determining the faith of the believer in the way we once thought. But what of those beliefs we as a people have about the past that seem crucial in our self-understanding and decisive in terms of our commitment to church? Can we understand how records of these events have become central in the life and faith of the church without at the same time assuming that historians must justify our faith by their research? I think we can.

The answer, it seems to me, lies in a proper understanding of "truth" and of the method by which we say that something is true for the church, whatever conclusions seem dictated by the historian's research. Consider Jesus' parables. Are they not considered "truthful" because they reveal truths about our relationship to each other and to God? Yet none of these stories are history in any sense of that word. That we recognize their truth in our lives does not mean that we know they actually happened at some time in the past (as when we say of a story that it "rings true" or of a writer that he or she has a "true feel" for Mormon life and culture). If this is a proper way of looking at truth, one which is demanded by the Mormon concept that a living relationship with God is what matters not knowledge of a dead and inerrant Bible, then I think we have a clue to understanding what canonization and scripture mean for the church.

Consider the story of Joseph Smith's first vision with which this essay began. The church has canonized one version of the event, but historians cannot verify whether or not that description of the event is more or less reliable than the others. Might we not say then that the 1838 account became true for the church not because of what happened between 1830 and 1838 or between 1830 and 1880 when one particular version was canonized? Is it not more honest to say that this one account is true because it bears witness to the faith of the church better than any other? For example, the canonical version speaks of two separate material beings in hierarchical relationship to one another. Canonization thus underscored the importance of this description of our relationship to God as it has come to be understood in the church. Canonization is both an act of and a witness to the faith of the church and need not be justified by the social scientist's research.

Understanding this process of canonization also sheds some light on the meaning of scripture. The truth of scripture lies in its relationship to faith not history. We have been tempted to forget this because of a scientific world view that reduces meaningfulness to empirical verifiability. Once the primacy of scripture to faith is made clear, much else falls into line. Scripture is seen to reveal God to humanity, not humanity's past to the present. It provides a window through which the divine light might shed on our lives; thus it is God's word.

To see this better, consider the act of Jesus in the Atonement. Jesus' atonement was an event in the past. Making that event alive in our lives is an ongoing process. If the primary function of scripture is to teach us about past events, then we adopt a way of thinking which has led Protestantism to the belief that the historical Atonement is the central proof of God's relationship to humanity, the evidence for which is contained in a closed scriptural canon. Both of these beliefs are so alien to Mormonism that it is strange that we should ever have thought of adopting a view of scripture borrowed from this manner of theological thinking.

A remark by S. Dilworth Young distills the essence of what

scripture means for the church. He told a group of leaders to teach the youth that "every grove can be a sacred grove." The importance of the first vision is that it teaches us this great truth. If a fourteen-year-old boy with little schooling can have an intimate relationship to God—whatever its historicity—then so can we. This is the meaning of that part of our canon, and I think that a similar statement can be made about scripture in general.

NOTES

1. In this essay I realize that I do not discuss historical knowledge precisely. Specifically I do not discuss the degree to which all historical accounts are subjective in the sense of being interpretations rendered by historians. It has been argued that if this is true, then a believer's interpretation is just as valid as a non-believer's since both represent interpretations based on mutually incompatible but non-verifiable premises. While I believe there is some truth in this assertion about subjectivity, I have chosen examples that skirt the issue. The two cases I have chosen do not involve interpretation. For example, either the text of Daniel is right in what it says about the political history of the sixth century B.C. or it is wrong. This is a question of testable fact, not interpretation. To believe contrary to evidence that something in the past happened the way that tradition says it happened is not a matter of justified subjectivity but simply of incoherent commitment to the irrational.

5.
History and Theology:
The Mormon Connection

Edwin S. Gaustad

BRITISH HISTORIAN F. M. POWICKE HAS OBSERVED THAT "THE CHRIS-tian religion is a daily invitation to the study of history."[1] I believe that the same can be said, in italics, for Mormonism. Thus I would like to reflect briefly on some of the relationships between religious and historical understandings, first with respect to Christianity generally, then with respect to Mormonism more particularly.

Considering history and theology initially in the context of the Christian religion has some legitimacy. First, Christianity is in the western world a familiar item. Second, that faith option has a long and reasonably well documented history. And third, it is relevant to our specific subject which is after all the Church of Jesus Christ of Latter-day Saints, not the Church of Joseph Smith of LDS.

Christianity is indeed enmeshed in history. It has often been described as a religion "of the book," but it is also unmistakably a religion of history. "God was in Christ, reconciling the world unto Himself." While this is primarily a statement about theology, it is surely a statement about history as well. And so one has not only Christian philosophies of history but also Christian historians, most of whom these days carry an adjective of some sort around with them: intellectual, social, radical, statistical, political, economic, military, or what-have-you. But does being a Christian historian create special challenges? I think the answer is "yes"—special challenges as well as special opportunities.

One of the challenges is concealed in my glib use of the word

"Christian." Though the Protestant Reformation (or Revolt) is nearly half a millennium behind us, we have only recently ceased to ask of a biographer of Luther or an account of the Inquisition: Is the author Protestant or Catholic? To respond simply "Christian" would be to indulge in the most intolerable evasion and irrelevance. And in surveying the history of the Christian church, it once made much difference whether the writing was by Eastern Orthodox, Roman Catholic, German Lutheran, Scotch Presbyterian, or British Unitarian. As one Christian historian, E. Harris Harbison, remarked, "Sectarian prejudice has long been a notorious obstacle in the path of historical understanding."[2] Strident polemicism and narrow parochialism are familiar faults. Even more serious criticism was leveled against "Christian history" by the fierce *philosophes* of the Enlightenment. Christian historians, they averred, ignored those civilizations not dominated by the church, quarreled over petty differences, found a miracle for every difficulty of causation, and relied on revelation for every declaration of purpose. For example, one ninth-century bishop and biographer could write: "Where I have not found any history of any of these bishops and have not been able by conversation with aged men, or inspection of the monuments, or from any other authentic source, to obtain information concerning them,—in such a case, in order that there might not be a break in the series, I have composed the life myself, with the help of God and the prayers of the brethren."[3] Such a technique mars history, but fortunately this technique was more typical of an earlier time.

So admittedly Christian history is vulnerable to special criticism. It also however has powerful potential. First, as Augustine noted, the history of the City of God is one of meaning and direction. Rejecting notions of history as repetitive cycle on the one hand or whirling chaos on the other, the bishop of Hippo found in history a dynamism and purpose, even consummation. Indeed Christian theology emerges from history—from the intimations of God's dealings with humankind.

Herbert Butterfield in *Christianity and History* wrote: "the Christian must find that religious thought is inextricably involved in historical thought. The historical Jesus on the one hand brings to a climax [the developments of ancient history], gathering up the whole story and fulfilling the things to which the Old Testament had so often pointed. In this respect, His life, His teaching and His personality are the subject of an historical narrative which knits itself into the story of the Roman Empire. Over and above all this, however, Christianity is an historical religion in a particularly technical sense that the term possesses—it presents us with religious doctrines which are at the same time historical events or historical interpretations. In particular it confronts us with the questions of the Incarnation, the Crucifixion and the Resurrection, questions which may transcend all the apparatus of the scientific historian—as indeed many other things do—but which imply that Christianity . . . has rooted its most characteristic and daring assertions in [the] ordinary realm of history. . . . The fact that Christianity comes down to us as an historical religion in this sense . . . is bound to provide certain bearings for interpretation of the whole drama of human life on this earth, bound to affect, for example, any views or dim feelings that we may have concerning the scheme of things in time."[4] For the Christian historian, in other words, God is not dead and the world is not meaningless.

Second, the Christian historian approaches the vast canvas of the human past with a point of view, a perspective, a passion. In an earlier time this may have seemed more a liability than an asset. In our own day, however, total and impersonal objectivity is seen more as delusion and snare. Historians do not and cannot stand apart from the stream which they attempt to describe. They are not in the balcony watching life played on a stage, for they too are among the players. Enlightenment thinkers believed themselves totally objective, shorn of all prejudice and presupposition. But as Carl Becker demonstrated long ago in *The Heavenly City of the Eighteenth-Century Philosophers*, they too were captives of a prevailing climate of opinion, they too burned down one heavenly city only to erect another. The Roman Catholic historian Eric Cochrane believes that committed Christian historians have at least two advantages over their secular counterpart. One, they are likely to take religious issues and religious ideas and religious motivations seriously; they may even know a little theology! And two, such historians follow their scholarly pursuit as a holy vocation. Catholic historians, he writes, "must regard the work of historical inquiry not as a way of gaining social prestige, of building academic empires, or of making payments on suburban swimming pools." Rather he sees the enterprise, the calling, as a process of sanctification—both for historians themselves and for those they reach through their work. Cochrane acknowledges that "talent rains on the just and unjust alike" but sees the calling as an added incentive to hard work, diligence, and thoroughgoing honesty. With approval he quotes Guiseppe Alberigo, "All historical research conducted with scientific rigor is a spiritual adventure; and research into the history of the Church is also a religious experience."[5]

The third potential for Christian history is the capacity for universality, for empathy as broad as the human race. Unfortunately Christian history has often degenerated into partisan polemical history with the circle of sympathy so narrowed as to exclude nine-tenths of the human race. God's love, oceanwide, is meted out thimbleful by thimbleful. Contemporary Peruvian theologian Gustavo Gutierrez describes salvation as the communion of all human beings with God and among themselves. For him it is no longer useful to speak of a profane world, for grace—whether accepted or rejected—is present among all peoples, and all human activity comes within the scope of Christian concern. "There is only one human destiny," he writes, and "the history of salvation is the very heart of human history." This gives history its unity and salvation, its universality. Those who try to "save" salvation exclusively for their own group, their own class, their own nation, will end up "losing" it. The salvation of Jesus Christ, Gutierrez concludes, "is a radical liberation from all misery, all despoliation, all alienation."[6]

Far too often the message of salvation is fatefully linked to a particular cultural mode, to a single epoch. If Ptolemaic astronomy falls, then Christianity must fall. If Darwin be right, Jesus is of no avail. If capitalism collapses, the church is doomed. In its first 300 years, Christianity was rarely tempted to wed itself to the political or economic or even scientific system of the day. In its critically formative period, it profited from cultural alienation. Since that time, however, it has often succumbed to the dangerous temptation to identify God's will with its own, to make itself and its institutions the center of the universe.

This brief prolegomenon suggests then that the problems of Mormon history and theology are not unrelated to the larger question of Christian history and theology. Certainly some psychic distance, some historical perspective may be gained by seeing a single church in the context of the universal church. But one must not be oblivious either to the similarities or to the differences. Mormon theology like Christian theology generally sees direction and progress in history. But the development is without end, and nothing lies beyond time. Eternity, as Thomas O'Dea pointed out, is simply "indefinitely prolonged time" during which humans in cooperation with God gain mastery over the elements in nature.[7] Not just history but all reality is on the move—purposefully, progressively, and endlessly. Mormonism has a process philosophy quite apart from the underpinnings of Whiteheadian thought and a sense of time from which nothing in the universe is exempt. The Mormon view intensifies the connection between history and theology even more than does the orthodox Christian view.

Also relevant to the understanding of history are the Mormon concepts of God and humanity. God has more limits and humanity fewer than in traditional Christian thought. God is finite, not infinite, subject as all else to the vagaries of time, limited by the materials available to him for the creation of the world.

To employ the language of Sterling McMurrin on this point: "As a constructor or artisan God, not entirely unlike Plato's demiurge of the *Timaeus*, the Mormon deity informs the continuing processes of reality and determines the world's configurations, but he is not the creator of the most ultimate constituents of the world, either the fundamental material entities or the space and time that locate them. . . . it is a basic article of Mormon theology that God is related to a world environment for the being of which he is *not* the ultimate ground and by which he therefore is in some sense conditioned. This means that God is a being among beings rather than *being* as such or the ground of being, and that he is therefore finite rather than absolute."[8] McMurrin acknowledges that the language of absolutism and omnipotence is more emotionally satisfying and is therefore found in many Mormon sermons, but "like it or not, the Mormon theologian must sooner or later return to the finitistic concept of God upon which both his technical theology and his theological myths are founded."[9]

If the great gulf between God and humanity (in Augustinian or Calvinist thought, for example) is narrowed by the limits placed on God, it is further bridged by the high view taken of humanity. God was once as we are now, and we may eventually become as God is. We are not the fallen, depraved, impotent creature of much Christian thought, not the earthen pot complaining to the potter, "Why hast thou made me thus?" Original sin with all its potential for debilitation or irresponsibility is cast aside explicitly and boldly. Again in the words of McMurrin: "To fail to recognize that at its foundation Mormon theology is essentially a rebellion against especially the orthodox Protestant dogma of original sin, and the negativism implied by it for the interpretation of the whole nature and life of man, would be a failure to discern not only the distinctive character of Mormon doctrine but also of the Mormon religion itself. . . . The history of Mormon theology . . . has been at many points a recasting of Pelagianism, Socinianism, or Arminianism, in a nineteenth-twentieth-century role, but where reason and theological subtleties have counted for less than common-sense insights, practical necessities, and dogmatic certainties."[10]

Such a high view of human powers and potential could lead to romanticizing many of the hard facts in history and to wishing away the reality of evil. Nineteenth-century America offers several examples of just such romanticism and monism. Remarkably Mormon theology while exalting humanity does not obscure or minimize the force and fact of evil. Evil exists, but the freedom to do something about it also exists. Evil is not always the "blessing in disguise," not invariably an integral part of some overarching but hidden plan, not merely and evasively the absence of good without an independent existence of its own. Evil is for God and humanity alike a challenge, an occasion of struggle, endurance, and ultimate victory. Once again the importance of history is magnified not minimized; events are not merely some sort of pageant play or placement test for the world beyond.

And history is taken seriously within the Church of Jesus Christ of Latter-day Saints. Let me suggest four areas in which this is the case. First, ancient history. As Richard Bushman has pointed out, one cannot take Mormonism seriously as a religion without taking seriously its attention to ancient history in the Book of Mormon.[11] This certainly need not imply that only one window should be opened to the ancient world (single window history like single issue politics is a risky business). But it does imply that the timeline does not begin in 1830 and that the heritage of all human history is a legitimate and relevant part of the Mormon heritage. John Henry Newman once remarked that to be deep into history "is to cease to be a Protestant." While I do not accept that as binding truth, I acknowledge some force in the idea for those who see Protestantism as wholly the product of the sixteenth century—with nothing of relevance occurring in the 1,500 years between the apostolic age and the Reformation. So to steal from Newman, I might be tempted to say that to be deep into history is to cease to be a Mormon—but I hope that I have made clear in what sense I believe that to be both true and profoundly untrue. The Mormon past properly apprehended is an ancient and inclusive past.

A second area of historical concern for Mormons is that of America and the New World. Here Mormons can helpfully remind all of us that the history of this hemisphere does not begin in 1492 or 1565 or 1607. Beyond extending the timeline, Mormons also declare that America and the New World were being prepared for a new revelation, a timely restoration. After the period of persecution, the Mormon dream seemed tied to the American dream, and for a time both fared remarkably well. Now with the American dream faltering, it is increasingly important for Mormonism to guard against cultural captivity. But in any event America's history has been taken seriously, divinely guided in preparation for and fulfillment of the promises of Zion.

Third, Mormons consider their own particular history with deep earnestness. More than a century and a half of Mormon history in this country alone is filled with inexhaustible drama. The sources and resources brought to bear on this lively past are enormous. The point hardly needs to be labored. I would simply like to pay tribute to one man, Leonard J. Arrington, for the quality and the quantity of his labors. He has coaxed, cajoled, encouraged, guided, and inspired countless young Mormon scholars in doing their history in a manner that is responsible, open, probing, and devout. For non-Mormon scholars he has opened doors and reduced suspicions on a scale that can only bode well for the future of the church. Most of all he has personally set a standard of integrity for all the rest of us to follow—or to ignore at our peril. Of Mormon history as of Christian history generally, the question should not be whether the author was a Mormon or a non-Mormon but whether that author was a historian or a hack.

Fourth, it is no secret in the scholarly world that Mormons take seriously their individual and family history. This herculean enterprise is a matter of pride and justifiably so. The raw data accumulated—now also disseminated and preserved with the aid of modern technology—constitute a source of incalculable utility. Historians—a proud and arrogant lot—do point out, however, that genealogy is not history. In his recent book on the *Roots of Modern Mormonism*, Mark P. Leone indicates his reservations about Mormon "amateur history, basically chronicle and vignette, not interpretation; its skeleton is kinship, not politics or economics, and it is unreservedly uncritical."[12] While Leone concedes that the church makes every effort to ensure the accuracy of genealogical searches, he believes that the searches themselves give a strong egocentric perspective to all historical undertakings with one result being that the broadest human grouping acknowledged is that of the family. The past is not seen in terms of larger entities, broad social forces, subterranean causes, profound cultural conflicts. When the approach to the past is essentially, if not exclusively, autobiographical, history is "atomized." This kind of historical investigation also tends to be adulatory, an endorsement rather than judgment of the present. In Leone's words: "Mormons lock themselves into the present more effectively than the rest of society. . . . [They] never see profound change and are even prevented from seeing the causes of it because all history is an individual's reflection; and just as a mirror never tells a viewer what it saw yesterday, history never tells Mormons what they or their society looked like before. It cannot do so because the living Mormon is the image in the mirror."[13]

In all four areas of concern with the past—ancient history, New World history, denominational history, and family history—the attention is nonetheless keen. Thus to appropriate Powicke's remark: "The Mormon religion is a daily invitation to the study of history." That much, it seems to me, is fixed and sure. In scrutinizing the relationships between history and theology in the Mormon context, however, some problems or questions remain. In a tentative and exploratory way, let me suggest three areas in which historians and theologians might wish to focus their reflections on "the Mormon connection."

1. Mormon historians might ask, as I now do, whether an effort should be made, consciously and deliberately, to lengthen the time-line of historical consciousness. All American religion, as Sidney Mead long ago pointed out, suffers from historylessness. For so many groups, and conspicuously the utopian and restorationist ones, the world began anew with their own founding. For many reasons, as I

have suggested, Mormonism has largely resisted this dismissal of the past. Largely resisted but not totally. There is still a strong tendency to go back no further than a single century or to find authentication chiefly or solely in one's own experience. All American pietism did and does the same thing. Culture was undernourished and institutions collapsed and broke apart with breathtaking frequency. Mormonism has too strong a sense of institution and authority for collapse—at least in the twentieth century. But cultural and personal enrichment can still be denied. Mormonism, which takes time so seriously, should gulp down larger and larger chunks of it from all humanity's past.

Other religious bodies originating in nineteenth-century America share this need—and have responded to it variously. Christian Science, for example, turns far less to history than to philosophy. But in terms of its own denominational past, it has manifested great and often jealous concern. The writings of Robert Pell, however, help make possible a freer commerce between "in-house" historians and those who approach Christian Science from the outside. The movement led by Alexander Campbell, a contemporary of Joseph Smith, has suffered internal discord and dissension which has distracted the group from a steady concern with earlier Christian history. Yet several conferences and periodical papers have tried to place that restoration movement into the larger context of the primitive and free church precedents. Seventh-day Adventists have recently been dismayed by the efforts of Ronald Numbers to place their foundress, Ellen G. White, more solidly in the company of fellow health reformers of the mid-nineteenth century. Some of these historical ways of thinking are new and therefore shocking. They can also prove refreshing. A recent Adventist book looks at the question of Saturday and Sunday worship—surely nothing new here. But the look is not at nineteenth-century America; rather it is at second-century Rome and thence to the entire patristic period. The Adventist author is moreover the first non-Catholic graduate of the Pontifical Gregorian University in Rome (see Samuele Bacchiocchi, *From Sabbath to Sunday: A Historical Investigation of the Rise of Sunday in Early Christianity*). Scholarly barriers should be crossed with the same courage and zeal that missionaries have crossed ethnic and national barriers.

2. If history's time-line needs to be lengthened, its embrace can also be widened—to include non-Mormons both as the subjects

and authors of history. Meetings of the Mormon History Association and the annual Sunstone Symposium are examples of what I mean, and I would like to think that they could easily occur under the sponsorship of the church. Why might they not? Because there is a continuing defensiveness, an uneasiness, a "garrison mentality"—to use the phrase of Davis Bitton. And Mark Leone has commented that "Mormons seem at the moment to be the sole owners of their own past." Much of this is readily understandable. When others were owners of the Mormon past in earlier generations, they tended to distort or at least misunderstand that past. Common sense might suggest therefore that one not surrender a proprietary hold. Beyond the fact of that period of persecution and misrepresentation is the additional fact of this religion's visible and vulnerable youth. The formative years of a religion—consider Christianity once again—are turbulent and contradictory, filled with false starts and misdirections. Senior citizens can look back on the vagaries of puberty with philosophical calm—not so the adolescent, challenged without at every turn and tortured from within by self-doubt and insecurity.

Still another reason for being suspicious of the outsider is the theological novelty of the Utah church, and novelty is only another word for heresy. In an earlier period Mormons were condemned by a gentile world for being polygamous and un-American. Now they are emphatically monogamous and vigorously American. So all is forgiven and forgotten—at least until one begins paying attention to theology. There the traditional Christian, confronted by a finite God, an unlimited freedom, and a forbidding temple ritual, may respond with a new wave of accusation and diatribe. Perhaps fearing such a situation, the Mormon church keeps its guard up against the outsider.

But the church keeps its guard up against the insider too, against those who move beyond amateur history and amateur theology. In a world gone awry, intellectuals, perceived as threats to a restored faith and improved morals, can serve as convenient scapegoats. "It is in such a context," Davis Bitton has written, "that we can best understand various efforts to seal off students from 'worldly' ideas, the denunciation of pornography, the unwillingness in Church periodicals to include different points of view or even critical letters to the editor, the hypersensitivity to criticism, the thirst for praise, the patronizing editorials on 'professors,' the interminable self-congratulation at having the truth . . . and the suspicion greeting the historian who wishes to study Mormon history. 'Is it for us or against us?' The assumption is that the world is divided already between the sheep and the goats."[14]

So it is possible to understand the defensiveness; what is also required is an understanding of its cost. For history shortened in time and narrowed in scope loses its capacity to enlighten, to liberate, to offer that emancipation which comes with genuine self-understanding. If Calvinist theology has a tendency to sink into gloomy despair, Mormon theology may have a tendency toward Pelagian or Promethean pride. And since that is humanity's most threatened sin, perhaps Mormon history—if broadened and length-ened—can provide a needed corrective to this facet of Mormon theology. However, to be successful in this regard, the approach to history instead of reenforcing egocentricity must be one which tran-scends it. If our paths are to be guided by the light of experience, that light must shine as broadly and as brightly as possible.

3. A final arena for reflection has to do not so much with the length or breadth of history as with the attitude taken toward it. To put it succinctly history should be seen as an ally, not as a foe. Mormon theology should not be horrified by the notion that dogma has a history, that doctrine develops, and that revelation is not closed. Amateur history can become a liability when obscurantism and mindless literalism assume control. When properly embraced, his-tory is instructive for its examples of ambiguity, variety, possibility, and failure. The liberating power of history was demonstrated, I believe, by the publication in 1970 of Stephen G. Taggart's little book, *Mormonism's Negro Policy: Social and Historical Origins*, and three years later by Lester Bush's article in *Dialogue: A Journal of Mormon Thought*. Change, wrote Taggart, "must eventually come,"[15] and eight years later it did. I am not suggesting that Taggart or Bush directly effected the change, but recognition of the relativities of history certainly made easier the modification of doctrine. Clearly Mormonism has a mechanism for change and development in place.

Another way in which to manifest the embrace of history rather than its disdain has to do with church archives and access. In his book on the opening of the Vatican archives (*Catholicism and History*), Owen Chadwick details the elaborate intrigue, political and ecclesiastical, that kept these archives so long from the scholarly world (including even the kidnapping of the archives by Napoleon in 1810). Not until the final decades of the nineteenth century were these archives opened. In the height of a renewed conflict between science and religion, the Roman Catholic church even released all of the Galileo manuscripts, concluding—rightly I believe—that it had more to fear from imposing a rigid and authoritarian secrecy than it did from openness and honest scholarship. Leo XIII in 1883 said, "Let nothing untrue be said; and nothing true be unsaid."[16] Of course there are risks, as freedom always involves risks, but a church which emphasizes so eloquently the absolute freedom of humanity cannot gracefully thwart that freedom's honorable exercise.

History must be embraced. But this is far from a challenge to be set before Mormonism alone. A whole society is turning its back on history, is ignoring or dismissing its past. Such books as Philip Rieff's *Fellow Teachers* and Christopher Lasch's *The Culture of Narcissism* bemoan the loss of historical memory, the reversion in America to a kind of barbarism. As Lasch noted, a denial of the past at first and superficial glance appears "progressive and optimistic," but on closer analysis we see that it embodies the "despair of a society that cannot face the future."[17] So the problem is greater than that represented by a single church or a particular tradition.

Among the many deeds and pronouncements of that genial pontiff John XXIII are these words: "The best apology for the Church is the impartial history of its life."[18] Wise and welcome words for his or for any church. But they were a long time in coming, which is why—no doubt—patience will continue to be an admirable virtue for Mormons.

NOTES

1. In C. T. McIntire, ed., *God, History, and Historians* (New York: Oxford University Press, 1977), 407.

2. Ibid., 345.

3. See John Tracy Ellis, in *Church History* 41 (1972): 225-29.

4. *Christianity and History* (London: Fontana Books, 1957), 11-12.

5. In McIntire, *God, History, and Historians*, 453-54.

6. Ibid., 136-38, 150.

7. Thomas O'Dea, "Mormonism and the American Experience of Time," *Western Humanities Review* 8 (Summer 1954): 181-90.

8. Sterling McMurrin, *The Theological Foundations of the Mormon*

Religion (Salt Lake City: University of Utah Press, 1965), 29.

    9. Ibid., 35.

    10. Ibid., 66-67.

    11. In *Dialogue: A Journal of Mormon Thought* 1 (Summer 1966): 82.

    12. Mark Leone, *The Roots of Modern Mormonism* (Cambridge: Harvard University Press, 1979), 194.

    13. Ibid., 201.

    14. In *Dialogue: A Journal of Mormon Thought* 1 (Fall 1966): 128.

    15. Stephen G. Taggart, *Mormonism's Negro Policy: Social and Historical Origins* (Salt Lake City: University of Utah Press, 1970), 76.

    16. Owen Chadwick, *Catholicism and History* (Cambridge: Cambridge University Press, 1978), 99.

    17. Philip Rieff, *Fellow Teachers* (New York: Harper & Row, 1973); Christopher Lasch, *The Culture of Narcissism* (New York: W. W. Norton, 1978), xviii.

    18. Quoted by Eric Cochrane in McIntire, *God, History, and Historians*, 456.

6.
On Being a Mormon Historian (and Its Aftermath)

D. Michael Quinn[1]

LATTER-DAY SAINTS HAVE BEEN TRAINED AS HISTORIANS AT UNIVERSI-
ties outside of Utah for more than half a century and have been
publishing Mormon history during that entire period.[2] Only recently
have some church authorities and others publicly criticized the
motivations and publications of Mormon historians. In part, this is a
reaction to the increasingly high profile of scholarly and interpretive
Mormon history since 1965.

At a time of phenomenal increases in the numbers of new
converts to the LDS church in the United States and throughout the
world, there has been a growing crescendo of interest in researching,
writing, and learning about the history of Mormonism. However, this
historical inquiry has been particularly evident on the part of Latter-
day Saints with generations of experience in the church.

Among the most significant examples of this trend are the
organization of the institutionally independent Mormon History
Association in 1965 which has held annual conferences for the
presentation of scholarly papers and whose membership has grown
from a few dozen to more than a thousand. Then came the establishment of *Dialogue: A Journal of Mormon Thought* in 1966 with an
emphasis on interpretive Mormon history.[3] *Brigham Young University
Studies* began devoting whole issues to LDS church history from
1969 on.

Crucial to this flowering of Mormon history in the late 1960s
and early 1970s was the gradual opening of Mormon church archives.

Apostle and official church historian Joseph Fielding Smith began this process during the late 1960s. His successor as church historian, Elder Howard W. Hunter, accelerated that openness in 1970-71, during which time both non-Mormon and Mormon researchers had unrestricted access to such previously unavailable sources as First Presidency files, diaries of general church authorities, presiding quorum minutes, excommunication files, general and local financial records, and ordinance record books. Then came the First Presidency's unprecedented appointment in January 1972 of a professional Mormon historian, Leonard J. Arrington, to the position of official LDS church historian.[4] (Similar developments occurred within the Reorganized Church of Jesus Christ of Latter Day Saints during the tenure of RLDS church historian Richard P. Howard since 1966.[5])

For the next eight years, under the official auspices of LDS church headquarters, the professionally trained church historian, assistant historians, and their university-trained staff published scholarly and interpretive books and articles about Mormon history. In addition, independent researchers at LDS archives wrote prolifically. This resulted in two exclusively historical periodicals: the primarily LDS *Journal of Mormon History* in 1974 and the primarily RLDS *John Whitmer Historical Association Journal* in 1981.

In addition, the college student-oriented magazine *Sunstone* (established in 1975) featured interpretative Mormon history. Then in 1979 the Sunstone Foundation began holding in Salt Lake City annual symposia which included scholarly papers on Mormon history. In 1980 the B. H. Roberts Society was founded in Salt Lake City for monthly or quarterly presentations of "timely issues in Mormonism." By then more than ten thousand Latter-day Saints had direct exposure to a newly interpretative and rigorous Mormon history through these various academic journals, magazines, conferences, and symposia.

This explosion of professional, interpretive, and footnoted approaches to Mormon history has had even wider impact. This "New Mormon History" has reached beyond the community of Mormon scholars and history buffs. It has extended to the general membership of the LDS church through faculty members at Brigham Young University, Ricks College, and in church seminaries and institutes, as well as through scholarly-historical publications by Deseret Book

Company, the *Church News*, and the *Ensign* and *New Era* magazines and their international counterparts.[6]

Preoccupied with trying to assimilate hundreds of thousands of new converts annually into the LDS church's present theological, social, and administrative identity, some general authorities have viewed with misgiving this burgeoning exploration of Mormonism's fluid past. The concern of these leaders has not been assuaged by the fact that contemporary with the proliferation of Mormon historians and histories there has been a shift in anti-Mormon propaganda. A new generation of anti-Mormon writers has turned from doctrinal diatribe to the polemical use of elements from the Mormon past to discredit the LDS church today.[7]

In reaction to this confluence of developments, Elders Ezra Taft Benson and Boyd K. Packer of the Quorum of the Twelve Apostles specifically identified Latter-day Saint historians as a source of difficulty. Elder Benson gave two talks about this subject in 1976, one of which stated: "This humanistic emphasis on history is not confined only to secular history; there have been and continue to be attempts made to bring this philosophy into our own Church history. Again the emphasis is to underplay revelation and God's intervention in significant events, and to inordinately humanize the prophets of God so that their human frailties become more evident than their spiritual qualities."[8]

Five years later, Elder Packer expanded on this point of view in a message delivered to Church Education System faculty but directed to LDS historians.[9] As part of his indictment against Mormons who write scholarly, interpretive history, Elder Packer told his 1981 audience: "Unfortunately, many of the things they tell one another are not uplifting, go far beyond the audience they may have intended, and destroy faith. . . . One who chooses to follow the tenets of his profession, regardless of how they may injure the Church or destroy the faith of those not ready for 'advanced history' is himself in spiritual jeopardy."[10]

In addition to these jaundiced views, Louis C. Midgley, a political scientist at Brigham Young University, spearheaded an academic assault against recent scholarship in Mormon history. Midgley concluded a 1981 presentation on Mormon historians with the following statement: "It is depressing to see some historians now struggling to get on the stage to act out the role of the mature, honest

historian committed to something called 'objective history,' and, at
the same time, the role of faithful Saint. The discordance between
those roles has produced more than a little bad faith (that is, self–
deception) and even, perhaps, some blatant hypocrisy; it has also
produced some pretentious[,] bad history."[11] As one of the historians
Midgley describes, I would like to explore what he and others have
questioned: the motivations, rationale, intentions, and conduct of
Latter-day Saints who profess to write "fair and objective" Mormon
history.[12]

    I do not claim to speak for anyone aside from the one
Mormon historian I know best, although I believe his particular
pilgrimage parallels in some ways that of other LDS historians he
knows. His biography may be of little interest to anyone but himself,
but elements of his background are important for understanding his
activity of a Mormon historian, his motives, and his reactions to
criticisms of Mormon historians.

    To begin with, he was born with a split-identity: seventh
generation Latter-day Saint on his mother's side but of Roman
Catholic, Mexican origin on his father's side. Since his earliest childhood, self-identity was not the most important emphasis of his life,
but rather an intense personal relationship with God.

    As long as he can remember, he knew God as personage and
immediate influence, and on occasion heard God's voice. Long
before he had ever heard much about the Holy Ghost, this young
man seemed to have constant experience with a presence from God
in comfort and revelation "like a fire burning" within him. As an
adolescent he was surprised to discover scriptural descriptions of
others' experiences with the Holy Ghost that he had thought were
God's special gifts to him alone. Although he had always known God
as Father, Christ as Savior, and Holy Ghost as Comforter and Reve-
lator, at the age of eleven the young man realized that he had been
a member of the LDS church for three years without specifically
asking God about its validity. Therefore, he sought and received
knowledge through the spirit that the Book of Mormon was the word
of God, that the LDS church was true and necessary, and that its
president was indeed a prophet of God.

    Although his relationship with God and the spirit was the
primary dimension and sufficient epistemology of his life, the young
man felt impressed that it was necessary to explore the temporal

manifestations of God's dealings with his people and prophets, as well as their conduct. By age fifteen he had read the standard works of the church (except for half of the Old Testament), and at seventeen he was reading the *History of the Church* and *Journal of Discourses*. To the occasional discomfort of his LDS seminary teachers, he subjected any religious proposition to rigid analysis, particularly with reference to the complete scriptural context as he could identify it.

By age eighteen, he had completed several historical projects. He had prepared his own card index of the Old Testament and other standard works. He had also written independent studies of misconduct among Roman Catholic popes from Marcellinus to Leo XII and of unfaithfulness in LDS general authorities from Sidney Rigdon to Richard R. Lyman. In addition, he had compared all proper names in the Book of Mormon with the Bible and had made a line-by-line comparison of the 1830 Book of Mormon with later editions. "I will not accept any criticism of the Church on face value," this eighteen-year-old wrote in his journal, "but, instead, search and study (and if need be, pray) to find the truth."[13]

During these adolescent years, the young man often went on extended fasts. By this religious regimen, he sought to draw close to the comfort, strength, and guidance of God's spirit as he confronted the difficulties of maturation. At the same time, he needed this spiritual support as he submerged himself in the intricacies of scriptural study and the polemics of anti-Mormon literature.

A few months before his nineteenth birthday, the young man wrote: "At present my evaluation of what I am going to have to do to be spiritually educated in the Gospel is to become extremely well acquainted with the Standard Works, *Journal of Discourses*, *Times and Seasons*, *History of the Church*, and the discourses and writings of the Prophets. It is a monumental task at this alone, which requires more than a cursory reading or even a single, very detailed reading of these materials. I can now see clearly, for really the first time, that such a task will take a lifetime to encounter, and longer to master."[14] Over the next decade, a series of unforseen circumstances (which he now regards as divine intervention) caused him to abandon his life's ambition to be a physician and in turn to abandon his second-best decision to complete a doctorate in literature.

Instead, after much prayer and soul-searching, he decided to turn his intense avocation of scriptural and church history research into a life's work. He began graduate study in history and later played a minor role in the development of Mormon history writing following Leonard J. Arrington's appointment as official LDS church historian in 1972. This young historian spent a decade probing thousands of manuscript diaries and records of church history that he never dreamed he would see. He completed a score of publications in LDS history, several of which have been described as "controversial" by some people.[15] He has always researched and written about church history with a continual prayer for the Lord to guide him in knowing what to do and how to express things in such a way that they might be beneficial to the understanding of the Latter-day Saints.

He would have been satisfied to have remained indefinitely on Leonard Arrington's staff, but he quit his position to begin Ph.D. study at Yale University. He did this because he felt impressed that it was the Lord's will for him to do so. In order to attend Yale, he uprooted his family shortly after purchasing their first home, and he borrowed thousands of dollars to complete the doctorate.

Nevertheless, he found himself ready to abandon his Ph.D. in the middle of writing a dissertation about the "Mormon Hierarchy."[16] He worried that this study involved too many controversies about the church and its general authorities. He asked the Lord to tell him if he should stop writing about the "sensitive" information he had found during his research. He told the Lord that he would stop and even destroy his research if that was the Lord's will. He was in earnest and desired to listen to God's will, not his own nor any one else's.

This faltering young historian obtained a spiritual witness that it was right to complete his dissertation, despite the so-called "controversies" and "sensitive" areas of church history with which it dealt. He then asked for courage and strength to face criticism and consequences which might result from those who were hostile to the kinds of things he was researching and writing. He continued to "pray into print" everything he published.

It is from this background that he approaches criticisms concerning the writing of Mormon history by Latter-day Saints. I will proceed from smaller issues to more important ones concerning sacred history, secular history, pluralistic history, monistic history, and what I call "accommodation history."

In 1976, Elder Ezra Taft Benson objected to Mormon

historians' use of scholarly "expressions and terminology" in describing developments or characteristics of Mormon history. Among the terms he said "offend the Brethren and the Church members" were "alleged," "experimental systems," "communal life," "communitarianism," and "Christian primitivism."[17] He preferred that Mormon historians use traditional Mormon terms and phrases even when Latter-day Saint historians are writing for scholarly, non-Mormon publications.

One approach in responding to this criticism is to observe that many of the terms and phrases Mormons use have specialized meanings unrecognizable to outsiders.[18] This either requires cumbersome explanations of what is essentially Mormon jargon or substitution of words and phrases familiar to the rest of the English-speaking world. Historians usually adopt some combination of these two alternatives, just as do LDS missionaries who encounter blank stares as they casually use familiar Mormon terms in explaining the church to non-Mormons. There is no justification for regarding this necessity as subversive when Mormon scholars do it.

Several of Elder Benson's examples of offensive expressions were virtually the same as phrases used in earlier, official church publications. "Christian primitivism" is simply another form of "the primitive church" which appears in Joseph Smith's Sixth Article of Faith. In 1930, the First Presidency approved, copyrighted, and published *A Comprehensive History of the Church*, which described the United Orders of Utah as having a "communistic character" and the first high school LDS seminary as being "in the nature of an experiment."[19] It will be an awkward situation, indeed, if historians are expected to shun not only secular terminology in Mormon history but also terms which had approval of the First Presidency in former times.

Related to this question is Elder Packer's advice to historians not to publish or refer to sensitive or controversial items merely because they have already been published before.[20] The criticism regarding terminology is a minor issue compared to this second concern. Some church leaders in recent years have criticized Mormon historians for republishing in part or whole out-of-print church publications such as the 1830 Book of Mormon, the *Journal of Discourses* (edited and published for thirty-two years under the auspices of the First Presidency), and statements from former church

magazines published for children, youth, and the general membership.[21] It is an odd situation when historians are criticized for reprinting what previous general authorities regarded not only as faith–
promoting but as appropriate for Mormon youth and new converts.

Elder Packer specifically warns against using "the unworthy,
the unsavory, or the sensational" from the Mormon past, merely
because it has been previously published. He also berates historians
for their "exaggerated loyalty to the theory that everything must be
told."[22] This raises the question of personal honesty and professional
integrity. If I were to write about any subject unrelated to religion,
and I purposely failed to make reference to pertinent information
of which I had knowledge, I would be justifiably criticized for dis-
honesty.[23]

What is true outside of religion is equally true in writing
religious history. That is the reason First Presidency counselor J.
Reuben Clark, Jr., criticized church historian B. H. Roberts and the
seven-volume *History of the Church*. President Clark told a meeting of
the First Presidency and Quorum of the Twelve Apostles in April
1943: "The Documentary History of the Church unfortunately as
printed does not contain all of the documentary history as it was
written. Brother Roberts made some changes in it. We do not know
always what the changes were or what they are, so that, as an absolute
historical source, the printed Documentary History is not one that
we can invariably rely upon. . . . Brother Roberts' work is the work
of an advocate and not of a judge, and you cannot always rely on what
Brother Roberts says. Frequently he started out apparently to establish a certain thesis and he took his facts to support his thesis, and if
some facts got in the way it was too bad, and they were omitted."[24]
President Clark's evaluation of the *History of the Church* was harsher
than recent historical analysis of this official LDS publication.[25]

It does disservice to the church for LDS historians to render
themselves subject to the criticism that they have ignored readily
available and previously published materials. If such material is
sensitive, controversial, unworthy, unsavory, or sensational, then it is
a matter of the author's judgment of its importance whether the item
should be quoted, paraphrased, or only referred to in a note. It is
careless, if not dishonest, to write as if such evidence did not exist.

In connection with counsel to avoid reference to previously
published sensitivities, Elder Benson warned historians against envi-

ronmental explanations of the background of revelations and developments in LDS history. He gave as examples the discussion by historians of the American temperance movement of the 1830s as part of the circumstances out of which Joseph Smith obtained the Word of Wisdom revelation on health. He also referred to historians who explain the revelation on the three degrees of postmortal glory in terms of contemporary questions by philosophers about the afterlife.[26]

Any historian writing about a non-religious subject would be considered inept at best and dishonest at worst if he or she described someone's innovation or contribution without discussing the significance of previously existing, similar contributions and ideas.[27] Any LDS historian is vulnerable if he or she discusses the revelation to Joseph Smith about abstinence from tobacco, strong drink, and hot drinks but fails to note that during the 1830s religious and social reformers were involved nationally in urging abstinence from these identical things. In such a case, any reader has cause to criticize the historian's accuracy, to question his or her motives, and to doubt any affirmation the historian might give to the revelation's truth.

It is obvious that Elder Benson opposed the idea that Joseph Smith invented something he called revelation that was a product of his own mind and of his culture and environment. As both a believing Latter-day Saint *and* historian, I also oppose such conclusions. One can acknowledge the influence of environment and contemporary circumstance and still affirm the actuality of divine revelation. In Mormon doctrine, revelation comes because of specific questions that individuals or prophets ask God, and those questions usually arise in the minds of prophets because of conditions they observe or experience.

Without environmental influence or surrounding significant circumstances, there would be no revelations from God to the prophets. And the changing circumstances and environment of the world are the very reasons Latter-day Saints affirm that there must be living prophets to respond with the word of the Lord to the new circumstances. If we write Mormon history as though its developments occurred without reference to surrounding circumstances, we undermine the claims for the restoration of living prophets. This is one of many areas in Mormon history where an alleged defense is actually a disservice to the Saints.

In a more precise discussion of the concern about environmental explanations, Elder Packer warned Mormon historians: "There is no such thing as an accurate, objective history of the Church without consideration of the spiritual powers that attend this work . . . without consideration of spiritual guidance, of discernment, and of revelation. That is not scholarship."[28]

I agree fully with this observation, but in reference to LDS historians, Elder Packer has created an enemy that does not exist. It is impossible for even an atheist to write about Joseph Smith or any of his successors without acknowledging that they claim to be prophets of God, that they make pronouncements in the name of God, and that they proclaim specific documents to be divine instructions given by revelation. True, a writer can express a tone of ridicule or affirmation, hostility or sympathy, detachment or advocacy when writing about such prophetic claims, but no reputable historian (least of all a believing Latter-day Saint) excludes consideration of the spiritual dimension in writing about people like Joseph Smith. Influenced by psychological, social, economic, and other theoretical disciplines, historians may give alternate explanations for Joseph Smith and other prophets, but they must also acknowledge the prophetic claims of these men.[29]

Louis Midgley's central criticism of Mormon historians is that their writings about Joseph Smith do not positively affirm to the world their personal testimonies that he was God's prophet. Elder Benson apparently indicated this same expectation when he said, "We would hope that if you feel you must write for the scholarly journals, you always defend the faith."[30] But why is it necessary for LDS historians to do more than writers of sacred history did when they simply stated that Moses and others had said, "Hear ye the word of the Lord?" In fact, Elder Packer himself once counseled an LDS seminary teacher to use the words "The Latter-day Saints *believe*" and "they *claim*" in his Ph.D. dissertation rather than to portray the spiritual experiences as facts.[31] Most LDS historians simply report that Joseph Smith said he saw God and Jesus Christ, and that he announced numerous communications as direct revelations from God. Occasionally a Mormon historian writing to a general audience (primarily non-Mormon) may also suggest alternate explanations for prophetic claims without stating the historian's own beliefs about what is inevitably a question of personal faith.

Skeptics are often unmoved by the most ardent personal testimonies, and earnest inquirers have occasionally been converted to the church after learning about it from anti-Mormon publications. It is inconceivable to me that any Latter-day Saint with a personal testimony would begin to lose that faith simply because he or she read a publication by a Mormon historian who reported the revelations of Joseph Smith without including the historian's personal testimony of the truth of those revelations. That kind of scholarly detachment does not threaten testimony and is not subversive to the church.

Central to the above criticisms of Mormon historians and their writings is the assertion that they have adopted the assumptions of secular scholarship and abandoned the verities of the spirit. Elder Benson speaks "of this trend, which seems to be an effort to reinterpret the history of the Church so that it is more rationally appealing to the world." Elder Packer warns against the tendency for Mormon academics "to begin to judge the Church, its doctrines, organization, and leadership, present and past, by the principles of their own profession." Midgley writes that "it is now possible to find historians functioning within the Church defending the proposition that the Restored Gospel must be studied and evaluated entirely with what they choose to call the 'naturalistic assumptions' of certain wholly secularized professional historians."[32] In other words, they accuse Mormon historians of writing to accommodate non-Mormon assumptions. This involves distinctions between monistic history and pluralistic history.

As used here, monistic history refers to the willingness of historians to consider only one explanation for historical developments, and pluralistic history refers to the willingness of historians to consider more than one explanation. The former is closed and the latter open. Elders Benson and Packer and Professor Midgley ask that interpreters of Mormon history be "open" to the spiritual dimension of revelation, but in reality this call for "openness" is not a plea for pluralism. They ask that any interpreter simply change the monistic category of Joseph Smith as fraud, or religious genius, or personality disorder, for the equally monistic interpretation that Joseph Smith was a divine prophet. If asked to give a categorical definition of Joseph Smith, I (and most other LDS historians) would say that he was a divinely called prophet of God. However, in all honesty, we must also acknowledge the existence of other reasonable, honest, and conscientious interpretations.

Moreover, the requirement for a monistic interpretation of Mormon history does not stop with categories of definition but extends to process. For example, Elder Packer demands that Mormon historians demonstrate and affirm that "the hand of the Lord [has been] in every hour and every moment of the Church from its beginning till now."[33] This requires a single, monistic explanation for every event in the Mormon past, but there are compelling reasons why Mormons should consider alternative explanations as well.

Personally, I am not willing to simply say that "the hand of the Lord" is sufficient explanation for all events and developments in the Mormon past. In fact, there is scriptural precedent for considering pluralistic explanations for even the most crucial events in Mormon history. For example, one of the most important developments in the sacred history of the Book of Mormon was the destruction of the Nephite people, yet the prophet-writers of that history suggested several different causes: adultery (Jac. 3:3-7, 10), fornication (He. 8:26), the Gadianton band of robbers (He. 2:13), secret combinations in general (Eth. 8:21), unrighteous lawyers and judges (Al. 10:27), or pride (Moro. 8:27).

If we were to adopt secular terms to describe these Book of Mormon explanations by prophet-historians, we could substitute moral disintegration, social disorganization, political discontinuity, and socio-economic disparity. Which of the various explanations within the Book of Mormon is the "true" or "real" reason for the decline of the Nephite civilization? I do not know, and apparently the historian-prophets who wrote the record did not know, either. But they felt an obligation to examine the evidence, reflect on it, and offer the best explanation or interpretation they could.

In like manner, Mormon historians may share the conviction that the "hand of the Lord" operates throughout history and that "His purposes fail not." However, they also have an obligation to examine the evidence, reflect on it, and offer the best interpretations they can for what has occurred in the Mormon past. The human record is characterized by complexity, both among Book of Mormon peoples and Latter-day Saints. There is nothing subversive about interpreting these developments from different points of view, even from perspectives of secular disciplines.

A more serious problem of Mormon history is involved in the implications of the demand that historians demonstrate that "the hand of the Lord [has been] in every hour and every moment of the church from its beginning till now." Every Mormon historian agrees that "we must never forget that ours is a prophetic history."[34] However, there are problems in asserting or implying that the prophetic history of Mormonism requires "the hand of the Lord" in every decision, statement, and action of the prophets. This comprises a larger question than the historical exploration of environmental backgrounds of decisions and revelations, or the application of secular understanding to explain specific events in religious history. Central to the apparent demands of Elders Benson and Packer is the view that official acts and pronouncements of the prophets are always the express will of God. This is the Mormon equivalent of the Roman Catholic doctrine of papal infallibility.

The Catholic dogma of infallibility is not that the pope is incapable of human weaknesses but that his statements and decisions are infallible in matters of faith and morals. Not until 1870 did Roman Catholicism officially adopt this doctrine. The Mormon church would have to dispense with some of its fundamental theology in order to adopt a similar position of prophetic infallibility.

The LDS doctrine of free agency is central to the Mormon view of existence in time and eternity. Mormon theology is incompatible with the view that Latter-day Saints are free to make mistakes in what they say and do until they become prophets. If a prophet is incapable of personal opinion, human limitation, and error in his decisions and statements, then that prophet has no free agency and no personal responsibility. If an LDS prophet is incapable of making mistakes in his prophetic calling, then he is the only Latter-day Saint who is excused from "rendering an accounting of his stewardship unto God." That is the requirement of the Mormon doctrine that each individual is absolutely responsible for his or her own actions and for the callings given to him or her by God.

The apostle Paul wrote authoritatively to the Saints but noted that "I speak this by permission, and not of commandment." Although the Book of Mormon was written, preserved, and translated by prophets of God, the title page declares, "And now, if there are faults they are the mistakes of men." A Book of Mormon prophet expressed his "opinion" about doctrines only partially revealed to him. Joseph Smith specifically denied that everything a prophet said was the word of the Lord and affirmed, "A prophet was a prophet only when he was acting as such." When J. Reuben Clark announced a decision of the First Presidency to a general conference in 1940, he observed, "We are not infallible in our judgment, and we err, but our constant prayer is that the Lord will guide us in our decisions, and we are trying so to live that our minds will be open to His inspiration." To LDS seminary and institute teachers in 1954, he also declared that "even the President of the Church has not always spoken under the direction of the Holy Ghost."[35]

Mormon historians would be false to their understanding of LDS doctrine, the sacred history of the scriptures, the realities of human conduct, and the documentary evidence of Mormonism if they sought to defend the proposition that LDS prophets are infallible in their decisions and statements. Moreover, it would be hardly less false to allow readers of Mormon history to draw the implicit conclusion that LDS prophets were infallible, because Mormon historians presented church history as though every decision and statement came as the result of direct revelation.

Mormon historians have both a religious and professional obligation not to conceal the ambivalence, debate, give-and-take, uncertainty, and simple pragmatism that often attend decisions of the prophet and First Presidency. The historian has an equal obligation not to conceal the limitations, errors, and negative consequences of some significant statements of the prophet and First Presidency. In like manner, Mormon historians would be equally false if they failed to report the inspiration, visions, revelations, and solemn testimonies that have also attended prophetic decisions and statements throughout Mormon history.

A few observers have been more specific in their criticism of Mormon historians who portray the human frailties of LDS leaders. Elder Benson noted that Mormon historians tend "to inordinately humanize the prophets of God so that their human frailties become more evident than their spiritual qualities." Elder Packer made the following comments about a Mormon historian's talk: "What that historian did with the reputation of the President of the Church was not worth doing. He seemed determine to convince everyone that the *prophet* was a *man*. We knew that already. All of the prophets and all of the Apostles have been men. It would have been much more worthwhile for him to have convinced us that the *man* was a *prophet*; a fact quite as true as the fact that he was a man. He has taken something away from the memory of a prophet. He has destroyed faith."[36] This is, in part, related to the infallibility question.

Elder Packer rightly observes that omitting the spiritual, revelatory dimension from the life of a church leader is a virtual denial of the existence of the spiritual and revelatory. However, it is equally true that omitting reference to human weaknesses, faults, and limitations from the life of a prophet is also a virtual denial of the existence of human weaknesses and fallibility. Both approaches are distortions. Must church history portray LDS leaders as infallible, both as leaders and as men? This is not the sacred history we know.

Sacred history (which is contained in the Bible, Book of Mormon, Doctrine and Covenants, and Pearl of Great Price) is an absolute refutation of the kind of history Elders Benson and Packer seem to be advocating. Sacred history presents prophets and apostles as the most human of men who have been called by God to prophetic responsibility. Sacred history portrays spiritual dimensions and achievements of God's leaders as facts, but it also matter-of-factly demonstrates the weaknesses of God's leaders. Examples are scriptural accounts of Abraham's abandonment of his wife Hagar and son Ishmael, Noah's drunkenness, Lot's incest, Moses' arrogance, Jonah's vacillation, Peter's impetuosity and cowardice, Peter and Paul's mutual criticism, Lehi's doubt, Alma the Elder's whoredoms, Alma the Younger's apostasy, and the progression of Corianton from adulterous missionary through repentance to one of the three presiding high priests of the church among the Nephites. Moreover, the Doctrine and Covenants contains frequent condemnations of Joseph Smith by the Lord. Sacred history affirms the reality of divine revelation and inspiration but also demonstrates that God's leaders often disagree and do not follow divine revelations consistently. An example is Peter's continued shunning of Gentiles despite his revelation at Joppa, for which Paul publicly condemned him.

According to the standards of history required by those who have criticized Mormon historians, writers of scriptural history are suspect at best and faith-destroying at worst. To use Elder Packer's words, "Instead of going up to where [God's leaders] were, he devised a way of collecting mistakes and weaknesses and limitations to compare with his own. In that sense he has attempted to bring a historical figure down to his level and in that way feel close to him and perhaps to justify his own weaknesses."[37] In fact, the scriptures do exactly what Elder Packer condemns.

Sacred history presents God's leaders as understandable human beings with whom the reader can identify because of their weaknesses at the same time the reader reveres the prophetic mantle. This enriches the lives of readers by encouraging them to identify and empathize with fallible, human prophets. Sacred history does not discourage readers by presenting prophets as otherworldly personages for whom the reader can feel only awe and adoration.

A young contemporary of Joseph Smith expressed the importance of identifying with fallible prophets in this way. "I saw Joseph Smith the Prophet do things which I did not approve of; and yet," he said, "I thanked God that he would put upon a man who had these imperfections the power and authority which he placed upon him . . . for I knew I myself had weaknesses and I thought there was a chance for me." This young man, Lorenzo Snow, eventually became an apostle and president of the LDS church.[38] The biography of Spencer W. Kimball, by his son and grandson, is virtually sacred history in its presentation of a loveable human prophet of God.[39] On the other hand, a Mormon history of benignly angelic church leaders apparently advocated by Elders Benson and Packer would border on idolatry.

Mormon historians have been accused of writing church history to accommodate non-Mormon scholarship, but Elder Packer advocates another type of accommodation history. He assaults the philosophy and conduct of Mormon historians because their objective church history "may unwittingly be giving 'equal time' to the adversary," and because such history "may be read by those not mature enough for 'advanced history' and a testimony in seedling stage may be crushed."[40] In regard to this latter point, he takes historians to task for being "so willing to ignore the necessity for teaching fundamentals" before presenting advanced information, and observes that "teaching some things that are true prematurely or at the wrong time, can invite sorrow and heartbreak instead of the joy intended to accompany learning."[41]

But Elder Packer does not advocate the gradual exposure of Mormons to historical truth. He excluded that possibility by warning historians against publishing objective history even in professional journals that "go far beyond the audience that they have intended, and destroy faith." He also assails Mormon historians who "want to tell everything whether it is worthy or faith promoting or not."[42] Elder Packer is not advocating Paul's dictum of milk before meat (1 Cor. 3:3; Heb. 5:12), but he demands that Mormon historians provide only a church history diet of milk to Latter-day Saints of whatever experience.

No historian I know of is insensitive to prerequisites. We give presentations differently to high school students than to graduate students. We write about the same topic more complexly for professional journals than for church magazines. I am personally aware of the need to reassure church members by cushioning evidence that is controversial. Half my own family are Catholics, several are recent Mormon converts, and others are inactive. Nevertheless, a diet of milk alone will stunt the growth of, if not kill, any child. That is true in nutrition and in religion.

Aside from calling for the kind of church history which would not surprise or offend even the newest convert, Elder Packer urges that historians write church history from a siege mentality to deny any information that anti-Mormons could possibly use to criticize the church. By this standard, most of the Old Testament, the gospel of John, many of Paul's epistles, and the Book of Revelation would never have been approved for inclusion in the Bible.

In fact, even at its most embattled, sacred history of the early Christian church was candid about problems at church headquarters. At the very time the Romans were persecuting and martyring early Christians, New Testament writers included discussion of Peter's weaknesses, of disagreements between apostles, and of apostolic condemnations of whole communities of Christians.

In the mid-nineteenth century, Brigham Young and other LDS leaders published sermons which spoke openly about Joseph Smith's weaknesses at the same time they testified of his prophetic calling. For example, Brigham Young publicly stated that Joseph Smith "had all the weaknesses a man could have when the vision was not upon him."[43] This at a time when Mormons were persecuted and assailed in the public press. Why does the well-established and generally respected LDS church today need a protective, paranoid approach to its history that the embattled early Mormons did not manifest?

Mormon historians are told to write church history as elementarily as possible and as defensively as possible. This is accommodation history for the weakest of the weak Latter-day Saints, for the vilest of the vile anti-Mormons, and for the most impressionable of the world's sycophants.

The sacred history of the scriptures stands in stark contrast to the historical standards of Elders Benson and Packer. It is presented for the instruction and enlightenment of the Saints, with the affirmation that the weaker Saints can become strong by knowing difficult truths about the church, that enemies of God's truth will distort to their own destruction anyway, and that the praise of the world is seductive.

The latter point was of special concern to J. Reuben Clark. He told priesthood leaders in the 1950s that there "is a startling parallel" between second-century Christianity and second-century Mormonism. He also noted that in the early church the Saints "were extremely anxious for two things: First, to be well thought of by the pagans. Their ears itched for praise. Do any of you brethren know anything about such a tendency as that?"[44]

Sacred history is not timid, defensive, or public-relations oriented. Mormon historians are better to use it as their guide rather than the accommodation history that has characterized twentieth-century Mormonism and which some general authorities want to perpetuate indefinitely.

The accommodation history practiced by some LDS writers is intended to protect the Saints but actually disillusions them and makes them vulnerable. Elder Benson, reporting with irritation the fact that LDS seminary and institute teachers sometimes ask him, "When and where can we begin to tell them our *real* story?" observed, "Inferred in that question is the accusation that the Church has not been telling the truth."[45] The reality is that there have been occasions when LDS church leaders, teachers, and writers have not told the truth they knew about difficulties of the Mormon past but have offered to the Saints a mixture of platitudes, half-truths, omissions, and plausible denials.

We are told that distorting LDS history can be justified because "we are at war with the adversary" and must also protect any Latter-day Saint whose "testimony [is] in seedling stage."[46] But such a public-relations defense may actually be a Maginot Line of sandy fortifications which "the enemy" can easily breach and which has been built up by digging lethal pits into which the Saints will stumble. So-called "faith-promoting" church history which conceals controversies and difficulties of the Mormon past may actually undermine the faith of Latter-day Saints who eventually learn about the problems from other sources.

One of the most obvious demonstrations of that fact is the continued spread of unauthorized polygamy among Latter-day Saints during the last seventy-five years, despite efforts of church leaders to stop it. Essential to this church campaign is the official historical argument that there were no plural marriages authorized by the church or First Presidency after the 1890 Manifesto. This official position adds that whatever plural marriages occurred between 1890 and the so-called "Second Manifesto" of April 1904 were the sole responsibility of two renegade apostles, John W. Taylor and Matthias F. Cowley.[47]

As a lifelong opponent of post-1890 polygamy, J. Reuben Clark knew otherwise. He spearheaded the administrative suppression of polygamist Fundamentalists from the time he entered the First Presidency in 1933, but he ruefully noted in 1945 "that one of the reasons why the so-called 'Fundamentalists' had made such inroads among our young people was because we had failed to teach them the truth."[48] The truth was that more than 250 plural marriages occurred from 1890 to 1904 in Mexico, Canada, and the United States by authorization of the First Presidency and by action or assent of all but one or two members of the Quorum of the Twelve Apostles. The official denial of that fact in LDS church statements and histories has actually given credibility to Fundamentalists in their promotion of new plural marriages after 1904 in defiance of First Presidency authority.[49]

Despite his recognition of the problem, President Clark himself was trapped within an administrative policy of historical defensiveness which he did not create and which he decided not to resist. The continued battle of church authorities against present-day polygamy might have been more successful had they encouraged a full disclosure of authorized post-Manifesto polygamy that would enable a contrast to be made with the unauthorized polygamy that has continued to the present. This would have reflected LDS president John Taylor's philosophy: "Some people will say 'Oh, don't talk about it.' I think a full, free talk is frequently of great use; we want nothing secret nor underhanded, and for one I want no association with things that cannot be talked about and will not bear investigation."[50]

As a Mormon historian, I desire to use the skills of scholarship in research and documentation, to emulate examples of sacred history in approach and philosophy, and to help Saints understand the vitality of Mormonism from a position of knowledgeable strength. In warning Mormon historians against objective history and against telling too much truth about the Mormon past, Elder Packer says, "Do not spread disease germs!"[51]

I see Elder Packer's symbolism in another way. It is apostates and anti-Mormons who seek to infect the Saints with "disease germs" of doubt, disloyalty, disaffection, and rebellion. These Typhoid Marys of spiritual contagion obtain the materials of their assaults primarily from the readily available documents and publications created by former LDS leaders and members themselves.

To continue Elder Packer's symbolism, believing Mormon historians like myself seek to write candid church history in a context of perspective in order to inoculate the Saints against historical "disease germs" that apostates and anti-Mormons thrust upon them. The criticism we have received in our efforts would be similar to leaders of eighteenth-century towns trying to combat smallpox contagion by locking up Dr. Edward Jenner who tried to inoculate the people and by killing the cows he wanted to use for his vaccine.[52]

The central argument of enemies of the LDS church is historical, and if we seek to build the Kingdom of God by ignoring or denying problem areas of our past, we are leaving the Saints unprotected. As one who has received death threats from anti-Mormons because they perceive me as an enemy historian, it is discouraging to be regarded as subversive by those I sustain as prophets, seers, and revelators.

Historians did not create problem areas of the Mormon past, but most of us cannot agree to conceal them, either. We are trying to respond to those problem areas of Mormon experience. Attacking the messenger does not alter the reality of the message.

Dedicated and believing Mormon historians seek to build the Kingdom of God and to strengthen the Saints by "speaking the truth in love," as Paul counseled (Eph. 4:15). For this Mormon historian, the words of a familiar church hymn express his hope:

O Thou Rock of our Salvation,
Jesus, Savior of the world,
In our poor and lowly station
We thy banner have unfurled.
Gather round the standard bearer;
Gather round in strength of youth.
Every day the prospect's fairer
While we're battling for the truth.

Aftermath. About forty people attended the Phi Alpha Theta meeting where I gave the above remarks as a talk at Brigham Young University on 4 November 1981. I expected some local discussion but was surprised by the publicity this essay received.

As word of my presentation spread, academics and non–academics, active and inactive Mormons, and even non-Mormons advised me not to publish it. They were concerned about personal consequences. At that time, others in the same groups encouraged its publication, and *Sunstone* was preparing to print it with my permission. On 18 November 1981, the *Seventh East Press*, then BYU's unofficial student newspaper, ran a front-page story about the talk.

This publicity resulted in meetings with my college dean and with a member of the First Presidency. I met first with Martin B. Hickman in the dean's office of the College of Family, Home, and Social Sciences, and later with President Gordon B. Hinckley in his home on Sunday, 22 November. Neither Dean Hickman nor President Hinckley gave direct instructions, but both advised against publication of "On Being a Mormon Historian." A few days later, I asked *Sunstone*'s editors not to print the already-typeset essay. In the meantime Elder Packer's address against Mormon historians had been scheduled for publication in the February 1982 issue of the *Ensign* magazine, but at the last minute the First Presidency ordered the *Ensign* to remove his talk from the issue.

However, tape recordings and transcriptions of my talk circulated, and Jerald and Sandra Tanner, prominent critics of the Mormon church, published it without my permission. Then *Newsweek*'s issue of 15 February 1982 ran a story ("Apostles vs. Historians") about the talks by Elder Packer and me. A few days later, a general authority invited me to his office. He warned me that he found Elder Packer to be easily offended and vindictive years afterward.

In May, my stake presidency informed me that five former bishops had recommended me to be the ward's new bishop but that Apostle Mark E. Petersen had blocked the appointment. He asked the stake presidency, "Why is Michael Quinn in league with anti-Mormons," apparently referring to the unauthorized publication of my essay by the Tanners.

Elder Petersen arranged for the stake presidency to bring me to the Church Administration Building at 47 East South Temple to meet with Apostles Petersen, Benson, and Packer. The second counselor in the stake presidency accompanied me. The apostles were careful not to ask me a single direct question. In order of seniority (Apostle Benson first, me last), each of us expressed his own views of the *Newsweek* article, the "problems" of writing Mormon history, and the effects of all this on the faith of LDS members. The meeting was congenial and supportive.

President Hinckley telephoned in June 1982 to say that he was sympathetic about a request I had written to obtain access to documents in the First Presidency's vault but that my request could not be granted. Since I now knew all I ever would about post–Manifesto polygamy, I told him I would go ahead and publish the most detailed and supportive study I could of the topic. President Hinckley said the decision was up to me, that he had done what he could to help.

A few weeks later, Apostle Packer told one of my students that my biography of J. Reuben Clark, then in manuscript, "will never see the light of day because it dirties the memory of a good man." Brigham Young University Press published it thanks to the intervention of two senior apostles, Howard W. Hunter and Thomas S. Monson, who both carefully read the manuscript and made limited (and reasonable) suggestions for revision. I was in Europe when *J. Reuben Clark: The Church Years* went on sale in March 1983.

I was still abroad in April when Elder Petersen directed a brief inquisition against contributors to *Dialogue: A Journal of Mormon Thought* and *Sunstone*. This did not involve me, and I only learned about it when someone sent me the newspaper stories about it. When President Hinckley learned about this inquisition, he ordered the apostles to stop it.[53]

Following my return to Salt Lake City that summer, I met with apostles Hunter and Monson. They each indicated support for the kind of honesty involved in my biography of President Clark. Apostle Hunter said, "While we made suggestions for revision in your manuscript, we told the men at BYU that these were simply suggestions. We could not expect you to make changes in your biography which were incompatible with your standards as a historian."[54] Almost a year after its publication, Elder Monson intervened directly to spur the *Church News* to review the book. The previous silence had apparently resulted from the editor's knowledge of Elder Packer's dislike for the book.

In May 1984 my college dean told me he had been instructed by "higher authority" to ask me not to publish a paper I had just presented to the Mormon History Association. It was a historical survey of the public activity of general authorities in business corporations. The dean apologized for having to make this request. I agreed not to publish my presentation and told no one about the incident.

In 1985, after *Dialogue* published my article "LDS Church Authority and New Plural Marriages, 1890-1904," three apostles gave orders for my stake president to confiscate my temple recommend. Six years earlier, I had formally notified the First Presidency and the Managing Director of the church historical department about my research on post-Manifesto polygamy and my intention to publish it.[55] Now I was told that three apostles believed I was guilty of "speaking evil of the Lord's anointed." The stake president was also instructed "to take further action" against me if this did not "remedy the situation" of my writing controversial Mormon history.

James M. Paramore, the area president who relayed these orders, instructed my stake presidency to tell me that this was a local decision and reflected their own judgment of the state of my church membership. My stake president replied that he was not going to tell me something which was untrue. Unlike the area president, my stake president and one of his counselors had read the *Dialogue* article. They saw nothing in it to justify what they were being required to do.

I told my stake president that I would not tell colleagues or friends about this because I did not want to be the center of more publicity. However, I told the stake president that this was an obvious effort to intimidate me from doing history that might "offend the Brethren" (to use Ezra Taft Benson's phrase).[56] The stake president also saw this as a back-door effort to have me fired from BYU. He told me to tell BYU officials that I had a temple recommend and not to volunteer that it was in his desk drawer. He continued to sustain me in my stake calling and said he would not take the "further action" of disfellowshipping or excommunicating me for continuing to do Mormon history. He said he would not presume to instruct me how to do my job as a historian. (Ironically, for decades my stake president had been a close friend and protege of Elder Packer.)

At various stake and regional meetings, Apostle Packer began publicly referring to "a BYU historian who is writing about polygamy to embarrass the Church." At firesides in Utah and California, a member of BYU's religious education department referred to me as "the anti-Christ of BYU." Church leaders today seem to regard my post-Manifesto polygamy article (and much of the New Mormon History) as "speaking evil of the Lord's anointed" because they themselves regard certain acts and words of those earlier church leaders as embarrassing, if not actually wrong. I do not regard it as disloyal to conscientiously recreate the words, acts, and circumstances of earlier prophets and apostles.

In the spring of 1986, graduating history majors at BYU voted me "outstanding professor." That fall BYU's administration had my name dropped from a list of participants in an upcoming celebration of Mormonism in Britain. Then, for the second year in a row, BYU's administration denied my application for "Professional Development Leave." This time the college dean invited me to his office to explain why. He said the apostles on the executive committee of the Board of Trustees had prepared a list of faculty members and research topics which BYU administrators were forbidden to support. "I have always hoped that one day BYU will become a real university," the dean said, "but this makes me feel that day will never arrive."

By January 1987 pressures on me increased. BYU's administration required the history department and Charles Redd Center for the American West to withdraw funds they had promised me to give a paper on general American religion at the University of Paris. It did not matter that the advanced text of the paper, entitled "Religion, Rationalism, and Folk Practices in America to the mid-19th Century," made no reference to Mormonism. I paid my own way to France to represent BYU.

Despite all that had happened, until January 1987 I could not yet believe that my life's hopes were at an end. A new department chair let me know that my situation would improve only if I stopped doing research which implied Mormon studies. As an American social historian, I had many non-religious subjects of interest. Abandoning Mormon history may have been safe in the climate of repression but it was unacceptable to me, especially as an option of duress. "Publish or perish" is the experience of scholars at most universities, but for this Mormon historian it was "publish and perish" at BYU.

After publication of my *Early Mormonism and the Magic World View* in mid-1987, two members of BYU's history department circulated the rumor that my stake high council was excommunicating me for apostasy. The rumor was completely false, but more important, I had thought these rumor-mongers were my colleagues and friends. When a student asked the dean of religious education if BYU was going to fire me, he replied that the Board of Trustees had decided against it. "Like stirring up a turd on the ground," he told the student, "firing Mike Quinn would only make a greater stink." At this point I began applying for research fellowships that would allow me to leave BYU.

No one ever gave me an ultimatum or threatened to fire me from Brigham Young University. However, university administrators and I were both on the losing side of a war of attrition mandated by the general authorities. In separate interviews, my college dean and department chair each asked what I saw as my future at BYU. I said it did not look very bright. The dean then asked how I was coping with the pressures against me. "Not very well," was all I could say. He commented he would understand if I chose to go somewhere else.

On 20 January 1988, I wrote a letter of resignation, effective at the end of the current school semester. "Aside from areas regarded as non-controversial by BYU's Board of Trustees and those responsive to such anticipated or actual views," I explained, "the situation seems to be that academic freedom merely survives at BYU without fundamental support by the institution, exists against tremendous pressure, and is nurtured only through the dedication of individual administrators and faculty members." At the time of my resignation, I had tenure ("continuing status"), was full-professor of history, and was director of the history department's graduate program. My letter of resignation represented my formal acknowledgement of failure—personal and institutional.

The resignation stunned my colleagues. The chair of the history department immediately called a special meeting for me to explain the decision to the faculty. For the first time, I began telling others of the various incidents of intimidation from 1982 to 1987. I declined to follow the recommendation of some BYU faculty members that I file a formal complaint against BYU's accreditation. Also, at my request, a newspaper reporter stopped preparing a story about the intimidation which had led to my resignation. Several faculty members in various departments criticized my decision to resign and not to openly resist the attrition of my academic freedom. "Now they've tasted blood," one professor said, "and you're leaving the rest of us here to face the consequences. Self-censorship will increase."

Because I did not give my students any of the background which led to my resignation, some took the news very hard. A married returned-missionary had enrolled in his second course with me. He began crying as he spoke of his plans to take every class I taught. In leaving, I limited public statements to a farewell essay for BYU's students I had taught and loved for twelve school years: "A Marketplace of Ideas, a House of Faith, and a Prison of Conformity."[57] This was as close as I came to making a fight on my own behalf. I had just held on—until walking away was the only solution I could live with.

Three months after my departure, it angered me to learn that BYU had fired a Hebrew professor for his private views on the historicity of the Book of Mormon. Although I personally regard the Book of Mormon as ancient history and sacred text, I told an inquiring newspaper reporter: "BYU officials have said that Harvard should aspire to become the BYU of the East. That's like saying the Mayo Clinic should aspire to be Auschwitz. BYU is an Auschwitz of the mind."[58]

When BYU's associate academic vice-president asked me if that was an accurate quote, I confirmed that it was. "Academic freedom exists at BYU only for what is considered non-controversial by the university's Board of Trustees and administrators," I wrote. "By those definitions, academic freedom has always existed at Soviet universities (even during the Stalin era)."[59]

The extinction of free thought is more accurately a goal of some general authorities, some BYU administrators, and even some faculty members. By contrast, many BYU faculty are dedicated to the unfettered life of mind for themselves and students. If BYU were a real university, there would be no element of risk or courage in promoting a marketplace of ideas there. I admire those who remain at BYU to continue a quiet struggle for genuine academic freedom.[60]

It is also my conviction that God desires everyone to enjoy freedom of inquiry and expression without fear, obstruction, or intimidation. I find it one of the fundamental ironies of modern Mormonism that the same general authorities who praise free agency, also do their best to limit free agency's prerequisites—access to information, uninhibited inquiry, and freedom of expression.[61]

I again addressed this issue in 1991 after a rarely used joint declaration by the First Presidency and Quorum of the Twelve Apostles condemned the annual Sunstone Symposium.[62] Those who questioned this statement were being summarily dropped from church positions, and both church and BYU administrative pressure was directed against a junior professor of anthropology at BYU who had given a symposium paper. I observed in a newspaper story: "Consistently, from the beginning, the [LDS] church leadership has always been uncomfortable with open forums that have been organized by the rank and file." However, I added, "in the 19th century, the leadership recognized the existence of a loyal opposition and the 20th does not."[63]

During the following months, many contributors to *Sunstone* and *Dialogue* told me of being asked to meet with a bishop or stake president who presented marked copies of their published articles and symposium talks. In each case, the local leader said it was his own idea to meet with the individuals, to express concern about his or her participation in these intellectual forums, and to recommend an end to activity which "offends the Brethren" or "disturbs the faithful." One stake president even asked the person to consider voluntarily withdrawing from the church. The uncomfortable demeanor of the inquiring local leaders, the photocopies of articles with underlined passages, the awkward assurances of this investigation's local origin— all were familiar to me. In October 1991, I tried to put this in historical perspective as part of a panel discussion, "Let the Consequences Follow: Telling the Truth About Our History."[64]

Since leaving BYU and Utah, I have been an independent

free-lance writer. I still do Mormon history. People of various persuasions seem eager for it.

NOTES

1. As a Brigham Young University history professor, I delivered this
essay as an address at the 4 November 1981 meeting of Phi Alpha Theta (the
student history association). The organization's student president had asked
me to help history majors understand my perspective on Mormon history in
view of a recent address by LDS apostle Boyd K. Packer. After a decade,
Sunstone magazine (which had first right of refusal for this essay) consented
to publication of this essay by Signature Books. This first authorized publication of "On Being a Mormon Historian" has added some clarifications to
the early text, updated the notes, and made some corrections of style and
punctuation.

2. Leonard J. Arrington, "Scholarly Studies of Mormonism in the
Twentieth Century," *Dialogue: A Journal of Mormon Thought* 1 (Spring 1966):
15-32; David J. Whittaker, "Historians and the Mormon Experience: A
Sesquicentennial Perspective," *A Sesquicentennial Look at Church History*
(Provo, UT: Religious Instruction, Brigham Young University, 1980), 293-
327; Davis Bitton and Leonard J. Arrington, *Mormons and Their Historians*
(Salt Lake City: University of Utah Press, 1988), 87-107, 126-69; Henry
Warner Bowden, "From the Age of Science to an Age of Uncertainty: History
and Mormon Studies in the Twentieth Century," *Journal of Mormon History*
15 (1989): 105-20.

3. Leonard J. Arrington, "Reflections on the Founding of the
Mormon History Association, 1965-1983," *Journal of Mormon History* 10
(1983): 91-103; Maureen Ursenbach Beecher, "*Entre Nous*: An Intimate
History of MHA," *Journal of Mormon History* 12 (1985): 43-52; Davis Bitton,
"Taking Stock: The Mormon History Association after Twenty-five Years,"
Journal of Mormon History 17 (1991): 1-27; B. J. Fogg, "My Weekend with the
Mormon History Association," *Sunstone* 15 (Sept. 1991): 64-65; David J.
Cherrington, "Societies and Organizations," in Daniel H. Ludlow, ed., *Ency-
clopedia of Mormonism: The History, Scripture, Doctrine, and Procedures of the
Church of Jesus Christ of Latter-day Saints*, 4 vols. (New York: Macmillan
Publishing Co., 1992), 3:1388.

4. Leonard J. Arrington, "Historian as Entrepreneur: A Personal
Essay," *Brigham Young University Studies* 17 (Winter 1977): 193-209;
Arrington, "The Writing of Latter-day Saint History: Problems, Accomplish-
ments and Admonitions," *Dialogue: A Journal of Mormon Thought* 14 (Fall
1981): 119-29; Davis Bitton, "Ten Years in Camelot: A Personal Memoir,"
Dialogue: A Journal of Mormon Thought 16 (Autumn 1983): 9-35; Howard C.

Searle, "Historians, Church," in Ludlow, *Encyclopedia of Mormonism*, 2:591.

5. For the perspective of RLDS authors on this same transition in their institutional and interpretive history, see Richard P. Howard, *Restoration Scriptures: A Study of Their Textual Development* (Independence, MO: Herald House, 1969); Richard P. Howard, "Latter Day Saint Scriptures and the Doctrine of Propositional Revelation," and Paul M. Edwards, "Why Am I Afraid to Tell You Who I Am?" in *Courage: A Journal of History, Thought and Action* 1 (June 1971): 209-25, 241-46; Richard P. Howard, "The Effect of Time and Changing Conditions on Our Knowledge of History," *Saints' Herald* 120 (June 1973): 54; Paul M. Edwards, "The Irony of Mormon History," *Utah Historical Quarterly* 41 (Autumn 1973): 393-409; Robert B. Flanders, "Some Reflections on the New Mormon History," *Dialogue: A Journal of Mormon Thought* 9 (Spring 1974): 34-41; Richard P. Howard, "The Historical Method as the Key to Understanding Our Heritage," *Saints' Herald* 121 (Nov. 1974): 53; Paul M. Edwards, "The Secular Smiths," *Journal of Mormon History* 4 (1977): 3-17; F. Henry Edwards, "Engagement with Church History," *John Whitmer Historical Association Journal* 1 (1981): 30-33; Richard P. Howard, "Adjusting Theological Perspectives to Historical Reality," *Saints' Herald* 129 (Sept. 1982): 28; C. Robert Mesle, "History, Faith, and Myth," *Sunstone* 7 (Nov.-Dec. 1982): 10-13; Richard P. Howard, "Themes in Latter Day Saint History," *John Whitmer Historical Association Journal* 2 (1982): 23-29; Richard P. Howard, "The Changing RLDS Response to Mormon Polygamy: A Preliminary Analysis," *John Whitmer Historical Association Journal* 3 (1983): 14-28; Richard P. Howard, "The Problem of History and Revelation," *Saints' Herald* 131 (Oct. 1984): 24; Paul M. Edwards, "Our Own Story," *Sunstone* 10 (Jan.-Feb. 1985): 40-41; Alma R. Blair, "RLDS Views of Polygamy: Some Historiographical Notes," *John Whitmer Historical Association Journal* 5 (1985): 16-28; Paul M. Edwards, "The New Mormon History," *Saints' Herald* 133 (Nov. 1986): 12-14, 20; W. Grant McMurray, "'As Historians and Not as Partisans': The Writing of Official History in the RLDS Church," and Roger D. Launius, "A New Historiographical Frontier: The Reorganization in the Twentieth Century," *John Whitmer Historical Association Journal* 6 (1986): 43-52, 53-63; Don H. Compier, "History and the Problem of Evil: Reflections on the Philosophical and Theological Implications of the 'New Mormon History,'" and Flanders, "Review," *John Whitmer Historical Association Journal* 8 (1988): 45-53, 91-93; Roger D. Launius, "Whither Reorganization Historiography?"; Paul M. Edwards, "A Time and a Season: History as History," *John Whitmer Historical Association Journal* 10 (1990): 24-50, 85-90; and Paul M. Edwards, "A Community of Heart," *Journal of Mormon History* 17 (1991): 28-34.

6. The best evidence and catalog of this outpouring is the annual "Mormon Bibliography" which *Brigham Young University Studies* began publishing in 1961. The New Mormon History has similarly influenced RLDS

church membership through the official Herald Publishing House, the *Saints' Herald*, and instruction at the church's Lamoni College and Temple School.

7. Bitton, "Ten Years in Camelot," 17, makes a similar observation. The most well-known example is Jerald and Sandra Tanner's *Mormonism: Shadow or Reality?* which is approaching its 30th year of publication in various reprints and editions. For an evaluation of their work, see Lawrence Foster, "Career Apostates: Reflections on the Works of Jerald and Sandra Tanner," *Dialogue: A Journal of Mormon Thought* 17 (Summer 1984): 35-60. Less well-known but academically more influential were scholarly publications by the Reverend Wesley P. Walters such as "New Light on Mormon Origins from Palmyra (N.Y.) Revival," *Bulletin of the Evangelical Theological Society* 10 (Fall 1967): 227-44, reprinted in *Dialogue: A Journal of Mormon Thought* 4 (Spring 1969): 60-81; Walters, "Joseph Smith's Bainbridge, N.Y., Court Trials," *Westminster Theological Journal* 36 (Winter 1976): 123-55; and Walters, "From Occult to Cult with Joseph Smith, Jr.," *The Journal of Pastoral Practice* 1 (Summer 1977): 121-37.

8. Ezra Taft Benson, "God's Hand in Our Nation's History," in *1976 Devotional Speeches of the Year* (Provo, UT: Brigham Young University Press, 1977), 310, 313; also Sheri L. Dew, *Ezra Taft Benson: A Biography* (Salt Lake City: Deseret Book Company, 1987), 454-55.

9. Boyd K. Packer, "The Mantle is Far, Far Greater than the Intellect," presented 22 Aug. 1981 to seminary, institute, and Brigham Young University religion instructors, and published in *Brigham Young University Studies* 21 (Summer 1981): 259-78. This talk was also immediately published as a pamphlet by the Church Educational System. Similar, but less developed, views subsequently appeared in the following general authority talks: Gordon B. Hinckley, "Stop Looking for Storms and Enjoy the Sunlight," *Church News*, 3 July 1983, 10-11; Hinckley, "Be Not Deceived," *Ensign* 13 (Nov. 1983): 46; Packer, "Dedication of Museum of Church History and Art," *Ensign* 14 (May 1984): 104; Hinckley, "Keep the Faith," *Ensign* 15 (Sept. 1985): 3-6; Hinckley, Remarks at Priesthood Session in *October 1985 Conference Report*, 63-69; and Russell M. Nelson, "Truth—and More," *Ensign* 16 (Jan. 1986): 69-73.

10. Packer, "The Mantle," 265, 266.

11. Louis C. Midgley, "A Critique of Mormon Historians: The Question of Faith and History," mimeographed draft, 30 Sept. 1981, 54-55. For similar criticisms, see Joe J. Christensen, "The Value of Church History and Historians: Some Personal Impressions," *Proceedings of the Church Education System Church Historian Symposium* (Provo, UT: Brigham Young University Press, 1977), pp. 12-17; Neal W. Kramer, "Looking for God in History," *Sunstone* 8 (Jan.-Mar. 1983): 15-17; David E. Bohn, "No Higher Ground: Objective History Is an Illusive Chimera," *Sunstone* 8 (May-June 1983): 26-32; Scott C. Dunn, "So Dangerous It Couldn't Be Talked About," *Sunstone* 8

(Nov.-Dec. 1983): 47-48; David Earl Bohn, "The Burden of Proof," *Sunstone* 10 (June 1985): 2-3; Midgley, "Church Espouses Agency, Critics Accuse Authorities of Seeking Blind Obedience," *BYU Daily Universe*, 10 Dec. 1985, 18; Robert L. Millet, "How Should Our Story Be Told?" and Midgley, "Faith and History," in Robert Millet, ed., *"To Be Learned Is Good, If . . .* (Salt Lake City: Bookcraft, 1987), 1-8, 219-26; Keith W. Perkins, "Why Are We Here in New England?: A Personal View of Church History," in Donald Q. Cannon, ed., *Regional Studies in Latter-day Saint History* (Provo, UT: Brigham Young University, 1987); M. Gerald Bradford, "The Case for the New Mormon History: Thomas G. Alexander and His Critics," *Dialogue: A Journal of Mormon Thought* 21 (Winter 1988): 143-150; Midgley, "Which Middle Ground?" *Dialogue: A Journal of Mormon Thought* 22 (Summer 1989): 6-8; Arthur H. King and C. Terry Warner, "Talent and the Individual's Tradition: History as Art, and Art as Moral Response," and Midgley, "The Challenge of Historical Consciousness: Mormon History and the Encounter with Secular Modernity," in John M. Lundquist and Stephen D. Ricks, eds., *By Study and Also By Faith: Essays in Honor of Hugh Nibley on the Occasion of His Eightieth Birthday, 27 March 1990*, 2 vols. (Salt Lake City: Deseret Book, 1990), 2:484-501, 502-51; David Earl Bohn, "Our Own Agenda: A Critique of the Methodology of the New Mormon History," *Sunstone* 14 (June 1990): 45-49; Gary F. Novak, "Naturalistic Assumptions and the Book of Mormon," *Brigham Young University Studies* 30 (Summer 1990): 23-40; Louis C. Midgley, "The Myth of Objectivity: Some Lessons for Latter-day Saints," *Sunstone* 14 (Aug. 1990): 54-46; Louis Midgley, "Revisionist Pride," *Sunstone* 15 (Oct. 1991): 4-5.

12. For other (sometimes academic, sometimes personal) statements by historians of Mormon background concerning the writing of Mormon history, see notes 4 and 5 above, and also Leonard J. Arrington, "Preface," *Great Basin Kingdom: An Economic History of the Latter-day Saints, 1830-1900* (Cambridge, MA: Harvard University Press, 1958), esp. viii-ix; Marvin S. Hill, "The Historiography of Mormonism," *Church History* 28 (Dec. 1959): 418-26; Klaus J. Hansen, "Reflections on the Writing of Mormon History," *Dialogue: A Journal of Mormon Thought* 1 (Spring 1966): 158-60; Richard L. Bushman, "Taking Mormonism Seriously," *Dialogue: A Journal of Mormon Thought* 1 (Summer 1966): 81-84; Bushman, "The Future of Mormon History," *Dialogue: A Journal of Mormon Thought* 1 (Autumn 1966): 23-26; Arrington, "The Search for Truth and Meaning in Mormon History," *Dialogue: A Journal of Mormon Thought* 3 (Summer 1968): 56-66; Bushman, "Faithful History," *Dialogue: A Journal of Mormon Thought* 4 (Winter 1969): 11-25; Fawn M. Brodie, *Can We Manipulate the Past?* (Salt Lake City: Center for the Study of the American West, University of Utah, 1970); Richard D. Poll, "God and Man in History," *Dialogue: A Journal of Mormon Thought* 7 (Spring 1972): 101-09; Hill, "Brodie Revisited: A Reappraisal," *Dialogue: A*

100

Journal of Mormon Thought 7 (Winter 1972): 85; Hill, "Secular or Sectarian History? A Critique of *No Man Knows My History,*" *Church History* 43 (Mar. 1974): 78-96; William Mulder, "Fatherly Advice," *Dialogue: A Journal of Mormon Thought* 9 (Winter 1974): 77-80; "History Is Then and Now: A Conversation with Leonard J. Arrington, Church Historian," *Ensign* 5 (July 1975): 8-13; Mulder, "The Mormon Angle of Historical Vision: Some Maverick Reflections," and Marvin S. Hill, "The 'Prophet Puzzle' Assembled: Or, How to Treat Our Historical Diplopia Toward Joseph Smith," *Journal of Mormon History* 3 (1976): 13-22, 101-05; Poll, "Nauvoo and the New Mormon History: A Bibliographical Survey," *Journal of Mormon History* 5 (1978): 105-123; James B. Allen, "Line Upon Line," *Ensign* 9 (July 1979): 32-39; Charles S. Peterson, "Mormon History: Some Problems and Prospects," *Encyclia: Journal of the Utah Academy of Sciences, Arts and Letters* 56 (1979): 114-26; "Mormon History: A Dialogue with Jan Shipps, Richard Bushman and Leonard Arrington," *Century 2* [BYU] 4 (Spring-Summer 1980): 27-39; Richard Sherlock, "The Gospel Beyond Time: Thoughts on the Relation of Faith and Historical Knowledge," *Sunstone* 5 (July-Aug. 1980): 20-23; James L. Clayton, "History and Theology: The Mormon Connection: A Response," *Sunstone* 5 (Nov.-Dec. 1980): 51-53; Roger Elvin Borg, "'Theological Marionettes': Historicism in Mormon History," *Thetean: A Student Journal of History* (Provo, UT: Beta Iota Chapter of Phi Alpha Theta, Brigham Young University, 1981): 5-20; Arrington, "The Writing of Latter-day Saint History: Problems, Accomplishments and Admonitions," *Dialogue: A Journal of Mormon Thought* 14 (Fall 1981): 119-29; Davis Bitton, "Mormon Biography," *Biography: An Interdisciplinary Quarterly* 4 (Winter 1981): 1-16; Clayton, "Does History Undermine Faith?" *Sunstone* 7 (Mar.-Apr. 1982): 33-40; Ronald K. Esplin, "How Then Should We Write History? Another View" *Sunstone* 7 (Mar.-Apr. 1982): 41-45; Jay Fox, "Clio and Calliope: Writing Imaginative Histories of the Pacific," *Proceedings of the Mormon Pacific Historical Society, Third Annual Conference*, April 10, 1982, 12-19; Ronald W. Walker, "The Nature and Craft of Mormon Biography," *Brigham Young University Studies* 22 (Spring 1982): 179-92; Bitton, "Like the Tigers of Old Time," *Sunstone* 7 (Sept.-Oct. 1982): 44-48; Melvin T. Smith, "Faithful History: Hazards and Limitations," *Journal of Mormon History* 9 (1982): 61-69; Arrington, "Personal Reflections on Mormon History," *Sunstone* 8 (July-Aug. 1983): 41-45; Smith, "Faithful History/Secular Faith," *Dialogue: A Journal of Mormon Thought* 16 (Winter 1983): 65-71; Thomas G. Alexander, "Toward the New Mormon History: An Examination of the Literature on the Latter-day Saints in the Far West," in Michael P. Malone, ed., *Historians and the American West* (Lincoln: University of Nebraska Press, 1983), 344-68; Smith, "Faithful History/Secular Religion," *John Whitmer Historical Association Journal* 3 (1983): 51-58; Hill, "Richard L. Bushman: Scholar and Apologist," *Journal of Mormon History* 11

(1984): 125-33; Lavina Fielding Anderson, "The Assimilation of Mormon History: Modern Mormon Historical Novels," *Mormon Letters Annual, 1983* (Salt Lake City: Association for Mormon Letters, 1984), 1-9; Arrington, "Why I Am a Believer," and Walker, "A Way Station," *Sunstone* 10 (Apr. 1985): 36-38, 58-59; Grant Underwood, "Re-visioning Mormon History," *Pacific Historical Review* 55 (Aug. 1986): 403-26; Alexander, "Historiography and the New Mormon History: A Historian's Perspective," *Dialogue: A Journal of Mormon Thought* 19 (Fall 1986): 25-49; Alexander, "No Way to Build Bridges," *Dialogue: A Journal of Mormon Thought* 22 (Spring 1989): 5; Hill, "The New Mormon History Reassessed in Light of Recent Books on Joseph Smith and Mormon Origins," *Dialogue: A Journal of Mormon Thought* 21 (Autumn 1988): 115-27; Poll, *History and Faith: Reflections of a Mormon Historian* (Salt Lake City: Signature Books, 1989); Hansen, "Arrington's Historians," *Sunstone* 13 (Aug. 1989): 41-43; "Coming to Terms with Mormon History: An Interview with Leonard Arrington," *Dialogue: A Journal of Mormon Thought* 22 (Winter 1989): 39-54; Hill, "Afterword," *Brigham Young University Studies* 30 (Fall 1990): 117-24; David B. Honey and Daniel C. Peterson, "Advocacy and Inquiry in Mormon Historiography," *Brigham Young University Studies* 31 (Spring 1991): 139-79; Gary James Bergera, "The New Mormon Anti-Intellectualism," *Sunstone* 15 (June 1991): 53-55; D. Michael Quinn, "Editor's Introduction," *The New Mormon History: Revisionist Essays on the Mormon Past* (Salt Lake City: Signature Books, 1991); Malcolm R. Thorp, "Some Reflections on New Mormon History and the Possibilities of a 'New' Traditional History," *Sunstone* 15 (Nov. 1991): 39-46; Douglas F. Tobler and S. George Ellsworth, "History: Significance to Latter-day Saints," in Ludlow, *Encyclopedia of Mormonism*, 3:595-98.

13. Dennis Michael Quinn journal, 2 Aug. 1962. Compare Jeffrey R. Holland, "An Analysis of Selected Changes in Major Editions of the Book of Mormon, 1830-1920," M.A. thesis, Brigham Young University, 1966; Dean C. Jessee, "The Original Book of Mormon Manuscript," *Brigham Young University Studies* 10 (Spring 1970): 259-78; Janet Jenson, "Variations Between Copies of the First Edition of the Book of Mormon," *Brigham Young University Studies* 13 (Winter 1973): 214-22; Stan Larson, "Textual Variants in the Book of Mormon Manuscripts," *Dialogue: A Journal of Mormon Thought* 10 (Autumn 1977): 8-30; Stan Larson, "Conjectural Emendation and the Text of the Book of Mormon," *Brigham Young University Studies* 18 (Summer 1978): 563-69. The most detailed presentation of all changes in the Book of Mormon's published 1830 text is the non-scholarly study by Jerald and Sandra Tanner, *3,913 Changes in the Book of Mormon* (Salt Lake City: Modern Microfilm Co., [1965]).

14. Quinn journal, 21 Nov. 1962.

15. Since delivering this essay in 1981 I have published two books. For reviews of *J. Reuben Clark: The Church Years* (Provo, UT: Brigham Young

University Press, 1983), see *Deseret News*, 1 May 1983, E6; *Salt Lake Tribune*, 15 May 1983, E2; *BYU Today*, Dec. 1983, 39; *Utah Historical Quarterly* 52 (Winter 1984): 94-95; *Sunstone Review*, Jan. 1984, 13; *Deseret News "Church News"*, 4 Mar. 1984, 14; *Western Historical Quarterly* 15 (July 1984): 350; *Journal of American History* 71 (Dec. 1984): 665-66; *American Historical Review* 90 (Dec. 1985): 1293-94; *Journal of Mormon History* 12 (1985): 129-33. For reviews of *Early Mormonism and the Magic World View* (Salt Lake City: Signature Books, 1987), see *Logan Herald Journal*, 27 Sept. 1987, 9-10; *Deseret News*, 4 Oct. 1987, E4; *The (San Bernardino) Sun*, 10 Oct. 1987, D4; *Rocky Mountain News*, 17 Oct. 1987, 106; *BYU Daily Universe*, 22 Oct. 1987, 7; *Utah Holiday*, Jan. 1988, 26-28; *Sunstone* 12 (Jan. 1988): 36-40; *Journal of the West* 27 (Apr. 1988): 106; *Saints' Herald* 135 (Apr. 1988): 14; *Utah Historical Quarterly* 56 (Spring 1988): 199-200; *Dialogue: A Journal of Mormon Thought* 21 (Summer 1988): 157-59; *Brigham Young University Studies* 27 (Fall 1987): 87-121; C. Wilford Griggs, "The New Testament of Faith," 3-4, in *New Testament Symposium Speeches*, 1988 (Salt Lake City: Church of Jesus Christ of Latter-day Saints, 1988); *The John Whitmer Historical Association Journal* 8 (1988): 85-87; *Pacific Northwest Quarterly* 79 (Apr. 1988): 80; *Small Press Review* 5 (Apr. 1988): 67; *Contemporary Sociology* 17 (Sept. 1988): 682; *Christian Century* 106 (25 Jan. 1989): 84-85; *New Mexico Historical Quarterly* 64 (Apr. 1989): 242-43; *Western Historical Quarterly* 20 (Aug. 1989): 342-43; *Pacific Historical Review* 58 (Aug. 1989): 379-80; *Critical Review of Books in Religion: 1989*, 336-38; *Church History* 59 (Mar. 1990): 110-12; and *Brigham Young University Studies* 31 (Spring 1991): 161-62.

16. Quinn, "The Mormon Hierarchy: An American Elite, 1832-1932," Ph.D. diss., Yale University, 1976.

17. Ezra Taft Benson, *The Gospel Teacher and His Message* (Salt Lake City: Church Educational System, 1976), 11-12. "Communitarianism" also appears in the transcript copy of the talk, page 8, Special Collections, Harold B. Lee Library, Brigham Young University, Provo, Utah. Specifically, Elder Benson objected to classifying Joseph Smith "among so-called 'primitivists,'" but his objections were to James B. Allen and Glen M. Leonard, *The Story of the Latter-day Saints* (Salt Lake City: Deseret Book Co., 1976), 12-14, 45, which used the terms "Christian Primitivists" and "Christian Primitivism." See also Bitton, "Ten Years in Camelot," 17.

18. The newly published *Encyclopedia of Mormonism* 4:1764-73 provides a glossary of 275 Mormon terms and phrases. However, the glossary and entire encyclopedia make no reference to such official terms (puzzling to non-Mormons) as "endowment company," "mission field," "sacrament gem," "scripture chase," or "second anointing." For the little-known (but important) latter ordinance, see David John Buerger, "The 'Fulness of the Priesthood': The Second Anointing in Latter-day Saint Theology and Practice," *Dialogue: A Journal of Mormon Thought* 16 (Spring 1983): 10-46. The

Encyclopedia of Mormonism also makes no reference to historically significant slang terms like "Jack-Mormon," "golden contact," and colloquialisms like "stake house" or "going through the temple." However, the *Encyclopedia's* essay by Robert W. Blair, "Vocabulary, LDS" (4:1537-38), provides a summary of differences.

19. B. H. Roberts, *A Comprehensive History of the Church of Jesus Christ of Latter-day Saints*, 6 vols. (Salt Lake City: "Published by the Church," 1930), 5:487, 6:519.

20. Packer, "The Mantle," 271.

21. An example is Joseph Fielding Smith's letter to me, dated 9 Aug. 1962, in which he enclosed a form letter decrying Wilford Wood's reprinting of the 1830 edition of the Book of Mormon. Elder Mark E. Petersen frequently complained about the reprinting of *Journal of Discourses* and wanted Mormons to neither read from it nor purchase the volumes. An example is Elder Petersen's letter to Ernest Cook, 30 Nov. 1976, in response to Cook's of 22 Nov. which referred to such remarks. Some authorities objected to my 1978 article in *Brigham Young University Studies* which quoted the *Improvement Era's* description of the use of "signs and tokens" in the temple's "holy order of prayer." Also, the pre-publication review committee for *J. Reuben Clark* asked me not to quote from Clark's "Home, and the Building of Home Life," *Relief Society Magazine* 39 (Dec. 1952): 793-94. In addition, staff members of the LDS church magazines informed me of repeated instances from the mid-1970s on in which the church's Correlation Committee required the deletion of "non-faith-promoting" quotes from such former church publications as *Juvenile Instructor* and *Young Woman's Journal*.

22. Packer, "The Mantle," 272, 263. When Elder Packer interviewed me as a prospective member of Brigham Young University's faculty in 1976, he explained: "I have a hard time with historians because they idolize the truth. The truth is not uplifting; it destroys. I could tell most of the secretaries in the church office building that they are ugly and fat. That would be the truth, but it would hurt and destroy them. Historians should tell only that part of the truth that is inspiring and uplifting."

23. Elder Dallin H. Oaks has identified the tension between the approach of traditional Mormon historians and that of New Mormon Historians: "*Balance is telling both sides. This is not the mission of official Church literature* or avowedly anti-Mormon literature. Neither has any responsibility to present both sides. But when supposedly objective news media or periodicals run a feature or an article on the Church or its doctrines, it ought to be balanced. So should a book length history or biography. Readers of supposedly objective authors and publishers have a right to expect balance in writing about the Church or its doctrines" ("Reading Church History," an address delivered at the Church Educational System's Symposium on the Doctrine

and Covenants, Brigham Young University, Provo, Utah, 18 Aug. 1985, emphasis added). By contrast, New Mormon Historians such as I believe that "official Church literature" is not exempt from the requirement to tell "both sides" and to be balanced.

24. J. Reuben Clark statement, 8 Apr. 1943, in "Budget Beginnings," 11-12, Box 188, J. Reuben Clark Papers, Archives and Manuscripts, Harold B. Lee Library.

25. Dean C. Jessee, "The Writing of Joseph Smith's History," *Brigham Young University Studies* 11 (Summer 1971): 439-473; Jessee, "The Reliability of Joseph Smith's History," *Journal of Mormon History* 3 (1976): 23-46; Howard C. Searle, "Early Mormon Historiography: Writing the History of the Mormons, 1830-1858," Ph.d. diss., University of California at Los Angeles, 1979; Jessee, "Authorship of the History of Joseph Smith: A Review Essay," *Brigham Young University Studies* 21 (Winter 1981): 101-22; Jessee, "Return to Carthage: Writing the History of Joseph Smith's Martyrdom," *Journal of Mormon History* 8 (1981): 3-19; Jessee, *Has Mormon History Been Deliberately Falsified?* (Sandy, UT: Mormon Miscellaneous, 1982); Van Hale, "Writing Religious History: Comparing the *History of the Church* with the Synoptic Gospels," in Maurice L. Draper and Debra Combs, eds., *Restorations Studies* III (Independence, MO: Herald Publishing House, 1986), 133-38; Dean C. Jessee, "Priceless Words and Fallible Memories: Joseph Smith as Seen in the Effort to Preserve His Discourses," and Howard C. Searle, "Willard Richards as Historian," *Brigham Young University Studies* 31 (Spring 1991): 19-40, 54-60. Jessee, Searle, and Hale all emphasize the conscientious efforts of early church historians to reconstruct sermons and accounts from sketchy originals.

However, these authors have generally ignored the more essential problems in the seven-volume *History of the Church*. First, it deleted significant entries in "The History of Joseph Smith," as originally published by *Times and Seasons, Deseret Evening News*, and the *Millennial Star*. Jerald and Sandra Tanner have produced the only extensive comparison of those published versions in their *Changes in Joseph Smith's History* (Salt Lake City: Modern Microfilm, [1964]).

Second (and more important), the *History of the Church* deleted evidence, introduced anachronisms, even reversed meanings in manuscript minutes and other documents which were detailed and explicit in their original form. In 1835 the Doctrine and Covenants began a policy of retroactive editing by reversing previous meanings, adding concepts and whole paragraphs to the texts of previously published revelations. The official alteration of pre-1835 revelations is the more fundamental context for the later pattern of editing in the *History of the Church*. For an analysis of changes in revelatory texts, see Melvin Joseph Peterson, "A Study of the Nature and Significance of the

Changes in the Revelations as Found in a Comparison of the Book of Commandments and Subsequent Editions of the Doctrine and Covenants," M.A. thesis, Brigham Young University, 1955; Richard P. Howard, *Restoration Scriptures: A Study of Their Textual Development* (Independence, MO: Herald House, 1969), 196-263; Robert J. Woodford, "The Historical Development of the Doctrine and Covenants," 3 vols., Ph.D. diss., Brigham Young University, 1974; and Woodford, "The Story of the Doctrine and Covenants," *Ensign* 14 (Dec. 1984): 32-39.

26. Benson, *The Gospel Teacher*, 11. His specific target was Allen and Leonard, *Story of the Latter-day Saints*, 69, 95. On the Word of Wisdom, see also Leonard J. Arrington, "An Economic Interpretation of the Word of Wisdom," *Brigham Young University Studies* 1 (Winter 1959): 37-49; Lester E. Bush, Jr., "The Word of Wisdom in Early Nineteenth-Century Perspective," and Thomas G. Alexander, "The Word of Wisdom: From Principle to Requirement," *Dialogue: A Journal of Mormon Thought* 14 (Fall 1981): 47-65, 78-88. On the similarities between Joseph Smith's teachings about "Three Degrees of Glory" and the available teachings of Emanuel Swedenborg and Thomas Dick, see also Mary Ann Meyers, "Death in Swedenborgian and Mormon Eschatology," *Dialogue: A Journal of Mormon Thought* 14 (Spring 1981): 58-64; Quinn, *Early Mormonism and the Magic World View*, 174-75; and Rick Grunder, *Mormon Parallels: A Preliminary Bibliography of Material Offered For Sale, 1981-1987* (Ithaca, NY: Rick Grunder Books, 1987), 30, 32, 58-61, 150.

27. In the 1830s Joseph Smith was acquainted with the Eleusinian Mysteries and the teachings of both Emanuel Swedenborg and Thomas Dick. See *Latter Day Saints' Messenger and Advocate* 3 (Nov. 1836): 422-23, and 3 (June 1837): 526; William E. Hunter, *Edward Hunter: Faithful Steward* (Salt Lake City: Mrs. William E. Hunter, 1970), 51.

28. Packer, "The Mantle," 262.

29. See, for example, Jan Shipps, "The Prophet Puzzle: Suggestions Leading Toward a More Comprehensive Interpretation of Joseph Smith," *Journal of Mormon History* 1 (1974): 3-20; T. L. Brink, "Joseph Smith: The Verdict of Depth Psychology," *Journal of Mormon History* 3 (1976): 73-83; Klaus J. Hansen, *Mormonism and the American Experience* (Chicago: University of Chicago Press, 1981), 18-24; C. Jess Groesbeck, "The Smiths and Their Dreams and Visions: A Psycho-historical Study of the First Mormon Family," *Sunstone* 12 (Mar. 1988): 22-29.

30. Midgley, "A Critique of Mormon Historians," 27-32; Benson, *The Gospel Teacher*, 11.

31. Packer, "The Mantle," 260; emphasis in original.

32. Benson, *The Gospel Teacher*, 10; Packer, "The Mantle," 259; Midgley, "A Critique of Mormon Historians," 42.

33. Packer, "The Mantle," 262.

34. Benson, *The Gospel Teacher*, 10.

35. 1 Cor. 7:6; Book of Mormon, title page; Al. 40:20; *History of the Church* 5:265; *April 1940 Conference Report*, 14; *Church News*, 31 July 1954, 8. I tried to present a balanced view in my "Decision-Making and Tension in the Mormon Hierarchy," Sunstone Symposium, Salt Lake City, 8 Aug. 1991, summarized in "Periodic Dissent at Top Big Part of LDS History," *Salt Lake Tribune*, 9 Aug. 1991, B-2.

36. Benson, "God's Hand in Our Nation's History," 310; Benson, *The Gospel Teacher*, 10; Packer, "The Mantle," 265; emphasis in original.

37. Packer, "The Mantle," 266.

38. George Q. Cannon journal, 7 Jan. 1898, in Stanley B. Kimball, *Heber C. Kimball: Mormon Patriarch and Pioneer* (Urbana: University of Illinois Press, 1981), xv n1; also similar statement of Lorenzo Snow in Abraham H. Cannon journal, 29 Jan. 1891, Western Americana, Marriott Library, University of Utah, Salt Lake City.

39. Edward L. Kimball and Andrew E. Kimball, Jr., *Spencer W. Kimball, Twelfth President of the Church of Jesus Christ of Latter-day Saints* (Salt Lake City: Bookcraft, 1977).

40. Packer, "The Mantle," 267, 271.

41. Ibid., 265.

42. Ibid., 265, 263.

43. *Journal of Discourses*, 26 vols. (Liverpool: LDS Book Depot, 1855-86), 7:243.

44. *April 1952 Conference Report*, 81; Clark's remarks to Bishops' meeting, 29 Sept. 1950.

45. Benson, *The Gospel Teacher*, 10; Benson, "God's Hand in Our Nation's History," 310.

David B. Honey and Daniel C. Peterson, "Advocacy and Inquiry in Mormon Historiography," *Brigham Young University Studies* 31 (Spring 1991): 153, defend Mormon historians of faith-promoting motivation who "leave out less-than-desirable episodes, tell only one side of the story, or are incomplete in their treatment." In support of that, on page 176, note 76, they argue "that 'suppression of evidence' is in fact an essential step in the application of a 'viable tradition' of interpretation, not, we may add, merely an editorial right to be exercised." They cite Peter Novick, *That Noble Dream: The "Objectivity Question" and the American Historical Profession* (New York: Cambridge University Press, 1988), 527, in support of this. Novick himself quotes without comment or evaluation, an extended argument in favor of the suppression of evidence.

Withholding or suppressing evidence does not refer to omitting evidence that is unimportant or irrelevant to one's subject, as Honey and Peterson indicate. Worse yet, Novick, Honey, and Peterson seem to actually endorse the view that one can withhold evidence from the reader that contradicts a writer's theory or contradicts evidence the writer does present. Since our views of "withholding evidence" are indebted to legal concepts, it is well to remember that the legal process requires the "suppression" of irrelevant evidence. History itself exists as the exclusion of everything unnecessary to tell the story or examine the subject as defined by the historian.

On the other hand, the legal process prohibits the suppression of "material evidence," in other words evidence which directly bears on the case at hand. Contrary to Honey and Peterson (p. 153), writers are certainly "dishonest or bad historians" if they fail to acknowledge the existence of even one piece of evidence they know challenges or contradicts the rest of their evidence. If this omission of relevant evidence is inadvertent, the author is careless (as I have been on occasion). If the omission is an intentional effort to conceal or avoid presenting the reader with evidence that contradicts the preferred view of the writer, that is fraud whether by a scholar or non-scholar, historian or other specialist. If authors write in scholarly style, they are equally dishonest in failing to acknowledge any significant work whose interpretations differ from their own.

Dishonest apologists typically insist on those standards for everyone but themselves and in every subject matter aside from their protected one. Honest apologists avoid suppressing material evidence, even as they seek to downplay the significance of this controversial information. Traditional Mormon history has had (and continues to have) both honest apologists and dishonest apologists. Many "New Mormon Historians" are also honest apologists for what they see as essential truths of Mormon theology and the basic goodness of the Mormon experience. These New Mormon Historian apologists often seek to downplay the significance, or "put into context," any evidence they find which may discomfort believing Mormons. Traditional Mormon apologists discuss such "sensitive evidence" only when this evidence is so well known that ignoring it is almost impossible. In my view, I have always written as a New Mormon Historian and as an honest apologist for the Mormon faith and experience.

    46. Packer, "The Mantle," 268, 271.

    47. Examples are Roberts, *A Comprehensive History of the Church* 6:399-400; Joseph Fielding Smith, *Essentials in Church History* 24th ed. (Salt Lake City: Deseret Book, 1971), 512-13; J. Max Anderson, *The Polygamy Story: Fiction and Fact* (Salt Lake City: Publishers Press, 1979), viii. See also Allen and Leonard, *The Story of the Latter-day Saints*, 443-44; and Leonard J. Arrington and Davis Bitton, *The Mormon Experience: A History of the Latter-day Saints* (New York: Alfred A. Knopf, 1979), 245-46. In the LDS church's new *Encyclopedia of Mormonism* Harvard S. Heath's "Smoot Hearings" (3:1363)

focuses on Taylor and Cowley, who were not the only apostles accurately implicated by the hearings. In contrast, Paul H. Peterson's "Manifesto of 1890" (2:853) gives a brief but accurate statement about the continuation of new plural marriages.

48. Quinn, *J. Reuben Clark*, 183-86, for this quote and its context.

49. Kenneth L. Cannon II, "Beyond the Manifesto: Polygamous Cohabitation Among LDS General Authorities After 1890," *Utah Historical Quarterly* 46 (Winter 1978): 24-36; Victor W. Jorgensen and B. Carmon Hardy, "The Taylor-Cowley Affair and the Watershed of Mormon History," *Utah Historical Quarterly* 48 (Winter 1980): 4-36; Cannon, "After the Manifesto: Mormon Polygamy, 1890-1906," *Sunstone* 8 (Jan.-Apr. 1983): 27-35; D. Michael Quinn, "LDS Church Authority and New Plural Marriages, 1890-1904," *Dialogue: A Journal of Mormon Thought* 18 (Spring 1985): 9-105; Jessie L. Embry, *Mormon Polygamous Families: Life in the Principle* (Salt Lake City: University of Utah Press, 1987); Fred C. Collier and Knut Knutson, eds., *The Trials of Apostle John W. Taylor and Matthias F. Cowley* (Salt Lake City: Collier's Publishing Co., 1987); Jessie L. Embry, "Two Legal Wives: Mormon Polygamy in Canada, the United States and Mexico," and B. Carmon Hardy, "Mormon Polygamy in Mexico and Canada: A Legal and Historiographical Review," in Brigham Y. Card et al., eds., *The Mormon Presence in Canada* (Edmonton: University of Alberta Press, 1990).

On Mormon fundamentalism, see Dean C. Jessee, "A Comparative Study and Evaluation of the Latter-day Saint and 'Fundamentalist' Views Pertaining to the Practice of Plural Marriage," M.A. thesis, Brigham Young University, 1959; Lyle O. Wright, "Origins and Development of the Church of the Firstborn of the Fullness of Times," M.S., Brigham Young University, 1963; Jerold A. Hilton, "Polygamy In Utah and Surrounding Area Since the Manifesto of 1890," M.A. thesis, Brigham Young University, 1965; Robert G. Dyer, "The Evolution of Social and Judicial Attitudes Toward Polygamy," *Utah State Bar Journal* 5 (Spring 1977): 35-45; Verlan M. LeBaron, *The Lebaron Story* (Lubbock, TX: Keels & Co., 1981); Dorothy Allred Solomon, *In My Father's House* (New York: Franklin Watts, 1984); Penelope W. Salzman, "Potter v. Murray City: Another Interpretation of Polygamy and the First Amendment," *Utah Law Review* (1986): 345-71; Richard S. Van Wagoner, *Mormon Polygamy: A History* (Salt Lake City: Signature Books, 1986), 190-222; Kahile Mehr, "The Trial of the French Mission," *Dialogue: A Journal of Mormon Thought* 21 (Autumn 1988): 27-45; Ogden Kraut, *The Fundamentalist Mormon* ([Salt Lake City: Pioneer Press, 1989]); Martha S. Bradley, "Changed Faces: The Official LDS Position on Polygamy, 1890-1990," *Sunstone* 14 (Feb. 1990): 26-33; Ken Driggs, "After the Manifesto: Modern Polygamy and Fundamentalist Mormons," *Journal of Church and State* 32 (Spring 1990): 367-89; E. Jay Bell, "'Living the Principle': Then and Now," *Sunstone* 14 (Aug. 1990): 62; Martha S. Bradley,

"The Women of Fundamentalism: Short Creek, 1953," and Ken Driggs, "Fundamentalist Attitudes toward the Church: The Sermons of Leroy S. Johnson," *Dialogue: A Journal of Mormon Thought* 23 (Summer 1990): 15-37, 38-60; Ken Driggs, "Twentieth-Century Polygamy and Fundamentalist Mormons in Southern Utah," *Dialogue: A Journal of Mormon Thought* 24 (Winter 1991): 44-58; Dirk Johnson, "Polygamists Emerge From Secrecy, Seeking Not Just Peace but Respect," *New York Times*, 9 Apr. 1991, A-22; Ken Driggs, "Utah Supreme Court Decides Polygamist Adoption Case," *Sunstone* 15 (Sept. 1991): 67-68; Ken Driggs, "Who Shall Raise the Children?: Vera Black and the Rights of Polygamous Utah Parents," *Utah Historical Quarterly* 60 (Winter 1992): 27-46; D. Michael Quinn, "Plural Marriage and Mormon Fundamentalism," in Martin E. Marty and R. Scott Appleby, eds., *Fundamentalisms and Society: Reclaiming the Sciences, the Family, and Education* (Chicago: University of Chicago Press, 1992); Martha Sonntag Bradley, "Joseph W. Musser: Dissenter or Fearless Crusader of Truth?" in Roger D. Launius and Linda Thatcher, eds., *Differing Visions: Biographical Essays on Mormon Dissenters* (Evanston: University of Illinois Press, forthcoming).

50. *Journal of Discourses* 20:264.

51. Packer, "The Mantle," 271.

52. For the successful effort (led by Elders Benson and Packer) to close the LDS church archives to open research, see Lyn Ostler, "Access to Church Archives: Penetrating the Silence," *Sunstone Review*, Sept. 1983, 7; Davis Bitton, "Ten Years in Camelot"; Robert Gottlieb and Peter Wiley, *America's Saints: The Rise of Mormon Power* (New York: G.P. Putnam's Sons, 1984), 240-41; Jan Shipps, *Mormonism: The Story of a New Religious Tradition* (Urbana: University of Illinois Press, 1985), 107; Richard D. Ouelette, "Reading Sealed Books at the Archives," *Sunstone* 11 (Sept. 1987): 40-44; and Richard E. Turley, Jr., "Confidential Records," and Searle, "Historians, Church," in Ludlow, *Encyclopedia of Mormonism* 1:310, 2:591-92. In June 1986 the staff of the church historical department announced it was necessary to sign a form which Elder Packer declared gave the right of pre-publication censorship for any archival research completed before signing the form. I and several others refused to sign the form and have not returned to do research at LDS church archives since 1986.

53. "LDS Church Threatens Writers," *Salt Lake Tribune*, 23 May 1983, A-10; Dawn Tracy, "LDS Leaders Challenge Y Professors' Faith," *Provo Herald*, 25 May 1983, 3; "Mormon Brethren Silencing Scholars?" *Salt Lake Tribune*, 26 May 1983, B-4; *Utah Holiday* 12 (Aug. 1983): 77; Gottlieb and Wiley, *America's Saints*, 81-82.

54. Later during this private meeting in his office, Elder Hunter commented on relationships within the Twelve. While discussing his pro-Arab philosophy in connection with the BYU Jerusalem Center, he noted

that he usually acquiesced to the Twelve's unnamed "zealots." He preferred to avoid conflict—even with junior apostles who promoted views contrary to his own. Elder Hunter was not anti-Jewish but described fellow apostles who were so pro-Jewish that they overlooked sensitivities and needs of Arabs, both Christian and Muslim. Elder Hunter dedicated the BYU Jerusalem Center on 16 May 1989.

55. In a 1979 letter to G. Homer Durham, managing director of the church historical department, I summarized my findings concerning post-1890 plural marriages. In the twelve-page letter and in a conversation with Elder Durham a few days later, I expressed my intention to publish this information. I also described my research about post-Manifesto polygamy in letters to the First Presidency in 1979 and 1980, and in detail to Gordon B. Hinckley in 1981. Elder Durham authorized me to examine many restricted documents during the six years after I informed him. In fact, just days before his death in January 1985 he authorized me to examine First Presidency materials for the upcoming *Dialogue* article.

56. Ezra Taft Benson, *The Gospel Teacher and His Message*, 11-12.

57. Originally published in BYU's off-campus paper, *A Student Review*, this essay also appeared in *Sunstone* 12 (Mar. 1988): 6-7.

58. "Ex-BYU Professor Claims Beliefs Led to Dismissal," *Salt Lake Tribune*, 30 July 1988, B-1. For Jeffrey Holland's comparison of Harvard with BYU, see Gary James Bergera and Ronald Priddis, *Brigham Young University: A House of Faith* (Salt Lake City: Signature Books, 1985), 341.

59. Quinn to F. Lamond Tullis, 29 Aug. 1988.

60. For a recent discussion of this topic, see "Academic Freedom Still Questioned on BYU Campus," *Daily Universe*, 20 Nov. 1991, 1, 10; "Professors' Freedom Questioned," *Daily Universe*, 21 Nov. 1991, 1, 8; "Combine Secular With Spiritual, Hafen Says," *Daily Universe*, 22 Nov. 1991, 1, 10.

61. See also Mark S. Gustavson, "Truth as Meaning: Faithful History and the Interests of the Mormon Church," *Sunstone* 14 (June 1990): 52; J. Frederic Voros, Jr., "Freedom of Speech in the Household of Faith," *Sunstone* 15 (Oct. 1991): 16-22.

62. *Deseret News*, 23 Aug. 1991, B-1; "LDS Church Decries Sunstone Sessions, Calls Content Insensitive, Offensive," *Salt Lake Tribune*, 24 Aug. 1991; "Church Issues Statement on 'Symposia,'" *Sunstone* 15 (Oct. 1991): 58-59.

63. "LDS Church Turns Up Heat In Feud With Intellectuals," *Salt Lake Tribune*, 5 Oct. 1991, A-6.

Ironically, the church's new *Encyclopedia of Mormonism* gives a positive description of *Dialogue*, *Sunstone*, the Sunstone symposia, the B. H. Roberts Society, and other independent forums. Cherrington, "Societies and Organizations" (in Ludlow, *Encyclopedia of Mormonism* 3:1389), concludes that these "unofficial organizations and their publications may serve at least six important functions for Church members and/or for the Church." One of the six is that they "provide an opportunity to learn and distribute new insights regarding theology, the scriptures, ancient cultures, historical events, and current practices. Dedicated members wanting to combine their religious beliefs with their professional training have made significant scholarly contributions, and unofficial journals provide outlets for publishing them."

64. This presentation at a meeting of the B. H. Roberts Society on 17 October 1991 was summarized in "Panel Confronts Role of LDS Intellectuals," *Salt Lake Tribune*, 19 Oct. 1991, A-10. The first of these papers to have been printed is David C. Knowlton, "Of Things in the Heavens, On the Earth, and In the Church," *Sunstone* 15 (Oct. 1991): 12-15. An earlier discussion is Davis Bitton, "Anti-Intellectualism in Mormon History," and James B. Allen, "Thoughts on Anti-Intellectualism: A Response," *Dialogue: A Journal of Mormon Thought* 1 (Autumn 1966): 111-33, 134-40; also see Poll, *History and Faith*; Bergera and Priddis, *Brigham Young University*; and Bitton and Arrington, *Mormons and Their Historians*.

7.
New Perspectives on the Mormon Past: Reflections of a Non-Mormon Historian

Lawrence Foster

UNTIL THE PAST THIRTY-FIVE YEARS THE VERY IDEA OF MORMON HIS-
tory was viewed as something of a joke by most professional historians. Despite the massive outpouring of dissertations and books
devoted to studying Mormon history, virtually none were known or
treated seriously outside the ranks of a handful of western history
buffs, social historians, and other enthusiasts with highly specialized
interests. Brigham Young University dissertations were seen as providing the classic stereotype of the genre. No matter what the topic,
each dissertation seemed to begin with Joseph Smith's first vision
and end with a reaffirmation of the author's faith in the restored
Mormon gospel. In between, almost as an afterthought, were sand-
wiched enormous masses of undigested data with no apparent organizing principle. Sober Mormon scholars could spend inordinate
amounts of time trying to find evidence that Joseph Smith had really
seen an angel—an argument that had about as much interest for
non-Mormon historians as the debates of medieval scholastics over
how many angels could dance on the head of a pin. Though Mormon
history *was* written in English, it might just as well have appeared
in an undeciphered foreign tongue for all the sense it made to the
secular American scholar.

As a non-Mormon historian initially trying to get through this
massive body of writing in order to better understand the controver-

sial origin and early development of Mormon polygamy, I struggled to comprehend the basis for this seemingly pointless collection of data. What was it that made Mormon historical writing so dull to an outsider yet of such importance to an insider? Why, I wondered, did Mormon historians characteristically take their complex and fascinating history and turn it into pablum? Above all why were Mormons so preoccupied with detail and so uninterested in larger conceptual frameworks? Why did Mormons never do anything intellectually with their history?

The answer was a long time in coming, but eventually it became clear to me that in the last analysis to be a Mormon meant to accept the idea that Mormonism explained everything. Mormons did not use theories from other disciplines—with some rare exceptions—because they felt that they already knew all the answers (at least all the answers that really mattered). Most Mormon scholarship thus was simply a footnote which added more evidence to an already well-known and well-loved story. Mormon control and insularity extended even to the thinking of historians themselves and to their writing. It seemed that there were almost no intellectuals within Mormonism—or outside it for that matter—who could step back and view it freshly. Most Mormon scholars still appeared to think almost exclusively within old categories. Disaffected Mormons did no better; they simply stood traditional Mormon arguments on their head. Instead of being a pasteboard saint, for instance, Joseph Smith was a malicious fraud. Even Fawn Brodie in her path-breaking biography *No Man Knows My History* spent too much of her time carping that her Sunday school image of Joseph Smith had not been the full picture. And as always the vast majority of non-Mormons outside the areas of Mormon cultural influence remained largely uninterested in such internal squabbles.

This isolation of Mormon scholarship from the mainstream of American historical writing was, it seemed to me, a most unfortunate situation. For in Mormonism, if anywhere in recent American life, was the sort of group that could provide almost "an ideal laboratory" for the social and intellectual historian of the sort that Perry Miller had found in earlier New England Puritans. Growing out of deeply American roots, Mormon people rejected the pluralism of the dominant culture, and indeed of the modern world. They instead set up a distinctive way of life and in their own manner challenged a host of commonly held assumptions about the way modern society inevitably must develop. And notwithstanding the great difficulties that they faced, Mormons had been remarkably successful—not simply in their own terms but also in terms of the wealth and power that the external society viewed as so significant. Surely both Mormons and non-Mormons could learn something of value about the extraordinary complexity of social change and the varied options for human development from the rich experience of the Latter-day Saints.

Fortunately during the past thirty-five years numerous scholars have begun raising such questions and taking steps to bridge the gap between Mormon history and the scholarly world. Thomas O'Dea's fine sociological study in 1957, *The Mormons*, showed that an outsider could write sympathetically and fairly about Mormons as a people among peoples, raising a host of issues with broader implications. Leonard Arrington's economic analysis in *Great Basin Kingdom*, a year later, showed that a committed insider could place the epic Mormon struggle to develop the Intermountain West into a larger context with meaning for other developing societies. Much of the best scholarship in Mormon history began to focus on the group's political aspirations and activities and the ways that those had been related to American values. Klaus Hansen in *Quest for Empire* started to reconstruct the activities of the secret Council of Fifty, a body which was potentially revolutionary in its rejection of American pluralism. Robert Flanders, in *Nauvoo: Kingdom on the Mississippi*, portrayed the social and economic life of Nauvoo, Illinois, viewing it as an unconventional Jacksonian boom town. And Jan Shipps used sophisticated sampling techniques to study attitudes toward Mormonism in the popular press—showing that however strange Mormonism might appear, it still could be subjected to statistical analysis.

By the mid-1960s and early 1970s, three closely related developments emerged out of the growing interest in Mormon history. First, chronologically speaking, was the founding of the Mormon History Association in 1965. Representing all varieties of Mormon, RLDS, and non-Mormon perspectives, the MHA has grown into an organization of more than a thousand members, publishing its own journal and attracting hundreds of participants to its annual meetings. Second, and almost simultaneous with the founding of the MHA, was the establishment of *Dialogue: A Journal of Mormon Thought* in 1966. Seeking genuine dialogue not simply between Mormons of different persuasions but also between Mormons and non-Mormons who shared their ideas within its pages, *Dialogue* has continued to tackle important and often controversial issues which could not receive full consideration by in-house publications. Third, and in many ways most important, was the appointment in 1972 of a highly respected professional historian, Leonard Arrington, to head a reorganized and revitalized LDS Church Historical Department in Salt Lake City. Convinced that full and well-informed accounts could only strengthen the Mormon church in the long run, Arrington and his associates—who at their peak numbered nearly twenty full-time historians—encouraged the opening of the church archives to serious scholars, both Mormon and non-Mormon alike, and began to put out many important studies themselves. A sense of excitement and exhilaration was generated as increasing numbers of Latter-day Saints began to develop a direct, personal sense of their own history, a deeper appreciation of the richness and complexity of the Mormon past.

Great strides have certainly been made by Mormons during the past two decades in developing a truly informed, professional, and compelling history of their faith. Increasing numbers of non-Mormons scholars too have come to appreciate more fully the enormous social vitality of Latter-day Saints. In the face of such achievements, it is particularly disappointing that so few non-Mormons have also become interested in the scholarly investigation of Mormonism as a religious movement. With the exception of Jan Shipps and a handful of others, non-Mormon scholars have shown little serious interest in the inner religious life that has given meaning to the external social activities of Latter-day Saints.

This oversight is not accidental. To state the situation bluntly, most educated non-Mormons still find the religious side of Latter-day Saints (as opposed to their purely social achievements) at best opaque. The growing respect for Mormon social history has not spread as yet, except in rare cases, to respect for Mormon beliefs. During the past two decades I have been at many informal non–Mormon gatherings in scholarly conferences at which the subject of Mormonism has arisen. Almost invariably at least one individual has turned to me and said something along the following lines: "One thing about them has always puzzled me. I have a valued Mormon colleague who seems to be an otherwise fine and intelligent person, but frankly it baffles me how any thinking individual could believe what he does. I just can't understand it."

I can understand this sense of disbelief as well. After all this was my own initial reaction both to Mormons and to their history. Before I got to know Mormons better, they chiefly appeared to be hardworking, clean-cut, loyal, thrifty, brave, clean, reverent—and utterly boring. No group ever talked more about free will (or in Mormon parlance "free agency") yet in practice seemed to exercise free will less in important matters. I was vividly reminded of a cartoon that showed a large, overbearing woman talking with her neighbor while her small, shy husband dutifully sat on the couch, his hands meekly folded. The woman was saying: "Hubert has a will of iron; he just seldom gets a chance to use it." This for me was the epitome of Mormonism and why I found it basically uninteresting and even sometimes distasteful.

Popular Mormon history merely reinforced this stereotype. Mormons throughout history, it seemed, had always been paragons of virtue, dedicated to the faith 100 percent or more. They had never had any doubts or problems except how better to spread the "gospel" among non-Mormons, who for inexplicable reasons were adamantly opposed to accepting the "truth." For me to give any credence to such Pollyanna-ish writing was impossible. Even without any knowledge of what had actually gone on, I was certain that the official version could not be the full story. Surely there must be more to Mormon history than such naive accounts indicated if their church had been able to achieve the remarkable degree of success that it had.

My investigation of what has sometimes been called "the New Mormon History" finally led me into real appreciation of the Mormon past and what Mormonism might become in the future. In beginning research for a 1973 paper on the origin of Mormon polygamy, I fortuitously decided to read systematically through all the back issues of *Dialogue* to see what the current historical and religious concerns of Mormonism were. The result was a minor revelation. Latter-day Saints clearly were not simply a bunch of zombies but in fact were real people who were struggling with many of the same questions that in a different religious tradition had also baffled and challenged me. Perhaps by studying Mormons I could gain insight not simply into their past but into my own as well.

The Mormon past came even more vividly alive as I began to work closely in printed and manuscript records, especially those in LDS church archives. What a fascinating cast of varied and interesting people I encountered. These were not the modern-day stereotype of dutiful, unquestioning, and unbelievable "saints" but real men and women who struggled in new and more creative ways to understand themselves, their faith, and their place in the world. Figures such as Joseph Smith and so many others became real to me as I read first hand of their personal efforts, triumphs, and failures. Any group which could attract such talent and dedication was surely worthy of deeper investigation. What a pity that the poorly informed writers of Sunday school manuals and approved histories were evidently ignorant of the vitality and richness of their own faith.

Nowhere was such blindness to their own history more pronounced than in Mormon treatments of polygamy, the primary topic I was investigating. The most common approach seemed to be to say as little as possible about the subject, as though it was something of which to be ashamed. Only when talking about how inexplicably nasty and hostile non-Mormons were to the Saints was polygamy brought up, and then almost exclusively as a religious revelation that had been introduced to test the faith of the Saints. But working with manuscript records, I became vividly aware of the importance that polygamy had for nineteenth-century Mormons—not simply as a test of faith but also as an integral part of a total way of life. Although I personally found polygamy distasteful, clearly many of the men and women who practiced it were fine people who did so sincerely and to the best of their ability. Simply to ignore a practice for which they had struggled and sacrificed so long seemed to be doing fundamental violence to the history of Mormonism as a whole. I wanted somehow to recapture that past and help both Mormons and non-Mormons to achieve a more constructive understanding of this remarkable Latter-day Saint effort to restructure relations between men and women.

Despite the great achievements of Mormon historical studies over the past two decades, many Latter-day Saints nevertheless have remained fearful of realistic writing about the Mormon past or attempts to deal seriously with controversial issues such as polygamy. The repeatedly expressed anxiety is that such an open and honest approach might not be "faith promoting," that it might tend to raise questions which would cause Latter-day Saints to be less loyal to their church. As a result of such fears, the last few years have seen an increasing drive from some factions of the church to restrict or even put a stop to serious historical studies of Mormonism. Leaders of the church are now calling publicly for their historians to write only sanitized, saccharine accounts, treatments which would best be characterized as "propaganda" by an objective observer. Never in the past decade has the outlook for the serious writing of Mormon history appeared so grim.

I am convinced that this restrictive tendency can only be counterproductive. The writing of misleading yet supposedly "positive" accounts of the Mormon past will be neither faith promoting nor good history. Of course it all depends on what kind of faith one is trying to promote. If one wishes to promote uninformed, unthinking acquiescence to the church as an institution that can do no wrong, then clearly the propagandistic approach is most suitable. But if one wishes to promote a mature faith tested by a responsible exercise of free agency, then such an approach can only be destructive and self-defeating. All too many Saints seem to be less concerned with promoting faith in Mormonism and more concerned with promoting faith in the naive writings that have appeared *about* Mormonism, even if those accounts can be clearly shown to be misleading or inaccurate. It is indeed sad that for some Saints the horror of having any doubt is so great that they do not see the even greater horror of having a faith so small that they are afraid ever to doubt or test it for fear the whole structure would crumble. Realistic faith, it seems to me, must grow out of confidence rather than fear and defensiveness.

One of the most frequently voiced fears is that serious historical writings tend to "secularize" Mormonism. This view is a red herring, in my opinion. For believing Mormons to write either an exclusively "religious" or an exclusively "secular" version of their history is for them to make a false dichotomy since Mormonism, more than most contemporary religions, has refused to accept a religious-secular dichotomy at all. Mormon theology unequivocally states that the spiritual dimension is comprised of a form of matter too and presumably must also be subject to some form of natural law, if only we could understand it. Joseph Smith asserted: "All spirit is matter, but it is more refined and pure, and can only be discerned by purer eyes." "Spirit is a substance that is material but that is more pure and elastic and refined matter than the body. . . . It existed before the body, can exist in the body, and will exist separate from the body when the body will be moldering in the dust."

Growing out of this assertion is the Mormon belief that when properly sealed under church authority, earthly relationships will literally continue and develop further in the afterlife and for all eternity. Death then is only a transition to a higher realm of reality which nevertheless involves a type of physical order even though we normally cannot comprehend that order because of our earthly limitations. (The analogy presented in Edwin Abbott's *Flatland* would be useful here.) Moreover, because this life and the afterlife are believed to be indissolubly linked, it also follows that in the last analysis all religious and secular activities on earth ideally should be inseparable. The extraordinary Mormon effort to set up Zion in the American west during the nineteenth century reflected this drive to integrate all reality into a unitary whole. In short Mormonism paradoxically is the most overtly materialistic of all major offshoots of the Christian tradition. Yet at the same time it also emphatically affirms the reality of the spiritual dimension of life. Mormons might thus be said to believe in a form of "spiritual materialism."

This explicitly materialistic orientation has some important logical consequences for Mormons studying their own history. Naive Saints, of course, will undoubtedly continue to look upon events of their past as having happened due to unaccountable divine fiat. More mature Saints, however, have the important option of investigating even the seemingly miraculous or inexplicable elements of their history to try to understand their naturalistic dynamics insofar as that is possible. Such investigation need not reduce the sense of awe, mystery, and power in Mormonism. Anyone who has ever read widely among the great writers in the natural and physical sciences such as Loren Eisley, Stephen Jay Gould, or Carl Sagan is surely aware that deeper understanding heightens rather than reduces our sensitivity to the ultimate wonder that is life. Similarly human history itself when understood deeply and fully is an ever-unfolding miracle. Not ignorance but knowledge is ultimately the most effective in promoting a rich and vital faith. As Mormons would say: "The glory of God is intelligence."

The writing of good history is also necessary if the Mormon church is to deal constructively with the challenges it faces. Since the end of World War II, Latter-day Saints have entered a new period of crisis and transition brought about somewhat paradoxically by their very success in attracting new members. The seven-fold Mormon growth to over seven million members and the spread of that membership out of the intermountain west and into other parts of the United States and the world is already requiring significant institutional changes. The long-range intellectual changes will eventually be even more profound, however, probably greater than those which took place in the late nineteenth and early twentieth centuries. At that time Mormonism gave up polygamy and most of its political exclusivity in order to reach at least a working accommodation with American society as a whole. If Mormonism is successfully to reach out into the world in the latter part of the twentieth century, it must also eventually shed many of its parochialisms. As only one example, the remarkable Mormon success in Brazil, where limiting membership due to racial antecedents ultimately proved too complex to be practical, contributed significantly to eliminating the policy of excluding blacks of African descent from full participation in the church.

In this as in similar cases, historians and others may play a crucial role in articulating the need for change and providing evidence that may encourage and support leaders in making necessary changes. On the particular issue of race, the new policy itself may well have come about primarily because of the institutional demands of the church, but without the often unpopular writings of historians to prepare the way, elimination of this policy might have taken much longer than it did. In the future similar issues will undoubtedly arise. Historians and others both inside and outside the church will continue to be needed because of broader and more realistic perspectives they can provide on both past and present. As a non-Mormon historian, I shall watch with great interest as the Latter-day Saint movement continues to struggle to come to terms with itself and with the challenges of an ever-changing society. Much has already been accomplished in writing Mormon history, but much more remains to be done if Mormon historians are to help successfully in spanning the gap between the still insular confines of Mormonism and the larger world.

8.
History, Faith, and Myth

C. Robert Mesle

Historians live with uncertainty and ambiguity. The uncertainty and to some extent the ambiguity arise from an irony which philosophers have known at least since Socrates. We are committed to a search for truth according to rules which say we cannot ultimately find it. That is, we are striving to find an objective description of what actually happened knowing that we can only interpret what happened. The reasons are obvious. The past is never directly observable. What remains from past events is always partial. The process of selecting which evidence is relevant and helpful is limiting. And every observer and historian has some point of view, a set of conscious or unconscious presuppositions and concerns that make it impossible to ever be fully objective.

This dilemma is especially acute for historians who are members of a community of faith. We want to know what really happened in the Exodus, but we cannot. We want to know if Jesus really said that the kingdom would come within one generation, but we cannot. We want to know what Joseph Smith really experienced in his fifteenth or sixteenth year, but we cannot. Still we continually insist on doing what we insist we cannot do. And when we fail, as we must, to provide an absolutely safe historical foundation for our faith, we do not know whether to applaud our historical and theological sophistication or to weep for our lost souls.

As historical research gives us more adequate images of people and communities, historians become increasingly aware of the imperfections of those people and communities and hence of the necessary ambiguity of all human commitments. As many modern

123

theologians have pointed out, we can escape neither uncertainty nor ambiguity by appeal to the divine, for we never deal with the divine apart from humanity. Even if one believes that God brought a religious community into existence and directed it on how to structure itself, it is still a community of imperfect men and women who have perceived and responded to that divine initiative. While God may never mislead us or make a mistake, we can never be absolutely certain that the human end of the connection is as reliable.

Because of this inherent ambiguity, the historian who is expected to use historical research to defend the community of faith, to write histories which support that faith, is forced into a difficult position. His or her dilemma is made far more intense by the prevalent idea that faith is belief without sufficient evidence, or even belief against the evidence. Such a concept of faith makes it logically impossible for a historian to be both faithful and scholarly.

The reason should be clear enough. When faith is understood as belief without evidence, one begins with a belief and uses it as a criterion by which to select evidence. Evidence which does not support belief is suppressed, distorted, or ignored. An important expression of this position is found in Elder Boyd K. Packer's article, "The Mantle is Far, Far Greater than the Intellect."[1] Elder Packer asserts that no one can properly write Mormon history unless they believe that "God the Father and His Son Jesus Christ personally appeared to the boy prophet, Joseph Smith, Jr., in the year 1820" and that those heavenly beings "instructed [Joseph] according to the testimony that he gave to the world in his published history."[2] He insists that historians of the Mormon church must presuppose that they have the truth and then select only that evidence for their histories which supports that truth. In such a view there cannot be a genuine attempt to arrive at truth on the basis of evidence by means of scholarly inquiry. The historian is forced to choose between the integrity of faith and the integrity of inquiry.

I do not believe that such a contradiction between faith and inquiry need exist, because I do not think that one need define faith as belief without evidence or as any form of belief. Instead I intend to offer what logicians call a persuasive definition. I want to change the descriptive meaning of the word faith while keeping its positive emotional and value connotations. But I do not do so arbitrarily. I have two justifications. First, I believe the definition I wish to offer is truer to the traditional meaning of the word than modern usage. Second, the former, traditional usage still has a strong place in our language and is almost always at least partially intended by the word.[3]

I propose that we abandon use of the word faith to mean belief and instead use the word faith to indicate commitment, loyalty, concern, and love: the experience of "being grasped" by something of ultimate concern.[4] In order to emphasize this, I will use the word "faith" only in that manner or I will choose one of these synonyms or I will use a phrase like faithful commitment or faithful love.

I also propose that we shift the positive, virtuous connotations evoked by the word faith to this new meaning and try to develop a negative attitude toward the concept of belief without evidence. The former should be thought of as virtuous, the latter as non-virtuous.

This proposal is hardly original. The work of Wilfred Cantwell Smith[5] increasingly persuades me that the equation of faith and belief is a modern Western heresy. I am therefore proposing a "restoration" of the meaning of faith found in the Bible and in the Christian tradition up to the last three centuries.

This restoration will enable us to make great strides towards resolving our dilemma. There will no longer be any conflict between faith and inquiry for at least three reasons. First, since faith no longer designates belief, it does not tell us what factual claims we should presuppose. Second, if we are really committed to something, we will wish to discover the truth about it, so that we can act out our commitments more effectively. Third, we are enabled to see that faith can often survive and even be deepened by changes in belief.

Let me offer a simple comparison. Having faith is much like falling in love. We do not fall in love without having some beliefs about the person we love. But neither do we suffer from any confused idea that love is identical with belief. We want our beliefs to be accurate so that our love will be properly placed and so that we can express our love effectively. But our beliefs can certainly change without automatically destroying our love. Indeed since people change, beliefs about them must change as well. A person who refuses to deal with the realities of a loved one is not admired by us. We see it as rather pitiful because that person seems to be in love with a dream, an ideal, rather than with a real person. What we admire is the ability to face reality and to love in the midst of ambiguity.

The same is true for faith. And the historian who has faith in a particular community—is committed to, concerned about, grasped by, and in love with that community—is well equipped to help members of that community develop a more mature faith-commitment by helping them recognize and live with the uncertainty and ambiguity which inevitably exist in the life and history of that particular community. For a concrete example of what I am talking about, I would like to consider the way in which LDS and RLDS historians may help their communities to deal with our knowledge of Joseph Smith's first vision.

In 1977 official RLDS church historian Richard P. Howard authored an essay entitled "Six Contemporary Accounts of Joseph Smith, Jr.'s, Early Visionary Experiences."[6] Most of the paper compared six known accounts of the first vision, all of which claimed either direct authorship by Joseph Smith or at least his editorial approval. There are certainly many important similarities between these accounts. One might therefore argue that even the most striking differences need not be logically incompatible, that Joseph might have been recounting different parts of the vision, which taken together give a more complete picture.

Despite this possible compatibility of some parts, there are clear differences among them. Chronologically the second account (and the first published account) omits the first vision entirely. In this account Joseph, who is in his seventeenth year, wonders about the existence of a supreme being, seeks assurance that he has been accepted by such a being, and is visited by an angel. The visitation of the Lord is entirely skipped over, and the text is clearly written as if there were no vision at all prior to 1823.

But the earliest account of his visions does include the appearance of Jesus.[7] However, this account is different from the 1842 account published in the *Times and Seasons* as the "History of Joseph Smith." The first account does not mention the grove, an experience of darkness, or a combat with demonic powers. Nor does it single out the denominations, though Joseph says it was on his mind. He sees Jesus, who says, "Lo, I come quickly as it was written of me," but only Jesus appears. Three later accounts describe two unidentified personages. One tells about many angels. Only the 1842 account says that the two personages were the Father and the Son.

It seems to me that there is a general progression in these accounts. From no mention of any difficulties attending Joseph's experience, we move in subsequent accounts to Joseph's difficulties in speaking and to the noise of someone walking toward him, and then to being tempted by the powers of darkness. Finally Joseph is seized by a power which binds his tongue and envelops him with thick darkness and a foreboding sense of destruction. First, there is one personage—Jesus. In subsequent retellings there are angels, and then we see God the Father and his son Jesus Christ. At first Joseph is concerned about the sinfulness of the world and forgiveness of his own sins—a classic Protestant theme which is omitted in the final account. Later accounts include statements that denominations believe incorrect doctrines, and finally there are condemnations of denominational creeds and of those who profess belief in them. We do not seem to be dealing here with differences of emphasis or with partial accounts that can be fitted together to provide a complete picture. Rather we seem to have intentional efforts to build up the miraculous character of the events and to buttress Joseph's position as he comes into increasing conflict with other denominations. One thing is certain: we cannot factually know that the first vision occurred or when or what Joseph experienced.

Such a situation should not surprise the historian. It is a common human tendency to build up the miraculous or heroic character of an event in telling and retelling it. And it is certainly common to gradually shape stories so that they illustrate or support some point of view. It happens in thousands of sermons every week. Furthermore the Bible itself gives us a wealth of examples of just such a process—for example the multiple accounts of the Exodus or the four gospels. All four gospels demonstrate that their authors are motivated by theological rather than modern historical interests. Who, for example, can deny the growth of the miraculous from Mark through John? In the same way Joseph Smith was simply telling and retelling his story.

But we moderns are uncomfortable with this approach. Our sense of history and the integrity of the historian are different. We may not condemn pre-modern people for their views and uses of history, but we do not share their freedom to alter accounts to fit needs. And mostly I think this is to our credit. Since I am one who happens to believe that reality always has the last word, I am convinced that the more adequately and honestly we can discover the past the better off we will all be.

What then can the faithful Mormon or RLDS historian say to the church community about the first vision and about Joseph's accounts of it? I was told once by a friend, who is both philosopher and historian, that most books by modern theologians are like fairy tales with three parts. In the first part we are told that the author has fallen into an infinitely wide and infinitely deep pit. The bulk of the text describes the horrors of the pit and all the reasons why it is absolutely inescapable. And then in the last part, the hero or heroine climbs out of the infinitely wide and infinitely deep pit, leaps onto the white horse, and rides away with the beautiful young woman or handsome young man.

I agree that this is true of many texts. And it is certainly an accurate description of the first two-thirds of this one. But I hope I shall not be guilty of such an ending. Instead I want to ask, "Having fallen into this pit, or rather having discovered that we have always been in it, what possibilities are there for creativity and faith?" I want us to find solutions that admit and accept the ambiguity inherent in any commitment to a community of faith and to find ways to tell our story that are faithful so far as possible to our communities, to our scholarly integrity, and to reality.

I believe it may be helpful and fruitful to introduce to our communities the concept of myth—or, if that term is too threatening, faith story. To provide a context which can help clarify the concept of myth, I will briefly summarize two sets of meaning for the words history, faith, and myth. First, I will offer what I take to be the popular understandings of the terms and then the alternatives I am suggesting—noting that none of my definitions are original.[8] I am only trying to bring them together for us.

Popular definitions. History: What actually happened or an account of what actually happened; history is true or false depending on whether it accurately reports the events.

Faith: Belief, often without or against the evidence; true belief; belief about what actually happened.

Myth: False stories about the past; false and fanciful history.

Alternative definitions. History: An honest reflection of someone's perspective, interests, and concerns about something that "actually happened."

Faith: Commitment which involves belief, based on events as related in a community of faith.

Myth: Here is a progression of definitions: (1) stories about the gods; (2) stories about "the other side" (the Transcendent or Divine) told in terms of "this side"; (3) stories which serve as *symbols* of our faith commitments, or faith stories; (4) narrative which explains the meaning of one or more symbols for a particular community of faith.

Note that this last definition of myth does not make any judgment about the historical accuracy of a story. The "truth" of a myth, like the truth of a symbol, does not refer to factual accuracy but to the adequacy with which it expresses the living concerns and commitments of the community of faith. In evaluating myth we ask, "Does it really tell people what the event or symbols mean to us?" Myths are not proved or disproved as myths. Instead they are born and die according to the faith of the community.

The relationship between myth and historical "reality" (what "actually" happened) is complex. If our commitments really rest on a belief that a specific event occurred, then historical evidence refuting that belief may destroy faith. But if the event is symbolic, expressing the content of our commitments rather than our beliefs about history, refutation of the belief may still leave the symbol intact. Historical data that challenges the accuracy of a myth can only make the myth "false" by killing the faith commitment which the myth expresses.

Three examples will help to clarify this approach to myth.

The Jewish Passover is celebrated in part through the sharing of a special meal called the Seder. The meal consists of several specific and highly symbolic foods. The feast is structured around the reading of the story of the Exodus. This story—the Haggadah—answers four questions asked by people at the table. For example, the youngest child asks, "Why is this different from any other night?" By answering these questions about the meal, the Haggadah explains the meaning of the symbols of the life of the community and tells the story of Israel. In this sense the Haggadah is a classic example of a myth, regardless of one's historical view of the biblical account of the Exodus.

Like the Jewish Seder, the Christian celebration of the Lord's Supper is a ritual myth. There too we tell the story which explains the meaning of the symbols central to our community of faith. Even though there are differing gospel accounts of that event, the eucharist expresses the basic commitments of the Christian community.

In the same way the story of the first vision of Joseph Smith, Jr., is a myth. The most well-known account includes several symbols which have great meaning for all Latter-day Saints: the scripture James 1:5, "If any of ye lack wisdom. . ."; the grove; the pillar of light; and the counsel to "join none of them." Regardless of one's historical judgment regarding the first vision, there can be no doubt that the story of that vision became a central means by which Latter-day Saints explain to themselves and to others "who we are." In telling this story Joseph was acting not as historian but as theologian. We should realize this and present his accounts of the first vision as successive attempts to explain who he was, how he saw the world, and to what he was committed. In so doing I believe we will be telling a more accurate truth about Joseph's view of history and of himself and will thus be providing a more solid foundation for the faith of our communities.

We do not thereby deny the historical nature of faith. On the contrary, problems of historical faith are ignored and the historical character of faith is denied when we demand that faith be blind to historical evidence and accept beliefs on authority. To claim that we can discover truth through some means which is immune to our humanness is to deny that we live, move, and have our being and our faith within history. This we cannot do.

NOTES

1. *Brigham Young University Studies* 21 (Summer 1981): 259-78.
2. Ibid., 272-73.
3. Consider, for example, how we use the words faithful and faithfulness and especially the words unfaithful and unfaithfulness. In the latter cases especially it is obvious that we are dealing with failure to acknowledge and love a known truth—that a commitment has been made. When we speak of unfaithfulness, we speak of lying, cheating, betrayal, and adultery not of mere opinions about propositions. In international relations we often hear nations accused of negotiating in "bad faith."
4. See Paul Tillich, *Dynamics of Faith* (New York: Harper and Row, 1957), and also Tillich's other definitions.
5. Wilfred Cantwell Smith, see *Belief and History* (Charlottesville: University Press of Virginia, 1977) and *Faith and Belief* (Princeton, NJ:

Princeton University Press, 1979). Smith documents how meanings of the words "faith" and "belief" have changed dramatically over the last three and a half centuries. At the time the King James version of the Bible was produced, the word "believe" meant "to belove," obviously a radically different sense than it has now. The word "believe" did not mean to have an opinion about something. For example, Smith cites a thirteenth-century poem in which a knight is urged to believe the oath he had sworn. That is, he is asked to acknowledge and honor his oath, to belove it rather than reject it. Obviously in the modern sense of the word, it makes no sense to ask someone to believe her or his own oath (see *Faith and Belief*, 110ff). That this sense was still dominant in 1611 is also established by Smith (see *Belief and History*, 61ff). See also Rudolph Bultmann and Artur Weiser, *Faith* (London: Adam & Charles Black, 1961).

6. Howard's essay is available in *Restoration Studies I*, ed. Maurice Draper (Independence, MO: Herald House, 1981). This article contains the texts of the various accounts under discussion.

7. It may be worth noting that according to Dean Jessee, this first account is the only one in Joseph Smith's own handwriting. See *Dialogue: A Journal of Mormon Thought* 6 (Spring 1971): 86.

8. The approach I am taking to myth depends on the work of Mircea Eliade, Paul Ricouer, and Norman Perrin. An excellent and brief summary of their definitions is available in Perrin's *The New Testament: An Introduction* (Chicago: Harcourt, Brace, Jovanovich, Inc., 1974), 21-26. Rudolph Bultmann's approach may be found in his *Kerygma and Myth*, ed. H. W. Bartsch (London: S.P.C.K., 1953), 10.

9.
Looking for God in History

Neal W. Kramer

HOW TO WRITE HISTORY HAS BEEN A MAJOR TOPIC OF DEBATE FOR centuries. This is hardly surprising since concepts such as history and time vary widely from culture to culture. A striking example of such differences is found in Mircea Eliade's *The Myth of the Eternal Return.*[1] Eliade here contrasts the cyclical conception of time exemplified in Greek and Indian sacred mythology with the biblical conception of time as having a beginning and an end. The Greeks found solace in the continuity and regularity of nature and its cycles of life, while the Hebrews saw time as a limited sojourn apart from God. The early Christians continued the Hebraic tradition. They taught that the coming of Jesus Christ signified that God had created time and that history would continue only until the Second Coming.[2]

The Christians' teleological conception of history persisted in western civilization until the beginning of the Renaissance. At that time scholars began rediscovering and translating ancient texts. One aspect of their work was reevaluating the idea of history. The resulting conflict between Hellenistic and Christian ideas of history helped produce an atmosphere in which a new conception could be nurtured. This approach advocated by a group of non-clerical but university-trained historians was based on a developing methodology of science. Philosophers like John Locke and David Hume articulated theories of how truth could be uncovered through careful study of the past.[3]

In the nineteenth century attempts at writing empirically verifiable, logically coherent, cause-and-effect history were well under way. By this time there was no longer any need to interpret history with reference to God or to a divine plan because facts when properly organized interpreted themselves. History became a chronological narrative of events as they happened. All the historian required was tenacity, a set of rules for determining the validity of evidence, and access to the necessary primary sources. The past had become an object for scientific inquiry. Evidence was judged by empirical standards and whatever did not qualify as "real" under the new guidelines was considered the result of ignorance, illness, superstition, and so on.

Such notions were the foundation of not only the historiography practiced by German historian Leopold von Ranke but also the positivistic sociology of the French philosopher Auguste Comte and the materialisms of Marxists on the one hand and utilitarians on the other.[4] The second half of the nineteenth century marked the high tide of the belief in the all-encompassing ability of scientific methodologies to comprehend all things. Thomas Huxley's advocacy of Charles Darwin's theories of natural selection and the beginnings of Fabian economic socialism in England typify what was becoming the ideology of history in the western world. Logical positivists extended the limits of this epistemology to construct a theory of knowledge which in effect equated all knowledge with scientific knowledge.[5] That which could not be verified through sensory experience was declared cognitively meaningless.

A challenge to the underpinnings of logical positivism has been mounted in the twentieth century. Much of the critique has centered on assumptions about language. Positivism assumes that language is transparent, describing the world exactly as it is without being subject to conceptual bias. In contrast, Ludwig Wittgenstein has shown that use of language is based on a set of arbitrarily established rules.[6] The rules limit what a concept means and in which contexts it is meaningful. One who adopts a particular mode of thought interprets the world according to the rules of his or her conceptual mode.

Structuralists, the name applied to a diverse group of thinkers which includes Claude Levi-Strauss, Roland Barthes, Jacques Lacan, Jean Piaget, and Michel Foucault, developed similar ideas about how our use of language mirrors other human activities. Foucault, for example, offers a lucid account of "discourse" as a set of restrictions on what we are or are not able to say.[7] His work stresses that we are limited in what we can know by what we can say about the world.

Jacques Derrida, another French philosopher, has tried to demonstrate the tenuousness of writing as the medium through which the world can be understood.[8] Written language, according to Derrida, tends to "deconstruct." By deconstruct, he means that the meaning of something, which was temporarily so obvious, tends to disintegrate into possibilities for meaning that are incapable of describing the world as it is. Rather than opening the world to our understanding, language limits how we think about reality and what we can ever claim to know. Absolute knowledge becomes nothing more than a fleeting dream because of the limiting effects of language. Adopting a set of rules or conventions is thus more a gesture of what one wishes to talk about than of what it is possible to know.

This understanding of the limitations of language has implications for writing Christian history generally and Mormon history in particular. It demands a reevaluation of the basic philosophy and methodology of historiography. The originators of the positivist tradition effectively dismissed God from discourse about the past.[9] Though there was a sort of kinship between their "idea of progress" and the earlier teleological eschatology of Christianity, they denied any actual power behind historical movement and described instead a kind of "natural" historical inertia.[10]

It now appears to be the case that religious experience can be described within its own linguistic contexts and evaluated on its own terms. Religious history need not be intimidated by a value system that reduces the experiences religious writers describe to superstition. One can strive to include the deep spiritual power of the past in a narrative instead of seeking a representation of the scientific "facts."

Belief in scientific history still proliferates among some professional historians and sociologists writing about Mormons today. Since professional training in major graduate schools in the United States and Great Britain has tended to be dominated by the scientific approach, many professional scholars have adopted the epistemological values it seeks to inculcate. And since a large portion of the scholarly writing on Mormonism today comes from people trained in the methods described, it comes as no surprise that such writing tends to try to fit the writing of our history within the limits of positivism.

Professionally trained historians often write for a specific audience—other historians. They go to professional schools to master a particular kind of language which carries with it a peculiar way of thinking about the world. They then expect others who wish to communicate with them to adopt the same point of view in order to make sense of what is being said. That this limits what may be discussed is never brought up. Thus when a work is promoted for more general audiences, neither reader nor author is usually able to break the conceptual bonds imposed upon them by the conventions of modern professional history.

The limitations of positivistic historical discourse are too narrow to allow it to become the only conceptual framework behind writing the history of the Mormon church. For example some historians contend that there is no place in their work for non-scientific testimony of the role of God in the rise of Mormonism and the continuing guidance of his church and people. These historians suggest the creation of categories like sacred history and profane history. Elder Boyd K. Packer's speech to Church Education System employees represents the concerns some church leaders have with some of the histories of the church published in the last two to three decades.[11] I think that it is proper to infer from Elder Packer's remarks that he disapproves of the sort of methodology that leaves out what he and others see as the most important facets of the history of the church.

Because my own interest in Mormon history is avocational rather than professional, I hesitate to criticize works which evidence obvious expertise. Yet I feel that their authors must continue to be challenged to include the divine as they seek to explain the growth of the church and the accomplishments of the Latter-day Saints. By hedging our bets, couching our descriptions of spiritual experiences in ambiguous language, hiding our belief in the reality of revelation behind objective criteria, we may satisfy the expectations of colleagues but risk offending delicate testimonies. Such writing desacralizes a most sacred history.

The Mormon community at large has generally avoided the intrusion of positivism into its experience. Indeed Mormonism brought with it the reality of the divine in history. The Book of

Mormon itself testifies of this important facet of the religion. Some of the holiest experiences in church history have now become a sanctified part of scriptural record. One feels compelled to see in the restoration of the church the restoration of the knowledge that God plays a significant role in history and that the writing of it serves to reveal sacred truths about him to all people.

There have been some outstanding works of Mormon history written in the past. For me, however, the single most impressive aspect of each has not been its objectivity; rather it has been the simple presentation of human experience with the divine. My personal favorites include Orson F. Whitney's *Life of Heber C. Kimball*, Matthias F. Cowley's *Wilford Woodruff*, and B. H. Roberts's *Life of John Taylor*. The quintessential Mormon history, however, is the Joseph Smith story. For me, no single account of the Mormon past has ever matched the power and simplicity of Joseph's few words and pure testimony.

It must be more than obvious that one of my criteria for effective Mormon history is the straightforward narration of personal experience as it was perceived without the added embellishment of sophisticated, secular commentary meant to soften the impact of the situation. Part of the model I would adopt has its basis in the stories of Jesus presented by the writers of the gospels. Another part comes from Nephi's narrative of his father's experience in the Book of Mormon. Both types of narrative are characterized by attempts faithfully to describe single events in detail and then to testify of the admittedly subjective truthfulness of the occurrences depicted. The testimony may be presented through an aspect of style (such as Nephi's use of parallelism to describe similar experiences), the adoption of a particular interpretive mode (as in Matthew's incorporating the use of typology in his gospel), or simple exhortation (Mormon's comments at various points throughout his book). It should be noted that the scriptures are filled with other ways of telling and testifying. My intuition leads me to believe that spiritual maturity might produce more figurative histories, but I do not advocate the deliberate mystification of a text. Nephi's "plainness" is much more to my liking.

Plain or simple need not imply, however, that the writer strive to be naive. Evaluation of evidence must include careful consideration of all available materials and the consequent weeding out of sources of questionable value and/or veracity. Few people familiar with Joseph Smith or Brigham Young would maintain that their lives were simple or naive. But the histories of their lives and work should not be cluttered with speculative psychological diagnoses or objective evaluations of the quality of the revelations they received. These histories can be presented as the stories of real people engaged in what they perceived to be a holy work. The reader should not be asked to judge whether the narrative itself conforms to some transitory standards of professional propriety but whether the work described is authentic.

It seems to me that this is the sort of history we need to have written by Mormon historians. Unfortunately my experience with much of the history I have read dictates that most scholars resist this approach. Much of what happened in the early days of the church has not yet been written. When it is, it will more than likely reveal personal apostasy as well as personal testimony. It will reveal personal weakness at times as well as personal strength, even in the church's staunchest defenders. We need not gloss over aspects of people's lives that do not match our expectations of them, but we do need to include their personal spiritual triumphs unmasked by various rhetorical disguises. Ultimately we cannot move away from what is for us an undeniable reality—that the hand of God is revealed in the history of this church from its earliest days to the present. The same God who appeared to Joseph Smith and revealed the gospel to him reveals his pleasure to today's living prophet. If we claim any less, then we have forgotten what we really believe.

NOTES

1. Mircea Eliade, *The Myth of the Eternal Return or Cosmos and History* (Princeton, NJ: Princeton University Press, 1954). The entire work serves as a sort of prolegomenon to a philosophy of history, tracing the origins of the concept of history and differentiating between various archaic approaches and more modern counterparts.

2. Karl Lowith, *Meaning in History* (Chicago: University of Chicago Press, 1949), 182-90. Lowith examines "the theological implications of the philosophy of history" and offers an account of the rise of scientific historiography in relation to fundamental theological concepts.

3. Locke's empiricism, relating all knowledge to direct sense experience, is best formulated in *An Essay Concerning Human Understanding*—arguably the most significant philosophical work of the seventeenth century.

A perfect example of the skeptical approach is David Hume's *The Natural History of Religion*. Hume's definition of nature and the narrow context in which he defines the concept of natural law is typical of what I call the empirical/skeptical approach. Religious history is explained here as a set of superstitious responses to natural phenomena.

4. Both Lowith's book and Hayden White's *Metahistory* (Baltimore, MD: Johns Hopkins University Press, 1973) offer instructive accounts of the development of historiography in the nineteenth century, relating it to the evolution of the dominant epistemologies of the period. Patrick Gardner's *The Nature of Historical Explanation* (Oxford: Oxford University Press, 1961) offers a British account of scientific explanation in historiography.

5. One need only refer to Bertrand Russell's "Why I Am Not a Christian" to read the arguments of logical positivists against Christianity.

6. Wittgenstein's *Philosophical Investigations* is his most important work on epistemology. Its implications about how concepts are formed and used through "language games" as they relate to particular "forms of life" have fostered new and interesting attempts at understanding even the most basic notions about concept formation and our understanding of the world. Of value in understanding concepts from the historical point of view is Stephen Toulmin's *Human Understanding* (Princeton, NJ: Princeton University Press, 1972).

7. Michel Foucault, *The Order of Things* (New York: Random House, 1970).

8. Derrida's most important work on writing appears in his two books *Writing and Difference* (Chicago: University of Chicago Press, 1978) and *Of Grammatology* (Baltimore: Johns Hopkins University Press, 1976). An interesting account of Derrida and his relationship to French philosophy appears in Vincent Descombes, *Modern French Philosophy* (Cambridge: Cambridge University Press, 1980).

9. I have already referred to Hume above. David Strauss, Ludwig Feuerbach, and Ernest Renan offered historical critiques of Christianity. In each they built upon a scientific approach to what ought to be accepted as fact and strengthened the methodology they sought to defend.

10. The idea of progress still finds support in works like Robert Nisbet's *History of the Idea of Progress* (New York, NY: Basic Books, Inc., 1980).

11. Boyd K. Packer, "The Mantle is Far, Far Greater than the Intellect," *Brigham Young University Studies* 12 (Summer 1981): 259-78.

10.
Faithful History/
Secular Religion

Melvin T. Smith

THE DEBATE ABOUT FAITHFUL HISTORY HOLDS GREAT INTEREST FOR ME, both for personal and for academic reasons. I came to the history profession with the convictions of a "true believer," and my pursuit of professional stature as a historian has been fraught with a multitude of challenges.

I remember talking with a young professor of history at Brigham Young University after I had completed course work and comprehensive examinations for a Ph.D. program there. I asked him, "Well, now that I am a bonafide historian, what do I do with Joseph Smith?" I was surprised by his answer: for him Joseph Smith presented no particular problems. And frankly I felt a certain envy at his secure hold on faith, for I was by then seeing holes in my own faithful armor.

I am still asking myself the question, what do we do with Joseph Smith and with others who claim that they have had direct communication with God or other divine beings? I have also seen many of my colleagues struggle with their own versions of this issue.

There has already been considerable debate about faithful history—what it is and how Latter-day Saints and Mormons who are historians ought to write it. For me none of the arguments has proven wholly satisfactory. It is for that reason that I am continuing my own probing of the subject.[1] The primary purpose of this essay is to provide a rationale for believing historians whereby they can produce objective professional history rather than so-called "faithful history."

My basic premises are simple. First, I see history as a finite tool used by very human men and women to study the lives, behavior, and institutions of finite human beings. Even when one includes all of human learning, which in a sense is part of human history, it is still finite. Additionally the sources of history are only people, no matter how important or brilliant or wise or righteous they may be. Hence history can only tell us about our finite world and about its finite inhabitants—which message, however, makes the pursuit of good history worthwhile.

Now to premise number two. I accept that there may be an infinite reality, called the realm of God or the divine. I also allow that God may choose and may have chosen to communicate with finite human beings at various times and for his own purposes. However, witnessing to divinity is God's domain alone, if such a witness is to be given. Human beings cannot do it, and especially historians with history cannot do it. History tells us about people, not about God. The terms *faith* and *religion* as related to the faithful history debate are inexorably tied to a belief and hope in God. The acquisition of religious or faithful insights into reality are usually reported to be very good by those who have claimed them. Therefore one's quest for faith and religious witnessing seems worthy of one's best efforts. However this essay is not an attempt to explore or to explicate the value and meaning of such religious experiences.

My third premise suggests that there is value in keeping the information of these two worlds separate while pursuing the truths or insights to be gained from each. Since believing historians are both historian and believer, there will be for them a continuous interplay of information from each of these sources. Therefore the historians' major challenge will be to use only historic data in premising their research and in drawing their conclusions. Otherwise their history will be faithful history, about which I will be saying more later.

In my opinion, it is ultimately within each of us that our truths and realities are best dealt with—hopefully in positive, constructive ways. To further clarify let me add that it is after truths and insights of both human learning (history) and divine witnessing (God) are received that each person must struggle to give them meaning for her- or himself. Those so struggling may find the services of theologians or philosophers or ministers most useful. Perhaps the scriptural analogy that the kingdom of God is within us is relevant (Luke 17: 20-21).

Now to return to the faithful history issue. A basic problem arises for believing historians when they see themselves judging their historical data in light of perceived superior facts or truths. All historians of professional stature know the tenuous nature of their conclusions drawn from never-completed research. Thus when that superior truth is perceived to be God's word, faithful historians will become vulnerable, for it appears to them that they are challenging God himself. Additionally historians will probably feel that their community of believers sees them as challenging God—hardly a climate for objective, effective scholarship.

How can believing historians deal with those problems? The answer lies in desensitizing history. If we accept the fact that history cannot testify of God, we recognize that neither can it testify against God. This attitude allows believing scholars to pursue their historical research unrestrained by so-called superior wisdom or divine disfavor, providing a favorable climate in which to produce their best histories.

Perhaps it would be helpful at this point to suggest a more useful definition of faithful history. It is simply "history" (so-called) written either to prove or to disprove the things of faith and religion or God, his will and ways. Mormons find they have the well-known writings both of Joseph Fielding Smith, *Essentials in Church History* (proof positive), and of Jerald and Sandra Tanner, *Mormonism: Shadow or Reality?* (proof negative). Neither is good history; and it seems doubtful that either is a viable fountain for faith or disbelief.

One additional point on this issue. Many define faithful history as history written to promote the faith. At best such action is a use of history not a kind of history, and frequently it is simply propaganda and apologetics.

Desensitizing history also allows believing historians to extend the range of *historical* evidence. For example, what do historians do with Joseph Smith when he said that divine beings talked with him? (JSH 2:17, 30-42, 44-46, 49) How do historians handle that historic fact—namely his statement?

Some historians elect to go the way of superior truth and insight by declaring that they *know* Joseph Smith was God's prophet. Therefore they conclude he talked with God. The problem for such historians rapidly compounds when other conflicting historical evidences are produced that show a variation in what Joseph Smith said happened and when techniques of scriptural higher criticism[2] are applied to their claims. Faithful historians continually face challenges (both to their history and to their faith) because historical conclusions are made with the bias of their religious perceptions of reality, which bias distorts the message of history.

Next, a look at a second option for dealing with Joseph Smith. Some historians state that Joseph claimed he talked with God. Their presumption is that he did not; still they have not actually called him a liar. Others do call him a liar. Now I ask you how does one prove that Joseph Smith did not talk with God? How can historians call their witness a liar—unless the historical record itself clearly shows that he lied? Historians hardly have the luxury of saying to their historic source, "I'll use this, but I won't use that portion of the evidence." Granted we must bring to our scrutiny of Joseph's data the same careful evaluation we bring to any historical resource.

The key to using the historic witness of one who is testifying to divine experiences lies in desensitizing that witness's message. I reiterate, *history* can only measure the historicity of a prophet's statements not their divinity. So why look for divine evidence in history? Second, Joseph Smith's witness is itself not a divine witness; it is a historic witness only. It differs qualitatively from the witness he claimed he received of God. For example, Joseph was puzzled that people in Palmyra did not generally believe his visionary claims. They even persecuted him for "telling the truth" as he perceived it. Joseph identified with the Apostle Paul (JSH 2:24), whose message of a divine communication was also rejected by many who heard him. What these people heard was Joseph's and Paul's witnesses. It requires little effort to discern that our reading of their accounts (the history) is not in any sense a replication of the experience each claimed of direct, personal communication with the infinite.

Let us continue to explore Joseph Smith's desensitized historic witness for additional insights. Three of the people he testified to were Martin Harris, David Whitmer, and Oliver Cowdery. These three men proclaimed later that they saw an angel who showed them the gold plates and testified to them of the plates' divine purposes. These men bore witness of these experiences, which is written in the preface to the Book of Mormon. Does this mean the Book of Mormon is true? God's word? The answer is no, for remember that we are looking at the historicity of the record only, not at its divinity.

Joseph Smith reported to his mother soon after their angelic witness that the burden of testifying of God's work no longer was his alone. They now had to bear it with him. He was relieved to the point of ecstasy.[3] Does that prove they saw the angel and the gold plates? No, but this desensitized look at the history of these events leaves us with some interesting questions and with new historical insights. Joseph Smith clearly recognized the difference between his witness and the angel's, a distinction apparent to Harris, Whitmer, and Cowdery also. And I suggest that these kinds of experiences confirmed for Joseph Smith in significant ways his own sense of his prophetic role. For us the question still remains: What did these men experience anyway?

Let me turn to my second point, that God only can witness to the divine. I do not presume to judge, nor is this essay an attempt to judge whether or not people have had a divine witness. That is their own personal experience. Yet one often sees examples of "faith" premised on historical evidence or some rationalization made from such data. It is easy to make a qualitative distinction between one's reading of Joseph's account of the angel's visit (history) and one's experiencing an actual angelic visit. I suggest that it would be this latter kind of witnessing that gives substance to faith and divinity to religion. Perhaps some Saints may be foregoing genuine religious witnessing from divine sources, because they have been seduced into accepting the "lesser light" of history as witness for their faith. However this essay is not a formula for religious experiences nor an explication of them. Rather it is a rationale for desensitized rather than faithful history.

An additional problem arises for people who presume an understanding of God, of how he operates, or what his will is from history. Again to Joseph Smith for an example: many good Christians maintain that God would not speak to Joseph Smith, because he was a money digger, a peep stone artist, and a charlatan.[4] The historic record shows that Joseph Smith did dig for buried treasure, did use a peep stone, and could have some of his behavior "charlatanized." However, when these same critics look to the desensitized historical record of the scriptures, they discover that God spoke to Moses, who killed an Egyptian in a fight (Ex. 2:11-15), and to King David, the psalmist who committed adultery and sent the husband into the thick of battle so he would be killed (2 Sam. 11:2-17). There is also Saul of Tarsus who actively persecuted the early-day Saints (Acts 8:1, 3-4; 9:1-9). Had he lived in the nineteenth century, one may have found him at Haun's Mill or at least in Missouri's courts. Latter-day Saints find little relief when looking at sixteen-year-old Nephi, who beheaded Laban to obtain the brass plates (1 Ne. 4:6-18). Or Martin Harris, who was entrusted with the first 116 pages of the newly translated Book of Mormon manuscript and lost them. Yet still an angel visited him with a divine message (JSH 2:63-65; D&C 3:12-13; 10:1-7, 9; 5:26-29; 17:1-9).

Can Saints presume an understanding of God from the historic record? Better the message be from God. For history as God's message maketh uncertain sounds indeed.

Next I digress only slightly to reinforce my argument for desensitizing history. The scriptural record advises us that the worst fate that could befall any mortal would be to be cast into hell or outer darkness with the devil and his angels, to become a son (or daughter?) of perdition (D&C 76:31-37, 43-46). I ask you to recognize that scripturally this terrible damnation is assigned not to those who have denied the witness of faithful history but to those who have received the most profound and sacred of divine witnesses—a visitation from Jesus Christ himself—and then denied it (ibid., vv. 35, 43; 88:3-4). The other side of the coin suggests that the hoped-for rewards of heaven and eternal life will require more than merely believing in faithful history.

I have been attempting to elaborate some of the nuances implied in the title of this essay, "Faithful History/Secular Religion." I reiterate my rationale: history is finite, witnessed to by humans only. If one's religion is based on faithful history, it is only a secular religion.

Problem number one. Whom did God want to succeed the prophet Joseph Smith? The Reorganized Church of Jesus Christ of Latter Day Saints affirms that the prophet ordained his son to succeed him. But does Joseph III's ordination mean that his line was to provide all succeeding presidents for the RLDS church? Were successors to be only the first born or were other male heirs equally eligible?

I am neither proposing church policy nor trying to determine the will of God in these matters for the RLDS church or anyone else. What I think can be shown is that to read the "historic" record as

God's will and word clouds the issue unnecessarily. It shows also the extensive rationalization required to obtain acceptable answers. Rationalization itself is a proper human practice. I question, however, that God's witnessing submits to human rationalizations.

Now take the succession issue to the LDS church. Was Brigham Young, president and senior apostle in the Quorum of Twelve Apostles when Joseph the prophet was killed, to succeed him? Did he not hold the keys of authority and was not the seniority system God's way of choosing the next president of the church? Does not God still use that method? The church certainly has not run out of seniority. In fact, it faces the problem in a new dimension as people live longer and as life support systems are brought to them. Does God also speak through life support systems as an aspect of seniority?

I sense it is easier for RLDS students to answer the second set of questions than the first. Why? Because they are easier? I do not think so. Utah Mormons find the first set of questions easy to answer. Why again? Because when we look at each other's issues, we tend to see them wholly from a historical perspective, unclouded by suppositions of what God has in mind. I can verify that the LDS questions are for Utah Mormons very difficult, for they recognize that the prophetic office and presidency require not only spiritual qualities but enormous physical stamina and mental strength. On the other hand RLDS members could readily recommend retirement and emeritus status for apostles, as Utah Mormons would be ready to recommend practical, reasonable solutions for the RLDS succession issue also.

This kind of juxtaposing of issues allows one to see what desensitized history, free of religious/faith bias, is and how such distance allows historians to gain the insights that history can give—insights usually unperceived when faith or religion clouds their scrutiny.

Moving to a second problem: polygamy or plural marriage. Utah Mormons accepted Doctrine and Covenants section 132 as the will of God and can produce historical evidence that Joseph the prophet was polygamous. After 1852 they practiced and preached it publicly.[5] Thirty-eight years later Wilford Woodruff issued the Manifesto (1890),[6] which supposedly ended plural marriage. Still a second manifesto had to be issued in 1904 by Joseph F. Smith.[7] There are fundamentalists practicing polygamy in Utah today, though it is not LDS church policy.

Now what was God's will in the matter? Did God want it to end in 1890 or never? Is God influenced by the law of the land? Will cases before the courts today of Utah polygamists make any difference to God? If the cases go to the U.S. Supreme Court and that body finds anti-polygamy laws unconstitutional, would God change his mind again? And would Mormons again practice polygamy?

The questions raised here are only relevant to the perspective that faithful history produces. Desensitized history shows that Mormons in territorial Utah worked against themselves in their territorial politics. First, they wanted as much self-rule as possible, which after Utah territory was created in 1850 would be achieved by statehood status. The only way they could gain statehood and its self-rule advantages was to give up peculiarities such as polygamy, cooperatives, united order economics, and theocratic politics. By 1896 (statehood) they had done that generally. History provides evidence that neither Brigham Young nor his successor, John Taylor, could let go of their perceptions of God's will for his Saints. Young died in 1877 propounding all of them. Taylor died on the polygamy underground—hiding out—in 1887. He did not insist on continuing the United Order. Wilford Woodruff stated that God no longer required these sacrifices of his Saints and issued the Manifesto in 1890. The historic facts are that the national government had disfranchised Mormons, persecuted and prosecuted them, escheated their properties, threatened disincorporation of the church itself, and closed out the perpetual emigrating fund. The LDS church as an institution was on the brink of extinction.[8] Objective history shows that the pioneer legacy for Utah and the LDS church was not without problems.

What about the RLDS church on polygamy? Has there not been some embarrassment over denial of sound historic evidence of the practice by Joseph Smith? Today both churches support monogamous marriages, but what do they do when converts are made in lands where polygamy is practiced legally? A clouded view of faithful history is of little help. God's direct witness or even desensitized human history would be better.

Let me turn to a third and final example, which I believe provides a classic, if tragic, example of "faithful history/secular religion." It is early fall of 1857, the location is southwestern Utah territory. You are there because you believe God wants you there to build up the kingdom of God on earth. You know God's will in the matter, because your church leaders have told you that Joseph Smith prophesied the Saints would become a mighty people in the Rocky Mountains,[9] and you have received a call from Brigham Young to go south and help build up the Iron Mission. You believe the earth is the Lord's and the fullness thereof. You are one of the elect to help usher in Christ's millennial reign on earth.

You know that the Saints ought to be pure, and you responded to the reformation preachings of Jedediah Grant and others by confessing your sins and being rebaptized.[10] You recognized that something was at fault when crickets and grasshoppers came in 1855 and when heavy crop damage from late frosts occurred the next year. Why would God permit such bad things to happen to his Saints if there was indeed a law upon which all blessings are predicated (D&C 130:20-21), as you believe? It must be because of the sinners and the evil in Zion, as Brother Grant had proclaimed. Zion must first be cleansed. You try to be as faithful as possible, even to become perfect.

In August 1857 Apostle George A. Smith preached in your meetings, warning you of the coming of an army to destroy the Saints. Just how faithful would you prove to be, he asked. You recalled mobs at Nauvoo, the Missouri persecutions, and absence of protection and redress from the government. You wondered, what did all of this mean? What did God have in mind for you and his Saints? It is now September. What should you do when a wealthy company of Arkansas emigrants comes through southern Utah and camps at Mountain Meadows before heading into the desert en route to California?[11]

Some are arguing that these are bad people from Arkansas and Missouri and enemies of God's people. Others add that they might return from California with a second army to destroy the Saints. Isn't this the situation Apostle Smith alluded to? And where do Indians fit into the picture? Surely Mormons need an alliance with them to help in case of war and to avoid a second front.

What should you do when the matter finally comes to a vote, either to destroy the wagon train or to let it go? You believe murder is an unforgivable sin (Ex. 20:13). You are commanded to love your enemies, to do good to them that persecute you (Matt. 5:38-39, 43-44). You know these commandments and believe them devoutly.

Yet somehow you understand that church leaders would approve of the wagon train's destruction. You reason it really is war in some ways with your enemy the United States sending an army to destroy you. These are bad people, you rationalize. Some of them are even from Missouri. So what should you do? Follow counsel? And what is that counsel officially?

If you happen to be John D. Lee,[12] adopted son to Brigham Young, you elect to do what you understand church leaders approve of (and there were many, many others also making similar choices), for you believe that God's will comes to you through his anointed prophet.

So you join the Indians who attacked the wagon train. You see the Iron County militia arrive. You take part in the council to select a course of action. (Later at your trial you claim you tried to talk them out of their chosen course of action.) You are not successful, and so the next morning *you*, John D. Lee, take a flag of truce to the emigrants, disarm them, and set the stage for the brutal massacre that follows: Mormons killing white men, Indian allies killing women and older children. It does not take long. The next morning you return to the site and join your compatriots in a prayer circle, there taking the most solemn of oaths not to reveal the details of that event.

You become haunted by what you have done, even though in your report to Brigham Young two weeks later you carefully lay the main blame on the Indians. You note that you do not believe there was any "innocent blood" in the whole bunch. Hadn't you been careful not to kill the innocent little children?

You continue to ask yourself during the remaining twenty years of your life, why? But you hold fast to the position that church officials, who "ordered" you to do it, would be held accountable before God, not you, if only you remain faithful. This you try to do—fulfilling calls to serve, to pioneer, to build a ferry to cross the Colorado River. Perhaps you seek comfort in the scriptural assurance of Doctrine and Covenants 132 that though you commit all manner of sins (after receiving the covenant of celestial marriage), save the "shedding of innocent blood," you might be destroyed in the flesh and turned over the buffeting of Satan but still you will come forth with your blessings in the resurrection (D&C 132:19, 26). It seems to be all you have after your excommunication from the church in 1870.

Lee never did turn against church leaders, and on 23 March 1877 he was "destroyed in the flesh" by a firing squad at Mountain Meadows. Lee's is only one of the many tragedies of Mountain Meadows. Another is Nephi Johnson, age eighteen in 1857. He was also there. In his deathbed delirium as an old man, he cried out, "Blood! Blood! Blood!"[13]

How did it happen? I have not heard any historian, even writers of faithful history, argue that God commanded them to do it. Then how? I maintain this is a classic example of people misconstruing what they heard from leaders as the will of God. The results were the tragic deaths of more than one hundred California-bound emigrants, the debasing of the Mormon people, particularly those who were involved directly, and a stain on both the Mormon church and its leadership during those years.

The issue was not just the fault of bad leadership, although in this instance it was surely bad. It must be remembered that these faithful Saints also had to override their belief in the commandments of God—Thou shalt not kill. Do good to them that persecute you.

For those Mormons their versions of faithful history left them bereft of individual morality, human judgments, and values to be found in objective, desensitized history. It also secularized their religion with grievous consequences for all. Thus these faithful followers found themselves at Mountain Meadows in September 1857 with the worst of both their worlds.

As stated earlier my purpose is to provide a rationale to believers who are historians writing about Mormon history. Arguments that faithful history, as defined herein, secularizes religion, are made not to discredit any particular religion or religious rationale. Rather it is an attempt to provide a justification to believing historians for desensitizing their histories and concluding from their studies what history by itself can tell us. It is hoped thereby that all of us will have the best facts and insights that history can provide.

Those historic "truths," along with whatever divinely witnessed "truths" one may receive, present each believing student of history with the raw materials from which he or she will draw conclusions about life: What is it? What are its purposes? What does one really know? and What now does one do with what he or she knows?

It is not an easy struggle, at least not for me, but it is a fascinating one which provides us with a great range of choices—the choice to believe, to follow, to support, to affiliate, and to question, the choice to "be engaged in good causes," to explore fully both human wisdom and God's witnessing for what each can mean in one's life.

This attitude allows each of us to enlist the help of specialists, of those wiser than we are in these matters—theologians, philosophers, psychologists, geneticists, biologists, anthropologists, and so on. What does all that we know really mean anyway? The big, profound, and final question, the question which religions generally attempt to answer, and the question ever present in the minds of believing historians, is a question best answered by them when they acknowledge the limits of history, desensitize their study of those evidences which refer to God and the infinite, and draw their historical conclusions from historic data only. With the good history they produce thereby, they and others are better able to wrestle with that "big question" than if they produced faithful history.

The struggle will not disappear, but it is better to have good evidences (tools) with which to struggle, be they historic or divine. Neither faithful history nor secular faith or religion are useful tools in the human search for understanding.

NOTES

1. The reader's attention is called to two previous articles on this topic by the author: "Faithful History: Hazards and Limitations," *Journal of Mormon History* 9 (1982): 61-69; and "Faithful History/Secular Faith," *Dialogue: A Journal of Mormon Thought* 16 (Winter 1983): 65-71.

2. See William D. Russell, "History and the Mormon Scriptures," *Journal of Mormon History* 10 (1983): 53-63; and his "A Further Inquiry into the Historicity of the Book of Mormon," *Sunstone* 7 (Sept.-Oct. 1982): 20-27.

3. Lucy Mack Smith, *Joseph Smith and His Progenitors* (Rprnt. ed.; Independence, MO: Herald House, 1969), 164-65.

4. See Fawn M. Brodie, *No Man Knows My History*, 2d ed. (New York: Alfred A. Knopf, 1971) for a historical perspective on these activities of Joseph Smith.

5. See Brigham H. Roberts, *A Comprehensive History of the Church of Jesus Christ of Latter-day Saints, Century 1*, 6 vols. (Provo, UT: Brigham Young University Press, 1965), 2: chap. 64.

6. Ibid., 5:294-300.

7. Ibid., 401.

8. See Gustive O. Larson, *The "Americanization" of Utah for Statehood* (San Marino, CA: Huntington Library, 1971), for a historical review.

9. Roberts, *Comprehensive History*, 2: 210-12.

10. See Gene Sessions, *Mormon Thunder: A Documentary History of Jedediah Morgan Grant* (Urbana: University of Illinois Press, 1982).

11. Juanita Brooks, *The Mountain Meadows Massacre* (Norman: University of Oklahoma Press, 1962).

12. Juanita Brooks, *John Doyle Lee, Zealot, Pioneer, Builder, Scapegoat* (Glendale, CA: Arthur H. Clark Co., 1962).

13. Juanita Brooks, "An Historical Epilogue," *Utah Historical Quarterly*, 24 (1956): 71-77.

11.
Objectivity and History

Kent E. Robson

IN THE EARLY 1960S A CRISIS OCCURRED IN THE ACADEMIC FIELD OF THE
philosophy of science, spilling over into the philosophy of history and
the philosophy of social sciences. The crisis emerged from research
in the related fields of the philosophy of language, the philosophy of
science, epistemology, and metaphysics and can be dated to 1962, the
year that Thomas S. Kuhn's book, *The Structure of Scientific Revolutions*, appeared.[1]

Before attempting to describe this crisis, let me characterize
some of its outcomes. One is the claim that there is no objectivity in
history, science, or life. Another is that there is no rationality—that
changing perspectives and conceptual schemes are irrational and that
unpredictable events happen without causes. As a result some scholars have claimed that there is no longer any basis in science for saying
that one way of doing things is more rational than another. Some of
the questions that have been raised with this way of looking at
objectivity and rationality are: What do we really know? What should
we believe? What is evidence? What are good reasons? And is science
as rational as people used to think?[2]

Another way of describing this crisis has to do with "scientific
realism." Here we might ask: What is the world? What kinds of things
are in it? What is truth? Is there in fact any such thing as truth? Are
"facts" of science simply constructs of human minds which could be
supplanted by alternative organizing schemes? Could these organizing schemes be changed, since they are based on shifting paradigms
without being guided by objective causes, truth, or rationality? What
then is left of truth? And what remains of rationality?[3]

155

It should be obvious why this crisis is of concern to philosophers of science and to historians. If there is no truth, no objectivity, no basis on which to argue the rationality of one account over another, one can claim that different accounts are simply based on prevailing sociological prejudices and biases. There would be no basis for claiming that one piece of history is good, another poor; no basis on which to say that one kind of history is objective, another biased. The sociology of knowledge becomes the central criterion for evaluating all work. All writing would be judged only against changing perspectives within the community of historians, the community of scientists, the community of scholars, without there being any starting point which could reveal truth, objectivity, and rationality.

This is the crisis that science and history have confronted since the early 1960s. If we accept this perspective, we can assert, as has BYU political scientist Louis Midgley, that since we have no ability to discriminate, we can have no perspective from which to be objective, and Mormon historians should therefore be defenders of the faith.[4] Like Johann Gottlieb Fichte, who maintained that what I believe about the world is determined by my will, it is my obligation to show that I am free, and to announce to the world my commitment to subjective truth.[5] Midgley maintains that history is a matter of assertion without objectivity, rationality, or truth and that we should all therefore assert our faith. Since no one can do better than this, one person's biases are no better than another's.

In another essay, David Earl Bohn, also of BYU's political science department, maintained that there is no superior approach to history from which historians can defend their views. Since there is no objectivity, there is no truth, no rationality. The reference to a "higher ground" assumes that there is some basis on which historians, scientists, and other can ground their claims to truth, objectivity, and rationality. Bohn wrote, "The illusion of a higher ground is indeed seductive. If the ideal of neutrality and objectivity cannot be approximated, then the historian's distinction between 'good history' and 'bad history' evaporates, and the secular historian's claim that somehow his account is of a higher order can no longer hold."[6]

The logical outcome of this line of thinking is that we have no criteria for deciding between good and bad history, good and bad science, good and bad logic, good and bad philosophy, and good and bad values. Everything becomes relative to the people who assert this or that position; skepticism, relativism, and cynicism rule the day. From this perspective, if I take a position in history and you agree with me, you write good history. But if you disagree with me, you write bad history. There is no position independent of our own from which we can say that this is in itself good or bad history or good or bad science.

This same crisis has spread into the field of ethics, where the prevailing mood is relativism. Nothing is good or bad, right or wrong. Good and bad are relative to a particular culture, nation, religion, or ethnic group. There is no objective definition of good or bad against which to measure these judgments. Since nothing is good, bad, right, or wrong, it does not make any difference what people do. This crisis is widespread and has profound implications in ethics, history, philosophy of science, epistemology, and elsewhere.

I would like to argue against this relativism, this subjectivity, this lack of objectivity, this claim that there is no truth—that knowledge can be determined only within the context of the sociology of knowledge. While I do not intend in this essay to argue against relativism in ethics, I do hope to argue against the lack of objectivity in history, the lack of truth in history, and the lack of rationality in history and science.

There is a body of literature in philosophy and history which argues that there is no truth, objectivity, or rationality in history or science. In fact David Bohn quotes some of that literature.[7] He could have gone on to draw attention to the controversies concerning a theory of truth in the philosophy of language and a theory of right in ethics. In history Bohn might have used Carl L. Becker's relativism and lack of objectivity expressed in "What are Historical Facts?"[8] Or he might have gone back further to English Bishop George Berkeley and Scottish philosopher David Hume, both of whom argued that we not only have no sure knowledge that there is an external world, we cannot know that we ourselves exist, let alone others.

Mormon historians have joined in the thrust of the ideas underlying this crisis. In 1969 Richard Bushman published "Faithful History," an essay in which he wrote, "We have abandoned the naive hope that we can write objective history."[9] James Clayton claimed in 1982 that historians do not have a point of view from which they can achieve "total objectivity."[10] In another article, "The Future of Mormon History," Bushman wrote, "We should not be deceived, however, by the illusion that at long last we have learned to write objective history. . . . The myth of scientific history . . . has been discarded."[11] Ronald K. Esplin asserted that an approach to historical truth which assumes that a historian can be objective is unrealistic and naive.[12] And Thomas G. Alexander has said that no historian today believes that objectivity is possible, at least in a Cartesian or Kantian sense. Alexander focused our attention on what we mean by objectivity and raised the question whether there is any kind of objectivity or truth that we can make use of in our history to overcome the challenge that there is no truth whatsoever.[13]

The issues are broad ones. They concern not only history but all of science. We are just now beginning to see reactions against this attack on objectivity, truth, and rationality. More and more philosophers are arguing that there *are* some starting points, that there *is* such a thing as rationality and objectivity, that everything is *not* equally valid. If we could arrive at acceptable definitions of objectivity and truth, so the claim goes, we may discover that history is no more subjective than science and that science is no more objective than history. Part of this problem lies in the traditional misunderstandings of science by those in the humanities and social sciences, especially historians.

The traditional assumption has been that scientific events are repeatable and testable. The truth of the matter is that all events are confined to specific places and times which, when they are over, are never repeated. The best that one can do is to construct, possibly in the laboratory, a new event that is similar enough in relevant ways to the previous event; but the tie between the two events is conceptual and linguistic.

Before any testing can be done, these kinds of conceptual ties between events must be made in science as in history. Frequently these ties are made by words. General terms cover not just one event but several. If historians talk about a revolution, for example, there must be ways to link past and present revolutions or they could not call both of them revolutions. In the same way scientists hope to call a particular event in a linear accelerator an event of left- or right-handed electron spin, while another could be interpreted as a weak neutral event of left- or right-handed electron spin.[14] Only by connecting the two events are scientists able to make a scientific generalization because the events are spatially and temporally discontinuous. It is because of this discontinuity—and the fact that connections between events need to be made by conceptual ideas having a basis in language—that the crisis over objectivity, truth, and rationality has in part arisen.

Before this crisis in science and history occurred, scholars used to assume that there was a clear distinction between observation and theory, that the growth of knowledge was cumulative, and that it could lead to an increasingly adequate theory of the universe. In the context of these views, Thomas Kuhn's book was a bombshell. Kuhn charged that there is no distinction between observation and theory, that science and history are not cumulative, that scientific concepts are not particularly precise, and that the methodological unity of science is false. There is no one basis upon which we can strive for truth and objectivity. Kuhn did not want to assert that science is therefore irrational. But he did not believe that one could talk glibly about what is true or objective. One interpretation of Kuhn's paradigm as a set of shared values is that these values are merely social constructs and that they change without there being necessarily good reasons for change. It is here where one writer senses a "whiff of irrationality" in Kuhn's view.[15] This whiff can extend to the dismissal of historical objectivity and even in some cases to the dismissal of a concept of truth.

One reaction to this crisis can be found in the work of Imre Lakatos, a well-known philosopher of science at the University of London, who charged that Kuhn's vision was dominated by "mob psychology."[16] Larry Laudan, another prominent philosopher of science, thinks that scientific rationality lies in the power of science to solve problems and answer questions.[17] And Ian Hacking takes his response to Kuhn from the idea that the entities, states, and processes described by correct theories really exist and that scientific realism is true.

My own claim for objectivity, rationality, and truth in history is an amalgam of these views, in addition to other considerations deriving from the philosophy of language. In this I assert that David Bohn and Louis Midgley are wrong when they say that there is no higher or middle ground that can be used for testing good history. When one sets out to write history, he or she tries to describe and interpret objects, persons, and events. I assume contrary to Berkeley and Hume that these objects and events exist, that there are real people in the world, and that there is an external world. To assume otherwise would be perverse, because the assumption that there are real events and objects in the world has made possible scientific progress.

Furthermore I believe that there is a defensible theory of truth which says that one can truly describe objects and events in the world. These events can be described and redescribed, but the descriptions are either true or false. There is a distinction to be made between truth and falsity. In the philosophy of language, while I reject a naive correspondence theory of truth, I do subscribe to the view that there is a holistic interpretation of truth that makes sense.[18] The naive correspondence theory holds that each word stands for an object, person, or event and that the truth is a relation in which a word *does* stand for an object. A holistic theory argues that truth must be discovered only in the context of a whole language and its relation to the world. Already we have two firm starting positions for history. Either events occurred or they did not occur. If they occurred we can give true descriptions of them or we can give false descriptions of them. It *does* make a difference. And we can endlessly describe in true ways events that occurred.

Why is it that historians can continue to write new books about the same events, using different categories and different interpretations? Does this once again suggest that history is not objective and that there is no truth? To my mind it does not. It simply tells us that many alternative, true accounts of historical events can be given without lapsing into falsehood and irrationality because no complete description of any event, let alone any historical event, may be given by anyone.

Historians have sometimes claimed that we cannot give complete descriptions of past events. Although they are right, the truth is that we cannot give *complete* descriptions of any event, even contemporary ones. Complete descriptions are impossible, not only because of the many ways that we can use language to connect events with this object or that person but also because the recursive rules of language formation enable us to generate an infinite number of sentences after starting with finite vocabulary and a finite set of rules. To whatever description we use, we could add, "John believed that . . ." There are rules for constructing true sentences that enable us to take an endless number of persons and ascribe attitudes to them.

These rules enable us to describe events and objects endlessly because the rules are recursive.[19]

It was this phenomenon Richard Bushman described in "Faithful History" when he observed, "Written history rarely survives the three score and ten allotted to the men who write it. New evidence, new outlooks, new concepts for describing the events can give rise to new accounts of the events."[20] At every time however one can ask: Did the events occur and are the descriptions and interpretations of them true?

When Bushman wrote "Faithful History," he talked about facts. I prefer not to use the word *fact* because it conceals a crucial ambiguity. Facts can be taken both as events themselves and as true descriptions of events. By running these two ideas together, one can make the mistake of believing that changes in one's descriptions "change," "mold," or "sculpt" the events themselves.[21] Once the event is over, it cannot be changed. But it can be endlessly redescribed. And among the endless redescriptions of the events are those that are true. If facts are taken as linguistic entities, then they relate to these descriptions and redescriptions of the events. But if facts are interpreted to be the events themselves, then they are unchanging and not in any way "plastic."

This brings me to my suggestions as to how we might make sense of objectivity in history or in science. Methodologically sophisticated historians like Thomas Alexander talk about objectivity in a Cartesian or Kantian sense, specifying the difference between subjects and objects. Here we know nothing about the objects unless we experience them as subjects. There is therefore a connection, as Kuhn suggested, between our experience and the way we conceptualize that experience. We do not know the events independent of epistemologically experiencing them.

In his 1967 book, *Science and Subjectivity*, Israel Scheffler argues for several definitions of objectivity in opposition to Kuhn's view. The first definition Scheffler provides is that objectivity means that independent tests can be made of any individual's assertions in any field. This is the assertion that any serious historian or scientist must make his or her work available to other historians and scientists for independent, impartial, and detached assessment. Scheffler says such a process is entirely compatible "with passionate advocacies, strong faith, intuitive conjecture, and imaginative speculation."[22]

This ideal cannot be limited to science but applies to history, mathematics, and other disciplines. It presupposes that people of differing points of view may yet talk intelligently and intelligibly to each other.

The next concept of objectivity suggested by Scheffler has to do with observation and objectivity.[23] Here he claims that assertions are objective if they are true, that is if they truly describe events that have occurred. This concept presupposes that the events and objects described and interpreted really exist and that there are true and also false ways of talking about them. In this Scheffler and Hacking have a common interest in defending "scientific realism," the view that there are real objects and events in the world. Scheffler asserts this concept despite his realization that observation is never independent of conceptualization, that what is observed may not be altered by conceptual change, that observation is not ineffable, and that observational descriptions are not, just because they are observational, certain. Even so there is a foundation for a kind of objectivity in realism.[24]

A third definition of objectivity has to do with meaning.[25] Donald Davidson has provided by far the most thoughtful discussion of this concept. Davidson construes the central problem in the philosophy of language to be developing a semantics that makes sense of concepts such as meaning, naming, referring, and asserting.[26] Davidson's answer to these questions lies in the development of a holistic theory of truth in language. Davidson writes for example that "language is an instrument of communication because of its semantic dimension, the potentiality for truth or falsehood of its sentences, or, better, of its utterances and inscriptions."[27] Davidson believes that this view helps us to understand that different languages are not relativistic—that is, not just derivative of cultures, times, and places as many writers have claimed. True sentences correspond to actual relations among things to which I refer by my sentences. As Hacking suggested, "This attitude brings a comforting antidote to relativism and anti-objectivity."[28]

A further interpretation of objectivity has to do with the growth of scientific knowledge.[29] This concept presupposes a scientific or historical community. Over a period of time, one can look back and ask: Are there problems that have been solved in science? Are there problems that have been solved in history? This, Lakatos asserts, is the key to understanding objectivity. Is it the case that knowledge does grow? Do we for example now know that polygyny was practiced in Nauvoo? There was a time not too many years ago when the answer was unclear. We have now reached a point where we can answer with firmness, "Yes." In this regard, as Laudan suggests, a solution has been found to a problem that gives us a concept of rationality.[30] We may still argue about what polygyny in Nauvoo among Mormons meant or what the intentions of the practicing individual were. Still we now know things about history, including Mormon history, that we did not know earlier. We can thus affirm that there is cumulative knowledge. No historian today can afford to overlook the sources, the documentation, the evidence, and the interpretations of others in arriving at new assertions. This gives us a demarcation between rational activity, even in history, and irrationalism. It could also be described as a demarcation between objectivity and subjectivism.

In light of these suggestions, one can argue against the assertions by some Mormons that there is no objectivity in history. When David Bohn contends that there is no ground for claiming that one history is better than another, I can suggest, because of the above definitions of objectivity, that Bohn's claim is false.

Bohn strenuously objects to "New Mormon Historians" and, after listing some of them, including philosopher Sterling McMurrin, categorizes all of them as "positivists" or "those expressing the positivist's paradigm," which he then dismisses on the grounds that there is no objectivity, truth, or rationality.[31] McMurrin's account of his own position suggests that he takes seriously the idea that some sentences about the world are true and can be distinguished from those that are false. To think otherwise would plunge us into a morass of irrationality, even in religious matters, and we should defend a concept of "reasonableness" and a commitment to "rationality."[32]

Some of what Bohn writes is not accurate. For example he alleges, "The historian who approaches the record realizes that his text constitutes his only avenue of access to the past."[33] I have previously pointed out that every record of every event is incomplete, not only of past events but of contemporary events as well. However every historian brings more to the event than simply the text. He or she brings a knowledge of a language that enables him or her to read the text and an understanding about events, objects, and current events which, by drawing analogies, he or she can bring to bear on the event. Furthermore there are aspects of language, such as truth and reference, contrary to what Bohn says, that remain stable over time and place. Davidson suggests this in his theory of truth.[34] Whatever historians arrive at may be tested, reexamined, and reevaluated by other historians. Over a period of time, this enables us to make fairly firm assertions about what is known and what is still problematic. The accounts can be interpreted in this sense as being more or less "adequate."[35]

There is another problematic suggestion in Bohn's essay. He suggests that "New Mormon Historians" mutually support the view that one should defend a "secular middle ground" in doing history. Such a middle ground, he asserts, would be one which is "objective and neutral."[36] In my reading in Mormon history, I have not seen the word *neutrality* widely used. In fact, some New Mormon Historians argue against objectivity in history and do not describe their own work as "secular." For example Ronald Esplin suggests that scholarship should be evaluated based on acquaintance with "relevant sources, honesty in the use of documents, integrity in presentation, quality of insights and adequacy of interpretation."[37] I see no assertion here that this must somehow be "secular." Lawrence Foster, a non-Mormon, in "New Perspectives on the Mormon Past: Reflections of a Non-Mormon Historian," argues that "labeling the recent historical writings as secular Mormonism is a red herring, since it suggests a false dichotomy between a position that is exclusively religious and a position that is exclusively secular."[38] James Clayton in "Does History Undermine Faith?" answers with this quote, "I believe that the study of history seldom directly threatens fundamental religious beliefs, because history and religions seldom meet."[39] And Richard Bushman suggests that the New Mormon History may be both "faithful and scholarly, informed, and intelligent."[40]

Bushman goes on to suggest that Mormons should write history. I firmly agree. By virtue of their religious perspectives, Mormons can bring an orientation to and an analysis of historical issues different from those of non-Mormons so long as they describe events that happened in ways that are true and submit their work to others for independent evaluation. I see no way to maintain that Mormons—just because they are Mormons—are incapable of offering insights on historical problems and even resolving them in ways that would be acceptable to non-Mormons as well as Mormons. In this Mormons may use models adopted from the social sciences, or they may attempt to make their work intelligible to non-Mormons by explaining the terms, conditions, and perspectives from which they write. But they may still write of issues as insiders in ways that non-Mormon historians may not have previously understood. Just because Mormons write to communicate their insights to Mormons and non-Mormons, this cannot mean that their work lacks faith, that it undermines faith, or that somehow it is innately "positivistic."

Both Clayton and Bushman address the issue of how religious values impact the writing of history. On the one hand I do not believe a Mormon historian needs to write history only according to a program of religious perspectives that have to be defended. Even though Bushman suggests that Mormon historians might consider some ways of organizing their historical research along lines called "Faithful History," his book *Joseph Smith and the Beginnings of Mormonism* does not suggest that he is writing narrow, programmatic history that cannot be taken to be true, rational, and intelligent also.

Bushman describes these possibilities when he writes concerning the discovery of the Book of Mormon plates and their translation: "The story to emerge from these accounts may in one respect perplex readers who are not Mormons. . . . Some readers may wish to separate the easily believable mundane details from the extraordinary supernatural events and to find other explanations for the unusual experiences. The account that follows does not make that separation or attempt an explanation beyond that *given in the sources.* It tells the story as the Mormons remembered it, in the hope that an account reconstructed from the participants' memories will be useful in some degree to every reader."[41]

Clayton's assertion that "historians and advocates of a particular religion do clash when the historian perceives that the advocate is not being loyal to historical as opposed to religious truth, when the religious advocate does not have a high sense of intellectual honesty or lacks a sense of balance, proportion, and common sense," suggests that Clayton may believe that a person who believes in religious truth cannot have the kind of honesty, sense of balance, proportion, and common sense needed to write history which would not clash with adequate historical perspectives. I believe that it is clearly possible to do that.

Clayton further argues that historians have no tools for dealing with the supernatural.[42] This is not completely accurate. Historians have the same tools as any other human beings. They have their normal faculties, their ability to understand language, their ability to assess information and to draw conclusions. If they themselves have not experienced certain kinds of events, at least they know what it is like to experience events. They can at the minimum report on what others have said they have experienced.

If one wishes to go beyond reporting what participants said, one could for example build a case based on the usual evidentiary rules used in the law. Are the accounts eye-witness accounts? Are they contemporary? Were they experienced by several individuals? Were the accounts repudiated? Are the descriptions of the event accurate? Are there additional descriptions of the events that would be true of the events and compatible with other descriptions? Did participants believe the descriptions to be true?

All of these questions might be used in assessing uniquely Mormon events such as the first vision, the discovery of the gold plates, and the translation of the Book of Mormon. At the same time one can take account of the perspectives of the writers of the events. Do they exhibit accuracy and honesty in dealing with the evidence available to them? Is the evidence first-hand or something else?

Lawrence Foster claimed concerning the writing of Jerald and Sandra Tanner, "On the one hand I agree with many of the Tanners' criticisms of the inadequacies of much Mormon writing until recently. On the other hand I am equally critical of the narrow-minded Protestant Fundamentalism which the Tanners have substituted for the Mormonism that they decry."[43] There is still a great deal to be said for honesty that does not become special pleading, for integrity that exhibits a sense of proportion and balance, and for careful research that has not decided that the purpose of writing is propaganda or indoctrination. If it is incumbent upon historians to do the best, most detailed, and most careful research they are capable of, one might also expect it to be incumbent upon those who possess sources of information to make them accessible and available.

In short, there are constraints on writing history. The first has to do with whether the event or events occurred. The second relates to whether descriptions of these events are true. An additional constraint has to do with the "multiple jeopardy" that any historical writer is subject to concerning the adequacy of historical research, the care and handling of sources and documentation, and the way in which peers from all areas in history may have access to the histories written and may assess them from many perspectives over an unlimited period of time.[44] If Lakatos's claims are correct about the growth of knowledge, the superior accounts will emerge over time after multiple testing and examination, and new problems will be solved. These constraints on history and science enable us to make sense of objectivity, truth, and rationality, and undercut relativism.

NOTES

1. Thomas S. Kuhn, *The Structure of Scientific Revolutions*, 2d ed. (Chicago: University of Chicago Press, 1970).

2. Ian Hacking, *Representing and Intervening: Introductory Topics in the Philosophy of Natural Science* (London: Cambridge University Press, 1983), 1.

3. Ibid.

4. Louis Midgley, "A Critique of Mormon Historians: The Question of Faith and History," Western History Association annual meeting, 14-17 Oct. 1981, San Antonio, Texas, 13, 28, 31.

5. Johann Gottlieb Fichte, *The Vocation of Man* (La Salle, IL: Open Court Publishing Co., 1906), Bk. 3.

6. David Earl Bohn, "No Higher Ground," *Sunstone* 8 (May-June 1983): 27; revised version printed in this compilation.

7. Ibid., 32, n23.

8. Carl L. Becker, "What are Historical Facts?" *Western Political Quarterly* 8 (Sept. 1953): 327-40.

9. Richard Bushman, "Faithful History," *Dialogue: A Journal of Mormon Thought* 4 (Winter 1969): 16; revised version printed in this compilation.

10. James Clayton, "Does History Undermine Faith?" *Sunstone* 7 (Mar.-Apr. 1982): 34.

11. Richard Bushman, "Introduction: The Future of Mormon History," *Dialogue: A Journal of Mormon Thought* 1 (Autumn 1966): 24.

12. Ronald K. Esplin, "How Then Should We Write History?" *Sunstone* 7 (Mar.-Apr. 1982): 41.

13. Thomas G. Alexander, "Historiography and the New Mormon History: A Historian's Perspective," *Dialogue: A Journal of Mormon Thought* 19 (Fall 1986): 25-49.

14. Hacking, *Representing and Intervening*, 266-71.

15. Ibid., 11.

16. Ibid., 112.

17. Larry Laudan, "A Problem-Solving Approach to Scientific Progress," in *Scientific Revolutions*, ed. Ian Hacking (Oxford: Oxford University Press, 1981), 144ff.

18. Donald Davidson, *Inquiries into Truth and Interpretation* (Oxford: Clarendon Press, 1984), 215-25.

19. Ibid.

20. Bushman, "Faithful History," 11.

21. Kent Robson, Letter, *Dialogue: A Journal of Mormon Thought* 5 (Summer 1970): 8.

22. Israel Scheffler, *Science and Subjectivity* (Indianapolis: The Bobbs-Merrill Co., Inc., 1967), 2.

23. Ibid., 21-44.

24. Ibid., 36.

25. Ibid., 45-66.

26. Davidson, *Inquiries into Truth*, 219.

27. Ibid., 201.

28. Ian Hacking, "On the Frontier," *New York Review of Books*, 31 Dec. 1984, 57.

29. See Scheffler, *Science and Subjectivity*, 67-89; Hacking, *Representing and Intervening*, 112-28.

30. Laudan, "A Problem-Solving Approach," 144ff.

31. Bohn, "No Higher Ground," 27-28.

32. Sterling M. McMurrin, *Religion, Reason, and Truth* (Salt Lake City: University of Utah Press, 1982), 18-19.

33. Bohn, "No Higher Ground," 28.

34. Davidson, *Inquiries into Truth*, 199-214.

35. Lee K. Lambert and G. Brittan, *An Introduction to the Philosophy of Science* (Englewood Cliffs, NJ: Prentice Hall, 1970), 88-91.

36. Bohn, "No Higher Ground," 27.

37. Esplin, "How Then Should We Write History," 4.

38. Larry Foster, "New Perspectives on the Mormon Past," *Sunstone* 7 (Jan.-Feb. 1982): 44; revised version printed in this compilation.

39. Clayton, "Does History Undermine Faith," 37.

40. Bushman, "Faithful History," 16.

41. Richard Bushman, *Joseph Smith and the Beginnings of Mormonism* (Urbana: University of Illinois Press, 1984), 80-81; my emphasis.

42. Clayton, "Does History Undermine Faith," 38.

43. Larry Foster, "Career Apostates: Reflections on the Works of Jerald and Sandra Tanner," *Dialogue: A Journal of Mormon Thought* 17 (Summer 1984): 36.

44. J. H. Hexter, *Doing History* (Bloomington: University of Indiana Press, 1971), 83.

12.
Two Integrities:
An Address to the Crisis in
Mormon Historiography

Martin E. Marty

MORMONS HAVE ACQUIRED AS DISTINCTIVE A CHARACTER IN THE larger public as Judaism possesses. Often overlooked in assessments of American religious demography, this "new religious tradition" increasingly demands separate analysis. A striking feature of Mormonism is that while "differentiation" is an aspect of modernity that challenges other sets of people, the current Mormon crisis has to do with the challenge of modern historical consciousness and criticism. Such a burden of history assaults all fundamentalisms and conservatisms, but it confronts Mormons most directly, for reasons that we shall shortly point out.

Mormon thought is experiencing a crisis comparable to but more profound than that which Roman Catholicism recognized around the time of the Second Vatican Council (1962-65). Whatever other changes were occurring in the Catholic church, there was a dramatic, sometimes traumatic shift in ways of regarding the tradition. One of the conventional ways of speaking of this shift comes from the observation of philosopher Bernard Lonergan. He and others argued that Catholicism was moving from a "classic" view of dogma to a thoroughly "historical" view of faith.

In the classic view Catholic teaching has come intact, as it were, protected from contingency, from a revealing God. Deposited in scripture, church tradition, and especially dogma, it was protected from anything but ordinary or trivial historical accidents. In the new vision this classic understanding gave place to an approach which saw Catholic events, thought, and experience as being at all points and in every way colored by the contingencies and accidents of history. God was revealed in the midst of this history.

Mormonism never was constituted around anything so formal and, it was believed by Catholics, uncontingent as dogma. From the beginning this faith was always characterized by its thoroughly historical mode and mold. Yet almost inevitably this understanding after a century took on what we might call an "historically classical" form. Today in what some might regard as a dramatic and traumatic shift among Mormon intellectuals, there is a move so expansive and sudden that it hardly needs chronicling. While tautology might sound cute, one could say this shift is from an "historical classical" to an "historically historical" understanding. A focus on this issue can serve for reexamination of the historian's vocation—whether this be of the believing "insider" or the non- or other-believing "outsider." At the same time the inquiry can point to some of the limits of historical contributions to issues of faith and certitude.

Whatever else historians do, there are at least two components in their work. They deal with the past and they tell stories. As G. J. Renier[1] reminds us, their subject is the human social past (in contrast to, say, "natural history"). And while today various structuralisms and "cliometric" statistical approaches may obscure the story character, yet over all the historical mode is one of narrative, of story. Stories have subjects. Here things begin to get interesting.

The ethics of the profession calls historians to do careful research, not to hide evidence, to be suspicious when handling sources, and then to be fair. People used to say they should be "objective," but objectivity seems to be a dream denied. This means that historians have to be reasonably aware of their assumptions, the viewpoints they bring, the thought worlds of the people they are representing at second hand. What results, all thoughtful historians agree, is not a reproduction of reality, which cannot even be grasped by people on the scene during events, but "a social construction of reality." The historian invents.

Historical construction or invention is more delicate when the subject is the experience of the sacred in the life of a people. The sacred, Rudolf Otto's *mysterium tremendum et fascinans,* appears in the midst of the mundane and ordinary world with an Otherness which sometimes threatens, often eludes, forever beguiles the historian who comes in range of it. Because people who respond to the sacred stake their arrangement of life and their eternal hopes on this experience, they bring to it a passion which often leads them to want to be protected from historians and other social scientists. "Our" sacred, "our" Otherness, we think, is different—pure, uncontingent, protected from accident, beyond the scope of inquiring historians, be they insiders or outsiders.

Most of the time both those internal to the history of a people and a faith as well as those external to it can go about their business without creating suspicion or arousing a defensive spirit. So long as the life of the people proceeds routinely, they may not pay much attention to what historians discover and publish. It is when people are in a period of crisis that they notice historians. Renier has a charming passage on how historians, used to obscurity, become suddenly relevant when people "stop to think." They are especially on the spot when what they discover and publish *causes* people to "stop to think." They have successfully done so, from within and without, in the case of Mormonism in recent times.

The Mormon ferment of today, like the Catholic analogue during and after Vatican II, is a species of a genus we might call "the crisis of historical consciousness." This crisis cut to the marrow in the Protestant body of thoughtful scholars in western Europe in the nineteenth century and continues, though it has been lived with in various ways and thus seems more domesticated, in the late twentieth. Before the Enlightenment and the rise of a critical history focused on Christianity, professional historians were ordinarily cast as storytellers who were defenders of the faith. A few learned to direct their suspicions against forgeries and frauds like the Donation of Constantine. Most were called, if they were Catholic, to summon events from the past to certify the truth of Catholicism over against Protestantism. Needless to say, *vice versa*.

This meant that ordinary historians were much like other believers in respect to the people's past. It is useful here to introduce Paul Ricoeur's concept of "primitive naivete,"[2] by which he means nothing pejorative or condescending, merely something which designates. Children have such a naivete: they receive and accept more or less without question a world, a world view, and views, from parents and nurses and teachers. Tribal people can sustain a similar naivete; they know other tribes with other ways only from a distance, at best. Or they find no threat in these because they see no lure; other ways belong to the enemy. Isolated people, whether in a valley or an urban ghetto in a pluralist society, even in the age of mass media, can sustain the naivete. So can people in massive isolations of the sort which bind together every fifth human, religions like Islam. Most places where it is strong it has a monopoly, and the Muslim never knows and need never consider alternative ways of being or believing.

The primitive naivete of Catholic Europe, protected by space from the Muslim and contrived space in the form of ghetto walls from the Jews, was challenged with the introduction of variety by the Protestant Reformation on western soil. Yet it waited for the Enlightenment to introduce the full-fledged assault on this naivete. The Enlightenment brought other religions close to home: one thinks of Lessing's *Nathan der Weise* as a typical attempt to see rough parity between Christianity, Judaism, and Islam. The Enlightenment went further: while beginning to relativize Christian distinctiveness in the face of other ways, it also used critical tools on Christian texts and traces from the past.

In the nineteenth century, the age of modern critical history, the crisis of historical consciousness became intense and drastic. Now no events, experiences, traces, or texts were exempt from scrutiny by historians who believed they could be value-free, dispassionate. Today of course no one sees them as being successful in their search. They were tainted by radical Hegelian dialectics, neo-Kantian rigorisms, or the biases of a positivism that thought it could be unbiased. We may see these critical historians as naive in this respect. Otherwise they were highly successful at destroying the primitive naivete among those who read them seriously. The responses could vary among these readers. Some lost faith while others shored it up with defensive fundamentalisms which focused on papal infallibility or biblical inerrancy. Most adapted their way of looking at faith and lived with it in transformed ways. Whatever else happened, however, the believer who made the passage beyond primitive naivete was very busy picking and choosing responsive attitudes.

Protestantism, like Catholicism, had a "classical" aspect through its own dogmatic structure. All Christians then, like the Latter-day Saints now, had much at stake because their faith was so thoroughly historical in character. It lived by reference to events like the Creation, the call of Israel through its exodus and exile, the happening of Jesus Christ and especially his death and resurrection within calendrical history, and the calling into being of an historical people, the church. To see these events as shaped by historical forces, their traces and texts unexempt from critical examination, altered responses of faith and practice.

The clash between classic and historical views was stated classically by Lessing (1729-81), the Lutheran minister's son who became an Enlightenment philosopher. He argued what has since become commonplace: historical truth was not capable of logical demonstration. Reported miracles from creation through the signs and wonders which accompany biblical accounts of Israel and Jesus and through the visions which led to the vocations of prophets and apostles down to the resurrection of Christ could never thus demonstrate the truth of Christianity. "Accidental truths of history can never become the necessary truths of reason." Lessing called the gulf between the truths of history and the truths of reason "the ugly broad ditch which I cannot get across, however often and however earnestly I have tried to make the leap."[3]

Henceforth whoever believed in God and the integrity of God's people, while aware of what Lessing and his successors posed, clearly had to believe in a different way—Ricoeur would say through a "second naivete." After criticism people believe not in spite of but through interpretation. Much of educated catholic (Catholic and Protestant) Christianity is made up of people who thus believe. They would not call themselves "literalists" about history and would even question whether self-styled literalists are really literal or whether these do not select which events to protect from scrutiny under the leaky canopy of historical contingency.

The transit of the second mode of being and believing was not easy; a little garland of testimonies should suffice to recall it. John Viscount Lord Morley[4] spoke of the subsequently developed "triumph of the principle of relativity in historic judgment," the "substitution of *becoming* for *being*, the relative for the absolute, dynamic movement for dogmatic immobility."

The result was what historian Friedrich Meinecke called "one of the greatest spiritual revolutions which western thought has experienced." Ernst Troeltsch, a great Christian scholar, personalized it in a way that speaks to and for many. He had come with a solid belief in the events and the demonstrability of events which made up the Christian story, protected from and within the rest of history. Like others he personally had felt the "demand of the religious consciousness for certainty, for unity, and for peace." But: "I soon discovered that the historical studies which had so largely formed me, and the theology and philosophy in which I was so immersed, stood in sharp opposition, indeed even in conflict, with one another. I was confronted, upon the one hand, with the perpetual flux of the historian's data, and the trustful attitude of the historical critic towards conventional traditions. . . ." So Christianity was henceforth "a purely historical, individual, relative phenomenon." Further, the inference from all this was "that a religion, in the several forms assumed by it, always depends upon the intellectual, social, and national conditions among which it exists." Gone for him was "the absolute validity of Christianity."

Not all scholars took Troeltsch's course. Critical historians who are Christian believers abound in most Catholic and Protestant communions. Yet the testimony of a profound and empathic figure like Troeltsch has led them not to be disdainful of people who take "literalistic" or "fundamentalistic" ways of responding to the crisis—just as they have to hope for sympathy and understanding from those who resist and, in resisting, show the depth of "the crisis of historical consciousness."

Similarly, from the earliest years, there have been Mormons who left the faith because their view of the historical events which gave shape to it no longer permitted them to sustain it. Others remained with the Mormon people but were uneasy and made their own adjustment. We may safely assume that all thoughtful people must have some struggles with elements of a complex history. Faith attached to or mediated through historical events has always had some dimensions of an "offense" or "scandal" to the insider just as it has been *only* that to the outsider who despises. Awareness of pettinesses and peccadillos among leaders or injustices in the record of a people—one thinks of the Christian Crusades and Inquisition or papal corruption in many ages—has to be some sort of threat to the clarity of faith's vision, though it clearly has not meant the loss of faith or abandonment of peoplehood on the part of so many who are aware.

As far as the profession as a whole and the intellectual community at large are concerned, however, the crisis has been noticeable only in the past two decades and urgent only in very recent years. The hostility of the gentile world, geographical remoteness from alien forces, and the necessarily defensive agenda of the Mormon churches and people long protected the Saints. Serene in their grasp of Mormon faith, historians could busy themselves marshalling evidences to defend the integrity of the people. More often they simply chronicled the story of the amazing formation, trek, colonization, and expansion of a people—subjects that have to stir the hearts of either insiders or outsiders who have a musical ear for human drama.

Someday the crisis had to come. Few others of the 20,870 separate denominations listed in the most recent encyclopedia of Christianity have as much at stake so far as "historicness" is concerned as do Mormons. The character of their shaping events takes on a different nature in that these occurred so recently, on familiar soil, in check-outable times and places, *after* historical "science" had become developed. The shaping events of classic Christianity, whose story Mormons share, are accessible almost entirely through insider Christian sources alone. The Romans ignored them. Mormon events, meanwhile, occurred inside a history chronicled by small-town newspaper editors, diarists, hostile letter writers, contemporary historians. The beginnings are not so shrouded in obscurity as are Christian beginnings which were recorded especially in the New Testament. People now alive in their nineties who talked as little children to people then in their eighties have "memories" which link them to the years of Mormon beginnings. There is no place to hide. What can be sequestered in Mormon archives and put beyond the range of historians can often be approached by sources outside them. While Mormon iconography developed impressively early in its history, the images of Mormon beginnings are not yet haloed or sanctioned the way Christian beginnings are by their reflection in stained glass, their inspiration in centuries of classical music. There is little protection for Mormon sacredness.

Whoever knows how Christian faith survives and can survive knowledge of all the evidences of fallibility and scandal that occurred through history will understand why the outsider historian finds trivial the question of whether the faith is threatened by the revelation of human shortcomings in the later administration of the Mormon churches. Of course, for public relations reasons, one likes to portray one's heroes and Saints as saints. Lives of quality and character and policies of justice and fairness enhance one's identification with them and the people at large. Yet intellectually these are not of much interest. One can cut through all the peripheral issues and see that most of the writing on Mormon history which poses the issue of the crisis of historical consciousness focuses finally on Joseph Smith's First Vision, often capitalized to set it apart, and then, many agree, more importantly on the later vision which led to a second capitalization, the Book of Mormon.

Let me clear the air with a stark, almost crude, but still light-hearted and well-intended analogy: "When Cardinal de Polignac told Madame du Deffand that the martyr St. Denis, the first Bishop of Paris, had walked a hundred miles carrying his head in his hand, Madame du Deffand correctly observed, 'In such a promenade it is the first step that is difficult.'"[5]

By analogy, if the beginning of the promenade of Mormon history, the First Vision and the Book of Mormon, can survive the crisis, then the rest of the promenade follows and nothing that happens in it can really detract from the miracle of the whole. If the first steps do not survive, there can be only antiquarian, not fateful or faith-full, interest in the rest of the story.

When the historical crisis comes it can, of course, be addressed by fiat. Authority can invoke authority and silence questions, suppress curiosity, rule inquiry out of bounds, close off sources, purge questioners. Now and then rumors and reports of policies somewhere in this range of "heteronomy," to use Paul Tillich's term, reach the ears of gentiles. If these occur ecclesiastically, they are "none of our business." Intellectually, professionally, and personally of course, one cares and feels sympathy for Mormon historians, who are believers and belongers through "secondary naivete" or "after criticism" or "through interpretation." At the very least, one will also hear the whisper of those driven away or silenced: *eppur si muove.* Galileo kept integrity by murmuring such a truth after authority forced him to recant, to say that against all evidence the world did *not* move. "And yet it moves!"

Suppressed historians may busy themselves trying to comprehend the integrity of those who guard the tradition, eager as these are to protect the faith of Mormons who live in "primitive naivete."

Yet historians can be understandably frustrated if they feel that their gift, which would help people pass to another, secondary mode of being and believing, is *a priori* denied. Still this is a matter of internal ecclesiastical concern, and it would come with bad grace for an outsider to intervene or pursue the matter much beyond the point of observation.

It *does* belong to the historian's vocation, however, to say that alongside the unreflective faith of Christian believers who have not come to the crisis of historical consciousness, there are reflective, historically conscious people who do believe. There may be something of worth in their history, a history of great complexity, which might serve Mormons through analogy and precedent. There can be more than one kind of integrity in faith and peoplehood.

Having dismissed as secondary, late stages in the promenade, both what we might call "political embarrassments" and "borderline religious issues" (like the role of Masonry, the development and demise of polygamy), we can concentrate on what I will call the *generative* issues. They come down to what historians of religion call "theophany," the appearance of gods or godlike figures, and "revelation," the disclosure from one order of being and reality to another. The First Vision belongs to the category of theophany, the Book of Mormon to revelation.

The four primary accounts of the First Vision do not quite match, a fact no less and no more interesting than that details in the four Christian gospels do not always match. What matters is the event, which is accessible only through these traces. It is hard to read Mormon history as I have for twenty years without coming to agree with Neal E. Lambert and Richard H. Cracroft that this First Vision is "that pivotal event which is so central to the message of Mormonism that belief therein has become a touchstone of faith for the orthodox Mormon and Mormon convert." James B. Allen says that it is "second only to belief in the divinity of Jesus of Nazareth," and "next to the resurrection of Christ, nothing holds a more central place in modern Mormon thought than that sacred event of 1820."[6] Reflective Mormons have to cross Lessing's "ugly ditch" as they face up to such events.

Second, more urgently, the vision of 1823, the story of golden plates and seer stones and the text translated and published as the Book of Mormon, is both theophany and revelation. While the book may go unread by many Mormons—it always surprises gentiles to see how little awareness of much of its content there is among their Mormon neighbors—it is the event itself, the whole generative shape of the discovery, translation, and publication, which has made up a single base for Mormon history. When historians call into question both the process and the product, they come to or stand on holy ground. Not all Mormon historians devote their energies to these generative events, just as I as a historian of twentieth-century Christianity do not have to do research on the resurrection of Jesus: "It's not my period." Yet the basis for faith and concerns for events which follow are at stake when professional colleagues converge on these focal issues.

After 150 years when historians inside or outside the Mormon community focus on the generative events, it has become conventional to see them as concentrating on a direct, simple question. It is all supposed to come down to "Was Joseph Smith a prophet or a fraud?" To say "prophet" made one a Saint, for how could one then stay away from the history and people which issue from these events? To say "fraud" is precisely what made one leave Mormonism or never convert in the first place. That was that.

Then two things happened. Many non-Mormon historians bracketed (put in brackets, suspended) that question. Seeing four million and more people shaped by Smith's theophanic and revelational vision, people who in many cases were as intelligent and "modern" as they, the historians asked a new range of questions. If they would get hung up on the prophet/fraud dialectic, however much it may have nagged or tantalized them, they could not get to another range of questions: what sort of people are these people, what sort of faith is this faith, what sort of prophet with what sort of theophany and revelation was Joseph Smith? His consciousness, his "myth," and his effect could be pursued if one refused to be tyrannized by the literal stark prophet/fraud polarity in the question.

Meanwhile Saints historians asked more radical questions than before. They had to move through history and interpretation toward a "second naivete" which made possible transformed belief and persistent identification with the people. They brought new instruments to their inquiry into Mormon origins; shortly I shall detail what strike me as the three main approaches used by outsiders and insiders alike.

For now a very obvious and important point needs to be made. According to the norms and approaches of the historical profession, the "ground rules" accepted by historians, it would be impossible to prove that Smith was a prophet. As Renier reminds us, past events are as events wholly lost to us. We have only traces, testimonies, texts. As historians we cannot get behind those testimonies to the New York hills where the visions occurred, and we cannot regress in time. There is no way in which empirical evidence can produce for our verification the "two personages" or the later angel of the visions. If by some now-inconceivable time machine device we could be there, we might be duly impressed that *something* was happening beyond the ordinary. But in 1820 and 1823 as in 1983, we would be suspicious of visions—and Smith called them that—because they can be contrived, can elude ordinary analysis without themselves being extraordinary. We can see some things more remarkable on television or on stage any day of a week, yet these do not inspire the response of faith.

Conversely, of course, historians may find it possible to prove to their own satisfaction that Smith was a fraud. This is hard to do with the First Vision, if we grant that somewhat different accountings of detail on four occasions are no more challenges to its integrity than are the four Gospel accounts to the gospel event. It could be easier to do, and many have done so to their own and others' satisfaction in respect to the Book of Mormon, both so far as its external circumstances and internal character are concerned. Yet this proving of fraudulence has not been compelling, not "proof," to millions of Saints, who do not really lie abed in suspense lest the next discovery or assault achieve what the first eight score years of attack could not achieve. For our purposes it is more important to note that the issue of fraud, hoax, or charlatanry simply need not, does not, preoccupy the historical profession most of the time.

It is not necessary here to detail fully two of the three approaches to questions beyond the prophet/fraud issues addressed to generative Mormon events. I need only cite them and point to major statements of the issue. The first family has been familiarly summarized in Klaus Hansen's *Mormonism and the American Experience*.[7] We might call the studies summarized and enlarged upon there "consciousness" studies, contributions to the question of the consciousness of a modern prophet. After reference to social and environmental contexts and explanations, Hansen moves to the consciousness sphere.

Quoting Jan Shipps, he develops first "the analogy of musical genius" and then more speculatively Julian Jaynes's hypotheses about consciousness as it relates to hemispheres of the brain. Other "possible explanatory frameworks for getting a handle on Smith's revelations" include non-Mormon T. L. Brink's summaries of four alternatives derived from "depth psychology." On their basis Brink can assume that Joseph Smith "was a man of sound mind and sincere religious convictions." Sigmund Freud, more plausibly C. G. Jung, and then Alfred Adler and Erik Erikson are called as witnesses to make plausible the prophethood and throw light on prophetic character.

Emphatically in my understanding of the historical approach, none of these produce proof that Smith was a prophet or fraud. Instead they make possible a different level of urgent inquiry and make plausible the concepts of Smith's "soundness" and "sincerity." I should add that Larry Foster[8] has developed his own approaches to prophetic consciousness, approaches which have made it possible for him sometimes to speak up more emphatically for Smith than many Mormons can or do. These scholars show that one can use psychological instruments to illumine without falling into a reductionism which would insist that Smith was "nothing but" an exemplar of this or that stage of adolescent psychology or whatever.

The second address to the crisis of Mormon historical consciousness comes from a cluster of scholars whose work is focused in and summarized by another non-Mormon, Jan Shipps. Aware, as is Hansen from within, that the issue of prophet/fraud is in many ways a question of faith which can be illumined but not proven by historical inquiry, Shipps employs still another discipline for her work, *Religionsgeschichte*, which in America is usually translated as history of religion. (History here is not the same as ordinary "history of religions" but implies a somewhat different set of methods and has far less interest in narrative. It may be more taken with synchrony than diachrony, with structure than with happening.)

For Shipps's purposes, to begin with the First Vision casts the questions in an inappropriate light; the Book of Mormon here (as in Foster's work) is determinative. With the Book of Mormon the public career of the prophet began, and here it becomes accessible to the historian. Shipps is interested explicitly in shifting the focus from the prophet/fraud questions to the notion that Smith's story is "best understood in the context of his sequential assumption of positions/roles that allowed the Saints to recover a usable past." That was his *religious* function and achievement. She can go on to say that when one sees how this endeavor legitimated the prophetic task, "the question of whether Smith was prophet or fraud is not particularly important."

The fourth chapter of Shipps's book, "In and Out of Time," suggests the promise of the history of religion approaches for ordinary historians.[9] The sacred and non-sacred, wrote Mircea Eliade, are "different modes of being in the world." Historians using their ordinary canons have to be aware of this difference. They must be aware that the original Mormons saw their prophet and themselves stepping outside ordinary time and space, beyond the reach of conventional critical criteria. Temporally they wanted to live "once again at the beginning, *in illo tempore*," the kind of time which lies beyond empirical evidence.

Guilford Dudley has written that "the mystic time of beginnings is sacred by definition." The experience on the hill in New York or, for Shipps more important, the Mormon entry into the promised lands was "entry into sacred space" *and* sacred time. This did not mean that the Mormons ever were anything but practical people; they were not insubstantial or otherworldly. Yet their special kind of millennialism removed many of their claims beyond the realm of the mundane and practical and has served to provide extraordinary interpretations for the life of the people. Mundane Mormons even today "possess the means of reentering sacred time and space" in their temples and special times. These help endow their peoplehood with value and guarantee that the mythic dimensions of their history, which remain beyond the range of historians' destruction, also become a part of their historical constructions.

A third approach, not yet fully developed but rich in promise, is the hermeneutical. This version of "interpretation theory" helps Mormon intellectuals make the passage from primitive to secondary naivete or from belief before criticism to belief through criticism and interpretation. It also helps both Mormons and non-Mormons in the historical profession understand each other and do some justice to the generative events without being mired in the prophet/fraud polarity or posing.

I propose a hermeneutical approach to the problem of Mormon texts. By texts I mean both those which impart Joseph Smith's visions and the Book of Mormon itself. Contemporary hermeneutics, the focus of so much philosophical passion today, can be treated extremely technically in ways which would seem alien to most historians. Yet the subject has on occasion been rather simply introduced, and I shall depend upon a summary by a noted literary critic, E. D. Hirsch, to outline it.[10]

Hermeneutics, he points out, is associated with *Hermes*, the divine messenger between gods and men. (The parallel name is *Interpres* from which we get "interpretation.") God's hidden message needs such a conveyor to ordinary people. In 1927 Martin Heidegger in *Sein und Zeit* borrowed a term from hermeneutics, *Vorverstaendnis* or "pre-understanding." He showed that unprejudiced, objective knowledge was not possible. All knowledge is bound in part by "pre-knowing" which is determined by our historical, social, and personal backgrounds. Such pre-knowing for example determines in large measure what attitudes we have toward and what we derive from Islamic, Marxist, Christian, or Mormon texts.

"Pre-understanding," to step back further, derives from Wilhelm Dilthey (1833-1911), who showed how understanding of a text is a circular process. As a non-Mormon I can discuss the Book of Mormon in such terms: "First we encounter words and clauses which have no distinct meaning until we know how they function in the text as a whole. But since we can only know the whole meaning through the various parts of the text and since we cannot know before what the parts mean or how they work together before we know the whole text, we find ourselves in a logical puzzle, a circularity. This is the famous 'hermeneutical circle.' It can be broken only by resolving the question of which came first, the chicken or the egg, the whole or the part. By general agreement from which there has been virtually no dissent, the question of priority is decided in favor of the whole. The whole must be known in some fashion before we know the part. For how can I know that I am seeing a nose unless I first know that I am seeing a face? And from the doctrine of the priority of the whole came the doctrine of pre-understanding. Since we must know the whole before the part, we must assume some kind of pre-understanding in all interpretation."

Muslim children come to Muslim texts and Mormon children come to Mormon texts with pre-understandings which allow them to grasp the whole before they take apart the parts. These pre–understandings, no doubt often creatively, bias their understandings of the whole and the parts. Those who stand outside the circle have great difficulty sharing the understandings which come from the pre-understandings, although of course there can be and are conversions which bring illuminations of texts "from within" as it were.

Fortunately for our purposes, philosophers Jean Nabert and Paul Ricoeur have developed the theme of a "hermeneutics . . . of testimony."[11] The philosophy of testimony evokes an enormous paradox. Nabert in *L'Essai sur le mal* asks in the spirit of Lessing, "Does one have the right to invest with an absolute character a moment of history?" This must be addressed. Now testimony begins with a "quasi-empirical meaning"; it "designates the action of testifying, that is, of relating what one has seen or heard." Then comes the sort of transfer on which all Mormon faith depends: "there is the one who testifies and the one who hears the testimony. The witness has seen, but the one who receives his testimony has not seen but hears," and it is in this hearing that faith or unfaith is decided. The statement and the story constitute "information on the basis of which one forms an opinion about a sequence of events, the connection of an action, the motives for the act, the character of the person, in short on the meaning of what has happened."

When, asks Ricoeur, do we give testimony and listen to it? In a form of discourse called "the trial," which whether they have noticed it or not defenders and attackers of Joseph Smith so regularly establish. "Hence the question: what is a true witness, a faithful witness?" Ricoeur connects witness with the Greek word *martus*; the witness is linked with the martyr: "A man becomes a martyr because he is first a witness. . . . It is necessary, then, that the just die." And "the witness is the man who is identified with the just cause which the crowd and the great hate and who, for this just cause, risks his life." Thus "testimony is the action . . . as it attests outside of himself, to the interior man, to his conviction, to his faith."

This is the point at which the religious meaning of testimony is most clear. Historical faith connects what one "testifies *for*" a meaning with the notion that one is testifying *that* something has happened which signifies this meaning. There is tension between confession of faith and narration of things seen, but it is this tension that means that faith is dependent upon testimony, not sight, not "proof."

Mormons are people who, though aware of many historical ambiguities in the record and fallibilities in the prophet Joseph Smith, also see in his character, vocation, career, and witnessing—finally martyrdom—a credentialing which leads them to connect confession of faith with "something that has happened."

We have connected Jean Nabert and Paul Ricoeur with the hermeneutics of being the testifier, the witness. When one deals with the text of the Book of Mormon, the issue now becomes the hermeneutics of testimony. Ricoeur asks, "Do we have the right to invest a moment of history with an absolute character? One needs a hermeneutics, a philosophy of interpretation." Here Nabert remarks that "consciousness makes itself judge of the divine and consequently chooses its God or its gods." Testimony gives something to interpretation, but it also demands to be interpreted. There is the story of an event and a demand for decision, a choice that the testimony functions to awaken faith in the truth. "The judge in a court makes up his mind about things seen only by hearing said."

It is interesting to this gentile to notice the Book of Mormon is not widely read in the church. People come to faith because living witnesses base their speaking and way of life on what they have read, "heard," there—and a new generation of children or converts comes to faith by "hearing." None of them see golden plates to authenticate this faith. There is "no manifestation of the absolute without the crisis of false testimony, with the decision which distinguished between sign and idol." The Mormon believer and the non-Mormon rejecter are on the same terms, so far as material traces of actual past events are concerned.

Nabert speaks of this norm for judging the divine "the expression of the greatest effort that consciousness can make in order to take away the conditions which prevent it from attaining complete satisfaction." Faith is *not* absolute knowledge of an event that is forever lost except through testimony. Here is the break between "reason and faith, . . . philosophy and religion." And "this is what signifies the 'trial,' the 'crisis' of testimony." We must "choose between philosophy of absolute knowledge and the hermeneutics of testimony." The enforcer of orthodoxy who limits the inquiry of the historian wants history to do what a "philosophy of absolute knowledge" would do. The historian to whom past events are lost and for whom only traces in testimony remain lives with "the hermeneutics of testimony," which is in the end at the basis of all faith.

I must add a word on *how* a text like the Book of Mormon ministers in the tension and authenticates itself as testimony. To summarize almost to the point of cliché a very complicated set of developments in "interpretation theory," let us say that one moves through and beyond both historical and literary criticism to the interpretive level. That is, one wants to understand "the world behind the text," the world of Joseph Smith and the events described in the Book of Mormon. Yet having learned all that can be learned is not what either brings about or destroys faith. Second, one can use literary tools to understand the world "of the text." What is its genre or form? Yet here too is not the birth or death of faith. Instead one deals with "the world in front of the text," for here testimony forces its challenge.

Not was Joseph Smith a prophet or a fraud, but does the Book of Mormon connect confession and event in such a way that it discloses possible modes of being or thinking or behaving that the reader or better the listener (to a contemporary witness based on it) must entertain the risk of acceptance or rejection of the testimony? There is where faith or unfaith is born. David Tracy, employing an insight from Hans-Georg Gadamer, says that here is "the fusion of horizons": "the reader overcomes the strangeness of another horizon not by empathizing with the psychic state or cultural situation of the author but rather by understanding the basic vision of the author implied by the text and the mode-of-being-in-the-world referred to by the text."[12] One is henceforth freed of the burdens of "psychologizing" and is less burdened by concern over the exact reference to literal historical events.

Are there analogies in "ordinary Christians'" approaches to the issues of trace or testimony and event in respect to the resurrection of Jesus? How far does historical inquiry and doubt go and where must one make that leap "from trace to event" which is at the basis of narrative and in some respects of faith itself?

In a conservative Protestant survey, evangelical biblical scholar Daniel Fuller set forth a typology that began with "attempts to sustain knowledge of the Resurrection apart from historical reasoning" and then "partially from historical reasoning." Of greatest interest to Fuller is a third category, German theologian Wolfhart Pannenberg's "attempt to sustain knowledge of the resurrection wholly by historical reason."

Fuller's choice of Pannenberg was fortunate, because Pannenberg is an extremely formidable and sophisticated theologian, not someone to whom the term "fundamentalist" could be applied in any pejorative sense. "True faith is first awakened through an impartial observation of events," according to Pannenberg. "There should be no talk of supernaturalism, which is unacceptable for the critically oriented reason of the historians, because it arbitrarily cuts off historical investigation of immanental causes and analogies through the assertion of a transcendental intervention."

Fuller chooses to see the basis of faith better outlined by an earlier historian, the author of Luke-Acts: "Pannenberg, it will be remembered, wants to make faith the possibility for all men by having what is, virtually, a priesthood of historians. Theology's task, as he sees it, is to assert the credibility of the Christian proclamation, so that laymen can believe it because of the authority that the theologian, with special historical skills, can provide. It does not seem, however, that Luke, who finds the basis for revelational knowledge in history, makes historical reasoning the exclusive way to such knowledge. Acts 11:24 is a passage of particular interest in this connection because it tells how a number of people came to believe on the basis of the moral impact of the minister, rather than by accepting his authority or by employing historical reasoning to get back to the truth of the resurrection. '[Barnabas] was a good man, fully of the Holy Spirit and of faith. And [as a result] a large company was added to the Lord.'"

How frustrating all this must be to someone who wants to prove Joseph Smith a prophet or a fraud or to make that issue the only one to interest insider or outsider historians. We have argued that it is impossible for historians as historians to prove that Smith was a prophet and improbable that they will prove him a fraud. Instead they seek to understand. That is a modest but still important task in the communities of both faith and inquiry. Similarly historians cannot prove that the Book of Mormon was translated from golden plates and have not proven that it was simply a fiction of Joseph Smith. Instead they seek to understand its revelatory appeal, the claims it makes, and why it discloses modes of being and of believing that millions of Saints would otherwise not entertain.

If what I have outlined makes any sense at all, it might be a contribution to a lowering of suspicions of historians by Mormon guardians. At the same time it does not try to pretend away the depth of the crisis of historical consciousness for history-based Mormondom. The motive for this all is not to commend Mormon history to the secular academy, as if Mormon historians had to be driven by a push for relevance and respectability. The secular academy which despises Mormonism also has to despise Islam, Catholicism, Protestantism, all of which make theophanic and revelational claims similar to those of Mormonism. Yet Islamic, Catholic, and Protestant historians have found means of pursuing their work and displaying their integrity.

There are many kinds of integrity. Some of these are appropriate to insiders and others to outsiders, some to church authorities and some to historians, some to those with "primitive naivete" and others to those who live in "second naivete." Confusing these integrities is almost as destructive to them as is dismissing those sorts which are appropriate to other people in other callings. Discernment of them and empathy across the lines of the vocations of people who display them seem to be the most promising forms of address to the present crisis of historical consciousness.

NOTES

1. G. J. Renier, *History: Its Purpose and Method* (Boston: Beacon Press, 1950), chaps. 1:i (for the social or collective character of history), 1:ii (for its story character), and 2:i (for "events and traces"). See p. 14 on "stopping to think."

2. On "primitive" and "second" naivete, see Paul Ricoeur, *The Symbolism of Evil* (New York: Harper & Row Publishers, Inc., 1967), 351-53. His exact words on the second naivete (352): "For the second immediacy that we seek and the second naivete that we await are no longer accessible to us anywhere else than in a hermeneutics; we can believe only by interpreting. It is the 'modern' mode of belief in symbols, an expression of the distress of modernity and a remedy for that distress. . . . This second naivete aims to be the postcritical equivalent of the precritical hierophany." Again (351): "If we can no longer live the great symbolisms of the sacred in accordance with the original belief in them, we can, we

modern men, aim at a second naivete in and through criticism. In short, it is by interpreting that we can *hear* again."

3. The Lessing passages are quoted in Daniel Fuller, *Easter Faith and History* (Grand Rapids, MI: William E. Eerdmans Publishing Co., 1965), 33-35.

4. Morley, Meinecke, and Troeltsch are cited in Franklin L. Baumer, *Religion and the Rise of Skepticism* (New York: Harcourt, Brace and Co., 1960), 156-59.

5. Paul Elmen, *The Restoration of Meaning to Contemporary Life* (Garden City, New York: Doubleday, 1958), 189.

6. See *Journal of Mormon History* 7 (1980): 31, 43. The articles are Neal E. Lambert and Richard H. Cracroft, "Literary Form and Historical Understanding: Joseph Smith's First Vision in Mormon Religious Thought," and James B. Allen, "Emergence of a Fundamental: The Expanding Role of Joseph Smith's First Vision in Mormon Religious Thought."

7. Klaus J. Hansen, *Mormonism and the American Experience* (Chicago: University of Chicago Press, 1981), 15-27.

8. Lawrence Foster, *Religion and Sexuality: Three American Communal Experiments of the Nineteenth Century* (New York: Oxford University Press, 1981), 128-30, and elsewhere in Foster's writings.

9. Jan Shipps, *Mormonism: The Story of a New Religious Tradition* (Urbana: University of Illinois Press, 1985).

10. E. D. Hirsch, "Carnal Knowledge," in *The New York Review of Books*, 14 June 1979, 18.

11. "The Hermeneutics of Testimony," in Paul Ricoeur, *Essays on Biblical Interpretation* (Philadelphia: Fortress Press, 1980), 119-54 passim.

12. David Tracy, *Blessed Rage for Order: The New Pluralism in Theology* (New York: Seabury Press, 1975), the section on "Interpretation Theory," 72-79, esp. 78.

13.
The Acids of Modernity and the Crisis in Mormon Historiography

Louis Midgley

COMING FROM OUTSIDE THE LATTER-DAY SAINT COMMUNITY, MARTIN E. Marty[1] situates the current Mormon controversy over faith and history in a larger context by demonstrating that the struggle over how best to approach the Mormon past resembles one that has taken place in the larger Christian and Jewish communities. In addition, Marty is not burdened with a narrow secular parochialism in his approach to Mormon historiography. Hence his analysis is perhaps better grounded than that taken by those who tend to focus their attention on a narrow slice of American history. Marty's identification of "the crisis in Mormon historiography"[2]—a quandary of faith among Mormon historians—thus constitutes a sound starting point for further probing of key issues. This crisis concerns Joseph Smith's prophetic claims and the Book of Mormon which are now being debated in an academic arena in which a struggle is being waged for control of the Mormon past. I believe that this debate is both theoretically challenging and central to the faith.[3]

Though Marty does not describe the emergence of a presumably "new" history of the Mormon past, he demonstrates that a discussion is taking place of issues that have significant practical consequences for the life of the community of faith and memory. What is at stake in the current debate is the possibility and content of faith as Latter-day Saints have known it. Before turning to the

189

details of Marty's essay, I will sketch the background of the crisis he sees in Mormon historiography, a crisis that has drawn public attention during the period since 1974 in which historians have employed the label "new Mormon history."[4] What constitutes this New History? When and why did it start? What are its characteristics? In what way might New History be in any way linked to a "crisis"?

In 1983 Thomas G. Alexander, a respected prize-winning Mormon historian and advocate for the so-called New Mormon History,[5] indicated that a distinctively new approach "started in the 1950s among both Mormon and non-Mormon scholars," who believed "that secular and spiritual motivation coexist in human affairs and that a sympathetic but critical evaluation of the Mormon past, using techniques derived from historical, humanistic, social-scientific, and religious perspectives, could help in understanding what is at base a religious movement."[6] "Thirty years ago," according to Robert B. Flanders, "Leonard Arrington in *Great Basin Kingdom* raised for Mormons a fundamental question of epistemology: can empiricism, the secular method of modern history, stand with or even shoulder aside prophetic insight as a means of describing and understanding the saints' experience with the Kingdom in time and space?"[7] If Flanders is correct, as early as 1958 an effort was made within the Mormon community to characterize the controlling assumptions that ought to govern what historians write about the Mormon past.[8]

Others, however, have held that Fawn M. Brodie[9] and Dale L. Morgan[10]—two secular critics of Mormon origins—set the stage, provided "the bridge" to the history that followed, and furnished some of the crucial vocabulary in which the discussion is conducted.[11] In 1986 Paul M. Edwards, director of curriculum and clergy training at the Temple School Division of the Reorganized Church of Jesus Christ of Latter Day Saints, claimed that "this new approach to Mormon history started with Fawn Brodie's *No Man Knows My History* (1945)."[12] Earlier, in 1974, Flanders claimed that "the 1945 publication of Fawn M. Brodie's *No Man Knows My History* was a landmark" in the emergence of a New Mormon History; her book was "a transitional work. A new era dawned with her book. All subsequent serious studies of early Mormonism have necessarily had Brodie as a reference point."[13] In 1991 William D. Russell, also RLDS, traced the development of a New Mormon History as follows: "Beginning with

Fawn Brodie's biography of Joseph Smith in 1945 and continuing with Leonard Arrington's *Great Basin Kingdom* (1958) and Robert Flanders' *Nauvoo: Kingdom on the Mississippi* (1966), professional historians began to write church history by the standards of their profession. A great volume of professional works has been produced by these 'New Mormon Historians'."[14]

There are, of course, disparate views even on whether there is a New Mormon History,[15] and, if there is, what exactly characterizes and distinguishes it from its antecedents, and hence where exactly it began. For example, one apologist for the kind of secular, naturalistic accounts provided by Brodie and Morgan flatly rejects the view that "the rise of a scientific, objective Mormon history began . . . barely thirty years ago," a stance he attributes to Davis Bitton and Leonard J. Arrington. From his perspective, Mormon history "turned an important corner in the 1940s."[16] For various reasons, LDS historians, unlike RLDS, have stressed the role of Arrington in New Mormon History, downplaying or ignoring earlier authors like Brodie and Morgan. For example, Alexander, writing in 1983, insisted that "an explicit application of social-scientific concepts to a Mormon problem had to await what is probably the single most significant bellwether of the New Mormon History, Leonard J. Arrington's *Great Basin Kingdom*."[17]

Charles S. Peterson has recently drawn attention to the dilemma faced by New Mormon Historians who seem increasingly isolated from Latter-day Saints and their leaders; he attributes this to the narrowing of intellectual horizons generated by the attention of New Mormon Historians in the 1980s to distinctively "Mormon concepts"—to what he calls "questions relating to revelation, otherworldly influences or the matter of ultimate loyalty." From his perspective the apologia for the New Mormon History are flawed because they are "defensive and assertive rather than analytical or philosophical."[18] Responding to a growing criticism directed at the more secular, naturalistic accounts, in 1986 Alexander for the first time distinguished among (1) history written from within the categories of faith that he feels is being defended by those he labels "Traditionalists,"[19] (2) a "New Mormon History,"[20] and (3) history written by "Secularists." His defense of New Mormon History bolsters it against criticisms from "Traditionalists" as well as "Secularists."[21] New Mormon Historians, from Alexander's perspective, while acknowledging "religious" motivations, endeavor to explain the Mormon past with categories of secular religious studies and from current fashions in social or behavioral sciences.[22] Alexander spurns the history he assumes "Traditionalists" defend because he sees it as apologetic, faith-promoting, pietistic and polemical, while he also shies away from history done by "secularists" because it tends not to give sufficient attention to "religious" motivations.[23]

The symptoms of the historiographical crisis Marty describes turn out to be, from my perspective, primarily the work of those Alexander describes as "Secularists." The work of many of those he labels "New Mormon Historians" seems to raise few fundamental issues except by inadvertence. But it is different with those whom Marvin S. Hill describes as "middle ground historians,"[24] for he denies that their secular, naturalistic accounts of Mormon origins challenge the integrity of faith,[25] while Alexander, by designating some historians as "Secularists," seems to sense that at least some accounts may dissolve the grounds and contest the content of faith.

Marty understands Mormon faith to be characterized by a "thoroughly historical mode and mold" [190] which opens it to both inquiry and controversy.[26] He recognizes that Latter-day Saint faith has both historical content and grounding. Why? Joseph Smith told a strange story. Was it the truth? If he was a faker or victim of illusion and hence his prophetic message false, ultimately we have nothing that places us in touch with deity. But if he told the truth, and if foundational texts like the Book of Mormon are genuine, then we have something. History is therefore the arena in which the truth claims of the restored gospel are contested. Those who have received the Book of Mormon and the story of Joseph Smith's prophetic gifts have found therein grounds for faith in God. Others do not receive the message, and, according to Marty, "there have been Mormons who left the faith because their view of the historical events which gave shape to it no longer permitted them to sustain it" [174]. The Book of Mormon and Joseph Smith's story are clearly a stumbling block, but they also furnish grounds for a distinctive community of memory and faith.[27]

As the writing of Mormon history has moved since 1945 from cottage to academic industry, Marty believes that the discussion of the historical foundations of the Latter-day Saint faith has grown in both intensity and urgency [170-71, 175] to the point where it has reached a critical stage. Some of the questions being debated concern the core of faith. "Mormon thought is experiencing a crisis comparable to but more profound than that which Roman Catholicism recognized around the time of the Second Vatican Council (1962-65)" [169]. The Catholic crisis was dogmatic; the Mormon agitation is historical in the sense that it involves the understanding of the historical foundations of the faith [169-70]. According to Marty, "when Latter-day Saints argue, they argue about morals based on history, or about historical events and their meaning—and about how the contemporary community acquires its identity and its sense of 'what to do and how to do it' from the assessment of the character, quality, content, and impetus of that story." In addition, and more to the point, he also recognizes that "Mormons have not made much of doctrine, of theology: They especially live as chosen and covenanted people in part of a developing history. Much is at stake when the story is threatened, as it potentially could have been when [Mark Hofmann's] forged documents concerning Mormon origins agitated the community and led to tragedy a few years ago."[28]

The reason for the crisis in Mormon historiography, according to Marty, is that a "faith attached to or mediated through historical events has always had some dimensions of an 'offense' or 'scandal'" [174]. Some find unseemly the account of Joseph Smith's prophetic gifts, visits with angels, the Book of Mormon, and other revelations. But why should the ferment now reach inside the community and touch the faith of some intellectuals? It was inevitable, according to Marty, since the faith is thoroughly historical, that crisis would overtake some Saints as they confront their past under the impact of elements of modernity. The primary source of the present crisis is the appropriation by a few intellectuals of competing or conflicting ideologies that began to dominate the thinking of educated people beginning with the Enlightenment [171]. The crisis is thus a conflict between the substance of Latter-day Saint faith, especially the prophetic claims upon which it rests, and certain of the dominant or at least fashionable ideas found in the secular culture.

Though it is widely recognized by competent observers both outside and inside the Mormon community that the faith of the Saints is profoundly historical,[29] some writers argue that this is not so, or, if it is so, it is a tragic mistake.[30] Perhaps in order to avoid what is assumed to be an unfortunate historical grounding of faith, or because of presumably unseemly contents, these writers claim that faith is not (or should not be) tied to accounts of the past. Entailed in such a stance is the view that faith should have neither an historical grounding nor content. Instead, texts like the Book of Mormon or Joseph Smith's reports of plates and visits with angels merely appear to credulous believers to constitute a genuine past made up of actual events. In addition, it is sometimes claimed that a past understood as essentially fictional, and in that sense mythical, cannot be examined other than by looking at its possible effects in the lives of its adherents, that the story of Mormon origins cannot be told from the perspective of the believer because an essentially mythical past grounded in what are thought to be illusions or delusions or at best ineffable mystical experiences does not yield to genuine historical scrutiny, that is, as they often say, it cannot be "proven" to be true. By adopting such a stance historians take a position on historical issues crucial to the faith, for it is clear that a radically different strategy must be adopted for dealing with texts that are thought to be fraudulent or that are believed to report ineffable mystical intuitions or that merely constitute grounds for a fictional "foundation myth" than the strategy for reading non-fictional texts that strive to record realities. These two strategies have, of course, generated a debate, and this controversy constitutes part of what Marty describes as the "crisis in Mormon historiography" [169].

Marty maintains that the current crisis centers on the attempts of a few Latter-day Saint historians to assess the historical foundations of the faith in the light of categories and assumptions borrowed from the larger culture. Instead of following the recommendation of Richard L. Bushman,[31] or following his example in *Joseph Smith and the Beginnings of Mormonism* by telling the story of Mormon origins from within categories of faith, some historians tell the story of the Mormon past from within a horizon provided by assumptions essentially foreign to the faith—assumptions borrowed from the social or behavioral sciences or from secularized religious studies. Such assumptions tend to compete with the faith, if they do not flatly contradict it. Such secular (or naturalistic) explanations may also provide intellectual justifications for radically altering the grounds, form, and content of faith or for unbelief. Marty thus holds that the crisis in Mormon historiography is not generated by the discovery of new texts, for they only complicate or enhance the picture of the past, or by inquiries into polygamy or other such issues. The difficulties he sees at the heart of the crisis arise in the way texts, especially the Book of Mormon, are to be understood, and this necessarily involves a network of assumptions held by the historian. This is the case precisely because what is brought to the interpretive task colors and controls the way texts are read. It is not even what historians call "facts" or "evidences" that are decisive, for there is nothing much evident about the past that is non-trivial without theories and assumptions that make it so by opening up in different ways the possible meanings of the texts upon which historical accounts necessarily depend. Thus background assumptions, as well as interpretative theories, determine in large measure how a story is told. The crisis that Marty describes is, therefore, not a difficulty forced on historians by some dramatic discovery that suddenly unravels the truth claims of the faith. Marty describes the difficulty confronting Mormon historians as a crisis of understanding, and hence of faith, and not of history as such.[32]

Marty rejects as "trivial the question of whether the faith is threatened by the revelation of human shortcomings" of the Saints or their leaders [175-76]. Such issues have fascinated a segment of historians, but from Marty's perspective such matters raise only public relations and pedagogical issues, or constitute what he calls "political embarrassments" or address merely "borderline religious issues" [177]. As important as such issues may be, "intellectually these are not of much interest" [176]. Marty thus attempts to "cut through all the peripheral issues" [176] that plague the discussion of the Mormon past in order to address what is really at stake. He shows that the crisis of faith does not center on peripheral issues like polygamy, but on the way founding events are to be understood. Nor is it brought on by the refutation of something essential to the faith. Rather it centers on how founding events—Joseph Smith's gifts, special revelations, and the Book of Mormon—are to be understood. It is foundational questions (for example, is the Book of Mormon what it claims to be?) that are crucial and these issues are essentially historical in that they are open to scrutiny by historians. It is therefore a mistake to assert, as some do, that the way history is written "seldom directly threatens fundamental religious beliefs because history and religion seldom meet,"[33] especially if one has in mind Latter-day Saints. To begin with such a premise ends up begging important questions by tacitly assuming what should be demonstrated: that nothing really important is at stake when the history of the faith is being radically transformed or challenged.

Marty traces the impact of certain of the dominant ideas of the larger culture that deny the possibility of the truth of Latter-day Saint faith, that compete with explanations internal to the faith, or that reduce such matters to mere expressions of sentiment. In addition, Marty argues that both the content as well as the possibility of faith are linked to the way the past is understood. He concludes that "if the beginning . . . , the First Vision and the Book of Mormon, can survive the crisis, then the rest of the promenade follows and nothing that happens in it can really detract from the miracle of the whole. If the first steps do not survive, there can be only antiquarian, not fateful or faith-full interest in the rest of the story" [176]. This is a clear statement of the decisive issue in the current controversy generated by recent efforts to fashion secular (or naturalistic) understandings of the foundations of the faith of Latter-day Saints.

Marty grants that it has not been proven that Joseph Smith was a fraud or the victim of illusion or that the Book of Mormon is fiction [178, 179, 186]—there is only a crisis of faith. The roots of this crisis he traces to ideologies that began corroding Protestant and Roman Catholic piety with the Enlightenment. According to Marty, the challenges to the historical foundations of the faith of the Saints are analogous to those corroding Christian and Jewish faith. Elsewhere, he describes the challenges to Christian faith from "modernity,"[34] a term commonly used to describe a cluster of related, though also competing, secular ideologies that distinguish the modern from the pre-modern world. Marty maintains that religious controversies in America are mostly internal to the churches simply because "so many of the battles seem to have to do with matters of faith." The reason for this is that such quarrels have "grown up on the sparse soil of modernity."[35] From Marty's perspective, European Protestants, like French Catholics, "have stared into the face of practical and metaphysical atheism and have seen what modernity has done to the meaning of faith itself." He finds that modernity eventually comes to fruition in the writings of Marx, Nietzsche, Darwin and Freud—the so-called "God-Killers."[36] He thus uses the expression "acids of modernity"[37] to describe "the process of corrosion which affected the vessel of apostolicity."[38]

Modernity yields scientism—a new secular religion of science—as well as Secular Fundamentalism: ideologies that dislodge God from history and from the world generally. Modernity also includes the new understanding of history that challenges the historical foundations of biblical faith among both Christians and Jews, as well as the rise of an historical consciousness which plunges all elements of culture into a sea of relativity. The source of the malaise that challenges the claims of historically grounded and mediated faith is the radical Historicist belief in the relativity of all positions, especially those resting on special revelations, and even of those grounded in unaided human reason. The problem is not generated by merely holding that the truths of history cannot be demonstrated or finally proven, that they are not somehow "objective," for even that understanding of truth, from the perspective of a radical Historicism, is itself only a part of the perpetual flux of ideas in history [173].

The "crisis of historical consciousness" that troubles the Christian world is one that Marty believes has "cut to the marrow in the Protestant body of thoughtful scholars in Western Europe in the nineteenth century" [171], and is analogous to one the Saints now face as they emerge from prereflective naivete. One of the chief sources of the crisis is a remnant of Enlightenment-grounded fear of superstition. The assault on Christian piety also came from ideologies linked to an historical consciousness which began "to relativize Christian distinctiveness in the face of other ways . . ." [172]. Modernity thus includes the Romantic reaction to the Enlightenment commonly known as Historicism, but it also includes other ideologies that have found their way into the hearts and minds of historians:"In the nineteenth century, the age of modern critical history, the crisis of historical consciousness became intense and drastic. Now no events, experiences, traces, or texts were exempt from scrutiny by historians who believed they could be value-free, dispassionate. Today, of course, no one sees them as being successful in their search. They were tainted by radical Hegelian dialectics, neo-Kantian rigorisms, or the biases of a positivism that thought it could be unbiased" [172]. This now seems naive, but it was once "highly successful at destroying the primitive naivete among those who read them seriously" [172].

Marty thus traces the crisis among Latter-day Saint historians to ideologies with roots in the Enlightenment: to a deep confidence in reason and even deeper fear of superstition, to naive Positivist notions of historical objectivity, and to the Historicist insistence on the relativity and hence equality of all faith or of all religions. These ideologies have now fallen on hard times, though their remnants are still at home among a few Latter-day Saint historians. Should these intellectual fashions serve as the foundation for the understanding of the Mormon past? On that issue Marty is silent.

The most common justification for efforts to transform what Latter-day Saints believe is historical reality into fiction (into myth understood as something other than authentic history, or into instances of mysticism) has been the assumption that the historian must strive for detachment from the faith, coupled with the notion that a presumably "objective" historian cannot deal with prophetic truth claims. Some writers have assumed that it is necessary and possible to achieve a measure of balance, detachment, or objectivity. And, as a corollary, they sometimes maintain that an historian cannot assume the truth of the faith, hence the story of the Mormon past cannot be told from the perspective of faith.[39] In the extreme case, they insist that the presumed need for detachment from the faith requires treating the prophetic truth claims of Joseph Smith as false, or at least that they cannot be assumed to be true when telling the story of the Mormon past. Some denigrate telling the Mormon story from within the categories of faith as apologetic or faith-promoting and hence, from their perspective, not genuine history. Or they may hold that historical inquiry has (or will) somehow disprove those historical truth claims unless they can be insulated from the scrutiny of historians by converting them into instances of mysticism or into myths which are not the same thing as the study of real places, persons, and things.

Marty places the delicious ironies of the various encounters between faith and modernity near the core of his interpretation of American religiosity. He expresses apprehension about the capitulation of believers to certain of the fashions of modernity. He also argues, and from my perspective persuasively, that Christian faith, whatever its content and contours, has a legitimate place in the doing of history.[40] The corrosive effects of modernity impact diverse types of religiosity in different ways. The particular "aspect of modernity" that has generated the current crisis of faith among a few Latter-day Saint historians "has to do with the challenge of modern historical consciousness and criticism" [169].

Christians confronted by the corrosive ideologies of the nineteenth century responded in various ways: "Some lost faith," Marty explains; while others affirmed their faith in seemingly more satisfactory ways; others transformed the content of faith to accommodate as best they could the pressures of secular ideologies; and some turned to "defensive fundamentalisms" [172]. Unfortunately, when Marty examines the impact of modernity in the Latter-day Saint setting, he does not acknowledge the same range of responses. These have issued as dissent and denial, loss of faith, or radical alterations to the content of faith to accommodate competing secular ideologies. But it has also yielded more adequate accounts of the Mormon past that are also fully consonant with faith.[41]

The crisis, Marty realizes, does not involve secondary or peripheral issues [176, 177-78], like the faults of the Saints or their leaders, but does involve what he calls *"generative* issues" [177]. The primary question concerns the veracity of Joseph Smith's "theophanies" and "revelations." Joseph's epiphanies—the prophetic charisms, visits with angels, the seer stones—are linked to the founding revelation, the Book of Mormon. These work together to constitute "a single base for Mormon history. When historians call into question both the process and the product, they come to or stand on holy ground" [178]. If these revelations do not survive historical inquiry "there can be only antiquarian, not fateful or faith-full, interest in the rest of the story" [176]. The primary issue thus becomes a combination of two related questions: Was Joseph Smith a genuine seer and prophet? and Is the Book of Mormon true? Hence a fateful response to the Mormon past depends upon the founding events being simply true. "To say 'prophet' made one a Saint" and to deny or reject the prophetic claims "is precisely what made one leave Mormonism or never convert in the first place" [178].

But the "stark prophet/fraud polarity" [178] troubles Marty, as it has others. For historians to ask if Joseph Smith was a genuine prophet exerts a chilling effect on discussions between believers and sympathetic unbelievers, and it seems unlikely that it is a question that can be resolved to the satisfaction of everyone, though it is a question that historians can address either directly or indirectly. In any case, most historians do not concentrate on that particular question. Perhaps a different way of formulating or conceiving the fundamental question might facilitate attention to secondary issues with which historians, especially those in the grasp of modernity, would feel somewhat more comfortable. Reasoning in this way, Marty struggles to move outside or "beyond the prophet/fraud issue addressed to generative Mormon events" [179]. But he also explains why Joseph Smith's claims are such that they ultimately demand either a prophet or a not-prophet answer. When dealing with generative events, Marty senses that one cannot have it both ways, and one cannot entirely avoid the issue of whether they are authentic.

Marty strives to avoid the prophet/fraud dialectic, while still addressing Joseph Smith's prophetic claims. He proposes two ways to do this. First, historians might simply bracket or suspend the question of whether Joseph Smith was a genuine prophet and the Book of Mormon an authentic ancient history. They could do so in order to deal with "a new range of questions," which include: "what sort of people are these people [who believe such things], what sort of faith is this faith, what sort of prophet with what sort of theophany and revelation was Joseph Smith?" [178] Those interested in the Mormon past often address secondary questions. For the most part, the issues Latter-day Saint historians deal with stand outside the controversy over whether the Book of Mormon is true and Joseph Smith a genuine prophet. Yet opinions on these questions may still be reflected in or even control the way historians address secondary issues. The primary question can, of course, be bracketed in order to inquire into such secondary questions. But whether it is possible to deal with secondary questions without an implicit answer to the primary issue coming into play has not been settled.

Marty also holds that in addressing the primary question it is unlikely that historians are going to disprove Joseph Smith's prophetic claims. They "may find it possible to prove to their own satisfaction that Smith was a fraud" [179, also 178, 186] but may have difficulty convincing others that they have succeeded. In any case, "the issue of fraud, hoax, or charlatanry simply need not, does not, preoccupy the historical profession most of the time" [179], but that is not to say that it does not occupy the attention of historians some of the time, or that opinions of historians form on the truth of Joseph Smith's prophetic claims do not wield subtle influence on answers to the questions that preoccupy them most of the time. Marty grants that historians who bracket the question of the truth of Joseph Smith's claims are still "nagged or tantalized" [178] by it. And the answer to the question of whether Joseph Smith was a genuine prophet and the Book of Mormon true may influence if not control what they make of the rest.

Marty's second way around the question of the truth of Joseph Smith's prophetic claims has been fashioned by historians who have started asking "more radical questions than before. They had to move through history and interpretation toward a 'second naivete' which made possible transformed belief and persistent identification with the people. They brought new instruments to their inquiry into Mormon origins . . ." [178]. He grants that these historians have achieved a "transformed belief" through the categories informing their "interpretation" [178]. For such historians the accounts of events which may have once shaped their participation in the Mormon community of faith and memory may no longer sustain it, and yet some have "remained with the Mormon people" for various reasons. They have, he feels, "made their own adjustment" [174]. Hence some historians who have experienced the corrosive power of the ideological acids of modernity still desire for sentimental or other reasons "persistent identification with the people"of faith [178].

According to Marty, some historians have "brought new instruments to their inquiry into Mormon origins" [178] with which they picture Joseph Smith as a sincere though superstitious rustic with a genius for addressing the religious concerns of his age, instead of charging him with blatant fraud. In such revisionist accounts[42] he is pictured as a mystic, a magician, a myth-maker who eventually managed to found a "new religious tradition." The new revised standard version differs from the old standard version in that it does not accuse Joseph Smith of fraud or deceit, as did the line of critics running from Alexander Campbell through Fawn M. Brodie and Dale L. Morgan to Wesley P. Walters. Instead, Joseph Smith is seen as an inventive, conflicted, dissociative, sincerely superstitious scryer or magus. This is, of course, one possible way around the "prophet/fraud dialectic" [178]. In that sense, there is a middle ground between prophet and fraud. But these revisionist accounts end up denying the historical foundations of the faith by compromising Joseph Smith's prophetic claims—there can be no equivocation on that issue. For to begin to understand the foundations as essentially mystical,[43] mythical,[44] or magical[45] is to deny that they are simply true. Why is that so?

Abraham Joshua Heschel, from within Judaism, has examined the range of possible explanations of special revelations. For Heschel, one who confronts the core message of the Bible is presented with certain claims. "The problem concerning us most is whether revelation has ever taken place," and again, "Is revelation a fact? Did it actually take place?"[46] Heschel finds that "there are only three ways of judging the prophets: they [a] told the truth, [b] deliberately invented a tale, or [c] were victims of an illusion. In other words, a revelation is either a fact or the product of insanity, self–delusion, or a pedagogical invention, the product of a mental confusion, or wishful thinking [that is, an outgrowth of 'the spirit of the age'] or a subconscious activity."[47] The New Mormon History, at least in its secularist mode, entertains or embraces one or more of these alternatives but without always carefully considering whether they are inimical to a faith-full response to the Mormon past.

Marty describes three approaches to Mormon history that go "beyond the prophet/fraud issue [and that can be] addressed to generative Mormon events" [179]. The first of these he calls "consciousness" studies or psychological explanations of Joseph Smith that would "make plausible the prophethood and throw light on prophetic character" [180].[48] The second approach is most attractively advanced by Jan Shipps,[49] who avoids the question of whether or not Joseph Smith was a genuine prophet by opining that "as far as history is concerned, the question of whether Smith was prophet or fraud is not particularly important."[50] Obviously this question is not important for those with only antiquarian curiosity about Mormon things. Nor does it make a difference from an essentially Historicist or radically relativist perspective. Though her recent book is insightful, especially about the place of the Book of Mormon in the faith of the Saints, and she approaches her subject matter with a measure of sympathy, Shipps does not manage to suspend unbelief; she merely strives to make questions of truth seem irrelevant to her questions. The chief weakness in her approach is that it does not genuinely allow the possibility that Joseph Smith's prophetic claims or the Book of Mormon are simply true, and until one has faced that possibility, one has not begun to penetrate the heart and mind of the faithful.

From the point of view of the believer or potential believer the question of whether Joseph was a genuine prophet and whether the Book of Mormon is true is decisive. Shipps insists that the Saints cannot *prove* that the Book of Mormon is true or that Joseph Smith was a prophet. From that she concludes that the Book of Mormon "has never lent itself to the same process of verification that historians use to verify ordinary accounts of what happened in the past. The historicity of the Book of Mormon has been *asserted* through demonstrations that ancient concepts, practices, doctrines, and rituals are present in the work. . . ." However, she claims that "such demonstrations point, finally, only to plausibility. Proof is a different matter."[51] Historians, from her point of view, deal in proofs and not merely in plausibility; they seek "intellectual verification" and try to know "what really happened."[52] On this issue she is simply wrong, for plausibility is about as good as one can expect from historical accounts that confront more than trivial issues. The crucial question is whether accounts of human and divine things, and hence myth in that sense, disclose historical reality. Bushman shows that the strength and "staying power of the Latter-day Saints from 1830 to the present rest on belief in the reality" of certain crucial events, including "that the Book of Mormon was true history. . . ."[53] Bushman's account of Mormon origins has, of course, drawn attention precisely because he writes candidly as a believer and explicitly defends the historical authenticity of the Book of Mormon and the prophetic truth claims of Joseph Smith. Hence he has been seen by some as an apologist, which he clearly is, and either praised or faulted for assuming that role. Though their positions have some things in common, in the decisive respect Bushman's position differs from that of Shipps, who holds that what the Saints have in the Book of Mormon is myth, at least when seen from the perspective of history. Her stance implies that faith is not in touch with a genuine historical reality.

Marty does not examine the background assumptions at work in the history done by Klaus J. Hansen, Lawrence Foster, and Jan Shipps, the historians whose works he mentions.[54] Instead, he bestows "integrity" on both the radical mythological and psychological accounts of Mormon foundational texts and events. He admits that such accounts have obviously "transformed belief" [178], but neglects to examine the extent or consequences of the transformation of belief or the reasons for the transformation in revisionist literature. From my perspective, both what is believed and faith itself are altered when the story of Lehi and his people is understood as fictional and the messenger with the plates transformed into crude magic, or into a product of a dream of surcease of a troubled rustic, or into an expression of mysticism, or when the message or teachings of the Book of Mormon are seen as Joseph Smith's imaginative effort to deal with sectarian controversies in his age through expansions on various theological themes drawn from his environment.

Marty's "two integrities" identify, first, the integrity of the faith that a child might have (or an entirely unreflective adult) and, second, the integrity of one whose faith has survived an encounter with ideas in the outside world which compete with the content or ground of faith. Marty uses Paul Ricoeur's expression "primitive naivete" to describe the beliefs of the child or isolated tribe or unreflective adult, and uses "secondary naivete" to describe the faith of one who has faced a crisis of faith and has managed to retain them. Marty makes much of the "primitive naivete" [171] of what he calls "unreflective" Saints [177].A crisis of faith is brought on by threats to naive faith through the recognition of competing possibilities. But, because their faith is tied to a controversial history, the Saints have always been involved with issues that seem to have taken them somewhat beyond a primitive naivete to a measure of reflective understanding. A more mature faith—Marty's "second naivete"—has faced and overcome doubts brought on by the confrontation with the modernity. The crisis Marty depicts is thus a turning point in which either the desire for faith or the presence of faith, or both, eventually disappear in a loss or denial of faith, or are affirmed in a more complete and mature faith. When the troubled one is healed of unbelief by a new and deeper affirmation of faith, one could speak of a new secondary integrity. If the grounds and contents of faith were radically compromised, there would be no genuine faith or a transformed belief with an alien content. This seems to be the reason that the "generative events" must survive for there to be a "fateful or faith-full" response to the Mormon past. "If the first steps do not survive, there can be only antiquarian, not fateful or faith-full interest in the rest of the story" [176]. Marty's "two integrities" thus identify a soundness of faith on either side of the crisis of faith.

Some Latter-day Saint historians have advanced explanations of the crucial generative events and founding texts similar to those advanced by Shipps and Foster. For instance, Shipps did not invent her account—she borrowed its outlines from Marvin S. Hill. She drew upon his opinion that there is a "middle ground" between genuine prophet and conscious fraud and hence a way around what she once described as the "prophet puzzle"—the "charlatan-true prophet dichotomy which has plagued Mormon history from the beginning."[55] One of Shipps's explanations of Mormon origins is that Joseph Smith began his career as a magician and, eventually, became a kind of "religious genius" and powerful myth-maker. Presumably such an explanation avoids the old quarrel over the truth of the Mormon faith, which Hill now thinks cannot be resolved with proofs and hence should be abandoned by presumably objective historians.

Hill began his career noting that the "recurrent conflict between Saint and Gentile has generally divided historians into two groups, forging a cleavage in sentiment which is evident in the debates over the origin of the Book of Mormon," as well as Joseph Smith's prophetic claims.[56] He argued that the most important issue concerns "the nature of that unique American scripture, the Book of Mormon. Acclaimed by the faithful as a sacred history of a Christian people in ancient America, the book has been labelled a fraud by non-believers. Bernard DeVoto recognized the fundamental character of this controversy when he said 'it is inseparable from one's explanation of Joseph Smith'."[57] Apparently Hill saw only two major ways of explaining the Book of Mormon. But by 1974 he attempted to fashion an explanation of the Book of Mormon and an account of Joseph Smith's prophetic claims situated somewhere between the prophet or fraud alternatives he had outlined fifteen years earlier. In 1974 he claimed that "in attempting a psychological explanation of Smith rather than that of daring deception, the mature Brodie seems to be telling us that her old interpretation was too simple. Perhaps what Brodie may have recognized at last is that her original interpretation perceived Joseph Smith in falacious [sic] terms, as either prophet in the traditional Mormon sense or else as a faker. Her original thesis opens considerable room for speculation because its either-or alternatives were precisely the same as those of the early Mormon apologist and missionary, Orson Pratt. . . ."[58]

Brodie thought that the key to Joseph Smith was the Book of Mormon.[59] Once one determined that the book was fiction, what remained was to work out a plausible explanation of how and why Joseph Smith made it up. Hence, in *No Man Knows My History*, she toyed with a number of related explanations for what she considered the Mormon imposture. In 1959 Hill provided a brief paraphrase of her explanation, which he described as "the most plausible exposition of the Smith hypothesis."[60] Following a line of explanations that began with Alexander Campbell,[61] she argued that Joseph Smith's prophetic claims began as a tale which later took on the trappings of religion. In contrast, Hill has tried to locate a "broad, promising middle ground" between the traditional prophet-fraud alternatives.[62] Such a stance runs counter to the traditional understanding, which is that, when confronted with the Book of Mormon, "there is no middle ground. This book is either false or true. If it is false, everybody ought to know it," but if it is true, then it is appropriate that it serve as "the cornerstone of the Church."[63]

Hill has, of course, elaborated a "Smith hypothesis" in ways that distinguish it from Brodie's account. For example, more than Brodie, he stresses Joseph Smith's sincerity and mystical or magical religiosity, though like Brodie he leaves that language undefined. He explains Joseph Smith's "religion" as the product of elements common in nineteenth-century folk culture; it was all a product of superstition, confusions, and later embellishments of youthful half-forgotten dreams and hence a product of magic, myth, and mysticism rather than Brodie's gross imposture, deception, or charlatanry. Hill's "broad, promising middle ground" between prophet and fraud seems to be the notion that Joseph Smith was sincere and vaguely "religious." Shipps has, from time to time, appropriated some of Hill's position on these issues, but she goes further in the direction of a mythological rather than a psychological-environmental explanation.

In 1988, however, Hill claimed that he had "used the term 'middle ground' to describe a position between those who said Mormonism is untrue and those who insisted on conclusive proof that it is true."[64] But neither in his 1959 nor his 1974 essays does he search for a middle ground between a conservative "right" among Mormon historians and an anti-Mormon "left."[65] It seems that the mode of explanation he called for in 1974 was between prophet and faker. What he now offers as a "middle ground" is a methodological agnosticism about the Book of Mormon and Joseph Smith's prophetic claims, and his "middle ground historians" are those who do not try to *prove* either that Joseph Smith was a prophet or a fraud.[66] Hill seems to deny that a text like the Book of Mormon can be examined by historians. He thus appears to skirt the question of whether Joseph Smith's prophetic claims are within the arena of history. But to treat the historical grounds and contents of Mormon faith as anything but firmly rooted in history, which is what his stance entails, is to rob the faith of something essential. In 1959 Hill had no doubt that "the faithful" regard the Book of Mormon "as a sacred history of a Christian people in ancient America." He now proposes that because some who reject it as authentic ancient history still find it "inspired" or inspiring, historians might be justified in pursuing that line of reasoning.[67] Yet he also holds that to adopt a radically relativist position robs the faith of something essential: "if it is not possible to say anything truthful about the past, the missionary message of the restoration would be included. A position so cynical would destroy all Mormon claims to historical truth,"[68] which he is not willing to, and yet he claims that a fictional Book of Mormon might be considered "inspired." Unfortunately, he does not avoid rejecting traditional Mormon claims to historical truth.

Until recently, the standard non-Mormon explanation of the restoration was that Joseph Smith was a conscious or intentional fraud. Joseph Smith, as I have shown, is now sometimes pictured as a sincerely religious victim "of an illusion."[69] Such alternative perspectives on Joseph Smith (and the Book of Mormon) preclude the possibility of his prophetic claims being simply true. Revisionists "suggest" that Joseph Smith was "perhaps" confused, caught up in the spirit of his age, even dissociative or some combination of such possibilities, all of which tend to render the prophetic claims questionable or even false. One can, of course, fashion explanations of the Book of Mormon and of Joseph Smith's prophetic claims that render them false without picturing them as instances of conscious deception and fraud and, in that way, work around the "prophet/fraud dialectic" [178], as Marty calls it. But the prophetic claims will still present the believer and unbeliever alike with either a prophet or not-prophet alternative.

One way to treat the historical portions of the foundational texts is to read them as myths and not as genuine historical realities. Some writers explain the Book of Mormon and Joseph Smith's epiphanies as parabolic, allegorical, metaphorical, and hence not as actual events in an authentic past. But what meaning and authority would the Book of Mormon have when read that way? Anthony A. Hutchinson claims that the founding stories, understood as myths, have "in some ways gained a new power because of their newly acquired clarity of meaning," though he personally "suffered a sense of loss" and "experienced a certain disappointment" as he rejected "the claim of many of Joseph Smith's works that they not only have a divine origin but also have an ancient origin."[70] For Hutchinson, divine revelation consists of "imaginative appropriation," "imaginative reworking," or "creative reworking" of older beliefs, stories, or traditions by "inspired" redactors. The product of such "imagination"[71] is "myth," understood as "the casting of theology in story form" or "*inspired fiction.*"[72] And yet, Hutchinson acknowledges, "one may freely agree that a myth's power in part depends upon the historical reality of events or persons within it." An historical reality must stand behind myth "only when this historical reality is somehow directly related to the reality the myth seeks to meditate." When and why might that be? "The power of a myth about redemption through Christ crucified and resurrected," he admits, "seems directly dependent on whether Jesus in fact died and then bodily reappeared to his disciples."[73] But the authority and power of the restored gospel, for Hutchinson, is *not dependent* upon whether angels actually visited with Joseph Smith, or whether certain of his works have an ancient origin. The Book of Mormon, Book of Abraham, and Book of Moses (including the Enoch materials) are, for him, "myths" generated by Joseph Smith's "creative reworking" of biblical and other lore.

Some Latter-day Saints who advance naturalistic accounts seem inclined to turn to what Sterling M. McMurrin denigrates as "sophisticated theories of symbol and myth,"[74] turning prophets into mystics or imaginative myth-makers in order to salvage some semblance of "religious" meaning from stories no longer believed to be simply true. McMurrin will have nothing of such legerdemain. Instead, he has a more radical program which if systematically followed would retain only fragments of a culture resting on abandoned beliefs about the crucial elements in the past. He insists that the church must abandon the traditional understanding of the beginnings of the faith. He opines that a failure to do so is dishonest because an objective scrutiny of the historical foundations of the faith by genuinely competent historians discloses "a good many unsavory things." Hence he charges "that the Church has intentionally distorted its own history by dealing fast and loose with historical data and imposing theological and religious interpretations on those data that are entirely unwarranted."[75] From his perspective the Mormon "faith is so mixed up with so many commitments to historical events—or to events that are purported to be historical—that a competent study of history can be very disillusioning. Mormonism is a historically oriented religion. To a remarkable degree, the Church has concealed much of its history from its people, while at the same time causing them to tie their religious faith to its own controlled interpretations of its history." His premise is that "nothing can produce a more rapid deterioration of religious faith than the honest study of the history of religion."

The problem, as McMurrin sees it, is a "fault of the weakness of the faith" which should not be tied to history.[76] He recommends a separation of faith from history, or rather what he calls "religion" (defined as sentiment) from history, substituting "naturalistic humanism"[77] for prophetic faith. If something "religious" remained, since its links with the past would be effectively severed except for essentially sentimental purposes, it would be one determined entirely by current intellectual fashions. We should, from McMurrin's perspective, begin with the dogma "that you don't get books from angels and translate them by miracles; it is just that simple."[78] That dogma presumably takes care of Joseph Smith and the Book of Mormon. A history resting on such a premise would require, among other things, a fundamental reordering—if not outright abandonment—of the content of faith. McMurrin thus provides the least sentimental statement of the intellectual grounds for a secular (or naturalistic) and hence revisionist Mormon history. But would a program of turning the Mormon past and sacred texts into myths do any better? At least part of the difference between these programs seems to be the degree of sentimentality about elements of the faith whose historical grounds have been compromised or abandoned.

The justification for revisionist history is that an unbiased, detached, objective look at the Mormon past and at the Book of Mormon calls for a modification in the traditional links between faith and history. Sometimes it is assumed that detachment (or objectivity) and honesty (or truth) are necessarily aligned. But there should be no illusions about objectivity or about the possibility or desirability of avoiding bias. "People used to say," according to Marty, "they should be 'objective,' but," he claims, "objectivity seems to be a dream denied" [170]. Still, some Mormon historians, especially those who advocate drawing upon categories and modes of explanation found in secular religious studies or borrowing explanations from the social sciences, tend to see their work as more balanced, detached, or objective than the accounts they denigrate as faith-promoting, pietistic, or apologetic. For example, Hill defends "the possibility of an objective history" against the belief "that historians can never escape their own culture and personal biases."[79] Abandonment of historical objectivism would, he believes, lead to a destructive nihilism.[80]

Competent scholars outside and some writers within the Mormon community have questioned historical objectivism by probing the assumptions upon which that so-called "noble dream" (or professional "myth") rests. They criticize the use of objectivist language while calling attention to the political function of such language.[81] Thus a debate has erupted over the possibility or necessity of detachment or objectivity—ideas that were previously more or less taken for granted both by segments of the American historian profession and by some historians with interests in the Mormon past. It turns out that historical objectivism (or positivism) lacks coherence, and talk about the necessity of avoiding bias—of detachment, neutrality, and objectivity—is illusory precisely because the historian always brings formal and informal preunderstandings, assumptions, biases, theories, and viewpoints to the task of interpreting texts and providing explanations.[82] This is not, as some may assume, a limitation that has to be overcome but a necessary condition for finding meaning in texts and text analogues.

After describing several possible strategies for avoiding what he calls the "prophet/fraud dialectic," none of which is entirely satisfactory, Marty sets out an approach to doing religious history which rests on a different understanding of the method and limits of history [170-71] than that employed by the historians for whom he offers an apology. He seems to claim a superiority—not merely a distinction—for his approach. He also claims that his way has been used successfully by some Mormon historians to achieve a "second naivete" but does not cite any instances.

Drawing on portions of the current literature on textual exegesis or hermeneutics, Marty maintains that historical understanding rests on preunderstandings brought to the text by historians [181-82]. Revisionists tend to be uncomfortable with discussions of hermeneutics. "Although," according to Hutchinson, "the recent discussion is needed and somewhat helpful, I think that some basic cautions are needed," though he has not indicated what they might be. Still he grants that a presuppositionless exegesis of texts is impossible.[83] Hill provides a second example by affirming that he "is not as skeptical as certain hermeneuticists" about an essentially Positivist approach to the past.[84] He holds that "there is grave danger in any Mormon historian adopting their perspective: the possibility that we can say anything with validity beyond our own cultural mind-set is then wiped out and with it hope that we have a true history to tell the world. It is indeed paradoxical that any Mormon would advance such a relativistic theory and assume that doing so is in the interest of the Church. This theory reflects, I think, what amounts to an intellectual crisis in Mormonism in which all are involved, albeit some without awareness."[85] But there is nothing necessarily nihilistic about careful textual exegesis. The more competent discussions of hermeneutics show that historians must necessarily strive to understand the meaning of the texts that provide the only windows to the past through the lens of formal and informal preunderstandings.[86]

These brief discussions of hermeneutics show, I believe, that some of the speculation of Mormon historians about their enterprise is still "tainted" by ideologies about which historians tend to be naive and uncritical precisely because they believe that they can or even have avoided having the bias introduced by faith. Some of these writers are still more or less enthralled by what Marty calls "the biases of a positivism that thought it could be unbiased" [172]. Such a bias still fuels the demand for objectivity, neutrality or detachment from faith found in revisionist Mormon history. For example, though the thrust of one of Alexander's essays is the claim that those doing New Mormon History are not in any way Positivists, he grants that "the term 'objectivity' has become so weighted with the positivistic connotation of full detachment . . . that it should be abandoned." Furthermore, he admits, "it is clear that some historians, including some of the New Mormon Historians—in the search for objectivity—have tried to detach their personal religious and moral views from their writing."[87]

Some of the pressure on Mormon historians to leave their beliefs out of their history—for detachment or objectivity in that sense—comes from those who simply do not believe. The demand for objectivity or detachment from faith and the demand for naturalistic treatments of Mormon origins originally came from those who thought they had avoided the corrupting commitments of apologists engaged in writing what they denigrate as apologetic, faith-promoting history. Morgan and Brodie, both writers with roots in Mormon culture, were flush with that illusion. But both Morgan's work, as well as the recent seemingly more neutral or detached history, suffers in comparison with that done by those who do not hold illusions about the possibility of objectivity and who are therefore not embarrassed to have their faith play a role in their history. However, the strength of Morgan's position is that he sensed that when dealing with the Book of Mormon and Joseph Smith's prophetic claims it had to be one way or the other—that there is what he called a Great Divide necessarily separating those who write naturalistic accounts from those who allow the possibility that Joseph Smith's prophetic claims could be simply true. Ironically, when Bushman's *Joseph Smith* is compared with Morgan's efforts—both cover somewhat the same ground—it turns out that Bushman's work is superior in content, style, and plausibility. Furthermore, Bushman's book does not manifest the affectation of seeming detachment or neutrality that leaves the reader guessing about his assumptions or biases; nor does it suffer from the assumption that an account of the Mormon past, in order to be well-grounded, must be detached from the faith, nor does it manufacture paper heroes or skirt difficult or controversial issues. Bushman's book is a fine exemplar of how I believe Mormon history ought to be written.

History "is not a reproduction of reality" from Marty's perspective—"the historian invents" [170]. When historians tell their stories they provide the plots and fill in everything not accessible through texts or text analogues; they must necessarily interpret or explain what they try to take from texts. Since historians are necessarily involved in a "social construction of reality," they cannot expect to discover exactly what happened—Marty clearly rejects that illusion, as well the notion that historians provide proofs.[88] Only "traces" of the past remain and from these only more or less plausible accounts are open to us; these are accessible only through texts colored by understanding and hence they constitute interpretations and are not merely neutral reports. Even plausibility depends on a network of assumptions and preunderstandings. And every text (or set of texts) remains open to more or less plausible though sometimes radically competing interpretations and explanations. Marty's account of method is clearly unlike that of historians currently enthralled by some variety of historical objectivism.

Marty's description of the method, limits, and situated character of historians contributes to clarifying the current debate over Mormon historiography. He has helped to identify certain of the ideologies that control the way in which the Mormon past is approached. Historians may not be aware of at least some of the assumptions upon which they operate, because these form, for them, a kind of natural horizon. Marty sets out a modest version of an historical skepticism which makes room for the possibility of faith in the face of scientism, naturalistic humanism, and dogmatic unbelief—all of which are manifestations of the "acids of modernity."

A measure of modesty leading to a suspension of unbelief makes possible a sympathetic understanding of the categories, norms, and explanations internal to faith. This is especially true when faith rests on historical claims that clearly run against the grain of assumptions common in our world, for example, that angels bring books that are translated by the gift and power of God. However, the dogmatisms of modernity stand in the way of the suspension of unbelief that is necessary for the truth of the faith to shine through when prophetic messages are encountered. Ironically, it turns out that every genuine historical understanding rests on suspending unbelief, on a willingness to grant the possibility that things are other than what the controlling ideas of an age demand.

I agree with Marty that final proof is not possible in historical accounts and I hold that it is neither possible nor necessary in matters of faith [184]. Still, faith, if it is an "historical faith," is one in which texts witness to divine things.[89] The texts upon which Mormon faith rests confront us with a message that makes claims upon us. Marty holds that we can, if so disposed, hear the message contained in texts; we must then judge whether or not it will be true for us. He calls this, following Paul Ricoeur, the "hermeneutics . . . of testimony" [183-84].[90] Assuming that he is correct on this issue, how then does one come to believe? How is faith justified? What is it that is believed when faith has as its object a complex network of events in the past?

We are, of course, shielded from direct access to the past and can only encounter a small segment of it already interpreted for us through texts. The historian, like everyone else, is confronted with the question of whether or not certain of these texts open a window to the past—a real and not merely a fictional one. In the case of the Saints or potential Saints, the decisive question is ultimately whether the Book of Mormon witnesses to the truth. An historical faith, like that of Latter-day Saints, comes by listening to its messages, by suspending unbelief and seeking with the aid of deity the truth found in the witness contained in the sacred texts. The Book of Mormon makes claims upon us concerning a then-and-there in which deity acted. These claims ultimately must be judged by hearing the witness and receiving the testimony of the message for our own here-and-now. In that way, the Book of Mormon bears the memory of divine things that we may begin to appropriate through the interpretative enterprise.

When viewed as a fictional-mythical account, and not as reality, the Book of Mormon neither has authority nor provides genuine hope for the future. To treat the Book of Mormon as a strange theologically motivated brand of fiction, and in that sense as myth, is to alter radically both the form and content of faith and thereby fashion a new "church" in which the texts are told what they can and cannot mean on the basis of some exterior ideology. To reduce the Book of Mormon to mere myth weakens, if not destroys, the possibility of it witnessing to the truth about divine things. A fictional Book of Mormon fabricated by Joseph Smith, even when his inventiveness, genius, or "inspiration" is celebrated, does not witness to Jesus Christ but to human folly. A true Book of Mormon is a powerful witness; a fictional one is hardly worth reading and pondering. Still, the claims of the text must be scrutinized and tested, then either believed or not believed always without a final proof.

The truth of the prophetic message in the Book of Mormon is linked to both its claim to be an authentic history and to Joseph Smith's story of how we came to have the book. To be a Latter-day Saint is to believe, among other things, that the Book of Mormon is true, that there once was a Lehi who made a covenant with God and was led out of Jerusalem and so forth. Such an historically grounded faith is, of course, vulnerable to the potential ravages of historical inquiry, but it is also one that can be true in a way that makes a profound difference. It seems that we are left, by God, with a witness to mighty acts on our behalf, but we must judge, for we are always at the turning point between two ways. And listening to the text to discover its truth for us, not proving it true—an impossibility if not a presumption—both reveals its truth and makes the sacred in the past plausible and thereby gives substance and meaning to the deepest longings of the believer. It is in this way that the Latter-day Saint community of faith and memory is now, as it has been in the past, both formed and sustained.

Marty feels that to begin to understand the message of a text like the Book of Mormon frees us so that we are somehow "less burdened by concern over the exact reference to literal historical events" [185]. He is correct if he means that a deeper, more profound understanding of the Book of Mormon removes obstacles that seekers may confront in grasping its prophetic message. But when the Book of Mormon is understood as fiction, and in that sense an element in a "Mormon myth," we have, at best, one more melancholy instance of human folly and not the word of God. To begin to suppose that the Book of Mormon is true requires that the text be taken with genuine seriousness in all its various aspects. Therefore, it is a mistake to hold that a mature faith calls for or yields a lessening of concerns about historical or literary details in the Book of Mormon or that it somehow allows the faithful to abandon the question of whether or not there was a Lehi colony with whom God made a covenant, or whether angels really visited Joseph Smith, or whether Jesus was resurrected and so forth. Only when faith has become an empty routine or mere sentimentality, and thereby shorn of its substance and meaning, does it no longer matter if the Book of Mormon is an authentic ancient history and its teachings simply true. For Latter-day Saint faith to have what Marty describes as a "thoroughly historical mode and mold" [170] includes the assurance that Joseph Smith's story constitute genuine history and that the Book of Mormon is an authentic record of the past providing a prophetic access to divine things and not merely a kind of "Mormon myth" entertained in some allegorical or sentimental sense.

NOTES

1. Marty, Fairfax M. Cone Distinguished Service Professor of the History of Modern Christianity at the University of Chicago, is perhaps the leading authority on American religiosity.

2. Page numbers in brackets refer to Marty's "Two Integrities: An

Address to the Crisis in Mormon Historiography," included in this volume, 169-188. His essay was originally the Tanner Lecture at the 1983 Mormon History Association meeting and was previously published in the *Journal of Mormon History* 10 (1983): 3-19 and again under the title "History: The Case of the Mormons, a Special People," in Marty's *Religion and Republic: The American Circumstance* (Boston: Beacon, 1987), 303-25, 337-78.

3. See Midgley, "The Challenge of Historical Consciousness: Mormon History and the Encounter with Secular Modernity," in *By Study and by Faith: Essays in Honor of Hugh W. Nibley on the Occasion of His Eightieth Birthday*, John M. Lundquist and Stephen D. Ricks, eds. (Salt Lake City: Deseret Book and FARMS, 1990), 2:502-51, for a more richly documented version of my argument.

4. The label "new Mormon history" was first used as the title of a review essay by Moses Rischin, a Jewish historian, in *The American West Review* 6 (Mar. 1969): 49, however the significant use of the label began with Robert B. Flanders in 1974. See his "Some Reflections on the New Mormon History," this volume, which first appeared in *Dialogue: A Journal of Mormon Thought* 9 (Spring 1974): 34-41. Flanders characterized what he understood as the "new" history, but others have employed the label without giving his views sufficient attention.

5. See, for example, Thomas G. Alexander's "Toward the New Mormon History: An Examination of the Literature on the Latter-day Saints," in *Historians and the American West*, Michael P. Malone, ed. (Lincoln: University of Nebraska Press, 1983), 344-68; "Historiography and the New Mormon History: A Historian's Perspective," *Dialogue: A Journal of Mormon Thought* 19 (Fall 1986): 25-49; and "Introduction" to *Great Basin Kingdom Revisited: Contemporary Perspective*, Thomas G. Alexander, ed. (Logan: Utah State University Press, 1991), 2-3, 14-17, 19. Leonard J. Arrington seems to have avoided use of the label, even though Alexander and others have identified his work as the beginning or at least a significant milestone in New Mormon History.

6. Alexander, "Toward the New Mormon History," 344.

7. Flanders, review of *New Views of Mormon History: A Collection of Essays in Honor of Leonard J. Arrington*, Davis Bitton and Maureen U. Beecher, eds., in *John Whitmer Historical Association Journal* 8 (1988): 91.

8. See Arrington's "Preface" to his *Great Basin Kingdom: Economic History of the Latter-day Saints, 1830-1900* (Cambridge: Harvard University Press, 1958; pap. ed., Lincoln: University of Nebraska, 1966), vii-xi; cf. Arrington, "Scholarly Studies of Mormonism in the Twentieth Century," *Dialogue: A Journal of Mormon Thought* 1 (Spring 1966): 28, which is the most widely quoted statement setting forth his program for explaining "the Mormon history and its religion" in what he called "human and naturalistic

terms." He seems to have assumed that the meaning of such language was self-evident and did not require an explicit definition.

9. Brodie, *No Man Knows My History: The Life of Joseph Smith the Mormon Prophet* (New York: Alfred A. Knopf, 1946; 2d ed. 1985).

10. Morgan worked for seventeen years on what he projected to be a three-volume history of Mormonism. He produced a draft of four chapters and some fragments of three other chapters for his first volume. See *Dale Morgan on Early Mormonism: Correspondence & A New History*, John Phillip Walker, ed. (Salt Lake City: Signature Books, 1986), 219-319. For a sympathetic review, see Gary Topping, "Dale Morgan's Unfinished Mormon History," *Dialogue: A Journal of Mormon Thought* 20 (Spring 1987): 173-74.

11. See Davis Bitton and Leonard J. Arrington, *The Mormons and Their Historians* (Salt Lake City: University of Utah Press, 1988), especially the chapter entitled "The Bridge," which deals with Brodie and Morgan. For an examination of the key language in the programmatic statements by Brodie and Morgan, see Gary F. Novak, "Naturalistic Assumptions and the Book of Mormon," *Brigham Young University Studies* 30 (Summer 1990): 23-40.

12. Edwards, "The New Mormon History," *Saints Herald* 133 (Nov. 1986): 14. For Edwards, Brodie's "biography of Joseph Smith was an open, honest, generally objective, yet strangely limited account. Her position has often been misunderstood and her motives seriously questioned. But she raised the significant question of Mormonism as a new religious experience in the Western world."

13. Flanders, "Some Reflections on the New Mormon History," this volume, citing Marvin S. Hill, "Secular or Sectarian History: A Critique of *No Man Knows My History*," *Church History* 43 (Mar. 1974): 78-96. Hill indicated that Brodie's book "falls short of greatness because of fundamental weaknesses which no amount of patching in a later edition can correct," but "that Brodie had written an immensely important book, a powerful book, which greatly influenced the thinking of Mormon liberals and conservatives with respect to the life of the prophet." Hill, "Brodie Revisited: A Reappraisal," *Dialogue: A Journal of Mormon Thought* 7 (Winter 1972): 73.

14. Russell, review of *Our Legacy of Faith: A Brief History of the Reorganized Church of Jesus Christ of Latter Day Saints* by Paul M. Edwards, *John Whitmer Historical Association Journal* 11 (1991): 91. Russell includes non-Mormon authors Thomas F. O'Dea, Mario S. DePillis, Jan Shipps, and Lawrence Foster among New Mormon Historians.

15. For example, one writer does "not believe that there actually exits an entirely 'new Mormon history' in terms of the issues argued or the points of view expressed, and certainly not in the negative sense that some would describe it." Hill, "The 'New Mormon History' Reassessed in Light of Recent Books on Joseph Smith and Mormon Origins," *Dialogue: A Journal of*

Mormon Thought 21 (Autumn 1988): 115.

16. Gary Topping, "History of Historians," *Dialogue: A Journal of Mormon Thought* 22 (Spring 1989): 157 (reviewing Bitton and Arrington, *Mormons and Their Historians*). LeAnn Cragun made the same point in her "Mormons and History: In Control of the Past," Ph.D diss., University of Hawaii, Dec. 1981.

17. Alexander, "Toward the New Mormon History," 354. However, D. Michael Quinn holds that New Mormon History starts with the 1950 publication of *Mountain Meadows Massacre*, by Juanita Brooks, rather than with Arrington in 1958 or Brodie in 1945. See his "Editor's Introduction" *The New Mormon History: Revisionist Essays on the Past* (Salt Lake City: Signature Books, 1992), viii.

18. Peterson, "Beyond the Problems of Exceptionalist History," in *Great Basin Kingdom Revisited*, 147-49.

19. See Alexander, "Historiography and the New Mormon History," 26-30, 34-8, 41-5. He identifies David E. Bohn, Neal W. Kramer, Gary F. Novak, and me as "Traditionalists." If we assume that "Traditionalists" defend something like the traditional believing accounts of the Mormon past, then Richard L. Bushman and numerous other contemporary LDS historians might be included in that category and the list of New Mormon Historians substantially reduced.

20. Alexander, "Historiography and the New Mormon History," 30, 45-46. For a criticism of Alexander's position, see M. Gerald Bradford, "The Case for the New Mormon History: Thomas G. Alexander and His Critics," *Dialogue: A Journal of Mormon Thought* 21 (Winter 1988): 143-50.

21. In 1985 Alexander complained that Klaus J. Hansen, "on the left, has joined forces with critics of the New Mormon History on the right who insist that history which accepts the Latter-day Saints on their own terms and then proceeds to interpret these people using models drawn from historical works on context, religious studies, and the social behavioral science are misguided because they do not try to resolve questions of faith." Alexander, "Substantial, Important, and Brilliant," *Dialogue: A Journal of Mormon Thought* 18 (Winter 1985): 186; cf. his "Toward the New Mormon History," 368n38, for an earlier version of this complaint.

22. If Alexander's account of New Mormon History is accepted, then Richard L. Bushman's *Joseph Smith and the Beginnings of Mormonism* (Urbana: University of Illinois Press, 1984), for example, is not part of that type of history but a much more plausible, accurate, and better written traditional account of the Mormon past.

23. Alexander, "Historiography and the New Mormon History," 24, 45. Alexander includes non-Mormon historians like DePillis as well as historians from the Mormon community like Hansen and Michael T. Walton in

the category of "Secularists." Accordingly, "New Mormon Historians have included both active Latter-day Saints . . ., and interested persons of other persuasions or of no particular religious conviction who studied the Mormon past from a combination of religious and naturalistic vantage points." Alexander, "Introduction," 2. If this is true, then religious conviction, persuasion, or activity is not necessarily relevant in the consideration of the competence and coherence of New Mormon History. But Alexander seems anxious to make the religious standing of LDS New Mormon Historians the chief grounds for his defense of their accounts.

24. Hill situates himself in a "middle ground" between a conservative right and an anti-Mormon left. Hill, "The 'New Mormon History' Reassessed," 115-27.

25. Ibid., 124-25; and Hill, in his letter in "Afterword," *Brigham Young University Studies* 30 (Fall 1990): 117-24. For an examination of some of the differences between Hill and Alexander, see Midgley, "Which Middle Ground?" *Dialogue: A Journal of Mormon Thought* 22 (Summer 1989): 6-9.

26. See Midgley, "Faith and History," in *"To Be Learned Is Good If. . ."*, Robert L. Millet, ed. (Salt Lake City: Bookcraft, 1987), 219-26. For a criticism, see Gary James Bergera, "The New Mormon Anti-Intellectualism," *Sunstone* 15 (June 1991): 54-55. For a response, see Midgley, "Revisionist Pride," *Sunstone* 15 (Sept. 1991): 4-5.

27. Marty drew attention to links between memory, history, and faith (especially in a Mormon context) in a lecture entitled "We Might Know What to Do and How to Do It: On the Usefulness of the Religious Past," *The Westminster Tanner-McMurrin Lectures on the History and Philosophy of Religion at Westminster College* (Salt Lake City: Westminster College of Salt Lake City, 1989), 1:11-12. His views parallel somewhat those found in Yosef Hayim Yerushalmi's *Zakhor: Jewish History and Jewish Memory* (Seattle: University of Washington Press, 1982; pap. ed., foreword by Harold Bloom, New York: Schocken Books, 1989). For efforts to draw parallels between Yerushalmi's work and developments in Mormon historiography, see Novak and Midgley, "Remembrance and the Past: Jewish and Mormon Memory and the New History," unpublished paper presented to the annual meeting of Mormon History Association, May 11, 1984; and the concluding remarks in Novak's "Naturalistic Assumptions and the Book of Mormon," 34-35.

28. Marty, "On the Usefulness of the Religious Past," 12.

29. See, for example, William F. Albright's summary of some of the reasons Mormonism is an historical faith in his "Archaeology and Religion," *Cross Currents* 9 (1959): 111. Edwin S. Gaustad, in addition to Marty, argues that Mormonism is a radically historical faith. See his "History and Theology: The Mormon Connection," in *Sunstone* 5 (Nov.-Dec. 1980): 44-50, reprinted in this volume, and also his "Historical Theology and Theological History:

Mormon Possibilities," *Journal of Mormon History* 11 (1984): 99-111.

30. See, for example, Sterling M. McMurrin, "Religion and the Denial of History," *Sunstone* 7 (Mar.-Apr. 1982): 46-49; with direct applications made to the Mormon setting in his "The History of Mormonism and Church Authorities: An Interview with Sterling M. McMurrin," *Free Inquiry* 4 (Winter 1983-84): 32-34, reprinted in an expanded version as "An Interview with Sterling M. McMurrin," *Dialogue: A Journal of Mormon Thought* 17 (Spring 1984): 18-43.

31. See Bushman, "Faithful History," *Dialogue: A Journal of Mormon Thought* 4 (Winter 1969): 11-25, reprinted in this volume.

32. I believe that Marty is on the right track when he maintains that historians cannot "prove that Smith was a prophet" and it is "improbable that they will prove him a fraud." "Similarly, historians cannot prove that the Book of Mormon was translated from golden plates and have not proven that it was simply a fiction of Joseph Smith" [186, see also 179].

33. James L. Clayton, "Does History Undermine Faith?" *Sunstone* 7 (Mar.-Apr. 1982): 37.

34. Marty, *A Short History of Christianity* (New York: Meridian, 1959, 1967), 296.

35. Marty, "Afterword," in *Where the Spirit Leads: American Denominations Today*, Martin E. Marty, ed. (Atlanta: John Knox Press, 1980), 231, 233.

36. Ibid., 298-301.

37. See, for example, Marty's *The Public Church: Mainline-Evangelical-Catholic* (New York: Crossroad, 1981), ix; and also *A Short History*, 294, 296.

38. Ibid., 296.

39. One writer has claimed, for example, that even believing historians must be neutral or detached from their faith when they write history. His reason is that historians "cannot prove historically" that their "beliefs are true and certainly cannot apply these beliefs to his or her scholarly research because there is no historically acceptable evidence of God, divine intervention, or life after death. Historians have no way to discern the hand of God or to measure the validity of inspiration because historians have no tools to deal with the supernatural. They can neither confirm nor disconfirm mystical experiences." Clayton, "Does History Undermine Faith?" 38.

40. Marty, "The Difference in Being a Christian and the Difference It Makes—for History," in *History and Historical Understanding*, C. T. McIntire and Ronald A. Wells, eds. (Grand Rapids: Eerdmans, 1984), 41-54. Marty's position seems quite unlike that advanced years ago by Van A. Harvey in *The Historian and the Believer* (New York: Macmillan, 1966), but it is not entirely unlike that advanced by Bushman in "Faithful History."

41. For example, Bushman's *Joseph Smith and the Beginnings of Mormonism.* Other titles could be listed.

42. I borrow the label "revisionist" from those who use it to describe essentially secular, naturalistic accounts of Mormon faith. See, for example, Edwards, "The New Mormon History," 14, and RLDS Church Historian Richard P. Howard's "Revisionist History and the Document Dealers," *Dialogue: A Journal of Mormon Thought* 19 (Winter 1986): 69.

43. Jan Shipps once claimed that Joseph Smith was a typical mystic and the Book of Mormon a typical mystical text. See "Mormons in Politics,"Ph.D. diss., University of Colorado, 1965, 31-32. See also Arrington and Bitton, *The Mormon Experience: A History of the Latter-day Saints* (New York: Vintage Press, 1979), 5, where Joseph's special revelations are described as mystical theophanies; Alexander, "Wilford Woodruff and the Changing Nature of Mormon Religious Experience," *Church History* 45 (Mar. 1976): 60-61, 69; *Things in Heaven and Earth: The Life and Times of Wilford Woodruff, a Mormon Prophet* (Salt Lake City: Signature Books, 1991), 49, 353-54n19, cf. 341n95 and n97; and also his "The Place of Joseph Smith in the Development of American Religion," *Church History* 5 (1978): 14-15. Edwards turns Joseph Smith into an Eastern mystic in his "The Secular Smiths," *Journal of Mormon History* 4 (1977): 3-17. He also accounts for the Book of Mormon as Joseph Smith's "speculative work that gives the story of his experience" which he understands as mystical. See Edwards, *Preface to Faith: A Philosophical Inquiry into RLDS Beliefs* (Midvale, UT: Signature Books, 1984), 31-34. In 1983 Anthony A. Hutchinson associated mysticism with fiction-fabrication or myth-production in Joseph Smith's dissociative personality to explain the Book of Moses and Book of Mormon, as well as the story of Moroni. See his "A Mormon Midrash? LDS Creation Narratives in Redaction-Critical Perspective," a paper presented at the Mormon History Association meetings in Omaha, Nebraska, in May 1983, 10-14; cf. his "A Mormon Midrash? LDS Creation Narratives Reconsidered," *Dialogue: A Journal of Mormon Thought* 21 (Winter 1988): 18n5. Hill once attempted to link superstition, mysticism, and magic in an explanation of Joseph Smith. See his "Secular or Sectarian History?" *Church History* 43 (Mar. 1974): 80, 86, 92; and "Brodie Revisited," 75, 76-78. Efforts to turn Joseph Smith into a mystic should be contrasted with the arguments presented by Hugh Nibley in "Prophets and Mystics," in *The World and the Prophets*, vol. 3, *The Collected Works of Hugh Nibley* (Salt Lake City: Deseret Book and FARMS, 1987), 98-107.

44. See Arrington, "Why I am a Believer," *Sunstone* 10 (1985): 36-38 (an edited version appeared in Philip L. Barlow, ed., *A Thoughtful Faith: Essays on Belief by Mormon Scholars* [Centerville, UT: Canon Press, 1986], 225-233); Shipps, *Mormonism: The Story of a New Religious Tradition* (Urbana: University of Chicago Press, 1985), 46. For specific application of the category of myth

understood as something other than authentic history to the Book of Mormon, see Richard Sherlock, "The Gospel Beyond Time: Thoughts on the Relation of Faith and Historical Knowledge," *Sunstone* 5 (July-Aug. 1980): 20-23, reprinted in this volume; see also his "B. H. Roberts's Voice from the Dust," *Sunstone* 11 (Sept. 1987): 39 (especially the final paragraph); and C. Robert Mesle, "History Faith and Myth," *Sunstone* 7 (Nov.-Dec., 1982): 10-13, reprinted in this volume.

45. Shipps, *Mormonism*, xii, 6-8, 18, 36, 68. She credits Marvin Hill with fashioning this explanation. The culmination of these efforts is D. Michael Quinn's *Early Mormonism and the Magic World View* (Salt Lake City: Signature Books, 1987). For an assessment of the presumed involvement of Joseph Smith with folk magic, see Bushman, "The Book of Mormon in Early Mormon History," in *New Views of Mormon History*, 3-4.

46. Abraham Heschel, *God in Search of Man* (New York: Meridian and Jewish Publication Society, 1959), 218.

47. Ibid., 223, itemizing letters supplied.

48. The two examples Marty mentions are Klaus J. Hansen, *Mormonism and the American Experience* (Chicago: University of Chicago Press, 1981); and Lawrence Foster, *Religion and Sexuality: The Shakers, the Mormons, and the Oneida Community* (Urbana: University of Illinois Press, 1984).

49. Shipps, *Mormonism*. According to Marty, Shipps holds that the Book of Mormon and Joseph Smith's story are "best understood in the context of his sequential assumptions of positions/roles that allowed the Saints to recover a usable past" by linking them with ancient and true Israel through the mythical history found in the Book of Mormon. "That was his *religious* function and achievement" [181].

50. Shipps, *Mormonism*, 39.

51. Ibid., 28.

52. Ibid., 29, 43.

53. Bushman, *Joseph Smith and the Beginnings of Mormonism*, 188.

54. A puzzling thing about Marty's essay is the attention he gives to the work of Shipps and Foster. Neither are Latter-day Saints. When they refer to Mormon prophets and special revelations they do so from outside the categories of faith; they are at their best when they ask what Marty calls secondary questions, for example, how the Book of Mormon functions in the life of believers. From their perspective the Book of Mormon is fiction, or what Shipps calls "myth," and not a text that makes accessible a genuine historical reality. One would expect no more from even a sympathetic outsider. Have either Shipps or Foster fashioned ways in which troubled Latter-day Saint historians might resolve their own crisis of faith? Presumably, from Marty's perspective, they have. Yet, Marty moves beyond, and even dismisses, their approaches in favor of another way of understanding and

doing history.

55. Shipps, "The Prophet Puzzle," *Journal of Mormon History* 1 (1974): 14.

56. Hill, "The Historiography of Mormonism," *Church History* 28 (1959): 418.

57. Ibid.

58. Hill, "Secular or Sectarian?" 96. He is citing Brodie's "Supplement," to her *No Man Knows*, 2d ed., 405-25. Hill may not have been aware of the subtle sophistication of Brodie's position because he did not have access to the discussions that took place within the Brodie-Morgan circle. For an examination of those discussions and their implications, see Novak, "Naturalistic Assumptions and the Book of Mormon," 23-40.

59. Brodie, "Fawn McKay Brodie: An Oral Interview," *Dialogue: A Journal of Mormon Thought* 14 (Summer 1981): 103-105, 111.

60. Hill, "Historiography of Mormonism," 418-19.

61. Alexander Campbell, *Delusions: An Analysis of the Book of Mormon* (Boston: Benjamin H. Greene, 1932).

62. Hill, "Secular or Sectarian," 96.

63. See Bryant S. Hinckley, *Some Distinctive Features of Mormonism* (Salt Lake City: Deseret Book, 1951), 10-11.

64. Hill, "The 'New Mormon History' Reassessed," 116n1.

65. Ibid., 115.

66. Ibid., 117.

67. Ibid., 125; cf. Hill's letter in "Afterword," 122, where he reiterates but tones down the suggestions he set forth earlier about the Book of Mormon.

68. See Hill, "The 'New Mormon History' Reassessed," 125.

69. Heschel, *God in Search of Man*, 218.

70. Hutchinson, "A Mormon Midrash: LDS Creation Narratives Reconsidered," 70.

71. Ibid., 12, 14-17.

72. Ibid., 16.

73. Ibid., 17n3.

74. McMurrin, *Religion, Reason, and Truth* (Salt Lake City: University of Utah Press, 1982), 143.

75. McMurrin, "An Interview with Sterling M. McMurrin," 22-23.

76. Ibid., 20.

77. McMurrin, *Religion, Reason, and Truth*, 279-280, cf. 166-167.

78. McMurrin, "An Interview," 25.

79. Hill, "The 'New Mormon History' Reassessed," 125. In 1986 Edwards, while defending revisionist Mormon history, employed the terms "objective" and "objectivity" ten times. See his "The New Mormon History,"

12-14, 20.

80. Hill, "The 'New Mormon History' Reassessed," 125; cf. Hill, letter in "Afterword," 122.

81. See Peter Novick, *That Noble Dream: The "Objectivity Question" and the American Historical Profession* (New York: Cambridge University Press, 1988), for a detailed examination of the enthrallment of American historians with what he calls the "myth of objectivity" from the beginning of professional history in America. For comparisons with the Mormon history profession, see Midgley, "The Myth of Objectivity: Some Lessons for Latter-day Saints," *Sunstone* 14 (Aug. 1990): 54-56, and Midgley, review of *That Noble Dream*, in *John Whitmer Historical Association Journal* 10 (1990): 102-104.

82. See Novick, *That Noble Dream*. One justification for continuing to talk about objectivity in the face of the kind of critique advanced by Novick (and others) is to grant the validity of the criticisms and then ignore the implications of having done so. For an example, see Philip L. Barlow, *Mormons and the Bible: The Place of the Latter-day Saints in American Religion* (New York: Oxford University Press, 1991), xv-xvi. Quinn has made a similar move. In his response to criticisms directed at the more secularized accounts of the Mormon past, he claims for New Mormon History a "functional objectivity," which he distinguishes from "ultimate" objectivity, which he grants is not attainable. See Quinn's "Editor's Introduction," viii. Quinn, unfortunately, does not address Novick's criticisms of appeals to seemingly modest versions of objectivity. Yet his "functional objectivity" appears to consitute a thin or soft version of a myth that Novick has shown lacks coherence even in its most truncated formulations. Much of Novick's *That Noble Dream* consists of exposing efforts by historians to save a weak or diluted notion of objectivity in the face of criticisms by granting the soundness of the criticisms and then advancing a less robust version of objectivity in an effort to warrant or certify certain accounts of the past. In both of these instances there is nothing approaching a confrontation with the issues raised by the critique of historical objectivism.

83. Hutchinson, "LDS Approaches to the Holy Bible," *Dialogue* 15 (Spring 1982): 119n9.

84. That is, Hill has more confidence in objectivity than any of his critics, some of whom have introduced a vocabulary and subtle analysis into the discussion of the assumptions upon which the new history rests that are drawn from a philosophical literature with which he seems unfamiliar. See Alexander, "Historiography and the New Mormon History," who seems to come from an Historicist and relativist perspective and who maintains that New Mormon Historians have not been influenced by the myth of objectivity; and Novak, "Naturalistic Assumptions and the Book of Mormon," coming from a perspective critical of both Historicism and historical objectivism.

85. Hill, letter in "Afterword," 122. Compare Hill's stance with my remarks about relativism in "Which Middle Ground?" 7.

86. Marty turns to some of the current literature on hermeneutics [181-85]. Martin Heidegger has shown, according to Marty, "that unprejudiced, objective knowledge was not possible" by identifying the pre-understandings that stand behind all interpretations and explanations. Marty assumes that what he calls hermeneutics is a special approach to texts. It is actually the attempt to understand the conditions necessary for understanding any text or text analogue. The literature on hermeneutics is, among other things, an endeavor to clarify historical method and it is not a special technique that can be set over against other interpretative techniques. Marty also seems to neglect the function of tradition in making the meaning of texts accessible.

87. Alexander, "Historiography and the New Mormon History," 39. He cites Hill and Melvin T. Smith as examples, but the list might be extended.

88. See, for example, Shipps, *Mormonism*, 28.

89. Bushman, *Joseph Smith and the Beginnings of Mormonism*, 187.

90. This portion of Marty's essay [182-86] is potentially the most fruitful because he has gotten to the crux of the issues and has separated himself from both relativistic historicism and historical objectivism.

14.
Unfounded Claims and Impossible Expectations: A Critique of New Mormon History

David Earle Bohn

THE WRITING OF HISTORY IS CENTRAL TO THE LATTER-DAY SAINT experience. Joseph Smith himself felt keenly the importance of keeping diaries and records and reminded his most intimate colleagues that their assignment to keep the church's history was by way of commandment. The language within which Latter-day Saints define themselves invokes a historical space defined by concrete events, past, present, and future. They include the Creation and Fall, the death and resurrection of Jesus of Nazareth, the apostasy and the restoration of the gospel, the Second Coming, the resurrection, and the final judgment of all humankind. The scriptures are historical texts which chronicle the relationship of God to his earthbound children. Their teachings are often expressed in stories which work within the larger framework of scriptural time, the understanding of which requires readers, aided by the Holy Spirit, to make present the ethical situations of scriptural people.

It is in both the scriptural and non-scriptural histories of the people of God that members of the Church of Jesus Christ of Latter-day Saints understand their past and, in so doing, their present and future condition. Again, aided by the Holy Spirit, each generation and each person must re-present the past—that is, make the past present for themselves—in order for it to live and to serve as a foundation for and guide to the future; indeed, in order for there to be any future at all.

Because Mormons believe that God participates in the unfolding of historical events and will eventually bring them to an appropriate end, every attempt to undermine the historical authenticity of the foundational events of the Mormon past constitutes an assault on Latter-day Saint self-understanding. Even when done with the best of intentions, efforts to de-literalize or mythologize the historical reality of the concrete occurrences that constitute the Restoration are never merely benign attempts to get this or that detail right. Rather they are nothing less than acts of intellectual violence[1] against the believing community.

It is not surprising then that many thoughtful Mormons have raised concerns about the claims of those sometimes referred to as "New Mormon Historians,"[2] a group of Mormon[3] and non-Mormon historians[4] that seems to argue for an essentially naturalistic or secular approach to the Mormon past. In an essay entitled "New Perspectives in Mormon History," Lawrence Foster provides a useful, if occasionally caustic, summary of the arguments in support of the New Mormon History.[5] Foster begins his essay with the contention that sectarian controversies over whether or not the church was divinely restored have distracted historians interested in Mormonism from their principal task: the pursuit of historical truth.[6] Foster notes that a few disaffected Mormons and many Fundamentalist Protestant critics have used history as a weapon with which to attack, rather than an aid with which to understand, the prophetic claims of the LDS church. From Foster's perspective, even "Fawn Brodie's pathbreaking biography" suffers because she spent too much time complaining that her naive Sunday school image of Joseph Smith had not been the full picture.[7]

At the other end of the spectrum, believing Latter-day Saints are accused of using history as an instrument of indoctrination to elicit the unquestioned acquiescence of its members. According to Foster, the church desires edifying histories, "sanitized, saccharine accounts, treatments, which would best be characterized as 'propaganda' by an objective observer."[8] As a result, otherwise "sober Mormon scholars" spend inordinate amounts of time trying to find evidence that Joseph Smith really saw angels. Foster judges these endeavors as akin to the "debates of medieval scholastics over how many angels could dance on the head of a pin."[9] Foster finds histories written from this point of view to be "deadly dull and pointless." He asks himself how an otherwise interesting subject matter could be turned into such "pablum."[10] This is why, according to Foster, "traditional" Mormon scholarship is simply a "joke" to professional historians. It has produced little more than an enormous mass of "undigested data with no apparent organizing principle." He charges that Mormon historians have been unwilling to use theories from other disciplines (presumably the social sciences), have ignored the broader social context, and on the whole remained blind to the rich "complexity," "social vitality," and insights of the Mormon experience.[11]

Foster then lauds what he calls the New Mormon History as a way out of such sectarian squabbling and into the mainstream of American historical writing.[12] The approach he advocates pretends simply not to be interested in the religious claims of the Mormon restoration; its focus is instead on the "facts." In what seems to me to be a clearly pejorative manner, Foster repeatedly contrasts the objective historical accounts produced by secular scholarship against faith-promoting ones; the former are portrayed as standing for maturity, understanding, rigor, and truth, while the latter are seen as inevitably naive, sentimental, one-sided, inaccurate, and mistaken.[13]

Despite this, Foster fears that the official policy of the Mormon church appears to be moving against the New Mormon History, making the writing of objective accounts of the Mormon past more difficult. He warns that this would be short-sighted and not in the best interests of the church. In his eyes, the type of history authorized by secular historians is preferable, even from the perspective of the church. First, it is believable. It tells the "real" story about "the real people who struggled to create Mormondom" rather than myths about "idealized paragons of virtue." Furthermore, Foster believes a secularized Mormon history would be compatible with Mormon theology in its naturalistic and materialistic assumptions, and would actually help the church meet constructively the challenges of the future.[14]

The argument supporting such a New Mormon History is by no means original with Foster. Indeed his article is merely one version of an argument that has been made regularly for over thirty years. This is not to say that New Mormon Historians and their supporters such as Leonard J. Arrington, Robert B. Flanders, Thomas G. Alexander, Jan Shipps, Marvin S. Hill, Davis Bitton, Klaus J. Hansen, Melvin T. Smith, D. Michael Quinn, James L. Clayton, Sterling M. McMurrin, Paul M. Edwards, Richard P. Howard, and others agree with Foster on every point. But they do seem to support the general argument for a secular middle ground between the extremes of sectarian history.[15] In addition, some New Mormon Historians seem to agree with Foster that the questions addressed in Traditional Mormon History are no longer of genuine interest and that they rest upon an approach that is neither conceptual nor objective but compromised on every side by personal bias and *a priori* commitments.

According to New Mormon Historians, their call for a middle ground is, among other things, a call for objectivity and neutrality. Leonard Arrington, for example, pleads for an "objective" history that will eschew "the author's personal feelings and opinions . . . and [the] prejudices of the time."[16] James Clayton celebrates the New Mormon History for its belief that "religious history . . . should be neutral . . . objective . . . and concerned with [the] consequences for . . . accumulations of wisdom." He sees historians as "objective and scholarly advocates of the truth . . . who respect objectivity more than orthodoxy."[17]

The detachment or neutrality called for by apologists for the New Mormon History rests on the assumption of a certain transparency in understanding the past; it demands a presuppositionless or objective vantage point—one above passion and polemic—which, we are told, allows the reality of the past to reappear as it really was, uncolored or undistorted by personal longings and biases. The "sectarian squabbles," as Foster calls them, that have generally characterized conflicting interpretations of the Mormon past deny the historian such neutral ground. Thus, in calling for a detached, neutral middle ground, New Mormon Historians are really calling for a movement to a "higher ground." From such heights, they implicitly claim that their versions of the past are objective reconstructions of what *actually* took place based upon obvious judgments of fact discovered through exhaustive work with the source materials themselves.

The allusion to a higher ground is seductive. But is it a chimera? Can secular historians rightly claim that their approach is truly objective and that their interests and questions reflect a higher order of significance than those of believers? Can they legitimately refer to their own accounts as mature, accurate, and insightful as opposed to what Foster among others labels as the "naive, narrow minded, pollyannish" histories written by Mormon historians who take their own religious categories as a theme for the understanding of the Mormon past?[18]

Such questions must be answered because if the ideals of detachment, neutrality, and objectivity cannot be reached or even approximated, then the kind of distinctions the objectivist historian wants to make between "good history" and "bad history" evaporates and the claim of secular history that its accounts are of a higher order no longer hold. Clearly Foster's advice to the church on the advantages of "good" history—that is, secular history, presupposes this distinction and depends on its validity.[19]

Exactly what assumptions are central to this objectivist position? I will treat at least two in this essay: (1) that historians can somehow achieve a detached, neutral state of mind and an objective attitude with regard to the subject matter under investigation; and (2) that the historical record is an independent and objective ground for the verification of properly constituted historical explanations. *Clearly, neither assumption can stand up to careful scrutiny. I hope to demonstrate why this is so.*

Let us examine what is being claimed in the first assumption. By assuming an objective and neutral posture—an attitude of detachment from the faith and hence a neutrality with no controlling values except a "passion for truth"—it is implied that the historian can gain a true and factual understanding of the past. The claim is literally that in some way historians can escape the biases of their own historical condition and view the past in its truth. Indeed, the assumption here seems to be that from such heights, the past can be apprehended in the truth of its self-evidence without the need for interpretation to constitute or integrate its elements. Such an assertion leaves the most fair-minded person asking, "How is that possible?" Historians necessarily work out their understanding of the past from within history, prejudiced by their own time's way of constituting the past. Of course, some historians may well disagree with the prevailing way in which the past has been put together by other historians, but every such disagreement will nonetheless be situated within a tradition of discussing how the past ought to be understood, and the provisional conclusions reached along the way will necessarily bear the stamp of the very age in which the various points of view were articulated; said differently, every such disagreement will reveal the possible ways the historical scholarship of a given time understood its own activity. Finally, not even "human rationality" is exempted from such temporal limits to stand as an objective ground for the writing of history, for every discussion that discloses the rational and seeks to characterize it reflects a given historical moment's own particular understanding of what reason is and how it operates.

The personal putting-together of the past, the questions and interests, the methods and procedures of historians may in some limited sense be authentically their own, but they will still be situated within the boundaries of their own time's way of making sense out of what went on before. For these reasons, the claim that adopting a neutral state of mind leads to "real history" requires that we believe the unbelievable. We must accept the notion that researchers can indeed rise to some higher plane beyond time and place and literally gaze upon a landscape of unchanging historical truths. In fact, historians achieve points of agreement that satisfy almost everyone for a time, only to break down eventually and be abandoned in the face of new arguments which themselves subsequently yield to later consensus. In the course of things, even the meaning of the original questions change as the horizon of the discussion moves on.

For the same reasons, *it is not even possible for historians to approximate neutrality and objectivity*. While people continuously approximate, few of us would claim that our approximations are objective, that they are working within some absolute universe or describing some deep structures of "reality." Rather we see them as working within agreed upon universes whose boundaries and standards of measure are defined by conventions which for one reason or another we find useful. If we define, for example, a uniform area and call it a "football field," and if we agree on a way of dividing it into sections, then we are in a position to approximate distances from various points on the field and invent games to be played within its boundaries. In all of this we realize that our approximations only have validity within the framework of the conventions upon which they are based. Similarly, historians need to acknowledge that instead of approximating objectivity that would necessarily presuppose a fixed standard of measure rooted in a historically unconditioned universe, they are only struggling to satisfy the conventions of the tradition of historical scholarship they have accepted or into which they have been socialized.[20]

Of course, hidden in this objectivist way of thinking are almost always implicit assumptions about universal human nature which is apparently law abiding and can supposedly be abstracted out of human experiences and then used to found the psychological and sociological principles or laws which constitute the social sciences. By drawing upon this conceptual language, the argument then follows, historians can produce objective histories precisely by moving beyond the particularities of cultural and personal prejudice in order to allow the underlying patterns that determine human reality to be seen. But again, are we expected to accept these assertions on the bases of self-evidence alone? How could such a position ever be validated? Clearly, efforts of historians to ground their conceptual language objectively on claims to having discovered a universal methodology, underlying laws, core social structures, or essential human nature fail to own up to the historically situated conventions that make possible and necessarily prejudice their historical accounts. In any case, such universal claims are inadequate and serve surreptitiously to give universal significance to what are otherwise merely our own personal and often arbitrary interpretations.

Finally, in the light of such deterministic language, how could historians ever speak in a defensible way about *human freedom* and thus also about *ethical behavior*? New Mormon Historians often criticize church policies and the conduct of the Saints, yet, strangely, naturalistic approaches to historical writing repress or rule out in advance the very possibility of authentic choice and thus responsibility, making legitimate moral and ethical judgments impossible. The problem is complex and touches all aspects of objectivist research. Nevertheless, I have always been struck at how naturalistic history leaves the reader with a rather odd scenario where evil is no one's fault. Rather, the impersonal socio-biological causes which are said to underlie history become responsible for the ethical failures that we individually and collectively suffer. In a sense, for objectivists, we are all "victims" of history and its causes.

At this point, and no doubt often even with the best of intentions, revisionist historians will redefine what they mean by a neutral and objective attitude. To define oneself as an objective and neutral observer is only a way of reaffirming one's commitment to honest and fair history, to giving a balanced account of things. But if this is all that is meant, then most of us would agree that the issue loses its force. Moreover, we are left to wonder whether the whole discussion of neutrality and objectivity does not boil down to an unwitting form of self-adulation. As a group, there is no clear evidence that New Mormon Historians are any more honest, fair-minded, or balanced in their judgment than those who write traditional accounts.[21] For example, while calling for objectivity and neutrality, Foster's characterization of Traditional Mormon History, which was quoted earlier, is neither "impartial" nor "balanced" but rather tendentious and derisive. What is more, I do not believe historians from any tradition would publicly advocate *lopsided, narrow, unfair,* or *distorted* history. Indeed the self-aggrandizing language of neutrality and objectivity may, in the long run, be counter-productive, leaving the reader to wonder whether such terms do not constitute merely a rhetorical device designed to privilege a given historian's productions, or those one wishes to advance, without having to deal with actual questions of merit.

This leads us back to our earlier conclusion that the critical issue has little to do with appeals for honesty and fair-mindedness but rather with the impossibility of overcoming the very way the ideas, world views, and practices of one's own time condition in advance the historian's personal disclosure of the past. Taken together they constitute the preunderstanding or historical prejudice that researchers necessarily bring to the historical record and in so doing undermine any claim to objectivity or neutrality that they might wish to advance. Indeed, I will endeavor to show that it is this very preunderstanding which allows the historical record to have meaning at all. Were reason somehow capable of gazing upon some objective past from a purely neutral vantage point, it would likely apprehend nothing at all.

This brings us to a critical juncture in our study. There is little doubt where writers of Traditional Mormon History stand. They have made no secret that at the most fundamental level their histories have been guided by a belief that Joseph Smith was a prophet of God, that the church was restored by the hand of God and is led by revelation to bring forth the fullness of the gospel of Jesus Christ. Nor have they concealed the fact that in the final moment the validity of these foundations will not be established by the convincing use of language, but also—and more decisively—by the witness of the Holy Spirit.

On the other hand, where do writers of the New Mormon History stand? What are the prejudices and preconceptions that pre-condition their writings and frame their conclusions? Peter Novick in *That Noble Dream: The "Objectivity Question" and the American Historical Profession* argues persuasively that the professional historical establishment resident in the graduate programs of America's universities is the most obvious and immediate institution which both constitutes and reflects the prevailing norms of acceptable historical research. Here the well-trained historian is portrayed as one who strives to produce a rational and objective version of the past rooted in a naturalistic understanding of human behavior with a strong bent toward some form of environmental explanation, that is an explanation in which the cause of human action is attributed to external circumstances. The last thirty years have seen a growth in the popularity of positivism as expressed in the methods and theories of the social sciences, which have been made to cohabit somehow with a more ingrained historicism.[22] The entire orientation seems to be pervaded with the ideology of humanism and at least a faint hope of progress.[23] Recently, this professional orthodoxy has been challenged on many fronts and can no longer be said to fully unify American historians, but it seems to remain dominant among New Mormon Historians.[24] Though some have striven to distance themselves from its more extreme manifestations, most continue to depend on its vocabulary and fundamental categories to justify their methods and conclusions.

This orthodox view of history embraced by most New Mormon Historians furnishes an overarching framework within which the world is disclosed in largely materialist terms. Its models and procedures are drawn for the most part from the non-human sciences. They include empiricism working within a defining framework of biological and environmental determinism. Presumably, the ultimate goal of this objectivist methodology is to provide causal explanations of human events. In the words of one New Mormon Historian, "It is far past the time when scholars can be satisfied with vague categories and glib generalization. Writers on complex topics like the development of important religious movements must be clear in their demonstration of causal connections between events."[25] Sterling M. McMurrin refers to these controlling methodological assumptions as naturalistic humanism with some flavor of positivism; and James L. Clayton asserts that the methodology of the inductive sciences is in principle appropriate for historical inquiry.[26]

It would seem then that it is simply not possible for historians of whatever tradition to occupy a detached and neutral stance with regard to the subject matter under investigation. The New Mormon History, like any other tradition of inquiry, works within historically defined prejudices which necessarily circumscribe the way in which those histories will be written.

But what of those historians who do have reservations about escaping their own historical condition and achieving neutrality? Could they not legitimately do an about face in order to sustain their objectivist position? Could they not assert that how historians actually come upon their explanations of the past is not important? They might willingly agree that scientists are driven by the same passions and interests as other people. What matters then would not be the attitudes and personal commitments of the researcher, but rather whether the historical explanations they proffer can be confirmed or disconfirmed. Do they correspond to the objective facts of history? Do they hold up against the evidence, against the facts? For this approach, it is in the possibility of confirming one's account against the hard facts that make up the historical record itself that the validity of the historian's claim to objectivity resides.

This position relates to the second basic assumption central to objectivist history presented earlier: *the historical record itself is an independent and objective ground against which properly constituted historical explanations can be tested and perhaps verified.* When secular historians are challenged, they make ready reference to "the record" and the "facts," to the "evidence," the "sources," and the "documents." The implication is that historians are simply letting the "facts speak for themselves" or that any rational individual could hardly infer different conclusions from the "evidence." Foster furnishes an excellent example. "The Mormon past," he writes, "came even more vividly alive as I began to work closely in the printed and manuscript records." These brought to mind the "real men and women" of the Mormon past.[28] We are left to conclude that if we could only get to the facts, the objective truth of the matter would be clear and apparent. This is what Foster believes the New Mormon History is doing—getting to the facts which, according to Sterling M. McMurrin, are precisely what faithful members of the church and their leaders do not want to face.[29]

Nevertheless, the thoughtful person would be well advised to examine these claims more closely. It is not at all clear that it is possible to verify historical accounts objectively against historical evidence or the historical record. The point certainly should not be conceded on the basis of self-evidence. What is a fact? How does mere information rise to the status of a fact? What is the relationship between historians and the facts which supposedly confirm their accounts of the past? Do historians have unmediated access to the facts? If not, what kind of access do they have?

To better understand the discussion about the "factual" claims historians can make, it is important to get one thing clear: the past is not really like a picture that can be approximated if one just has enough information, or a puzzle the pieces of which can be assembled presumably on the basis of perception alone. This is because, strangely enough, the meaning of a "picture" is not self-evident but can only be worked out if one already understands its components. For example, when it is pointed out to students both through discussion and reading what a diesel injector is, they can readily recognize one in a photograph. Otherwise such a photo would seem strange, and its content only recognizable as some kind of gadget based on some prior understanding of gadgetry. But in turn the meaning of gadgetry is not self-evident. It would likewise rest on previous discussions or reading about mechanical devices or instruments, and so on. This is why the meaning of visual objects in the historical record cannot simply be "pictured." Such meaning is not objectively manifest. Rather it is arrived at through interpretation that is always led by some kind of preunderstanding. In a sense, visual objects, like a text, are "read" and "interpreted." But the issue is more complex.

Human history is itself not really about visual objects. Instead it is an accounting of human activity, intentional and historical, rooted in our common possibility for language—that is for shared meaning. The past never appears as merely a fixed or static "picture" but is disclosed through the mediation of historical interpretation as a rich and ever-changing complexity of human interactions arising out of this sharing of meaning and the way of life in which it is embedded.[30] Thus human possibilities—inherent in the indeterminateness of language and the common world it discloses—can be encountered only through interpretation. Properly worked out, such accountings reveal the ambiguity of human being, an ambiguity concealed by objectivist approaches that work within the visual metaphor of objects, a terminology more appropriate to the non-human sciences.

Returning to the role of "facts" in writing historical accounts, most historians would point out that "facts" themselves are contained in the historical record, which is the mass of inherited information that historians draw upon to write their histories. The record consists of a variety of artifacts all of which can be read and interpreted as texts or as text analogues. The obvious but critically important aspect which all these diverse texts and text analogues have in common is that they happened to have survived.

The problem is that although the textual record is the historian's only avenue of access to the past, the meaning of the specific documents it contains cannot be said to be objective characterizations of the time in which they were produced; rather they represent the opinions, beliefs, and ideas of those who wrote them. Furthermore, the textual record will always be incomplete, never containing more than fragments and traces from the past whose accuracy can never be fully verified. Nor can the historian always depend on the record being a representative sample of what occurred in the past. For this reason scholars frequently lament that the data they need simply were not recorded or that what was recorded seems irrelevant to their research. In the end, the historian fleshes out an account of the past from conjecture of what an imaginary textual record—somehow objectively complete and fully accurate—might have contained.

But obviously our ability to disclose the past is not limited solely by the fragmentary and temporal makeup of the textual record. It is also mediated by the very character of language and the understanding it bears. Language is much more than a set of empirically stipulated definitions. It is in our common possibility for language that we as human beings are able to collectively disclose and share a "world." It is in language that we are able to participate in a tradition of understanding and a given way of life.[31] Thus language is not merely the medium in which understanding is transmitted; it is the very way in which people arrive at meaning, coordinate a shared way of life, and disclose a common world. Furthermore, in the same way that people in their individual and collective activity are not fixed, static, or inert but are ever-changing in how they disclose the "world" and work out their lives within it, so too is language always in transformation, since language and the understanding it brokers are the very means of that change, are the very foundation of the future. But as Martin Heidegger has shown, language renders possible the future by preserving the past. It is in language—in its very structure and content—that the understanding of one historical moment is passed on to the next; it is in the collective remembering—the very being of language—that culture is possible. Every movement of language toward the future is by way of the past.

Since language is historical and always underway, since it is at one with the changes in the way of life and culture in which it is practiced, the meaning it bears necessarily changes. Even the formal meaning of words and statements becomes more and more ambiguous and indefinite as the world of the text—the way of life and the language within which a text was produced—becomes increasingly remote from the world of the historian who endeavors to interpret the text. Clearly, students of history can come to the language of the text only from across the horizon of their own time, pregnant with its own meanings, proffering its own way of life, and prejudiced by all that is understood to have happened in between. But at the same time we must keep in mind that the language practices we have inherited are themselves historical; our way of using language is constituted by the ways of using language which preceded it, and therefore we can in some measure read and understand texts authored at earlier points. We can begin to share in the understandings worked out in different historical moments, but never in the same way. We can never approach it from within their world. Making the meaning of the texts present always involves interpretation; it always involves getting clear on what the texts can mean for us, fusing their horizon to ours. The historical record does not interpret itself: it is the reader who explores the possible meanings of the texts, who interprets the text from within the language of his or her own time. Hence history is necessarily in part a discovery and in part an invention or creation.

Since interpretation always works within a linguistic horizon, even the most elementary ordering principles prejudice or structure in advance our access to the meaning of the historical record and define the field of study. For example, to order their materials historians will define the contents of the record vertically according to time and horizontally according to topic. In so doing, the mass of data is altered as researchers draw together into a whole, bits and pieces which otherwise seem only accidentally connected.[32] Few historians want to stop simply at doing chronology or archiving information. Most would affirm that to write history is to tell a story and give explanations of events. As they begin to craft their story, the very questions they ask and tools they use will in part determine what kind of past will get disclosed through their writings. As they introduce or accept an already existent chronology as well as cross-cutting categories of psychology, economy, politics, religion, culture, etc., and the related theories that map out those categories, the historian becomes more and more the creator of the past which will be remembered and not the midwife who lets the "facts" tell their own story.

In making this point, I wish in no way to demean historical scholarship. Quite the contrary. It seems to me that when historians deny the artistic character of their endeavor, when they work out their accounts in the indifferent, insensitive, and indeed inhuman and determinate terms of scientific discourse, they hide the genius, imagination, and inventiveness that constitutes the substance of the best historical narratives. It is no embarrassment that the vitality and spontaneity of human activity does not give itself without disfigurement and deformation to the necessarily rigid and programmatic vocabularies of the natural sciences but rather comes to life within the creative play of spirit and language. We must remember that art tells its truth too, but in a different way, speaking with a kind of richness denied to the pedantic: it discloses us as living, creative, and above all ethical beings. This is not to say that the historian can do whatever he or she pleases. The elements of texts do have a structure whose possible meanings will be worked out in one way or another within the interpretive horizon of the historian; but that is the point, the working out of these meanings can never be an objective enterprise.

In any case, every story requires a setting. Historians make theirs plausible by drawing on widely accepted prejudices about "human nature" and stereotypes of given historical periods such as the "Renaissance," the "Age of Discovery," "Western Americana," etc. This setting or context is rarely more than a ready-made backdrop to orient the reader to time and place and allow the writer to then sketch in the immediate background and flow of events. This done, historians must produce a script that relates the setting and events to the major and minor historical characters who will people the story. This is no small task. The writer must decide who will be heroes and who will be villains, who will appear and who will simply be lost like faceless props in the multitude. The characterization of the principals, of how they influence each other and affect the outcome of events, and the creation of a seamless narrative that can combine all of these elements into a plausible drama, challenges even the most skilled and creative authors.

Critical to the art of historical composition as described above is what Paul Ricoeur calls "emplotment."[33] The historian introduces a plot in order to give structure to historical narrative, to weave all the fragments drawn from the historical record together into a plausible and interesting story. The plot itself is a quasi-causal model which seeks to define and connect the elements (the so-called "facts") that make up the story-line, bringing them to some kind of climax or conclusion.[34] Simply understood, the plot functions as a kind of explanatory theory that links the parts of a story into a unity by defining how things happen and why people act as they do.

In the case of Mormon history, this involves weaving the disparate elements of what is understood to make up the Mormon textual record into a whole with regard to a given question. Historians must decide what is important and interesting. They must posit the "how" and the "why" of the past. They may raise such questions as: Why were the early Saints driven out of Missouri? Why did they adopt the practice of polygamy? How did Mormons come to believe in temples and associated ceremonies? Why did people join the LDS church in such large numbers in Great Britain? Why did persecution act to increase the fervor of many of the Saints? To answer these questions, secular scholars go beyond establishing events and dates and offer explanations. This requires the positing of a theory whose function it is to emplot the story and thus guide the interpretation of the text and organize its content. The theory assists the historian in deciding on and sorting out the relevant "facts" and fitting them together into a coherent response or conclusion. To understand how all of this is done requires that we explore in greater detail the relationship between "fact" and theory.

Most historians seem to use the word "fact" in at least two different ways without necessarily being consistent in what they mean. First, it is often used as a synonym for phenomena: "facts" are simply undifferentiated sensuous representations that appear to the conscious mind such as color, shape, and sequence. "Facts" understood as phenomena would supposedly require no interpretation to be encountered but would simply be there. But as mere phenomena, "facts" would have no meaning, no identity. For example, a house would appear as merely a dimensional entity occupying time and space in the broader matrix of a person's consciousness. Only in the measure that it is noticed and interpreted within the categories of understanding of a given historical moment does it acquire identity and get apprehended in its function as a shelter. Clearly, were it actually possible to encounter pure and unmediated phenomena, one would be about as close as imaginable to "true objectivity"—that is, the uninterpreted "facts"—but it is equally true that such objectivity would be vacuous. Without identity or meaning, such "facts" could never constitute a sufficient ground for the validation of truth claims.

Secular historians also use the word "fact" as a synonym for evidence—that which can prove or disprove a conjecture. But obviously not all "facts" understood as phenomena would be evidence. One need only think of the infinite and bewildering kaleidoscope of undifferentiated phenomena present in any historical moment to realize that only some would be legitimately considered evidence with regard to a given question. While still at least in one sense "facts," the remaining information would be defined as accidentally co-present. In short, the historian must decide which "facts" will count as evidence and which will not.

Karl Popper has shown that it is the theory one has chosen that determines which "facts" (phenomena) constitute the evidence and which do not.[35] "Facts" cannot be understood as a category of evidence until some hypothesized account has been posited, until some plot has been proposed. Obviously only those "facts" which are defined as relevant to this hypothesized account count as evidence. But since this distinction is achieved only by processing (interpreting or identifying) the "facts," they acquire the status of evidence only at the cost of losing their objective or phenomenal character. In sum, phenomena may or may not appear involuntarily to the conscious mind, but evidence does not; it is defined by theory and validated by argument. And of course without a theory, without a plot, without some idea of how to connect things together—that is, without a ground for interpreting the text—we would be hard pressed to make much sense at all out of the historical record.

For example, in seeking to give the how and why of Joseph Smith's prophetic claims, one might theorize that he was an epileptic and that his visions were the inevitable hallucinatory properties of his seizures. Such a theory would establish in advance that information relevant to seizures, as they are currently understood, constitutes the factual evidence on this subject. The researcher, eager to advance such an explanation, would then sift through the record for data that can be made to support his hypothesis. Other information ("facts") in the record would recede into the background. Were one to assert that Joseph Smith's visions were caused by delusions of grandeur arising from basic psychological disorders, the information relating to epilepsy would become irrelevant while the writer pieces together whatever in Joseph Smith's background might lend itself to such a psychological approach. There is no end to the theories that could be invented to emplot Joseph's story, to specify relevant "facts" and connect them together into a supposedly "true" and "real" account of his life. Each attempt would put into motion a new examination of the record specifying a search for different "facts" and arriving at different conclusions.

But theory does more than furnish explanations, identify what will count as evidence, and define criteria and standards of measure. It determines how to interpret the text appropriately, how to divide the record into periods, and how to develop categories for collecting and organizing information. Again, in so doing, theory will be used to distinguish the interesting and relevant from the unimportant and trivial. Finally, these various aspects of historical composition are not distinct, individual, and sequential; rather they are interdefining, interconnected, and circular. Thus even the most elementary ordering or interpreting of information, indeed, even the initial questions asked by the historian, will necessarily work within some kind of background theory or pre-understanding.

The way in which theory integrates the various aspects of

historical research into a whole can be seen in how Marxist historians interpret the language and periodize the content of the historical record differently than economic liberals. Drawing from the theory of dialectical materialism, Marxists use such categories as class, repression, revolution, mode of production, forces of production, capital, surplus value, and alienation to select from the record those "facts" which they see as important and believe stand as evidence in support of their way of disclosing the past. In the same way, so-called multi-culturalists are calling for the radical rewriting of the story of America and its peoples. Moving from widely differing premises, Americans of diverse racial and cultural backgrounds re-script the story with different plots, peopled by new casts of characters, and defined by a distinctive re-structuring of events. These divergent historical narratives arrive at conclusions that vary greatly from the academic accounts which orthodox professional historians are accustomed to writing.

For the most part, the theories used to emplot and organize historical accounts are not necessarily found anywhere in the textual record. They are rarely a part of the thinking or the explanations that the people under investigation gave of themselves or of their time. They are usually foreign elements, situated in the historians' own historical horizon, introduced by them to coordinate and give direction to their story of the past. And is not that the point? Theories reflect the horizon of understanding of a given circle of historians and the interpretive tradition in which they stand, situated as it is in their time's way of making sense out of the past.

Then too it is ironic how theories borrowed from other disciplines, few of which can lay claim to much predictability and none of which can adequately explain the phenomena of the present, always appear to fit so much better when applied to the past. For example, the usefulness of Freudian psychoanalysis is disputed in contemporary philosophy and psychology. A significant segment of the psychological profession rejects it outright. Yet for some historians it is an important source of insight for understanding Joseph Smith and his prophetic claims. More alarming is the fact that while a modern psychoanalyst may cautiously venture a reconstruction of what psychoanalytic theory defines as a patient's personality only after months of intimate consultation, a psychohistorian with almost no such information and across more than a hundred and fifty years tries to make transparent Joseph Smith's underlying motivations.

Finally the whole enterprise is subject to the caprice of fashion. Theories that once invoked great authority are abandoned and given the most derisive treatment by a later generation, only to be revived under new garb to widespread popularity by a subsequent age. And somehow each historical epoch tends to believe its understanding of the past (or at least its categories) to be consummate, so much so that the image projected by these categories appears as reality, the "truth" of what happened, the world as it "really" is. The categories themselves almost fade from view because of their very familiarity; the structure they have produced seems merely to be common sense and self-evident "reality," very much like a person used to wearing glasses who forgets that the vision she has of the world is the result of the curvature of the lenses.

For all the above reasons, the second argument on behalf of objective history, like the first, cannot hold. Historians inescapably face the necessarily circular character of historical understanding; no matter at what level they find themselves in their research, the textual record only acquires additional meaning by the further imposition of the historian's categories and criteria which are necessarily external to the supposed phenomena themselves. Clearly, then, the facts—the uninterpreted textual record—cannot stand apart from the enterprise of interpretation and explanation as an objective standard against which our understanding of the past can be verified. Indeed, there are no unmediated facts; a fact becomes evidence only if one accepts the theoretical framework which confers the status of evidence upon what is otherwise merely undifferentiated data that happen to have been preserved and would otherwise go unnoticed.

This brings the discussion full circle, for the theoretical framework of historians is not arrived at in a vacuum. Their questions, interests, categories, ordering principles, values, and commitments are situated within the medium of their own time's way of understanding the past. In the case of the New Mormon History, this means an objectivist tradition. For these reasons, secular historical scholarship cannot use neutrality and objectivity as a ground for claiming that its accounts are better or have higher standing. In a very real sense such historians have already come to their conclusion about the meaning of the textual record—of the facts—before having consulted them and all pretense to objectivity and neutrality is delusory. However, it is precisely this claim that is continually rearticulated both implicitly and explicitly to legitimate the objectivist and naturalistic accounts of the New Mormon History, and with it the equally unjustified impression that now, finally, progress is being made in the telling of the Mormon story.

This may account for the surprising degree of prejudice and disdain that secularized historians exhibit against traditional accounts, for to make progress and to advance in one's career, the professional historian must necessarily challenge established historical interpretations. This prejudice deteriorates into retrograde debunking when faced with religious histories not based on the secular historian's objectivist assumptions. Authentic religious history is quickly dismissed as myth, as the revisionist writer rescripts its content in the language of naturalistic explanation. In all of this, there is a strange fascination with the "new" as opposed to the traditional, and a tendency to exaggerate the importance of recently discovered material against a preponderance of "evidence" in the established record; thus a line in a letter here, or a rumor written down there, become the justification for a radical revision of traditional accounts. And when there are no documents, it is sufficient to invoke strange theories and bizarre conjectures to fill in the cracks.[36] In view of this, it is not altogether surprising that many New Mormon Historians were taken in by the Mark Hofmann forgeries. Hofmann knew how to invent the kind of documents such historians longed to find in order to flesh out their peculiar speculations about Mormon origins. So strong was their conviction of the authenticity of the Salamander letter and other counterfeit documents that the prosecution in the Hofmann case found it difficult to persuade these historians to "give up their attachment to the Hofmann forgeries," despite all the forensic evidence.[37]

In any case, it is this audience of professional historians who share the same kind of training and prejudice about historical understanding that writers of revisionist Mormon history have in mind when they craft their stories about the Mormon past. This, of course, can create difficulties for believing historians who write about Mormon things in secular terms. By applying the methods, using the theories and language, and appealing to the standards and criteria of naturalistic history, these historians may be able to meet the expectations of prevailing fashion found in certain academic circles. Nevertheless, they will find themselves ill equipped to write meaningfully about those most fundamental aspects of the Mormon past to which they are committed. This is because the language of the profane in which secular historiography is written represses that which is sacred; it cannot open up a space for a genuine discussion of that which is holy—it has no vocabulary for authentic spiritual experience and no words for the genuinely divine.[38]

The word *profane* itself means *before* [outside] *the temple*. Here, the temple is understood as the link between Heaven and Earth, the hallowed ground where God is present to and communicates with humankind. Otherwise, no matter how exquisite its design, it remains merely a building. The thick walls of the temple constitute an opaque boundary that excludes the unholy from God's presence. To be *outside the temple* is not to have access to that which is most sacred. From the outside, then, the temple is just a building and that which is most essential to its meaning cannot be encountered.

This imagery gives insight into why secular or profane language can only represent the sacred—the temple—from the outside and as something merely human, something only to be understood in the impoverished terms of psychological discourse. For believers who have felt the presence of the sacred in their lives, arguments which claim that in order to get clear on things spiritual we must implement a naturalistic language that denies the very possibility of the spiritual seem strange and unreasonable. Certainly with regard to religious histories, it is difficult to understand how naturalistic accounts that repress or qualify all information of a genuinely spiritual character could claim to be more informative and complete than believing ones.

All this leads one to wonder how Foster could ever gain an understanding of the "real men and women" of the Mormon past, how he could ever hope to get clear on a movement that was integrated in every respect by the spiritual, with a language steeped in the secular? In saying this, I have no desire to argue in behalf of narrow-mindedness. To the contrary, in a very real sense a believing Mormon can better grasp what is at work in the religious life of Catholics, Protestants, Jews, and non-Christian believers than those not open to the sacred. A non-believing account inevitably exhibits a certain hollowness which comes from its repression of the divine, its reduction of spiritual life to a kind of deviant form of psychological behavior.

In light of the foregoing discussion, the New Mormon Historian's criticism of Traditional Mormon History can be misleading. When New Mormon Historians criticize the Traditional Mormon Historian for not being conceptual or willing to use or depend on ordering principles from other disciplines, they show a lack of understanding of the larger question. Indeed traditionalists do use concepts to order their accounts of the Mormon past, for it is impossible not to do so. What I believe New Mormon Historians really object to is that traditional accounts do not use naturalistic concepts authorized by the world view currently in fashion among revisionist historians.

Clearly it is not simply a question of New Mormon Historians who presumably want to get to the "facts" and let them speak for themselves and Traditional Mormon Historians who want to manipulate the "facts" for their own religious ends. Psychological, sociological, and economic explanations of visions, texts (such as the Book of Mormon, the Pearl of Great Price, or the Doctrine and Covenants), and practices (such as temple work) do not constitute a neutral or objective way of getting to the bottom of things. The language underlying such theories is repressive. Subtly and sometimes not so subtly it denies *a priori* that the foregoing could authentically involve revelation and the divine and imposes its own explanation. And it is precisely because these theories are not objective or neutral and cannot deal authentically with the sacred that traditionalists have every right to take issue with the way such theories structure the Mormon past. Traditional Mormon Historians have every right to reject the unsubstantiated but still implicit claim that revisionist accounts are necessarily more interesting, significant, and true.

New Mormon Historians might well respond that no reputable historian believes it is possible to be objective and therefore the arguments I have made are directed at straw people. Perhaps, but aside from routine disclaimers about how perfect objectivity is unattainable, most revisionist historians continue to write as if they were barely aware there is a problem. Others admit that objectivity is not fully possible but continue to offer it as a worthy ideal that can be approximated. Even those who refuse to take a position still use methods, evolve categories, and develop explanations that presuppose some notion of objectivity. In addition, objectivist vocabulary is ubiquitous, lending a false sense of legitimacy and rigor to historical accounts.

If Foster and other New Mormon Historians do really reject the objectivist tradition, then it seems incumbent upon them to provide a clear justification of the methodology and related criteria they use. It is simply not enough to satisfy oneself with recognizing the limits and bias inherent in naturalistic explanation and then continue on as if there were none. The willingness of secular historians to admit discomfort with the logical implications of their methodology does not constitute of itself a clarification of or a remedy for its untenable ground. It is not enough to say that one is only trying to approximate objectivity when it is clear that objectivity and neutrality cannot be approximated. It is not enough to redefine objectivity as an effort to be fair, high-minded, and honest—all undeniably laudable qualities—but not ones which New Mormon Historians hold in any greater measure than Traditional Mormon Historians. In the end, all such efforts to parry criticism act to shroud the repressive character of naturalistic explanation and conceal the subjective nature of its accounts.

Since revisionist histories cannot justify themselves as being more objectively true than Traditional Mormon accounts, what does distinguish them from the latter? They cannot be said to be making "progress" by giving us the real picture of the Mormon past, since such a claim would require an unequivocal standard that is being progressively realized—which is precisely what is lacking. Rather the critical difference is that openly and without shame, Traditional Mormon History works out its accounts within a horizon of belief. This honest and straightforward approach does not hide its commitments or highest concern. At its best, Traditional Mormon History is a faithful history that seeks to authentically re-present our common past, our inheritance, to fuse the horizon of believing past and believing present. Traditional Mormon History is a history worked out within and for the believing community. Its central theme is the restoration of the gospel of Jesus Christ, the mission of the LDS church in the present dispensation of time, and God's power to unfold his purpose on earth. It is distinguished by the priority it gives to the sacred and the implementation of a language which can frame our common past in terms that take into account the spiritual. It recovers that which has been forgotten or repressed by secular discourse and displaces the "violence" done by vocabularies that disbelieve. In a very genuine way, the language of Traditional Mormon History resonates with the same meaning as that of the early Saints: it operates within the same tradition and is true to the same kinds of values and expectations, albeit made present along a later historical horizon.

Of course actual accounts of Mormon history written within the community of belief will necessarily vary in their merit and purpose. Obviously, this essay was not written to defend everything and anything that claims to be a believing account, only the possibility of high quality history soundly worked out within categories true to the faith. Nor do I wish to advance a narrow and limited perspective. Certainly believing histories will stress many different themes. At numerous junctures there will be relatively few areas of difference between a Traditional Mormon History and its revisionist counterpart; at other points they will diverge significantly. But as already noted, the decisive factor is that Traditional Mormon History is motivated by the community of belief which faithful Mormons share. It will necessarily work within an understanding animated by individual and collective encounters with the Holy Spirit. Indeed, for the faithful, an account of their past worked out from within some other framework would be a story robbed of its substance. Such a past would appear as something pointless, distant, and trivial, an alien production worked out within the hostile language of secular historiography.

At this point, thoughtful readers are probably wondering how apologists for the New Mormon History have responded to such assessments. Candidly speaking, none have remedied its methodological weaknesses or rehabilitated its claims. Even more disturbing is the defensiveness and general lack of openness to the discussion itself. For example, Malcolm Thorp's essay entitled "Some Reflections on New Mormon History" summarizes much of the reaction of New Mormon Historians to their critics.[39] On the whole Thorp, a historian specializing in British studies at Brigham Young University, concedes as correct the majority of criticisms made of the New Mormon History. But he then seeks to trivialize these admissions in order to reassert—without arguments—a weaker version of the same objectivist claim.

Thorp's efforts involve what we might call the *archival fallacy*. With more than a little disdain, he asserts that criticisms of the New Mormon History are uninformed because they are made by non-historians who have never done archival research and therefore cannot understand how the reading of the record flows more or less unproblematically from the documents themselves. In support, he cites Kellner who contends "most [historians] will assert that the guarantee of adequacy of the historical account is found in the sources. If the sources are available, scrupulously and comprehensively examined according to the rules of evidence, and compiled in good faith by a reasonably mature professional, the resulting work will more or less 'image' reality."[40]

From here Thorp insists that the New Mormon History arose from the availability of new sources which naturally produced new and apparently "stronger" interpretations of the Mormon past.[41] He scrupulously avoids using the term "objectivity" and interjects disclaimers along the way. Nonetheless, even a casual reader will see that Thorp reinserts the claim to an objective reading where the documents themselves determine the interpretation—that is, where the "facts" speak for themselves. To do this, he minimizes the role the historian plays in scripting historical accounts, a role we have already explored in this essay, arguments which Thorp himself concedes to be correct. Paradoxically, in asserting the autonomy of the texts he also places himself at odds with other New Mormon Historians, such as Foster, who laud the New Mormon History for modeling the Mormon past according to the naturalistic theories and concepts of the social sciences.

Dominique LaCapra, a historian at Cornell University, calls this kind of approach the "documentary model" that makes a "fetish of archival research" and relies on a relatively mundane and uninformed sort of "*Quellenkritik*" to get at the meaning of the documents. He finds that this obsession with documents fosters an insider mentality which LaCapra calls, "l'esprit de cénacle," a kind of clannishness that resists rigorous criticism and is satisfied with a narrow "cracker-barrel" logic for interpreting the intertextuality of the record.[42] Then LaCapra cites H. Stuart Hughes, who sees in all of this a "primitive positivism" unaware of how "*new readings*" [his italics] and not just new sources account for new interpretations.[43]

LaCapra does not wish to deny the value of archival research nor the practical skills necessary to conduct it. Rather the intention is to bring into view the controlling assumptions that lead to an unjustified privileging of historical accounts on the basis of having served time in the archive. He also wants to surface clearly the "objectivist model of knowledge"[44] implicit in this archival fetish and expose how it conceals the degree to which the meaning of the text is always worked out within an interpretive horizon that the historian brings to the archive.

Despite Thorp's contentions about the autonomy of the documents in determining interpretations, historians do come to the archive with certain research interests and questions, with an array of concepts and theories, and with methodological commitments and professional practices that guide in advance which documents they will choose and how they will interpret them. And it is in the light of these same prejudices that interpretations will be judged as either strong or weak. This does not mean that historians never change their mind about the meaning of sources, but most adjustments are minor and work within the historian's existing framework of reference. When fundamental shifts in understanding do occur, they are more likely to result from extensive philosophical or methodological discussions than some enlightening archival experience with a new document.

Simply put, Thorp's attempt to rehabilitate the New Mormon History's objectivist claim fails to show that archival research with its controlling methodology and references to some new document can actually "image" reality or produce necessarily "stronger" accounts than those advanced by Traditional Mormon Historians. But there is another point to be made. Has Thorp done anything more than obliquely assert that New Mormon Historians are masters of the archive? Indeed, has Thorp shown that the best traditionalist Mormon historians do not use archives well, read and process texts in a scrupulous manner, and demonstrate mature judgment and good will in arriving at their conclusions? And certainly, in the measure that the best traditionalists do demonstrate archival competence, then the difference between believing histories and secular ones cannot be reduced to the documents themselves; rather it must be the function of a difference in interpretive horizon.

There is a second, more troubling aspect to Thorp's essay. He insists that accounts of the Mormon past put together in terms that take religious claims seriously would necessarily be narrow and confining, indeed illiberal. He quickly demotes discourse involving the sacred to a radically restrictive and private kind of language, a sort of closed system, which in his view "denies all possibility of rational discussion."[45] His assertion seems to imply that languages of belief are necessarily irrational, belonging to the realm of sentiment rather than reason. In asserting such a position, Thorp necessarily reserves reason to secular discursive practices alone, thus privileging the methodology of the New Mormon History.

Of course, such a narrow, "logocentric," or "dichotomous" view of rationality would deny much of the richest scholarship found in the traditions of both East and West where rational discourse worked out its arguments from within a horizon of belief. It would deny rationality to the prophets of Israel and the Rabbinic tradition in their efforts to get clear on the meaning of the *Word*; to much of what constitutes the history of philosophy; indeed to our own Mormon tradition in which we are enjoined to seek wisdom through both Spirit and Reason.

Clearly, Latter-day Saints understand rational discourse in a much broader way. They are willing to explore all modes of discourse, even those that are blind to spiritual things in order to get clear on their past; but they realize that all "worldly" ways of understanding work within limits and are thus insufficient. Indeed, language left to its own devices comes to no final conclusion and the plenitude of reason is obtained only in a space opened up by the Holy Spirit. The horizon of understanding of believers is made richer not poorer by their openness to the sacred.

As previously argued, it was within the language of the sacred and its categories of faith that both early and contemporary Latter-day Saints have disclosed a world of common meaning and action. How incongruent and futile it would be to try to fuse horizons with that world, to interpret its documents and to write its histories in purely secular and naturalistic terms. How could such histories, *systematically closed* as they inevitably would be to the genuine possibility of the sacred, escape doing enormous violence to the meaning of the texts and to the very world they seek to disclose? This is why such naturalistic accounts are properly understood as repressive and hostile. It is for this reason that thoughtful members of the church will turn to more authentic histories written in a language that is open to the sacred and sympathetic to belief.

The *archival fallacy* and Thorp's unsatisfying portrayal of reason and its relationship to spiritual things are not the only problems. The essay is also troubled by a general lack of arguments, moving as it does from assertion to assertion. It attributes a wholly private meaning to critical terms such as "naturalistic." It misunderstands Gadamer, making him support an "ecumenical"—that is objectivist position—that he spent his life combatting. It denigrates Derridean deconstruction by improperly portraying it as some *sinister* threat to the church. And finally, rather than dealing straightforwardly with the arguments themselves, it resorts to portraying New Mormon Historians as innocent victims who have been laid low by malevolent critics. It is painful to probe these and other weaknesses apparent in the efforts of the New Mormon History to deal with fundamental questions of methodology. Nevertheless, it is necessary since these apologists display the same inclination that according to Hayden V. White characterizes orthodox historians everywhere: "a resistance throughout the entire profession to almost any kind of critical self-analysis."[46]

Peter Novick shows why by rightly pointing out that the crucial questions of methodology—in this case the objectivity question—fall into the domain of philosophy, not history. Since most historians are not trained in philosophy, and the history profession does not monitor such discussion with much rigor, the quality of the methodological debate often suffers.[47] But more than this, Novick argues that orthodox professionals have reacted strongly against critics of historical objectivism because it involves far more than just "a philosophical question. It is an enormously charged emotional issue: one in which the stakes are very high, much higher than in any dispute over substantive interpretations. For many, what has been at issue is nothing less than the meaning of the venture to which they have devoted their lives, and thus, to a very considerable extent, the meaning of their own lives."[48] How much more distressing the problem must be for believing New Mormon Historians who willingly use secular modes of discourse to please professional referents and yet somehow must integrate that understanding with more fundamental commitments of faith. To assuage those feelings Thorp's essay tries to redefine the Mormon community as one in which people can believe anything because Mormonism itself has no central tenets and no binding content.[49]

This leads us to the final and central issue: on what grounds can New Mormon Historians claim that their accounts are inherently superior and of greater relevance than accounts worked out from within categories that assume faith? What reasons can they advance to support the contention that their histories raise the right questions—the important questions—about the Mormon past, and that their methods allow them to provide "real" answers to those questions, thereby bringing New Mormon Historians closer to the "real human beings" who lived the Mormon experience? Can the New Mormon History actually justify the claim that somehow its plots are intrinsically more interesting and salient and should serve as a model for the rewriting of the history of the Mormon past?

As I have endeavored to show, New Mormon Historians have provided few arguments that speak convincingly to the question.[50] In any case, I think that all would admit that simply because objectivist history and positivist methodology have been fashionable among American historians, it does not seem to get to the heart of the problem. As noted earlier, and as we are seeing now in the present debate, history itself records that what is fashionable in one generation can fall out of fashion in the next. Nor should we be talked too quickly into believing that Mormon historians must use secular language in order to bring their secular counterparts to an understanding of Mormonism and its past. It seems obvious that if scholars do not come to understand us in our *own terms*, they will probably never come to understand us at all. In addition, one does not have to abandon one's beliefs to genuinely understand and occasionally find useful positions advanced by those of a more secular vein. But, if popularity and acceptance or professional advancement and recognition comprise the fundamental justification for revising the way we put together our past, then I think that sincere New Mormon Historians would join in declaring, "Who cares?"

Whatever the case, there is a real danger to writers operating within the community of belief. The danger is not that secular approaches to the past will somehow disestablish the truth claims of the Mormon restoration. Rather, it is that the challenge of secular historiography will distract them from their central concerns. Indeed, if Traditional Mormon Historians allow secular historians to set the agenda, to define what questions are relevant and what information is salient, if as a community we turn our attention away from the Restoration as the organizing principle of our self-understanding, we will end up defending our terrain with their language and trying to justify our beliefs by satisfying their standards and meeting their criteria. By doing so we assume a burden of proof which should be legitimately theirs. Indeed, it is for them to show that the traditional and accepted language used in telling the Mormon past should be discarded. They should give reasons satisfying to us why our understanding the Mormon past should undergo a wholesale revision and be retold in a naturalistic language.

Until that time Mormon historians should strive to produce an intelligent and carefully researched account of our common past: one of high quality that is safeguarded by honest efforts to meet demanding internal standards of excellence—certainly one subject to sincere and constructive criticism—but above all one centered by the interests and concerns of believing Mormons as they seek to better understand the unfolding of the Restoration.

NOTES

1. I use the term violence as it is used by post-modern thinkers, particularly Emmanuel Levinas, *Totality and Infinity*, Alphonso Lingis, trans. (Pittsburgh, PA: Duquesne University Press, 1969).

2. The first real use of the label "New Mormon History" was by Robert B. Flanders, a historian of the Reorganized Church of Jesus Christ of Latter Day Saints. See his "Some Reflections on the New Mormon History," *Dialogue: A Journal of Mormon Thought* 9 (Spring 1974): 34-41, reprinted in this volume.

3. This "new history" has been promoted by a number of prominent RLDS historians. See, for example, Paul M. Edwards, "The New Mormon History," *Saints Herald* 133 (Nov. 1986): 12-14, 20. For an LDS apology, see Thomas G. Alexander, "Historiography and the New Mormon History: A Historian's Perspective," *Dialogue: A Journal of Mormon Thought* 19 (Fall 1986): 25-49; and compare his "Toward the New Mormon History," in *Historians and the American West*, Michael Malone, ed. (Lincoln: University of Nebraska Press, 1983), 344-86.

4. Non-Mormon supporters of New Mormon History include Mario S. DePillis, Lawrence Foster, and Jan Shipps.

5. Lawrence Foster, "New Perspectives on the Mormon Past,"

Sunstone 7 (Jan.-Feb. 1982): 41-45, reprinted with revisions in this volume.

6. Ibid., 42.

7. Ibid.

8. Ibid., 44.

9. Ibid., 41.

10. Ibid.

11. Ibid.

12. Ibid., 42.

13. Ibid.

14. Ibid., 44-45.

15. I am not implying that "New Mormon Historians" agree on everything; nor am I impugning their religious commitments. My point is simply to suggest that beneath their differences seems to exist a fundamental agreement on methodological postulates.

16. Leonard J. Arrington, "Scholarly Studies of Mormonism in the Twentieth Century," *Dialogue: A Journal of Mormon Thought* 1 (Spring 1966): 17-18.

17. James L. Clayton, "Does History Undermine Faith?" *Sunstone* 7 (Mar.-Apr. 1982): 34-36. See also Edwards, "The New Mormon History."

18. Foster, 42.

19. Ibid., 45. Here again I would like to avoid being accused of "lumping everyone together" under the rubric of positivism. Surely there are important differences which separate "New Mormon Historians," but when it comes to the fundamental framework of analysis and methodological procedures there seems to be agreement, at least according to my reading of their works. Readers interested in investigating the problems of positivism more extensively might begin with works listed under n31. For a short treatment, see Joseph Bleicher, *The Hermeneutic Imagination* (London: Routledge & Kegan Paul, 1982), chaps. 1 and 2.

20. See Philip L. Barlow, *Mormons and the Bible* (New York: Oxford University Press, 1991), xv. Here Barlow talks about "attain[ing] a certain level of objectivity." While rejecting talk of an absolute objectivity, he asserts that the concept retains meaning for him without advancing an argument to sustain that position at a more public level. Unfortunately, historians often similarly assert their opinion on foundational issues without also demonstrating or justifying their position. Barlow argues from effect to cause on page xvii, where he asserts—erroneously in my opinion—that nihilism is inherent in every argument against objectivity. But it is often the case that historians repeat statements they have heard others make without fully understanding the import of the claim. The question is resolved by Heidegger and Gadamer; see Kockelmans, *On the Truth of Being* (Bloomington: University of Indiana Press, 1984), 5-17.

21. Barlow, xvi-xvii. Note also a redefinition of objectivity by D. Michael Quinn, "Editor's Introduction," *The New Mormon History: Revisionist Essays on the Past* (Salt Lake City: Signature Books, 1992), vii-xix. Here Quinn introduces a kind of "functionalist objectivity" which seems to me to be an arbitrary and subjective standard that does not fit either the standards New Mormon Historians have used in this methodological debate over history or Quinn's own efforts to reestablish a common "functionalist" standard. Quinn's language, in particularly how he understands "truth," continues to betray a controlling objectivist metaphysics. In addition, he does not realize that even a "functionalist objectivity" needs to be grounded. If not, it risks appearing as another effort to elevate the claims of New Mormon History without dealing with more fundamental philosophical issues—for this is first a philosophical question and only second a historical one. On the other hand, Quinn's short essay does invite genuine discussion.

22. See Alexander, "Historiography and the New Mormon History." Some New Mormon Historians defend their approach by appealing to ingrained historicism which in the end presupposes a kind of hidden objectivism.

23. See Peter Novick, *That Noble Dream: The "Objectivity Question" and the American Historical Profession* (New York: Cambridge University Press, 1988), 379-80. This work contains a comprehensive discussion of the American historical establishment; also see Dominique LaCapra, *History and Criticism* (Ithaca, NY: Cornell University Press, 1985), chaps. 1 and 4.

24. Novick, 627-29. In the early 1980s I had everyday contact with well known historians writing secular accounts of the Mormon past. I was surprised at what seemed to be a lack of understanding of the problems of historical methodology whether raised from an ontological or epistemological perspective. All seemed dedicated disciples of the historical establishment, unaware of the challenges already being made by historians elsewhere who were less willing to conform to professional orthodoxy.

25. Thomas G. Alexander, "The Place of Joseph Smith in the Development of American Religion: A Historical Inquiry," *Journal of Mormon History* 5 (1978): 17.

26. Sterling M. McMurrin, "On Mormon Theology," *Dialogue: A Journal of Mormon Thought* 1 (Summer 1966): 136. I have difficulty in determining how such a position fits McMurrin's own way of understanding; see his *Religion, Reason, and Truth* (Salt Lake City: University of Utah Press, 1982), 1-19, esp. 17-19; also see Clayton, "Does History Undermine Faith?" 36.

27. Edwards, 12-14, 20. In few articles are objectivist terms so obviously used without any fundamental support to legitimate the author's point of view.

28. Foster, 43.

29. Sterling M. McMurrin, "Religion and the Denial of History," *Sunstone* 7 (Mar.-Apr. 1982): 48-49; republished in his *Religion, Reason, and Truth*, 133-44. In this essay McMurrin seems to take a rather strong position on objective methodology, yet in other places he qualifies his position in such a way that it is difficult to know where he stands.

30. This is because the idea of our historical past as a kind of static object detached from the historian and open for his or her inspection overlooks the historicity of the writing of history itself. It fails to take into account what Gadamer calls *Wirkungsgeschichte* or the ongoing effect of history at work in the historian's efforts to produce a history.

31. W. V. Quine, *Words and Objects*, D. Davidson and J. Hintikka, eds. (Dortretcht: Reidel, 1969), 221, 303-306. Richard Rorty, *Philosophy and the Mirror of Nature* (Princeton: Princeton University Press, 1979), 193-212; David Couzens Hoy, *The Critical Circle* (Berkeley: University of California Press, 1982), 20. For a more extensive treatment of the subject as well as the major sources used for the framing of the following arguments, see Imre Lakatos and Alan Musgrave, *Criticism and the Growth of Knowledge* (London: Cambridge University Press, 1976); Harold Morick et. al., *Challenges to Empiricism* (Belmont, CA: Wadsworth, 1972); Karl R. Popper, *The Logic of Scientific Conjectures and Refutations: The Growth of Scientific Knowledge* (Oxford: Oxford University Press, 1979); Thomas S. Kuhn, *The Structure of Scientific Resolutions*, 2d ed. (Chicago: University of Chicago Press, 1970); Frederick Suppe, The *Structure of Scientific Theories* (Urbana: University of Illinois Press, 1974); Carl G. Hempel, *Aspects of Scientific Explanation and Other Essays in the Philosophy of Science* (New York: Free Press, 1965); "Reason and Covering Laws in Historical Explanation," Sidney Hook, ed., *Philosophy and History* (New York: New York University Press, 1963); Ernst Nagel, *The Structure of Science* (London: Routledge & Kegan Paul, 1961); W. V. Quine and J. S. Ullian, *The Web of Belief* (New York: Random House, 1978).

It is my opinion that the most salient criticisms and alternative models can be found in the literature that deals with hermeneutics and deconstruction. See Martin Heidegger, *Being and Time*, John Macquarrie and Edward Robinson, trans. (New York: Harper and Row, 1962); Martin Heidegger, *Gesamtausgabe Die Grundprobleme der Phanomenologie*, vol. 24 (Frankfurt: Vittorio Klostermann, 1975); *Gesamtausgabe Beitrage zur Philosophie*, vol. 65 (Frankfurt: Vittorio Klostermann, 1975); Joseph J. Kockelmans, *On the Truth of Being* (Bloomington: Indiana University Press, 1984); Hans-Georg Gadamer, *Truth and Method* (New York: Continuum, 1975); *Philosophical Hermeneutics* (Berkeley: University of California Press, 1977); *Reason in the Age of Science*, Frederick G. Lawrence, trans. (Cambridge, MA: MIT Press, 1981); Maurice Merleau-Ponty, *Phenomenoligie de la Perception*

(Paris: Gallimard, 1945); Paul Ricoeur, *History and Truth* (Evanston, IL: Northwestern University Press, 1969); *Time and Narrative*, vol. 1 (Chicago: University of Chicago Press, 1983); Jurgen Habermas, *Knowledge and Human Interest* (Boston: Beacon, 1972); Adorno et al., *The Positivist Dispute in German Sociology* (New York: Harper Torchbooks, 1976); R. Bubner et. al., *Hermeneutik und Dialektik: Idealogiekritik* (Frankfurt: Suhrkamp, 1971); Josef Bleicher, *Hermeneutics as Method, Philosophy and Critique* (London: Routledge and Kegan Paul, 1980); also note an excellent book which reformulates Collingwood's ideas in even more powerful form, Rex Martin, *Historical Explanation* (Ithaca, NY: Cornell University Press, 1977). Probably Jacques Derrida, along with Gadamer, have done most to advance criticism inherent in Martin Heidegger, see Jacques Derrida, *Speech and Phenomena*, David B. Allison, trans. (Evanston, IL: Northwestern University Press, 1973); *Dissemination*, Barbara Johnson, trans. (Chicago: University of Chicago Press, 1981); *Margins of Philosophy*, Alan Bass, trans. (Chicago: University of Chicago Press, 1982); *Of Grammatology*, Gayatri C. Spivak, trans. (Baltimore: Johns Hopkins University Press, 1976). Certainly Foucault as a historian has shaped the language of objectivist criticism. A few of his more important works are *Madness and Civilization: A History of Madness in the Age of Reason*, R. Howard, trans. (New York: Vintage Books, 1973); *History of Sexuality*, vol. 1, Robert Hurley, trans. (New York: Random House, 1978); *The Order of Things: An Archaeology of the Human Sciences* (New York: Vintage Press, 1970). For an even more radical critique of objectivity from the point of view of the history of the other, see Levinas, *Totality and Infinity*.

32. Even in the beginning stages of constituting the record, staffs at libraries and archives carefully process received materials cataloging them in accordance with a taxonomy that anticipates what historians might want to see.

33. Paul Ricoeur, *Time and Narrative*, vol. 1 (Chicago: University of Chicago Press, 1983). In a sense, one should read the whole book to grasp the rich understanding of Historical Narrative that Ricoeur recovers for the reader, but most important is chap. 5, "In Defense of Narrative."

34. Ibid.

35. Karl Popper, *The Logic of Scientific Discovery* (New York: Harper Torchbooks, 1968), 97-120, 175-248.

36. See, for example, D. Michael Quinn, *Early Mormonism and the Magic World View* (Salt Lake City: Signature Books, 1987).

37. Among other places, see Robert Lindsey, *A Gathering of Saints: A True Story of Money, Murder, and Deceit* (New York: Simon and Schuster, 1988), 334-35.

38. Shipps, "The Mormon Past." Drawing from the work of Eliade,

Shipps tries to distinguish between "Ordinary" and "Sacred" history but at best only elevates "ordinary" history, which she apparently sees as recovering the objective truth about the Mormon past, and debases "sacred" history, which she sees as essentially mythological.

39. Malcolm R. Thorp, "Some Reflections on New Mormon History and the Possibilities of a 'New' Traditional History," *Sunstone* 85 (Nov. 1991): 39-48, reprinted in this volume.

40. Ibid., 39.

41. Ibid., 40.

42. LaCapra, *History and Criticism*, 18-20, 105.

43. Ibid., 20.

44. Ibid., 17.

45. Ibid., 41.

46. LaCapra., 31.

47. Novick., 11.

48. Ibid.

49. Thorp, 43-44. Thorp seems to want to define the Mormon community empirically in such a way that one need have no sense of conviction at all. Anyone who happens to have been born a Mormon or who might be interested in Mormon things would be a member. In this way Thorp avoids claims of a community that is unified by a common set of tenets and shared experiences of spiritual confirmation. For me, Thorp's position trivializes the meaning of genuine Mormon spirituality, reducing it to the status of a plaything in the grasp of secular discourse.

50. In "Historiography and the New Mormon History," Alexander seeks to defend the New Mormon History against detractors but, in my opinion, fails because of an inadequate understanding of historicism. He seems not to see that objectivism and positivism go hand in hand with historicist explanations—Marx, Freud, and modern structural-functionalism being obvious examples. He would have profited from James Faulconer and Richard Williams's excellent article, "Temporality in Human Action: An Alternative to Positivism and Historicism," *American Psychologist* 40 (Nov. 1985): 1179-88. See also their "More on Temporality," *American Psychologists* 42 (Feb. 1987): 197-199. Marvin Hill's "The 'New Mormon History' Reassessed in Light of Recent Books on Joseph Smith and Mormon Origins," *Dialogue: A Journal of Mormon History* 21 (Autumn 1988): 116-27. Here, Hill reviews a small number of books without addressing any of the fundamental problems of method.

15.
Some Reflections on New Mormon History and the Possibilities of a "New" Traditional History

Malcolm R. Thorp

IN THE LAST DECADE AN IMPORTANT DISCUSSION HAS OCCURRED ABOUT certain methodological assumptions underlying what has been called New Mormon History. This discussion has allowed historians to reflect on the ideas which underlie historical presentation, in spite of the fact that some of the discussion has been marred by personal attacks and strategies similar to sectarian pamphlet warfare. "The constructive task of the philosopher," said Oxford University philosopher of history Patrick Gardiner, "lies in sympathetic analysis rather than in justification and condemnation."[1]

David Bohn, a professor of political science at Brigham Young University, stands out as one of the most constructive critics in this debate. He has raised important considerations about the problems of objectivity.[2] He points out, "What the historian has access to is not the past but only texts and text analogues. The information they provide is fragmented, incomplete, unrepresentative, and ambiguous." Of course, it is an assumption that texts are "unrepresentative," but few historians would quibble with Bohn on these points.

Bohn's hermeneutic, which rejects the "false sense of legitimacy and rigor" found in objectivist historical accounts, is sensible.

But are historians as neolithic? To be sure objectivism is alive and well in American academia,[4] although serious reevaluation is already taking place within the discipline, but there are few "positivists" left, at least in the mainstream of the profession.[5] More important, Bohn's response to objectivist language in historical accounts represents an overreaction to a problem of some significance but perhaps not of the magnitude he would have us believe. Objectivism and its false grounding in a reality independent of the historian as creator cannot be defended on ontological grounds, but this still provides no reason for de facto rejection of such histories. Objectivist accounts still must be seriously considered on the basis of their contribution to the discussion and not summarily dismissed as methodologically defective.[6]

Most historians would also agree with Bohn that historical facts do not speak for themselves, for it is the historian who ultimately decides on the selection as well as the interpretation of sources.[7] While this may seem self-evident, some historians cling to entrenched ways of understanding history. Hans Kellner described this reluctance to acknowledge the flexibility of so-called "facts": "The historian's sources are, as we have been taught, those particles of reality from which an image of the past is made; while few historians object to the idea that histories are produced, most will assert that the guarantee of adequacy in the historical account is found in the sources. If the sources are available, scrupulously and comprehensively examined according to the rules of evidence, and compiled in good faith by a reasonably mature professional, the resulting work will more or less 'image' reality."[8]

Most practicing historians, even those who have abandoned the quest for historical certainties, will undoubtedly find difficulty with Paul Ricoeur's assertion (which Bohn ascribes to[9]) that history takes on the same characteristics as the novel.[10] Such an assertion does not take into proper consideration the extent to which historical arguments are shaped by textual readings, a point not always developed in theories comparing historical narratives to patterns of literary representation. The texts themselves remain important, even the dominant, determinants in historical construction, although there are also non-textual sources at work in writing history.[11] Kellner asserts that any story must arise out of an act of contemplation. "To understand history in this way is not to reject those works which make claims to realistic representation based upon the authority of documentary sources; it is rather to read them in a way that reveals that their authority is a creation effected with other sources, essentially rhetorical in character."[12] It logically follows that this resort to a-textual, rhetorical devices in the construction of narratives also applies (as we will see) to the methods of historical representation employed by traditional Mormon historians.

Bohn is also undoubtedly correct in pointing out the historian's use of models in the process of historical construction. No thinking can take place without such devices. According to him: "As historians begin to ask questions of the past, as they begin to craft their story, the very questions they ask and the very tools they use will in part determine how the past will be understood. As they introduce or accept an already existent chronology—cross-cutting categories of psychology, economy, politics, religion, culture, etc., and the related theories which map out those categories—the historian becomes more and more the creator of the past which will be remembered and not the midwife who lets the past tell its own story."[13]

Yet textual readings play a more significant role in historical construction than Bohn is willing to admit. Moreover, these "other sources" (models and literary strategies) likewise affect the outcome of traditional historical accounts, which are therefore not quite so "up front" in methodology as Bohn leads his readers to believe.[14] Traditional LDS historians might be more forthright in proclaiming the Restoration, but there is no recognition of the implicit objectivism of their works. Nor is there a comprehension of the rhetorical devises used in framing their narratives. The proclamation (*kerygama*) serves literary functions in such accounts and provides a sense of certainty to such histories that must be recognized as authorial perspectives and not necessarily historical reality.

What Bohn does not tell us is that the undercutting objectivist assumptions do not lead to a democratization of scholarship in which every man or woman is his or her own historian and every interpretation holds the same significance. Most historians would agree that there is not a single "right" interpretation of historical phenomena, since each account is conditioned by the situation of the interpreter and must include methodological and historiographical considerations. Still there will always be stronger and weaker formulations that will arise out of rigorous criticism of sources and the significance of interpretation.[15] Of course this process of evaluation is hardly new to historians. And as is also the current practice, historical accounts that stand out as insightful will be those which raise new and meaningful questions or which make available new or significantly different readings of familiar texts, thus carrying the discussion further.

The hermeneutical position developed by Hans-Georg Gadamer (which Bohn uses in his critique[16]) is an ecumenical endeavor aimed at clarifying the process in which understanding takes place. It is not an endeavor that creates battle lines between radically different approaches. As Gadamer says, mediation makes insightful sharing possible, thus throwing light on the conditions of understanding in all modes of thought.[17]

Bohn's definition of New Mormon History does not represent how these historians describe themselves. Indeed while some New Mormon Historians are products of the large American graduate schools, and obviously some of these scholars use models from the social sciences,[18] the *raison d'etre* of this approach lies elsewhere. New Mormon History arose out of new access to LDS sources in the 1950s and 1960s and an awareness of the possibilities for new questions and interpretations which were not possible within traditional approaches to the Mormon past. Indeed there was a feeling that traditional accounts, characterized by objectivist certainties, could no longer be entirely maintained and that many of the "truth claims" of this tradition contradicted archival sources. Thus what has characterized New Mormon History from its traditional counterpart has been the importance of texts and an openness in interpreting such sources for new ways of understanding the past.[19]

Bohn misses the point when he asserts that by asking new questions, New Mormon Historians were necessarily calling for "the wholesale abandonment of categories of self-understanding internal to the community in favor of a new set of standards external to the faith."[20] Bohn does not precisely explain what this "wholesale abandonment" is all about. Is he suggesting that such historians have denied the revelatory experience within the Mormon past? Simply stated, there is no evidence for this. Although pluralistic in composition, the general tenor of New Mormon Historiography has never been to destroy faith but to increase understanding of Mormon themes and experiences.

If Bohn is accusing historians of relying on external vocabulary and environmental explanations,[21] it can be argued that these have only enriched not diminished our understanding of the Mormon past. Mormonism did not arise *in vacuo*. It has always been seen as part of the American religious experience. Our understanding of the movement is conditioned by this obvious fact. Such categories as millenarianism, seeker, identity crisis, myth, primitivism, and even magic are not indigenous to Mormonism but are used by a wide variety of scholars, including traditionalists. In addition, one need not go far to find environmental explanations in support of the cause. Such an argument might be that social, political, and religious conditions made society "ripe" for the harvest by Mormon missionaries. To argue that Mormonism can be understood only through its own language, categories, and truth claims denies all possibilities of rational discussion.

Bohn further contends: "The head of the discussion rightly involves underlying assumptions and methodological commitments which determine the direction of historical inquiry, grounding the criteria by which questions are asked, theories selected, information is gathered, and conclusions are reached and validated." And all of this occurs, he argues, "in advance, before the historical record is even touched."[22] Here Bohn is half right. Tradition and methodology are determinants but not the only ones. Not a practicing historian himself, all this only demonstrates that Bohn has no practical understanding of how archival research is actually done by historians. He shows no comprehension of the possibility that scholars' minds are influenced by the texts they read, that new approaches are made possible by such readings which completely change the direction of one's thought and even break with previous historiographical assumptions.

Bohn's position, taken to a logical conclusion, rests on an anti-historical bias or at least on a low regard for the historian's craft. Consider, for example, this statement: "There is a strange fascination with the 'new' as opposed to the traditional, and a tendency to exaggerate the importance of recently discovered material against the preponderance of 'evidence' in the established record; thus, a line in a letter here, or a rumor written down there become the justification for a radical revision of traditional accounts." Historians are not the only ones to come under fire. Archivists are depicted as pandering to the whims of the historical profession, building collections and processing texts to please their trend-minded clientele.[23]

Any academic discipline is interested in recently discovered sources as well as in new interpretations of existing sources. This is hardly sinister. But do historians ignore the rigorous methods of textual criticism developed by their craft, and are they really collectively guilty of manipulating texts for their own self interest? This is a serious charge, but Bohn does not prove the case. Rather than provide allegations related to the role of historians in the Mark Hofmann forgeries,[24] clearly an exceptional case, Bohn should have provided concrete examples over a broad spectrum of writers to prove his point. To be sure there is shoddy work in history just as there are shoddy efforts in political science and philosophy.

His remarks suggest a certain nostalgia for the past, a fear that images from "the record" and "the story" will be destroyed by wolves in sheeps' clothing, hidden secularists ("cultural Mormons"), whose real intentions are to undermine traditions. These fears are hardly new. The only thing original is the strange connection to new critical methodologies, the purpose of which is to provide avenues for revisionism.

The traditional Mormon history has been aptly diagnosed by American historian Peter Novick. Using Thomas Kuhn's model of an internal paradigm, he describes how objectivist claims have become self-validating. Novick's concluding point was to raise the issue: Do New Mormon Historians really want to work within the confines of a contained objectivist paradigm with its narrow strictures and implicit authoritarianism?[25]

Bohn accuses New Mormon Historians of reaching conclusions before the examination of sources really begins. This is a more appropriate criticism when applied to traditional Mormon history, where the story line has been long established, and scholarly interpretation is concerned largely with finding props for an existing interpretation. Like such accounts, Bohn's version of history within the community of faith implies that there is "a story," which in itself presupposes that there is an objective, verifiable past.[26] The preservation of this story, with its authentic language and categories, constitutes his avowed purpose.

Bohn does not tell readers that this "story" was never brought down from Mount Sinai or revealed in a sacred grove but was crafted by scribes and early historians, including Willard Richards, George A. Smith, Wilford Woodruff, Orson F. Whitney, and B. H. Roberts. Like all historical writings, they reflect the age in which they were written, including positivist assumptions that were well entrenched in nineteenth-century American culture.[27] These early accounts are of historiographical value to us today, but they hardly represent the final word for historical understanding. Yet along with their twentiethcentury counterparts such as Joseph Fielding Smith's *Essentials of Church History* (1922), they continue to supply one of the "other sources" for traditional historical representation.

Because such traditional accounts tend to be repetitive, non-Mormon historian Lawrence Foster asserted that such histories are "boring," one way of saying that they are predictable.[28] Despite Foster's unfortunate choice of words, he never implied that the subject matter of interest to the believing Mormon community was either trivial or inconsequential.[29] Simply stated, Foster was asserting the obvious, that the bulk of traditional histories tend to depend on the same sources and do not cut new ground.[30] Consequently such accounts fail to open up new avenues for understanding.

Bohn's statement that traditional historians are more "honest" and "up front" than New Mormon counterparts is one of the most controversial aspects of the on-going debate.[31] In one sense, Bohn is correct. It is indeed easy to discover the ecclesiastical perspective of such writers. But in another sense he is wrong. Can he really claim that traditional historians have been as open and receptive to texts and the possibilities that are contained in such sources as their New Mormon counterparts have been? Is traditional Mormon history, either as now practiced or as Bohn would have it established, a serious encounter with the available texts bearing on the Mormon past? Bohn never really indicates what he would have traditionalists do with such sources—especially those not conforming to preconceived images of reality. It is one thing for Bohn to say that historical accounts should be "up front" and not be "public relations" jobs in which everything turns out "rosy."[32] It is quite another to argue for a dialogical encounter along the lines advocated by Gadamer in which a multi-perspective encounter with texts becomes the objective of scholarly interchange.

Nor does Bohn really explain who is to maintain historical standards within "the community of faith." Indeed how can historical purity be maintained within a church committed to precepts of human freedom and the right of individual choice? There will always be people who probe into discrepancies between the "faithful history" told by the closed community and discordant texts that inevitably make their way into our present world (memory holes have not yet been invented). Given the impossibility of such a task, perhaps the best solution is the present one: let historical pluralism flourish, recognizing that there never was "a story" but many stories open to a multiplicity of interpretations.

One may wonder, however, if Bohn's version would be satisfactory to Mormon traditionalists. Paradoxically his advocacy of history rising above image-making would be unsettling to some. For Bohn's version would not only exclude faith-promoting homilies but encourage probing into human cupidities, even in high places. It would also seemingly tie history to a doctrine of human nature, for in his view humankind displays a "general unwillingness" to choose the good and consequently to adhere to a moral life.[33] Of course this sounds suspiciously like Calvinism. Yet one of the attractive features of Mormonism has been its exalted view of humankind and the possibilities for eternal development.

The problem for the practicing historian is not so simple. Human activities are so mixed and muddled that history cannot be often described as a straightforward struggle between good and evil. This is especially true in dealing with collectivities such as nations and religious communities.[34] Thus to take but one example from the Mormon past, which Bohn raises, can the Mountain Meadows Massacre be seen from this simple right-versus-wrong paradigm, or would it be more appropriate to view this incident as a tragic predicament in which motives were so twisted and tangled on both sides that no mere historian will ever be capable of a moral assessment? All that is possible is for the historian to construct a narrative of events (recognizing even the finitude of this endeavor) based upon all the sources at his or her disposal.

Of course the idea of the historian as a moral judge has a long (and unfortunate) tradition. It was Lord Acton who most fully developed this attitude in the late nineteenth century. He took this task seriously, even to the point of asserting that we should weigh historical characters on the scales of justice, and if found wanting, they should be defamed for time immemorial as lasting examples for other reprobates. If the scales failed to tilt but remained at a position of equipoise, the individual should still be consigned to outer darkness so that firmness be shown, thus demonstrating a commitment to morality.[35] It is safe to say that few scholars today would want to delve into the murky waters of moral judgments. Most would undoubtedly agree with the admonition to judge nothing before its time (1 Cor. 4:4-5).

Perhaps the most problematic aspect of Bohn's model, however, is his advocacy of viewing history "as the stage upon which the power of God will pour forth to abolish in one last and final conflagration the confines of mortality and the forces of darkness."[36] Certainly millennial prophecies are part of Mormon beliefs, but one can reasonably ask why historians should be committed to futuristic projection (chiliastic or otherwise) when the subject matter of history is the past not the present or the future. Bohn's contention certainly suggests that somehow historians should know about how God has shaped the past and will shape the future. But how can one really know, for example, what role the Holocaust played in the divine scheme of history? Although it is acceptable to argue that God is in all human events, it is not for historians to assign divine significance to those events. Without resorting to wild historicist speculations, we can only say that God's purposes are woven into the texture of history even though this is invisible to mortal eyes.

We are left to wonder about the validity of Bohn's "otherworldly" approach: "the fundamental understanding which guides the faithful historian's reading of the historical record is always sure precisely because it does not derive from everyday discourse, but from genuine spiritual experience grounded in God's power to confirm and reveal truth."[37] Does this mean that all "inspired" historians will interpret the past the same way? If God reveals truths about the historical past to the faithful historian, is this not objectivism (revealed truth or "surety" about what actually happened)? If history can be written from the perspective of unambiguous revelation, why the need for rational discourse, including post-structural methodologies?

Indeed how does Bohn reconcile his advocacy of history as revelation with his espousal of post-structural methods? Bohn must realize that such approaches often lead to disturbing, even frightening results, far more unsettling than the rather calm, rational, soft objectivism of some New Mormon Historians. If historical studies are tied to post-structuralist methods such as Derridean deconstruction with its avowed purpose to tear apart structures of thought, reveal displacements in language, and question the effects of tradition on shaping interpretations, where will this lead Mormon studies? Using such a methodology, truth becomes multi-perspectival not mono-lithic—a fact that has bothered many in religious studies.[38] For in Derrida, interpretation becomes nothing more than a game or *jeu*.[39] Thus we find such results as Carl A. Raschke's statement: "Deconstruction is the dance of death upon the tomb of God; it is the tarantella whose footfalls evoke the archaism of the Great Mother, who takes back with the solemnity of the Pieta her wounded, divine son." He then continues into an area of contemporary concern to LDS church leaders: "Deconstruction, therefore, can be seen as a kind of Bacchic fascination with the metaphysics of decomposition and death, with the murky undercurrent of modern discourse; in this respect it serves as a simile for the return of the repressed feminine in the predominantly patriarchal academy."[40]

From the perspective of post-structural criticism, one would also have to concede the possibilities of Foucaultean probing into historical discontinuities in Mormon history as well as investigations into how structures of power have manipulated individuals.[41] It is not my purpose here to shock, only to suggest that these are real possibilities within such methodologies. Is Mormonism ready for this?

All language is essentially naturalistic (evolutionary) and historically situated. This indeed is at the root of one of the most serious problems in Bohn's essays. He assumes that because termi-nology employed by historians (and for that matter all other schol-ars) often originates from positivism and naturalistic disciplines, language use remains within the original mode of understanding. This is clearly not so. Language changes in meaning and context and hence in scholarly usage. Moreover the use of secular vocabu-lary does not necessarily presuppose any ontological grounds for belief or disbelief.[42]

If I were to use the term "myth" to describe Genesis 1, would this tell the reader anything significant about my religious convic-tions? One dictionary definition is "a commonly-held belief that is untrue, or without foundation."[43] But if I adopted Eliade's definition of myth (as does Jan Shipps),[44] this would likewise reveal only that I find such a concept useful to my understanding of Genesis. I could still be an atheist, an agnostic, or a theist. I could hardly be accused of dualism in thought (as Bohn accuses faithful LDS historians who write as professional historians).[45] There is no hidden ontological significance to my choice—other than confirming my belief in the value of models in human thought. Indeed I am no different than Bohn, who must also rely upon secular modes of understanding and language.[46]

This quest for discovering hidden meaning in language use is indeed disturbing. For example, Lawrence Foster stated that it was his purpose as a historian that "as much of the evidence as possible be investigated before conclusions are reached." He then explained that the perspectives one brings to historical inquiry only partially predetermine one's conclusions. He believes that the historian "who is sincerely interested in determining what happened in the past will continually test out different hypotheses and seek new evidence in attempting to explain and understand events." Foster has attempted to describe his research strategy, nothing more. On this flimsy pretext Bohn concludes that Foster is really a closet "soft positivist," that he believes the "facts" will prove the true past.[47] But Foster disavows such connections, which would seem to suggest that Bohn somehow knows Foster better than Foster knows himself. Certainly if Foster was a positivist, his article would contain references to either attempts to discover governing laws in history or statements concerning the historian's ability to recover the reality of the past. But we find neither.

According to Bohn, Foster and other New Mormon Historians "use methods, evolve categories, and develop explanations that presuppose objectivity."[48] Essentially Bohn's conclusions about Foster rest on an old logical fallacy: if A is found to exist, then it is *assumed* that B must exist.

However, Bohn is correct in his assertion that New Mormon Historians use the vocabulary of secular historiography and the underlying language of modern social sciences. But what other possibilities are there? Perhaps Bohn means that the imposition of models derived from the various humanistic disciplines somehow distorts the conceptualization of traditional stories. But he should be up front in recognizing that many of the same social science and environmental explanations are likewise used by traditional Mormon historians and apologists.[49]

Bohn assumes there exists an "other worldly" language and modes of understanding unique to Mormonism and unavailable to other traditions. In his view efforts at understanding LDS religious phenomena somehow become degraded if scholarly language and models are applied to Mormonism. In this he assumes a strange dualism which could be eliminated by realizing "The earth is the Lord's and the fullness therein" (1 Cor. 10:26).

Unfortunately Bohn never defines what a "community of faith" means. Instead he resorts to a rather vague metaphor about the "sacred" and the "profane," in which the profanators are seemingly the outsiders of the temple walls who look scornfully at proceedings within: "To be *outside the temple* is not to have access to that which is most sacred."[50] Presumably "sacred" history is to be written from the inner sanctum, and this accounts for why "secular" historians write about the Mormon experience as something merely human.[51] Certainly we might question if Gadamer, who does refer to communities of scholars with common methodological views, ever intended such communities to include only "true believers."

As we have observed, the purpose of hermeneutics is to make dialogical discussions possible between scholars of differing interests and approaches. Gadamer asserted that his version of textual explication demanded the suspension of faith as well as prejudice in order that the horizons of the text and that of the interpreter might come closer together.[52] Gadamer refers to the necessity of a "loss of self" which is crucial to theological hermeneutics. He compares hermeneutical understanding to a game in which each player "conforms to the game or subjects himself to it—that is, he relinquishes the autonomy of his own will. For example, two men who use a saw together allow the free play of the saw to take place, it would seem, by reciprocally adjusting to each other so that one man's impulse to movement takes effect just when that of the other man ends." Gadamer then goes on to say that "absorption into the game is an ecstatic self-forgetting that is experienced not as a loss of self-possession, but as the free buoyancy of an elevation above oneself."[53] Of course this applies to all of the traditions engaged in understanding the Mormon past. But it has special relevance to his argument because there is an explicit ecumenism in hermeneutical understanding that is apparently denied by Bohn and his counter-parts. Like the high priests of old who rigorously protected their own self-interest, those excluded from the temple of understanding would be all "secular" historians, cultural Mormons, and even faithful Latter-day Saints who do not understand Mormonism in quite the same way as Bohn or who use naughty language.[54]

I question whether this "community of faith" corresponds at all to the community one joins at the local chapel on Sunday. As demonstrated by a recent study, LDS wards are hardly monolithic communities of idealized Saints.[55] Rather they more often than not resemble a motley collection of human beings similar to the characters in John Bunyan's *Pilgrim's Progress*, some striving to reach the gates of the Heavenly City but many bogged down in life's problems along the way.

History cannot concern itself exclusively with the celestial but must move outside of the inner sanctum into the terrestrial world. For to believers in Providence, God reveals his purposes in all places and at all times.

Does Bohn's argument open up the possibilities for a New Faith-Promoting History? The answer must be an ambiguous one. He certainly suggests that the horizon of Mormon texts needs to be more fully understood. This would include transcendental experiences speaking to us in our present situation. This is an important point that should not be overlooked. Speakers from the past do carry messages of profound significance for us. They confirm the premise that God continually reveals truth to the church as well as to individuals. This does not mean that historians are not free to go beyond the textual horizon in their quest for understanding, but such messages deserve to be understood on their own terms.[56]

But Bohn does not apply his hermeneutic to a faithful history, at least not consistently. Traditional LDS history is based on the certainty of an objective past. By speaking of "a story," Bohn seemingly gives justification for this approach—but not for New Mormon versions of the story, some of which are likewise objectivist. What is even more confusing, however, is how he has also linked various modes of post-structural methodology with personal revelation as a method of textual explication. Bohn needs to explain how in practice he can advocate doing history by combining these seemingly incompatible elements into a workable synthesis.

NOTES

1. Patrick Gardiner, *The Nature of Historical Explanation* (Oxford: Oxford University Press, 1980), 24.

2. David Earl Bohn, "No Higher Ground," *Sunstone* 8 (May-June 1983): 26-32; "The Burden of Proof," *Sunstone* 10 (June 1985): 2-3; "Our Own Agenda," *Sunstone* 14 (June 1990): 45-49.

3. Bohn, "Burden of Proof," 2.

4. Peter Novick, *That Noble Dream* (Cambridge: Cambridge University Press, 1988).

5. For an example of continuing tradition of positivism in history, see Robert Fogel and G. R. Elton, *Which Road to the Past? Two Views of Scientific and Traditional History* (New Haven: Yale University Press, 1983). According to Novick, "The book constitutes a mutual nonaggression pact between two hitherto warring positivistic schools"; Novick, *That Noble Dream*, 610.

6. See, for example, Dominick LaCapra's critique of G. R. Elton's approach to sixteenth-century English history. Elton is considered to be the premier objectivist historian of his generation, and his handbook, *The Practice of History* (London: Fontana, 1969), stands out as the most significant practical defense of "soft positivism" among historians of today. LaCapra, the most forceful exponent of post-structural approaches to history in America, sees Elton's method as too restrictive and unresponsive to the demands of intellectual history. But otherwise he recognizes the importance (as well as the objectivist limitations) of Elton's work. See Dominick LaCapra, *History & Criticism* (Ithaca: Cornell University Press, 1985), 136-39.

7. One can also agree with Bohn that "the historian can only encounter the past from within history through his own time's way of understanding the past"; Bohn, "No Higher Ground," 27.

8. Hans Kellner, *Language and Historical Representation: Getting the Story Crooked* (Madison: University of Wisconsin Press, 1989), 9.

9. Bohn, "Our Own Agenda," 45.

10. Kellner, *Language and Representation*, 3-25, 325-33. He ultimately modifies Ricoeur by averring "the deepest respect for reality" but at the same time recognizing the function of rhetorical devices on the historical imagination. There is an interplay of both in historical representation.

Hayden White stands out as the most important American historian who attempts to impose literary models on historical writing. See *Metahistory: The Historical Imagination in Nineteenth-Century Europe* (Baltimore: Johns Hopkins University Press, 1973). For general reactions to White, see Novick, *That Noble Dream*, 624-25.

11. See Hayden White, *Tropics of Discourse: Essays in Cultural Criticism* (Baltimore: Johns Hopkins University Press, 1985), 121-34.

12. Kellner, *Language and Representation*, 10-11.

13. Bohn, "Our Own Agenda," 45.

14. Bohn, "No Higher Ground," 31.

15. David Couzens Hoy, *The Critical Circle: Literature, History, and Philosophical Hermeneutics* (Berkeley: University of California Press, 1982), 68-72.

16. Bohn, "No Higher Ground," n. 23, 32.

17. Hans-Georg Gadamer, *Truth and Method*, 2d rev. ed. (New York: Crossroad, 1990), xxiii.

18. Bohn seemingly ignores that his description would also characterize such traditional historians as Milton V. Backman and Richard Anderson as well as Hugh Nibley, who are all products of large American universities and who likewise apply models from the social sciences. Indeed is there a current intellectual writing on Mormon history who has completely avoided the use of such models?

19. For a useful summary of the historiography of New Mormon History, see Louis Midgley and David J. Whittaker, "Mapping Contemporary Mormon Historiography," book in progress; draft of 6 November 1990 is available in Special Collections, Harold B. Lee Library, Brigham Young University. Chapter 3 is an annotated bibliography of discussions on Mormon historiography since 1958.

20. See especially Bohn, "Our Own Agenda, 47-48.

21. Bohn asserts that secular historiography "has no vocabulary for authentic spiritual experience and no words for the genuinely divine." This flies in the face of the long tradition of biblical historical studies. Many of these scholars participate and publish in forums sponsored by Brigham Young University. See "Our Own Agenda," 47.

22. Bohn, "Burden of Proof," 3.

23. Bohn, "No Higher Ground," 47.

24. The one example used by Bohn to demonstrate this is the Mark Hofmann forgery affair. Bohn contends that the prosecution in the case found it difficult to persuade the New Mormon Historians to give up belief in the Hofmann forgeries. This was true at least until physical evidence on the forgeries was made available.

I was present at the BYU lecture given by George Throckmorton, a forensic document expert, in which he demonstrated how the Martin Harris "salamander" letter was shown to be a forgery. I discussed Throckmorton's presentation with my university colleagues, including a number of prominent New Mormon Historians. Not one scholar said that they still believed in the Hofmann forgeries, although questions were raised about why the FBI forensic experts earlier authenticated the document. Of course, historians were fooled by Hofmann, and this points to the need for more careful standards.

But this does not in itself prove that historians do not conscientiously try to be critical of their sources.

25. Peter Novick, "Why the Old Mormon Historians Are More Objective than the 'New,'" typescript of address given at the Sunstone Symposium, 23-26 Aug. 1989, Salt Lake City, Utah.

26. Bohn, "Our Own Agenda," 46.

27. See Howard Clair Searle, "Early Mormon Historiography: Writing the History of the Mormons 1830-1858," Ph.D. diss., University of California at Los Angeles, 1979; David Bitton and Leonard J. Arrington, *Mormons and their Historians* (Salt Lake City: University of Utah Press, 1988).

28. Lawrence Foster, "New Perspectives on the Mormon Past," *Sunstone* 7 (Jan.-Feb. 1982): 41-45; also in this compilation.

29. Foster's lampooning efforts were not an attack on revelatory experience. He merely questions the relevance of all such information.

30. An excellent example of this is in V. Ben Bloxham, James R. Moss, and Larry C. Porter, eds., *Truth Will Prevail: The Rise of the Church of Jesus Christ of Latter-day Saints in the British Isles 1837-1987* (Cambridge: Cambridge University Press for the Corporation of the President of the Church of Jesus Christ of Latter-day Saints, 1987). Chapters 3-5, the crucial chapters in early Mormonism in the British Isles, were largely written from printed sources such as Orson F. Whitney and the compilations of Andrew Jensen. The archival sources behind such stories were never consulted, nor were a wealth of material from diaries, journals, and reminiscences.

31. Bohn, "No Higher Ground," 31.

32. Bohn, "Our Own Agenda," 46.

33. Bohn, "No Higher Ground," 46.

34. Reinhold Niebuhr, *Moral Man in Immoral Society: A Study in Ethics and Politics* (New York: Scribner's, 1932).

35. See Herbert Butterfield, *The Whig Interpretation of History* (New York: Norton, 1965), 107-32.

36. Bohn, "Our Own Agenda," 46.

37. Bohn, "Burden of Proof," 3.

38. See Kath Filmer, "Of Lunacy and Laundry Trucks: Deconstruction and Mythopoesis," *Literature and Belief* 9 (1989): 55-64. This entire issue is devoted to new methodologies and belief.

39. Hoy, *Critical Circle*, 83.

40. Carl A. Raschke, "The Deconstruction of God," in Thomas J. Altizer, et al., *Deconstruction and Theology* (New York: Crossroad, 1982), 28-29.

41. For an introduction to this approach, see Raul Rabinow, ed., *The Foucault Reader* (New York: Pantheon Books, 1984).

42. A good example of such thinking is provided by Gary F. Novak, who in assessing Marvin S. Hill's studies on early Mormon origins has

"discovered" hidden sources of "atheism" in Hill's remarks: the "models from the social and behavioral sciences from which Hill draws—social stress theories of revelation, the cultural connections of teachings in the Book of Mormon with the Calvinism of Joseph's immediate environment—all involve implicit assumptions about such questions as the existence of God." Rather than atheism, such lines of reasoning can only be described as a *non sequitur*. See "Naturalistic Assumptions and the Book of Mormon," *Brigham Young University Studies* 3 (Summer 1990): 33 and passim.

43. *Chambers Concise 20th Century Dictionary* (Edinburgh: W & R Chambers, 1985), 640.

44. Jan Shipps, "The Mormon Past: Revealed or Revisited?" *Sunstone* 6 (Nov.-Dec. 1981): 55-58.

45. Bohn, "Our Own Agenda," 49, n. 17.

46. Hayden White has written, "Historical events, whatever else they may be, are events which really happened or are believed really to have happened, but which are no longer directly accessible to perception. As such, in order to be constituted as objects of reflection, they must be described, and described in some kind of natural or technical language." Hayden White, "New Historicism: A Comment," in *The New Historicism*, ed. H. Aram Veeser (London: Routledge, 1989), 297.

47. Lawrence Foster, letter, in Readers' Forum, *Sunstone* 8 (Nov.-Dec. 1983): 4-5; Bohn, "Burden of Proof," 2.

48. Bohn, "Burden of Proof," 2.

49. See for example, Milton V. Backman, Jr., *The Heavens Resound: A History of the Latter-day Saints in Ohio 1830-1838* (Salt Lake City: Deseret Book, 1983). Backman uses such terminology from the social sciences as seekers, primitive Christianity, revolution, as well as economic models and environmental explanations for persecution and internal dissent. This in no way casts aspersions on Backman's book but demonstrates that even traditional writers cannot (and should not) avoid such categories and modes of explanation.

50. Bohn, "Our Own Agenda," 47.

51. The basic meaning of profane seems to mean to desecrate or defile such things as the altar, the Sabbath, the sanctuary, and the name of God. It also has the more modern meaning of showing contempt for sacred things. Can it be argued that collectively New Mormon Historians have really shown contempt for sacred things? Is there evidence that New Mormon Historians argue that LDS history is "merely human"? Thus the appropriateness of Bohn's analogy of sacred and profane must be questioned.

52. Gadamer, *Truth and Method*, 277-307. Also germane to this discussion is Gadamer's contention concerning the possibilities of historical understanding of the New Testament and its authors. He maintains that the

kerygmatic meaning of the New Testament "cannot ultimately contradict the legitimate investigation of meaning by historical science." See Hans-Georg Gadamer, *Philosophic Hermeneutics* (Berkeley: University of California Press, 1976), 209-11.

53. Gadamer, *Truth and Method*, 51-56.

54. See especially Bohn, "Our Own Agenda," 49n17. He asserts, "Some committed historians seek to resolve the dilemma by clearly stating in advance that they accept the truth claims of the Church. Although this brings the dilemma to the reader's attention, it does not resolve it. In the measure that the historians rely on naturalistic language to account for fundamentally prophetic phenomena, they will offer explanations which are essentially at odds with the claims of the Church. As a result, the believing historian is forced to compartmentalize his understanding of the Church into seemingly unbridgeable categories of the *spiritual*, accepted on the basis of faith, and the secular, rooted in naturalist explanation." This becomes a serious matter, because he is suggesting that this is sinful (making statements at odds with the claims of the Church) to use naturalistic language to describe religious experience. Of course naturalistic language is commonly used in discourse through the church and is rooted in all human language. Perhaps what is needed is a new vocabulary (God-speak, perhaps) to keep us from such pharisaic sins.

55. See Stan L. Albrecht, "The Consequential Dimension of Mormon Religiosity," *Brigham Young University Studies* 29 (Spring 1989): 57-108.

56. For an approach that is critical of historians who "mine" texts for "facts" and advocates a broader, dialogical reading, see LaCapra, *Rethinking Intellectual History*, and his *History of Criticism* (Ithaca: Cornell University Press, 1985).

16.
Historiography of the Canon

Edward H. Ashment

IN CONTRAST TO OTHER PROTESTANT CHRISTIAN PRIMITIVISTS, JOSEPH Smith taught that the Bible was not inerrant and that appeal to scripture was not the final authority. Instead the Bible had been corrupted by "the great and abominable church," which removed "many parts which are plain and most precious" in order to "pervert the right ways of the Lord, that they might blind the eyes and harden the hearts" of men and women (1 Ne. 13:24-27).[1] To remedy this Smith announced that God had chosen him as a prophet to reopen the heavens after nearly two thousand years of silence. Smith said that "God ministered to him by an holy angel," who gave him "commandments which inspired him" and empowered him to produce the Book of Mormon, which "contains . . . the fulness of the gospel of Jesus Christ" (D&C 20:6). Smith hoped that the Book of Mormon would enlarge the canon of scripture, chiding objectors as "fool[s], that shall say: A Bible, we have got a Bible, and we need no more Bible"; just because God produced one book, the Bible, it did not mean that he could not produce more, because his "work is not yet finished" (2 Ne. 29:6, 9).

Shortly after publication of the Book of Mormon in March 1830, Smith's second canonical project was to correct errors and omissions in the Bible. His initial efforts provided the majority of textual "restorations." These changes demonstrated Smith's belief in a primordial Christianity first revealed by God to Adam and reflected an effort to legitimize the Book of Mormon and Smith's own prophetic vocation. But this ambitious undertaking soon dwindled to little more than minor corrections.[2]

Smith declared that many more ancient records would come to light as part of the "restoration of all things." For example, he promised that Oliver Cowdery would translate "records that contain much of [the] gospel"—those parts of the "scriptures which have been hidden because of iniquity" (D&C 6:26; cf. 8:1; 9:2). He announced that Warren Parrish would "see much of [the Lord's] ancient records, and shall know of hiden things, and shall be endowed with a knowledge of hiden languages."[3] The enthusiasm with which Smith welcomed the arrival of Michael Chandler and his mummies and papyri in Kirtland, Ohio, the Reverend Caswall with his Greek Psalter in Nauvoo, Illinois, and the Kinderhook plates, also in Nauvoo, reflect Smith's promises and early Mormons' consequent anticipation of more and more of God's ancient records coming to light.[4]

But he produced little. Oliver Cowdery wrote in the December 1835 *Messenger and Advocate* that Smith's third translation project, an exposition of the contents of Egyptian papyri, which contained the book of ancient Abraham, could result in large volumes.[5] But the project was virtually abandoned by 1836, and Smith's vocation changed from restorer of God's ancient records to builder of God's kingdom on earth.[6] Thereafter he spent only a day and a half producing ancient scripture even though his followers' enthusiasm to receive more of God's hidden truths remained high. He decided that it would be too much to produce another book and opted instead to publish installments of his interpretations of ancient papyri. Three installments appeared in Nauvoo in the *Times and Seasons* in 1842. Smith promised to publish more from time to time, but he never did.[7]

By the time of Smith's murder in 1844, only the first of the three scriptural projects—the Book of Mormon—had been accepted as canon by Mormons. Thereafter different paths to canonization were pursued. The Reorganized Latter Day Saint church published Smith's Inspired Version of the Bible in 1866 and authoritatively endorsed it as canon in 1878.[8] They never canonized the Book of Abraham. In contrast the Utah-based Latter-day Saint church never canonized Smith's Bible but in 1880 did canonize a small portion which had been included in the already published Pearl of Great Price. The Book of Abraham was canonized in the same process.[9] A century later the Utah church intercalated extracts from the Inspired Version into their scriptural apparatus cross reference system, thus indirectly giving it canonical status.[10]

The belief that more books could be added to the canon has continued in Mormonism and become one of its most exciting and controversial calling cards. Since Joseph Smith's death, however, the opening in the heavens has become more restricted. While the Reorganized LDS church has continued to add revelations to its Doctrine and Covenants, only four revelations and two "Official Declarations" produced since Smith's lifetime have been canonized by the Utah church.[11]

Much of the recent controversy over historiography in the LDS community has revolved around questions about the historicity of these canonized books. Mormonism's premier apologist, Hugh Nibley, issued the challenge for scrutiny of the canonized restored records which Smith produced: to test the "main hypothesis" of the Book of Mormon, that it "contains genuine history"[12]; to evaluate the historicity of the Book of Abraham and Smith's claim that it is an actual "TRANSLATION of Some ancient Records that have fallen into our hands, from the Catecombs of Egypt."[13] This hypothesis is based on the proposition that Smith's "work was divinely inspired."[14] Brigham Young University political scientist Louis Midgley added that the "primary issue" for Mormon studies is "a combination of two related questions: Was Joseph Smith a genuine seer and prophet, and is the Book of Mormon true? If either one or the other is true, because both are linked, the truth of the other is thereby warranted."[15]

Historians and others have taken up these challenges to consider canonized texts in the context of history. But the apologetic formulation of the relevant questions frames the issue in an impossible way. It requires presuppositions which would automatically disqualify any historical inquiry and thereby nullify conclusions that historical analysis might arrive at. As one scholar has explained, it represents "an attempt to resolve a nonempirical problem by empirical means" by "framing . . . a question which cannot be resolved before the researcher settles some central metaphysical problem."[16] In other words, one must first answer the question "Was Joseph Smith a prophet of God?" before historical research can proceed.

Christianity has struggled with issues raised by its canon, the Old and New Testaments, which are not unlike those encountered by Mormon theologians. Christianity accepted as genuine, inspired, and binding only certain books written by ancient Jews and early Christians. That list of books became known as the canon of scripture, the Bible of today, and assumed the position of an encyclopedic constitution governing all knowledge, belief, and action.[17] Those books in the canon known as the Apocrypha, which seemed to buttress the authority and some of the doctrines of the Catholic church, were jettisoned by the Protestant Reformation, in part so that Protestantism would not be bound by Catholic claims.[18] While still affirming the "sole right of the Church to interpret the Bible," the Catholic church eventually reduced the Apocrypha to semi-canonical status.[19] The Christian canon was thus reduced and remained "closed" or limited until Joseph Smith's affirmation that the Christian encyclopedia could be amended.

Canon makes certain historical claims on Christians. As Van Harvey has pointed out in his book, *The Historian and the Believer: The Morality of Historical Knowledge and Christian Belief,* many believers may doubt the historicity of such "stories of floating axes, suns standing still, asses talking, blood raining from heaven, supernatural births, [and] walking on water," but they insist absolutely that the unique event of the resurrection of Jesus is a historical "fact." But that "fact" is really a conclusion which does not follow from the usual historiographic methodology of collecting data and arguing from generalizations based on consistently observed data. It is a conclusion about a totally unique event which can be "grasped only in faith."[20]

Mormons can have a similar relation to their own distinctive canon. They may doubt the historicity of such claims as non-tarnishing, forever incorruptible brass plates anachronistically representing an already established Old Testament canon as early as 600 BCE[21]; shining stones in ancient semi-submarines; a magic compass which worked only for the righteous; archaeologically unverifiable civilizations; botanically unverifiable animals; linguistically unverifiable languages in the pre-Columbian New World; and the existence of an autobiographic papyrus of ancient Abraham in their church's vault.

But in addition to Jesus' resurrection, Mormons insist absolutely on further unique events, "facts" also to be grasped only through faith: God and Jesus actually appeared to Joseph Smith; Smith really was visited by an angel named Moroni, who revealed to him an authentic, ancient history of America's pre-Columbian inhabitants; Smith dictated an English version of this history to scribes and published it; and God inspired Smith to render in English an autobiographic document written by ancient Abraham when he was in Egypt.

According to Harvey, historiographic methodology is "based on assumptions quite irreconcilable with traditional belief. If the theologian regards the Scriptures as supernaturally inspired, the historian must assume that [they are] intelligible only in terms of [their] historical context and [are] subject to the same principles of interpretation and criticism that are applied to other ancient literature. If the theologian believes that the events of the [scriptures] are the results of the supernatural intervention of God, the historian regards such an explanation as a hindrance to true historical understanding. If the theologian believes that the events upon which Christendom rests are unique, the historian assumes that those events, like all events, are analogous to those in the present and that it is only on this assumption that statements about them can be assessed at all. If the theologian believes on faith that certain events occurred, the historian regards all historical claims as having only a greater or lesser degree of probability, and he regards the attachment of faith to these claims as a corruption of historical judgment."[22]

In other words, "History of religions cannot make pronouncements about God, His existence or His nature. The word revelation does not fit in with its terminology." As a result, "there is a marked difference between history of religions and theology in the way in which they deal with religious values. The theologian ultimately assumes a personal attitude towards religious values. The historian of religions acknowledges the existence of religious values and tries to understand their significance. But his method should be completely free from any value judgement."[23] Otherwise historians end up exempting their own theological system from the rigorous analysis used to scrutinize other systems and thus indulge in "special pleading."

However, this does not mean that the historian of religion must exempt theology as an object of study. As one scholar has argued, "a prime object of study for the historian of religion ought to be theological tradition, taking the term in its widest sense, in particular, those elements of the theological endeavor that are concerned with canon and its exegesis," at the same time "bracketing any presuppositions as to its character as revelation" from which "the historian of religion must abstain."[24]

The problem that theologians have with historiography is that it brackets the elements of faith and revelation—the cornerstones on which believers rest their unique facts. Midgley discusses the source of this conflict from the perspective of the believer: "The primary source of the present crisis of faith is the appropriation by some historians of competing or conflicting ideologies that began to dominate the thinking of educated people beginning with the Enlightenment. The crisis is rooted in conflict between the substance of Mormon faith, especially the prophetic claims upon which it rests, and certain of the dominant ideas found in the secular culture. Prophetic claims appear questionable, if not absurd, from the perspective of secular modernity, which also provides the ideological grounds of both rival explanations of the faith, and competing secular accounts of the meaning of life."[25]

To enter the debate and "attempt to vindicate the truth of the sacred narrative," the apologist "could no longer appeal to the eye of faith or to any special warrants."[26] But Mormon apologists, according to this articulation by Gary Novak, regard such a position as threatening: "For example, one cannot find anything like an appeal to 'facts' in any scriptural chronicle; the scriptural chronicles are written under an entirely different set of assumptions from those that govern modern histories. The appeal to 'facts' by modern historians is often symptomatic of positivism or historical objectivism, serving as a vehicle to subtly transform the faith and erode memory. Much of the New Mormon History is written in such a way as to exclude or bracket what scripture understands as the mighty acts of God. These mighty acts are precisely what are essential for the collective memory of the Saints."[27]

In other words, by submitting the Book of Mormon and the Book of Abraham to historical inquiry, historiography reduces their claims of uniqueness to the same level on which Mormons have already placed the unique claims of the rest of Christianity and other world religions, which they do not consider to be inspired. For an objectivist apologist such as Midgley, the consequences of such thinking to the Mormon canon is that the Book of Mormon "when viewed as a fictional or mythical account, and not as reality, no longer can have authority over us or provide genuine hope for the future. To treat the Book of Mormon as a strange theologically motivated brand of fiction, and in that sense as myth, is to alter radically both the form and content of faith and thereby fashion a new 'church' in which the texts are told what they can and cannot mean on the basis of some exterior ideology. To reduce the Book of Mormon to mere myth weakens, if not destroys, the possibility of it witnessing to the truth about divine things. A fictional Book of Mormon fabricated by Joseph Smith, even when his inventiveness, genius, or inspiration is celebrated, does not witness to Jesus Christ but to human folly. A true Book of Mormon is a powerful witness; a fictional one is hardly worth reading and pondering."[28]

In this objectivist view "the faithful" would be allowed to "abandon the questions of whether there was a Lehi colony with whom God made a covenant, . . . whether Jesus was resurrected or whether angels visited Joseph Smith."[29] Such fears help to explain why Mormon theologians regard historiography as inimical when it is applied to their dogma. They perceive history as attempting to destroy their house of faith. And because they have objectivistically identified their own perspective so completely with what is "True," they sometimes regard alternative perspectives as attacks against that truth and their advocates as deluded and enemies of God. Thus they often frame part of their response in *ad hominems*, for they feel compelled to defend what they believe has been attacked by those they perceive as enemies.[30]

The conflict between historians and theologians which has surfaced in Mormonism is not a new one. It has been staged in various guises already in the larger context of Christianity. That battle can provide a useful context for the Mormon controversy.

Mormon apologists have focused on the Enlightenment as the period when history writing went awry.[31] This has traditionally been the strategy of conservative Christians as well. The choice of the Enlightenment is no accident. Before the Enlightenment, as historians of religion have pointed out, one morality of knowledge prevailed in which "professional historians were ordinarily cast as story-tellers who were defenders of the faith. . . . Most were called, if they were Catholic, to summon events from the past to certify the truth of Catholicism over against Protestantism. Needless to say, vice versa."[32]

In contrast the Enlightenment introduced a new morality of knowledge which is similar to that of today's scholarly world. One of its major accomplishments was what one scholar has termed its "establishing once and for all the methodological priority of historiography as an instrument of liberation and a principle of interpretation."[33] One of the results of this shift, according to another scholar, was that "religion was domesticated; it was transformed from pathos to ethos. At no little cost, religion was brought within the realm of common sense, of civil discourse and commerce. [Its] impulse was one of tolerance and, as a necessary concomitant, one which refused to leave any human datum, including religion, beyond the pale of understanding, beyond the realm of reason."[34] Consequently historians could not make a special exemption of their own religion from historiographic method while at the same time subjecting all others to rigorous analysis.

Thus the Enlightenment was what one scholar has called a "declaration of independence against every authority that rests on the dictatorial command, 'Obey, don't think.'"[35] Theologians who demand unquestioning obedience not surprisingly support the trend to "dismiss the Enlightenment as intellectually and morally bankrupt"[36] or to "destroy its values and drive out its way of dealing with biblical materials."[37]

While making a special exemption for their own objectivism about the Truth of traditional claims,[38] some Mormon apologists adopt a deconstructionist strategy when it serves their purpose and label modern historians as "positivists" and "historicists." For example, one apologist asserts that "it is a crude and now rather widely rejected *positivism* that assumes that there is much of anything evident apart from theories, assumptions, or formal or informal pre-understandings," because those "familiar with the discussions of historical method" believe that these prejudgments "are necessarily brought to texts by the exegete or historian."[39] Further, the "positivist" historians of Mormonism have been slow to understand how discredited their method has become.[40] Another apologist objectivistically inveighs against what he terms an "empirical religion" of historians that he feels is hostile to "objective, propositional revelations from God or objective knowledge of future events" to which the Holy Spirit serves as "a witness."[41]

Thus Mormon objectivist apologists attempt to neutralize what they term the "revisionist history" of Mormonism. They claim that historiography is attempting to nullify traditionally unique Mormon historical-theological claims and reduce the theology of the Utah church to the status of the RLDS church, which now, thanks to its own revisionists, retains only "remnants" of its traditional faith. Thus today's historians of Mormonism would revise out of existence the traditional LDS church.[42]

Modern historiographical methodology is neither positivistic nor objectivistic. But because Mormon apologists rely so heavily on identifying historiography with positivism, it is important to consider how historiographic methodology evolved. According to Norman F. Cantor and Richard I. Schneider in *How to Study History*, historical process traditionally was considered "intrinsic in history" itself. As a result, no one focused on historians, who were regarded simply as the ones "to recognize and describe the inner reality that produced historical change." Classical writers "believed that history moved in ever-recurring cyclic patterns and that a process of growth and decay was the ultimate historical reality." Thus from the fourth to the eighteenth century it was widely believed that divine providence was the inner reality "that moved history." The primary effect of the Enlightenment was to separate that inner reality from the church.[43]

Still imbued with the notion that process was intrinsic in history, the nineteenth-century philosopher Hegel thought that he identified "an objective causal reality inside the process of history itself, a 'spirit' that moved inexorably forward." Philosophers spent the rest of the century developing an explanatory metaphysics and portraying "in various ways the historical reality" that they "assumed to exist outside the mind of the historical observer and beneath the surface of facts and to impel history forward to a goal of glory or damnation." But at the end of the nineteenth century, "doubt set in as to the ability of the human mind to get outside of itself and to focus upon a final and causal reality that stood over and against individual human minds." The resulting relativism, according to Cantor and Schneider, held that "Historical process was not an objectified reality: it was the act of thinking and writing itself. Historians did not discover history: they created it." Consequently, the question of what constitutes fact has become the "central focus of the philosophy of history since 1900."[44]

Relativism had, explain Cantor and Schneider, "reached extreme proportions" by the 1930s with Becker and Beard proclaiming "respectively that every man was his own historian and that writing history was simply an act of faith."[45] The terrible consequences of the extreme historical views of Nazis and Communists forced philosophers of history to again reconsider such a position.[46] The deconstructionism of today is a fossil of that extreme relativist school of thought—Allan Bloom has described it as "the last, predictable, stage in the suppression of reason and the denial of the possibility of truth in the name of philosophy."[47] Interestingly one Mormon apologist acknowledges that his post-philosophical "radical hermeneutics" are "deconstruction."[48]

According to Cantor and Schneider, today's historiography represents a "middle ground" between the ancient belief in the "absolute truth of history and the recent extreme relativism." Today's "historical analysis does follow 'probablistic' rules about human conduct," and "the historian employs a reasonable process of explanation and logic."[49]

In embracing relativistic arguments, Mormon apologists align themselves with conservative Christian apologists who employ similar strategies. Van Harvey identifies several Christian apologetic arguments—arguments which sound familiar to those acquainted with the current controversy in Mormonism:

1. Apologists accuse historians of "surrendering the [scriptural] conception of faith," while accepting a "naive philosophy of history" protected "by invoking the sanctity of intellectual integrity."

2. To apologists the central issue is "God's supernatural action in certain historical events," without which "the whole Christian edifice would be found to be built on sand" if those events did not occur "in the way they were reported."

3. Apologists employ the relativistic argument that "all interpretation presupposes some criteria, some principles of interpretation," which ultimately "reflect the faith-perspective of the historian."

4. Apologists accuse historians of not perceiving that "there is no impersonal objective standpoint; that disbelief, with its corresponding doubt about miracles, is not derived from an impartial study of the records but is itself based upon a faith-principle, albeit a positivistic and secular one."

5. Apologists insist that one must receive "some prior enlightening of the eyes of the mind before either the facts or their meaning can be seen in the true perspective." From a Mormon perspective, that would mean that only people with a testimony of the truth of Mormonism can truly understand Mormon history.

6. Apologists claim that miracles are matters of faith and are undetectable by scientific means. To assert otherwise is "to be committed to the view that the only forces in the universe are those [that] science can describe," which is "a metaphysical not a scientific belief."[50]

Addressing the apologetic claim that "historical narrative is necessarily selective" and thus the historian's selection of data "presupposes the interests, values, and beliefs of the historian," Harvey observes that such relativism "assumes that selection always involves distortion, that interest and purpose are necessarily antithetical to objectivity." He points out, however, that such assumptions require an impossible ideal: that the historian "should reproduce the past in the way some divine observer with no interests and purposes would." In other words the apologist maintains that the historian should "reproduce the past as it really was," which of course is how the apologist's "traditional history" and "traditional theology" already reproduce it. Thus historiography—selecting data according to its naturalistic presuppositions—can never be objective and can only distort what the apologist already knows by faith to be God's objective and true perspective "against which all human answers are measured and found wanting."[51]

Harvey regards the apologist's claim that a "historian's deepest convictions will dictate what and how he will write about the past" as both true and misleading. He acknowledges this is true "in the obvious sense that no scholar is apt to spend much time or labor studying that in which he has no real interest, although some doctoral dissertations seem to be exceptions to this truism." But it is misleading in the sense that one may be interested in something generally, without committing to it. Moreover, if as the apologist claims "historians cannot be objective in matters where their deepest convictions are at stake," then "we should generally distrust the work of [sectarian] scholars because their deepest convictions are obviously at stake in the inquiry."[52]

Perspectivistic apologetics does not recognize a difference between "explanation and the justification of [that] explanation, between getting into the position to know something and defending what we have come to know, between why we want to know something (psychology) and the grounds (logic) that can be given for saying that we know." The question is not "whether historians can be objective, but whether some selective judgments" about the past "are more entitled to credence than others"; whether self-transcendence is possible, which means that people can "arrive at unpleasant truths . . . at judgments which run counter to their treasured hopes and desires." On the one hand the apologist denies that possibility for the historiographer but assumes it for his or her own position.[53] After basing their case against historiography on relativism, apologists argue positivistically that their own perspective "is the true one because it enables us to see the facts as they really are," and their conclusion is not based on empirical argument but on faith and revelation.[54] Consequently they are convinced that their perspective is above rational evaluation.

What they fail to acknowledge is that nearly 21,000 other sectarian perspectives would thus be above rational evaluation too, and all other denominations would be as true as theirs, which of course they cannot accept. In other words, historians of Mormonism must accept Mormon Truth claims. In like manner, historians of Catholicism must accept Catholic Truth claims and the Catholic Holy Spirit as a reliable indicator of those claims, which of course would automatically nullify Mormon Truth claims. The same must obtain for historians of Eastern Orthodoxy, Lutheranism, and the remainder of the almost 21,000 Christian denominations. Since it would not be possible for historians of religion to write about other religions or denominations without accepting *their* Truth claims, no historian of one perspective could critically analyze another perspective with any validity because he or she would have to accept the latter's Truth claims which of course would naturally be self-validating of the other perspective. Historiographers would be turned back into pre–Enlightenment "story-tellers" or "defenders of the faith" called by the church "to summon events from the past" and write "faith-promoting history."

Harvey identifies the core idea of perspectivist apologetics as "the claim that it is meaningless to make a distinction between fact and interpretation in history," because "there can be no true historical understanding of [scripture] which is not also devotional, or religious, or theological."[55]

But there are facts in history that are separate from interpretation. Harvey points to police files and scientific notebooks that are full of facts "that we simply are unable to interpret in any meaningful way" and "the unintelligible cuneiform tablet, the discovery of a third-century Roman coin in a first-century ruin, the discovery of a diary that contradicts a widely accepted version of an event. All these require interpretation. They are facts in search of a meaning, so to speak." Moreover, "fact" is an important word in historiography because it draws attention to intentional and unintentional data. Intentional data reflect conscious intent. Unintentional data refer to "those types of things that witness to something in spite of themselves, so to speak, and that may be the basis for an interpretation quite foreign to the conscious intention of the author of a document. It is significant that historians rely far more on unintentional than intentional data."[56]

Mormon apologists focus almost exclusively on the intentional data of the Book of Mormon and the Book of Abraham, but the examination of unintentional data has led some historians to question the ancient historicity of those documents. Thus one apologist accuses historians of simply "jettisoning the traditional understanding of the Book of Mormon." He fears the specter raised by considering unintentional data: "without a real Lehi colony, how could there have been a real resurrected Nephite angel who later visited with Joseph Smith, or real plates, all of which are part of the controlling narrative of the Mormon faith."[57]

Harvey points to the death of Hitler as an example which demonstrates that facts exist separate from interpretation. The fact is that Hitler died. But "are we to argue that the history of this even is the meaning given to it by those Nazis who were most closely identified with him? Or should we say it is the meaning given to it by those Jews who were persecuted and survived? Or is the true meaning apprehended by the German people?" This example shows that "there is no *one* significance to any event. There may be as many meanings attributed to it as there are persons who interpret it. But it is precisely this diversity of interpretation *that forces us to use the rough distinction between fact and interpretation*. By using this distinction, we indicate that although the death of Hitler meant many different things to different people, his death was a fact alike for Nazis, Jews, Germans, Russians, and English historians." Likewise, "The life and death of Jesus have one sort of importance as events in the history of religions, another from the standpoint of Roman provincial justice, still another as an illustration of man's inhumanity to man, and still another as a disclosure of the meaning of life and death."[58] Harvey concludes that perspectivistic apologetics—"Hard Perspectivism"—is "the denial of self-transcendence" or "the ability of human beings to enter imaginatively into possibilities of understanding and valuation not their own, to appreciate alien claims, to evaluate and assess them, and to commit oneself to them."[59]

In contrast, it is this cultural and imaginative use of religion which the historian of religion can address. The canon and its exegesis provide an important focus for such study. One scholar has described the interest for historians of religion. They are fascinated by the "radical and arbitrary reduction" from a large range of possibilities into a limited list "represented by the notion of canon and the ingenuity represented by the rule-governed exegetical enterprise of applying the canon to every dimension of human life." Such application of the canon represents "that most characteristic, persistent, and obsessive religious activity," which is "at the same time, the most profoundly cultural human activity."[60]

What should Mormon historians do if such an enterprise seems to conflict with their faith? There are as many responses to that question as there are Mormon historians, although many resolutions have not been easy. Some move from Martin Marty's "primitive naivete" to his "second naivete."[61] Others conclude, as other Christian historians have, that they "can be a believer only at the price of sacrificing the standards of truth and honesty which have dominated the scholarly community since the Enlightenment."[62] While some make that sacrifice, others are compelled to make an odyssey into the lone and dreary world. Harvey's description of the difficulties for Christians in general is poignant: "It was, after all, Christianity itself which tutored the Western mind to believe that it should know the truth and the truth would make it free. But now that the student has learned to prize the truth, he has discovered, with pain both to himself and his teacher, that it can only be gained at the cost of rejecting the one who first instilled in him the love of it."[63] Not without significance, there are increasing numbers of non-Mormon historians who are fascinated by the colorful history and sincere people who call themselves Mormon. The result is a melody of voices that speaks the language of Mormon history.

Historiography is a marvelous debate based on pluralism in which historians discover, discuss, and examine various facts, events, warrants, and conclusions. Apologists do them a service when they challenge their methodology, because they must constantly keep it in good repair and relevant. And they are compelled to remind apologists, as one scholar has succinctly put the matter, that "any attempt to give a theological appraisal of historic facts means a transgression from historic study to theology."[64]

NOTES

1. James B. Allen and Glen M. Leonard observe: "Unlike many advocates of the primitive gospel movement, the Saints did not believe the Bible was an infallible, final religious authority. They agreed with the Campbellites that the King James Bible required correction, but also claimed new revelation to restore lost truths" (*The Story of the Latter-day Saints* [Salt Lake City: Deseret Book, 1976], 66). See also Marvin S. Hill, *Quest for Refuge: The Mormon Flight from American Pluralism* (Salt Lake City: Signature Books, 1989); and F. L. Cross and E. A. Livingstone, eds., *The Oxford Dictionary of the Christian Church*, 2 ed. (Oxford: Oxford University Press, 1983), 409.

2. See F. Henry Edwards, "Introduction" in *Joseph Smith's "New Translation" of the Bible*, ed. Paul A. Wellington (Independence, MO: Herald Publishing House, 1970), 27-115.

In Joseph Smith's additional text for Genesis 50 the biblical Joseph identifies Smith as a "choice seer" who will produce the Book of Mormon "in the latter days." This portion of Smith's restoration was based on the already-published 2 Nephi 3:6-18. However, the Bible addition omits 2 Nephi 3:8, which limits Smith's mission to the production of the Book of Mormon. A verse similar to the one in 2 Nephi also appeared in the Book of Commandments: "and he has a gift to translate the book, and I have commanded him that he shall pretend to no other gift, for I will grant him no other gift" (BC 4:2). This verse was later altered in the Doctrine and Covenants: "And you have a gift to translate the plates; and this is the first gift that I bestowed upon you; and I have commanded that you should pretend to no other gift until my purpose is fulfilled in this" (D&C 5:4).

In Smith's addition for Isaiah 29 (based on the already-published 2 Nephi 27) Isaiah provides a detailed prophecy of the history of the production of the Book of Mormon, specifically pointing out that the gold plates would be invisible except through the "power" and "will of God." By that means "three witnesses" and another "few" would "behold" and "view" them (v. 17). The "Testimony of the Three Witnesses" had already declared that "we have seen the engravings which are upon the plates; and they have been shown unto us by the power of God, and not of man." Smith described this process more clearly in Moses 1:11, in which Moses declares: "But now mine own eyes have beheld God; but not my natural, but my spiritual eyes, for my natural eyes could not have beheld." Martin Harris, one of the Three Witnesses, concurred, declaring that he had seen the plates only through spiritual means (see Marvin S. Hill, "Brodie Revisited: A Reappraisal," *Dialogue: A Journal of Mormon Thought* 7 [Winter 1972]: 83).

3. Dean C. Jessee, ed., *The Personal Writings of Joseph Smith* (Salt Lake City: Deseret Book, 1984), 83.

4. See my forthcoming book, *"The Papyrus Which Has Lived": The Joseph Smith Papyri and the Book of Abraham*, esp. chap. 2.

5. "When the translation of these valuable documents will be completed, I am unable to say; neither can I give you a probable idea of how large volumes they will make; but judging from their size, and the comprehensiveness of the language, one might reasonably expect to see a sufficient to develop much upon the mighty acts of the ancient men of God, and of his dealing with the children of men when they saw him face to face" (*Messenger and Advocate* 2:236).

6. Hill, *Quest for Refuge*, chaps. 3-4.

7. See Ashment, *An Introduction to the Book of Abraham*, chap. 2. As editor of the *Times and Seasons*, John Taylor later enticed renewals from many who first subscribed to the periodical "at the time when the translations from the Book of Abraham commenced," by stating that "we had the promise of Br. Joseph, to furnish us with further extracts from the Book of Abraham" (*Times and Seasons* 4 [1 Feb. 1843]: 95).

8. Edwards, "Introduction," 18, 19.

9. James Clark, *The Story of the Pearl of Great Price* (Salt Lake City: Bookcraft, 1955), 186ff.

10. Edward H. Ashment, "Making the Scriptures 'Indeed One in Our Hands,'" in *The Word of God: Essays on Mormon Scripture*, ed. Dan Vogel (Salt Lake City: Signature Books, 1990), 237, 253f.

11. None of the restored records that have "come forth from the dust" of Nag Hammadi and Qumran has found its way into either denomination's canon. See speculations about such a possibility in Hugh Nibley, *Since Cumorah: The Book of Mormon in the Modern World* (Salt Lake City: Deseret Book, 1967).

12. Nibley, *Since Cumorah*, v.

13. *Times and Seasons* 3 (1 Mar. 1842): 704; Hugh Nibley, *Abraham in Egypt* (Salt Lake City: Deseret Book, 1981), x, 1.

14. Nibley, *Since Cumorah*, v.

15. Louis Midgley, "The Challenge of Historical Consciousness: Mormon History and the Encounter with Secular Modernity," in *By Study and Also by Faith*, eds. John M. Lundquist and Stephen D. Ricks, vol. 2 (Salt Lake City: Deseret Book, 1990), 510. Similarly Alan Goff declares that "We

Latter-day Saints are in a position to accept the Bible and the Book of Mormon not only as literature but also as scripture and history. To insist that the text is only one or the other of the alternatives is to diminish it; to insist that the book has no power to transcend our own understanding or expectations about the book constrains us to what we think at the moment, without recognizing possibilities for growth" ("A Hermeneutic of Sacred Texts: Historicism, Revisionism, Positivism, and the Bible and Book of Mormon," M.A. thesis, Brigham Young University, 1989, 43). Stephen E. Robinson points out that there are "only two [interpretive issues] that are determinative for the Latter-day Saint view of scripture: the guidance of living prophets and the witness of the Holy Spirit." To separate the "scriptural texts from the interpretation of the apostles and prophets" would be "from a Latter-day Saint perspective a crippled view of scripture" ("Review of *The Word of God: Essays on Mormon Scripture*, ed. Dan Vogel," in *Review of Books on the Book of Mormon*, eds. Daniel C. Peterson and Shirley S. Ricks, vol. 3 [Provo, UT: Foundation for Ancient Research and Mormon Studies, 1991], 313).

    16. David Hackett Fischer, *Historians' Fallacies: Toward a Logic of Historical Thought* (New York: Harper Torchbooks, 1970), 12.

    17. The following books provide good summaries of the development of the Christian canon: Norman Perrin and Dennis C. Duling, *The New Testament: An Introduction*, 2d ed. (San Diego: Harcourt, Brace, Jovanovich, 1982), 435-46; James H. Charlesworth, ed., *Apocalyptic Literature and Testaments*, vol. 1 of *The Old Testament Pseudepigrapha* (Garden City, NY: Doubleday & Company, Inc., 1983), xxiii-xxiv; and Cross and Livingstone, *Oxford Dictionary*, 232.

    18. See Roland H. Bainton, "The Bible in the Reformation," in *The Cambridge History of the Bible: The West from the Reformation to the Present Day*, ed. S. L. Greenslade (Cambridge: Cambridge University Press, 1963), 6-9; Cross and Livingstone, *The Oxford Dictionary*, 70f.

    19. Cross and Livingstone, *The Oxford Dictionary*, 1392, xxiv.

    20. Van Harvey, *The Historian and the Believer: The Morality of Historical Knowledge and Christian Belief* (Philadelphia: Westminster Press, 1966), 229, 219. Jonathan Smith notes that in religious studies "unique" is "phoenix-like": "it expresses that which is *sui generis, singularis*, and, therefore, *incomparably* valuable. 'Unique' becomes an ontological rather than a taxonomic category; an assertion of a radical difference so absolute that it becomes 'Wholly Other,' and the act of comparison is perceived as both an impossibility and an impiety." He further observes that the "uniqueness" of the "death and resurrection of Jesus" is really a "double claim": "On the ontological level, it is a statement of the absolutely alien nature of the divine protagonist (*monogenes*) and the unprecedented (and paradoxical) character of his self-disclosure; on the historical level, it is an assertion of the radical

incomparability of the Christian 'proclamation' with respect to the 'environment.' For many scholars of early Christianity, the latter claim is often combined with the former, so as to transfer the (proper, though problematic) theological affirmation of absolute uniqueness to an historical statement that, standing alone, could never assert more than relative uniqueness, that is to say, a quite ordinary postulation of difference. It is this illicit transfer from the ontological to the historical that raises the question of the comparison of early Christianity and the religions of Late Antiquity" (*Drudgery Divine: On the Comparison of Early Christianities and the Religions of Late Antiquity* [Chicago: University of Chicago Press, 1990], 38).

21. It is curious, for example, that the Book of Mormon proclaims anachronistically that the brass plates contained "the five books of Moses," the histories, and "the prophecies of the holy prophets," including "many prophecies which have been spoken by the mouth of Jeremiah" (1 Ne. 5:11-13). Consequently, they would represent evidence that the text of the Pentateuch was completed before the time of Ezra. Yet the "full predominance of the Torah, seen as Mosaic law, comes from about the fifth century: it is still not there in Jeremiah, in Ezekiel, or in the latter parts of the Book of Isaiah; in Ezra-Nehemiah, however, in rough terms, it is already there." Moreover, the "religious recognition of much of [the later prophets] may have been earlier than the recognition of the supremacy of the Torah" (James Barr, *Holy Scripture: Canon, Authority, Criticism* [Philadelphia: Westminster Press, 1983], 52f).

22. Harvey, *The Historian and the Believer*, 5.

23. Ibid., 28.

24. Jonathan Z. Smith, *Imagining Religion: From Babylon to Jonestown* (Chicago: University of Chicago Press, 1982), 43.

25. Louis Midgley, "More Revisionist Legerdemain and the Book of Mormon," in *Review of Books on the Book of Mormon*, eds. Daniel C. Peterson and Shirley S. Ricks, vol. 3 (Provo, UT: Foundation for Ancient Research and Mormon Studies, 1991), 505.

26. Harvey, *The Historian and the Believer*, 105f.

27. Gary F. Novak, "Naturalistic Assumptions and the Book of Mormon," *Brigham Young University Studies* 30 (Summer 1990): 35.

28. Midgley, "The Challenge of Historical Consciousness," 525. Novak articulates the spiritual dilemma this way: "From the very beginning, the Book of Mormon has served as a vessel of memory and identity for the Saints. It sets them apart from the world and orients them in God's plan. If the Book of Mormon is true, if it is authentic history brought forth in the last days for the wise purposes of God, then the Saints have good reason for faith and a genuine hope for a trust in God. If the Book of Mormon is the product of deliberate deception or the sincere psychological delusion caused by

severe stress, *the Saints have no reason for faith or for hope*" ("Naturalistic Assumptions," 35).

29. Midgley, "The Challenge of Historical Consciousness," 526.

30. In this context, see Goff, "A Hermeneutic of Sacred Texts," 1-42; Midgley, "More Revisionist Legerdemain," 261-311; and esp. Robinson, "Review of *The Word of God*," 312-18.

31. Midgley, "The Challenge of Historical Consciousness," 505. See also Goff, "A Hermeneutic of Sacred Texts," 44, who cites Gadamer's assertion that "historicism . . . is based on the modern enlightenment and unknowingly shares it[s] prejudices."

32. Martin E. Marty, *Religion and Republic: The American Circumstance* (Boston: Beacon Press, 1987), 306; see also Harvey, *The Historian and the Believer*, 127. In modern Mormon terms, apologetic, believing historians rally to their leaders' summons to write only "faith-promoting history" (see Boyd K. Packer, *The Mantle is Far, Far Greater Than the Intellect* [Salt Lake City: The Church of Jesus Christ of Latter-day Saints, 1981], 4).

Robinson, a Brigham Young University professor of religion who castigates a collection of "empirical studies" on the Mormon canon "as a work of propaganda," would do well to analyze this morality of knowledge in the same way (see Robinson, "Review of *The Word of God*," 317). "Propaganda" is defined by the *Oxford English Dictionary* as: "The systematic propagation of information or ideas by an interested party, especially in a tendentious way in order to encourage or instil a particular attitude or response" (Sup. 3:837b). History that is "faith-promoting" seems to fit well within that definition.

33. Jaroslav Pelikan, *The Melody of Theology: A Philosophical Dictionary* (Cambridge: Harvard University Press, 1988), 70. See also Harvey, *The Historian and the Believer*, 127.

34. Smith, *Imagining Religion*, 104. Barr notes that the academy no longer was under control of the church, with the result that "theology itself could no longer count as the sole and absolute criterion for the evaluation of biblical studies" (*Holy Scripture*, 109).

35. Harvey, *The Historian and the Believer*, 39.

36. Pelikan, *The Melody of Theology*, 70. Goff claims that "a discussion of literary criticism, historiography, and method requires the adoption of a whole new vocabulary from [deconstructionist] philosophy," because "virtually all the social and humanistic disciplines face the prospect of having long-standing approaches questioned and overthrown" ("A Hermeneutic of Sacred Texts, 1).

37. Barr, *Holy Scripture*, 123.

38. See notes 27-29.

39. Midgley, "More Revisionist Legerdemain," 291; see also Midgley, "A Hermeneutic of Sacred Texts," 1-42. Midgley's proposition parallels

that of deconstructionist post-philosophers. See Kenneth Baynes, James Bohman, and Thomas McCarthy, *After Philosophy* (Cambridge, MA: The MIT Press, 1987), 2ff.

40. See Midgley, "A Hermeneutic of Sacred Texts," 1; Midgley, "More Revisionist Legerdemain," 295.

41. Robinson, "Review of the *Word of God*," 312, 313. On the other hand Stephen Ricks doubts that objectivity is even possible. To him it is "still the elusive—and unreachable—will-o'-the-wisp of many in the historical profession" ("Review of *Lehi in the Deseret, The World of the Jaredites, There Were Jaredites*," in *Review of Books on the Book of Mormon*, eds. Daniel C. Peterson and Shirley S. Ricks, vol. 2 [Provo: Foundation for Ancient Research and Mormon Studies, 1990], 130).

42. Midgley, "More Revisionist Legerdemain," 262n3, 295ff. Robinson refers to "five RLDS scholars and clerics who have already helped to 'correct' the views of that denomination" by infusing it with "liberal Protestant theology" ("Review of the *Word of God*," 312).

43. Norman F. Cantor and Richard I. Schneider, *How to Study History* (New York: Thomas Y. Cromwell Co., 1967), 255.

44. Ibid., 255, 256.

45. Ibid., 258.

46. Fischer, *Historians' Fallacies*, 42n4, identifies five categories of relativist error:

"First, there is a confusion between the way knowledge is acquired and the validity of that knowledge. An American historian may chauvinistically assert that the United States declared its independence from England in 1776. That statement is true, *no matter what the motives of its maker may have been*. On the other hand, an English historian may patriotically insist that England declared its independence from the United States in 1776. That assertion is false, and always will be.

"Second, relativism mistakenly argues that because all historical accounts must be partial in the sense of incomplete, that they must also be partial in the sense of false. An incomplete account can be an objectively true account; it cannot be the whole truth. In this respect, the relativists continued to bootleg the idea of telling the whole truth in their work.

"Third, relativism makes false distinctions between history and the natural sciences. Beard in particular did this, and his error consisted in rendering a special judgment upon historical science for its use of hypotheses, etc., which are also characteristic of natural science. Arthur Danto comments, 'It is as though a man were to lament that it is a sad thing to be a Frenchman, for all Frenchmen die. . . . History is no more and no less subject to relativistic factors than science is' (Danto, p. 110). Mannheim made the same error in *Ideology and Utopia* (p. 79).

"Fourth, relativists all argue that they and their friends were exempt from relativism in some degree. Thus, Beard's special pleading for an economic interpretation; and Mannheim's, for the intelligentsia. Both scholars were inconsistent, and understandably so. Cushing Strout has observed that 'a consistent relativism is a form of intellectual suicide' (*The Pragmatic Revolt in American History: Carl Becker and Charles Beard* [New Haven, 1958], p. 84).

"Finally the idea of subjectivity which the relativists used was literal nonsense. 'Subjective' is a correlative term which cannot be meaningful unless its opposite is also meaningful. To say that all knowledge is subjective is like saying that all things are short. Nothing can be short, unless something is tall. So, also, no knowledge can be subjective unless some knowledge is objective. (See Christopher Blake, "Can History Be Objective?" *Mind* 72 [1955]: 61-78.)"

47. Allan Bloom, *The Closing of the American Mind* (New York: Simon and Schuster, 1987), 379. For a discussion of Goff's type of deconstructionist radical hermeneutics as canonical criticism, see Barr, *Holy Scripture*, 76ff.

48. Goff, "A Hermeneutic of Sacred Texts," 1.

49. Cantor and Schneider, *How to Study History*, 258.

50. Harvey, *The Historian and the Believer*, 205-207. In a Mormon context, Robinson, for example, claims that "as both the scriptures and the philosophers know, genuine faith is belief in the absence of evidence or even belief that contradicts the evidence" ("Review of *The Word of God*," 316).

51. Ibid., 209-12.

52. Ibid., 212, 213.

53. Thus Mormon apologists plead positivistically to "let Joseph Smith speak for himself."

54. Harvey, *The Historian and the Believer*, 213, 214.

55. Ibid.

56. Ibid., 215, 216.

57. Midgley, "More Revisionist Legerdemain," 263, 299.

58. Harvey, 217, 219.

59. Ibid., 221.

60. Smith, *Imagining Religion*, 43.

61. Marty, *Religion and Republic*, 308.

62. Harvey, *The Historian and the Believer*, 308.

63. Ibid., 246.

64. C. J. Bleeker, *The Rainbow: A Collection of Studies in the Science of Religions*, Studies in the History of Religions (Supplements to Numen), vol. 30 (Leiden: E. J. Brill, 1975), 23.

Epilogue:
Myth, Symbol, and Truth

Leonard J. Arrington

MY PATH OF COMMITMENT TO AND BELIEF IN THE CHURCH OF JESUS
Christ of Latter-day Saints developed around four basic religious
questions I encountered as I grew up. First, is there a living God?
Second, was Jesus a teacher worthy to be worshipped? Third, was
Joseph Smith a prophet deserving of allegiance? And fourth, is our
Latter-day Saint culture meritorious—worth defending and working
for?

As these questions may reveal, I believed the intellect to be
enormously important—more important than the heart, more important than tradition. If my mind could not confirm the truth of my
religion, I felt I would be unsettled and apprehensive. Nevertheless,
I felt very comfortable with poetry, music, art, drama, testimony,
ritual, ceremony, and other expressions of religious feeling and
thought. I was also comfortable with people who contended that
religion was a matter of spirit, not mind, and that testimonies could
come only through the assurance of the Holy Ghost.

My struggle with the first question began when I was a
freshman at the University of Idaho and continued until the third
year of graduate school. I acted as a believer, willing to assume there
was a loving and powerful Creator. But I was not satisfied until I had
studied the matter through and came to a conviction that my intellectual could defend. My first satisfying experience was with Lowell
Bennion's *What about Religion?* This manual, used in the church's
Mutual Improvement Association for the youth, taught a crucial
truth, namely that the restored gospel represents truth and enlightenment, not superstition and ignorance. Scholarship and education

are part of the gospel; Mormonism undertakes to foster the discovery and spread of truth; God has commanded that we study and learn and become acquainted with all good books; the glory of God is intelligence; and it is impossible for a man or woman to be saved in ignorance (Doctrine and Covenants 90:15; 93:36; 88:118; 131:6). The manual also quoted with approval Brigham Young's statements in the *Journal of Discourses* that we accept truth no matter where it comes from, that Mormonism comprises all truth, and that there is an indissoluble relationship between religion and learning (1:334; 11:375; 15:160). These became articles of my religious faith and continue to remain so.

When I went to the university, my roommate, anxious to test my mettle, provoked me into reading *Why We Behave Like Human Beings*, by George A. Dorsey. This widely read treatise by a noted anthropologist and behavioral scientist gave a rather mechanistic interpretation of the ultimate questions and was not intended to inculcate faith in religion. Men and women were little more than complete biophysical machines. The book did not make me cynical, as it apparently had done to my roommate, but it did help to keep alive within me a quest for certainty. I vividly remember one phrase from it. Dorsey quoted Dr. John B. Watson, the famous behaviorist, as saying that thinking was no more than "laryngeal itch." That stimulated me to read several books on organic evolution, including *On the Origin of Species* and *The Descent of Man*, by Charles Darwin.

Dissatisfied with the superficial and uninformed views that were being conveyed in certain publications to which I was referred, I concentrated on the works of philosophers. First I read *The Story of Philosophy*, by Will Durrant, which introduced me to the names of the most prominent persons who had pondered the great issues. For the same purpose I read C. E. M. Joad's *Guide to Philosophy* and Wilhelm Windelband's brilliant but tedious *History of Philosophy*. I then systematically read some of the great thinkers—Plato, Aristotle, Thomas Aquinas, Spinoza, Immanuel Kant, Josiah Royce, and William James. I read some philosophical novels: Somerset Maugham's *Of Human Bondage* and George Santayana's *The Last Puritan*. I read Robert Shafer's *Christianity and Naturalism* and George Santayana's *Reason in Religion*. I read the autobiographies of St. Augustine, John Henry Newman, and John Stuart Mill. I read several books that reviewed what the great thinkers had said about God, humanity, and the universe, and had personal experiences that confirmed their views in an intimate way. By the time I began my third year of graduate work, I had satisfied myself about the existence of God. And my religious experiences in my mature years have merely served to corroborate what I had then come to believe. While philosophers have not always argued that the existence of God is demonstrable, they have presented arguments that have been persuasive to me. My experiences suggests that Francis Bacon was correct when he contended that "a little philosophy inclineth man's mind to atheism; but depth in philosophy bringeth men's minds about to religion."

My conceptions of Jesus emerged when I was still in high school. I must confess that I read the Bible through when I was thirteen but, country boy that I was, I was turned off by the King James Version, which was to me a strange and unfamiliar idiom. When I went to the university, George Tanner, my LDS Institute of Religion instructor, gave direction to my search for Jesus as a person, as a leader. He introduced me to new translations of the Bible, and I read through the New Testament version of James Moffatt and Edgar Goodspeed, and Richard G. Moulton's *Modern Reader's Bible*. These were very helpful and I still often use them. At his suggestion I also read Shirley Jackson Case's *Jesus: A New Biography*, Ernest Renan's *The Life of Jesus*, Albert Schweitzer's *The Quest for the Historical Jesus*, and James E. Talmage's *Jesus the Christ*. All of these persuaded me that Jesus was, indeed, a historical figure, that the values he taught were superior to anything humanity had ever devised, that Jesus was indeed a divine person, and that his life provided a model worth imitating in meeting today's difficult problems.

As to Joseph Smith, I am grateful that I was not introduced to some of the views of his philosophy and theology that are being advocated today—views of his life and thought that clash with impressions I have acquired and confirmed in my years of research in the Church Historian's Office. I was very fortunate in having been given, as a teenager, John Henry Evans's book *Joseph Smith, An American Prophet*. I read the books while still in high school and was very impressed with the prophet. I remember giving some two-and-one-half minute talks that were based on the book. Unquestionably Joseph had a marvelous intellect and also acute spiritual sensitivity. He honestly sought to resolve the many intellectual, spiritual, social, and personal problems that arose in his lifetime. He was an imaginative thinker and leader. He accepted truth from many sources. And he had good values; people were more important than money, and the law of eternal progression pointed us all in the right direction.

What about the prophet's accounts of his own experiences: the first vision? the visit of the angel Moroni to tell him about the golden plates of the Book of Mormon? the return of John the Baptist to confer the Aaronic Priesthood, and of Peter, James, and John to confer the Melchizedek? Can one accept all of the miraculous events that surrounded the restoration of the gospel? I was fortunate to have read Santayana's *Reason in Religion* before confronting these historical problems. I do not say that I fully understood it or that I agreed with his basic premise, but the book gave me a concept that has been helpful ever since—that truth may be expressed not only through science and abstract reason but also through stories, testimonies, and narratives of personal experience; not only through erudite scholarship but also through poetry, drama, and historical novels. Santayana used the term "myth"—a term well understood in recent religious literature—to refer to the expression of religious and moral truths in symbolic language.

The worth "myth" has some pejorative connotations in modern English. It can mean a story of belief asserted to be true but without any basis in fact. It can be an invented explanation of some natural or historical phenomenon or a wholly fictitious supposition or belief. However, this is not what Santayana had in mind. What he called myth was a traditional account of events and happenings that have religious significance. To say that something is a myth is not to say that it was deliberately fabricated but to identify it as an account that may or may not have a determinable basis of fact or natural explanation. The truth of a myth is beyond empirical or historical accessibility. Examples are the Christian story of the Resurrection, the Virgin Birth, and the creation of the world as described in the Book of Genesis. These are ways of explaining events or truths having religious significance that may be either symbolical or historical.

To go one step further, even in the Shakespearean tragedy where, unlike episodes of Mormon and Christian history the characters and events are wholly fictional, one can find philosophical and religious truth. Examples of novels disclosing religious truths that I had read during the formative stages of my religious beliefs include:

Pearl Buck's *The Good Earth*, Knut Hamsun's *Growth of the Soil*, William Henry Hudson's *Green Mansions*, Fyodor Dostoyevsky's *Brothers Karamazov* and *Crime and Punishment*, and Leo Tolstoy's *Anna Karenina* and *War and Peace*. And, for that matter, the philosophical drama in the Old Testament's Book of Job.

Because of my introduction to the concept of symbolism as a means of expressing religious truth, I was never preoccupied with the question of the historicity of Joseph Smith's first vision—though I find the evidence overwhelming that it did occur—or of the many reported epiphanies in Mormon, Christian, or Hebrew history. I am prepared to accept them as historical or as metaphorical, as symbolical, or as precisely what happened. That they convey religious truth is the essential issue, and of this I have never had any doubt. Ineffable experiences, messages, and value affirmations do not always lend themselves to scientific, literal, or precise articulation. It does not bother me at all that, in describing a religious experience that transcends his or her ability to express it, a narrator, a testimony-giver, often resorts to traditional phrases in presenting it. Indeed, I do it myself, as those who have heard me speak in testimony meetings can vouch. The Italians have a useful expression for this sort of thing: *"Se non e vero, e ben trovato,"* which means, roughly, "Whether it is literally true or not, it is still true."

This brings me to my fourth basic question: Are Mormon values, policies, practices, and leadership sufficiently superior to justify a lifetime of devotion? Can one work as effectively in furthering the work of God through Mormonism as through other causes? I came to the conclusion that Mormonism was indeed a positive influence worth contributing to and perpetuating.

In 1985 Alfred Knopf published *Brigham Young: American Moses*. In preparing that biography I learned that Brigham saw and read the Book of Mormon in 1830, when he was twenty-nine. Why then did he wait almost two years before joining the infant Church of Christ, as it was then called? When asked to explain this, he replied that he wanted time to observe the character of those who were leading the movement. "I watched," he said, "to see whether good common sense was manifest" (*Journal of Discourses* 8:38). After twenty-two months of observation and investigation, he decided that the movement did indeed manifest "good sense." He joined in 1832 and spent the rest of his life laboring on its behalf.

My examination of Mormon cultural institutions did not begin until 1941, when I was twenty-three and in my second year of graduate work. This study was the result of my surprising discovery at that time that there was a historically based Mormon culture. I had grown up on a farm in a non-Mormon community in southwestern Idaho, the son of parents who had grown up in North Carolina, Tennessee, southern Indiana, and Oklahoma. Neither parent had had any experience with the Mormon way of life. There were no Mormon schoolteachers or administrators in our local school system, and none of our close neighbors was Mormon.

Then I went to the University of Idaho, where there were few Mormons in attendance. (At that time, most Idaho Mormons went to Brigham Young University or to Utah State University in Logan.) After four years in Moscow, Idaho, I went to the University of North Carolina in Chapel Hill where I was the only Latter-day Saint in the university and the community. So all these years I was outside the Mormon cultural community.

My major at the University of North Carolina was economic theory. While doing some teaching at North Carolina State University in Raleigh, I took a minor in agricultural economics and rural sociology. One day, as I was perusing some books for a class, I happened to come across a description of the Mormon village in a new book on *The Sociology of Rural Life*, by the young sociology T. Lynn Smith. I did not know at the time that T. Lynn was a Latter-day Saint and a graduate of BYU, but I was absolutely fascinated with his pages on the Mormon village—something I had never heard of before. I hunted for discussions on the subject in other texts and was delighted to find that Mormon rural life was of great interest to sociologists.

About the same time, partly as the result of the curiosity aroused by discovery that there was a recognized Mormon rural life pattern, I ran across an article by Bernard DeVoto in *Harper's Magazine* which was about his grandfather, a Mormon farmer who had lived at Uinta, southeast of Ogden; and also two articles by Juanita Brooks, whom I had not heard of before, that were also in *Harper's*: "The Water's In" and "A Close-Up of Polygamy." These introduced me to the literature on Mormon culture—something I had not been aware of because I had not grown up in Utah or in a Mormon village. Basically, I have spent the rest of my life trying to keep abreast of this literature and trying to make some contributions myself to that body of writing.

My study of this literature very quickly told me that Mormon culture was praiseworthy—that my people did indeed believe in education and were willing to sacrifice to put their children through college; that Mormon educators were remarkably loyal to the church, were well respected, and sought to preserve the best values of the culture; that the people were not provincial but, partly because of missionary contacts, had an interest in the peoples of the world; and among the influential leaders of the faith were a number of impressive intellectuals. This was a great church, I came to believe. It perpetuated fine ideals of home, school, and community life; its approach and philosophy enabled its members to reconcile religion with science and higher learning; its strong social tradition taught its members to be caring and compassionate; and its strong organizational capability empowered its people to build better communities. As Brigham Young said, a central doctrine of Mormonism is that God's primary work is through people, and so our principal concern was with the here and now.

In short, it *was* a religion and a church worth working for. I went into the American armed services soon after reaching these conclusions, and upon my return at the end of World War II, I expected to live in a Mormon village to rear my children and to perform my life's labor.

After three years overseas in North Africa and Italy, I did return, obtained a professorship at Utah State University in the Mormon village of Logan, and remained there to rear our family in what Grace and I always regarded as sacred space, because in Logan we actually experienced the way of life we had read and dreamed about. Except for three sabbaticals, we did not leave our beloved Cache Valley until I was called to be Church Historian in 1972. With my appointment, as well as the appointments of others to the historical department, we inaugurated a number of books on aspects of Latter-day Saint history; began a series of important edited documents, beginning with Brigham Young's letters to his sons; discovered and catalogued previously unknown historical materials; assisted archivists with the preparation of registers and guides to archive collections; gave papers on LDS history at historical conventions; and produced articles for church magazines, professional journals, and encyclopedias. In my capacity as Church Historian I was able to examine the most intimate records of the church—records that are replete with faith-promoting incidents that served to strengthen my belief in the divinity of the latter-day work. Particularly meaningful to me was my private knowledge of the divine circumstances that led up to the announcement in 1978 by the First Presidency that the priesthood might be conferred on all worthy males without regard to race or color.

Although now released from the position of Church Historian, I am still devoted to carrying out responsibilities that I trust continue to help build the Kingdom of God on earth. Many satisfying spiritual experiences, as well as my continued study of the Saints and their leaders throughout our history, have intellectually and emotionally validated my decision to serve the faith that I committed myself to many years ago, and that I believe to be based on true principles. "Blessed is he who has found his work," wrote Thomas Carlyle; "he need to ask no other blessedness."

CONTRIBUTORS

LEONARD J. ARRINGTON served as Church Historian of the Church of Jesus Christ of Latter-day Saints for ten years beginning in 1972. He is author of *Great Basin Kingdom: An Economic History of the Latter-day Saints, 1830-1900* and *Brigham Young: American Moses.* "Myth, Symbol, and Truth" first appeared in *Sunstone* 10 (Jan. 1985): 36-38 as "Why I Am a Believer," and later appeared under the same name in *A Thoughtful Faith: Essays on Belief by Mormon Scholars*, edited by Philip L. Barlow (Centerville, UT: Canon Press, 1986), 225-33.

EDWARD H. ASHMENT, former coordinator of translation services for the Church of Jesus Christ of Latter-day Saints, studied Egyptology at the University of Chicago. "Historicity of the Canon" is published here for the first time.

DAVID EARLE BOHN is professor of political science at Brigham Young University in Provo, Utah. "Unfounded Claims and Impossible Expectations: A Critique of New Mormon History" is a revised and expanded revision of "No Higher Ground," *Sunstone* 8 (May-June 1983): 26-32; "The Burden of Proof," *Sunstone* 10 (June 1985): 2-3; "Our Own Agenda," *Sunstone* 14 (June 1990): 45-49.

RICHARD L. BUSHMAN is Gouverneur Morris Professor of History at Columbia University and author of *Joseph Smith and the Beginnings of Mormonism.* "Faithful History" first appeared in *Dialogue: A Journal of Mormon Thought* 4 (Winter 1969): 11-28.

PAUL M. EDWARDS, director of the Temple School, Reorganized Church of Jesus Christ of Latter Day Saints, Independence, Missouri, is author of *Preface to Belief: A Philosophical Inquiry into RLDS Beliefs*. "The Irony of Mormon History" was first published in *Utah Historical Quarterly* 41 (Autumn 1973): 393-409.

ROBERT B. FLANDERS is professor of history at Southern Missouri State University in Springfield. He is author of *Nauvoo: Kingdom on the Mississippi*. "Some Reflections on the New Mormon History" first appeared in *Dialogue: A Journal of Mormon Thought* 9 (Spring 1974): 34-41.

LAWRENCE FOSTER is professor of history at the Georgia Institute of Technology in Atlanta. He is author of *Religion and Sexuality: Three American Communal Experiments of the Nineteenth Century*. "New Perspectives on the Mormon Past: Reflections of a Non-Mormon Historian" was first published in *Sunstone* 7 (Jan.-Feb. 1982): 41-45.

EDWIN S. GAUSTAD is professor of religious studies at the University of California, Riverside. He is author of *Dissent in American Religions* and editor of *Atlas of American Religion*. "History and Theology: The Mormon Connection" was first published in *Sunstone* 5 (Nov.-Dec. 1980): 44-50.

NEAL W. KRAMER is professor of English at Ricks College in Rexburg, Idaho. "Looking for God in History" first appeared in *Sunstone* 8 (Jan.-Mar. 1983): 15-17.

MARTIN E. MARTY is Fairfax M. Cone Distinguished Service Professor of the History of Modern Christianity at the University of Chicago. He is past president of the American Society of Church History and co-editor of *Church History*. "Two Integrities: An Address to the Crisis in Mormon Historiography" was first published in *Journal of Mormon History* 10 (1983): 3-20, and subsequently reprinted in his *Religion and Republic: The American Circumstance* (Boston: Beacon Press, 1982), 303-25, 377-78.

ROBERT C. MESLE is professor of philosophy and religion at Graceland College in Lamoni, Iowa. "History, Faith, and Myth" first appeared in *Sunstone* 7 (Nov.-Dec. 1982): 10-13.

LOUIS MIDGLEY is professor of political science at Brigham Young University. A version of "The Acids of Modernity and the Crisis in Mormon Historiography" was first published as "The Challenge of Historical Consciousness: Mormon History and the Encounter with Secular Modernity," in *By Study and by Faith: Essays in Honor of Hugh W. Nibley on the Occasion of His Eightieth Birthday*, eds. John M. Lundquist and Stephen D. Ricks (Salt Lake City: Deseret Book and FARMS, 1990), 2:502-51.

D. MICHAEL QUINN was professor of history at Brigham Young University in Provo, Utah, until 1988. Since then he has held research fellowships from the Huntington Library, the National Endowment for the Humanities, the American Academy of Arts and Sciences, and Indiana University-Purdue University at Indianapolis. His recent publications are *The New Mormon History: Revisionist Essays on the Past*; "Religion in the American West," in *Under an Open Sky: Rethinking America's Western Past*; "Mormon Women Have Had the Priesthood since 1843," in *Women and Authority: Re-emerging Mormon Feminism*; and "Plural Marriage and Mormon Fundamentalism," in *Fundamentalisms and Society: Reclaiming the Sciences, Education, and the Family*. "On Being a Mormon Historian (and Its Aftermath)" is published here for the first time with the author's permission.

KENT E. ROBSON is professor of philosophy at Utah State University in Logan. "Objectivity and History" first appeared in *Dialogue: A Journal of Mormon Thought* 19 (Winter 1986): 87-99.

RICHARD SHERLOCK is professor of philosophy at Utah State University in Logan. "The Gospel Beyond Time: Thoughts on the Relation of Faith and Historical Knowledge" was first published in *Sunstone* 5 (July-Aug. 1980): 20-23.

MELVIN T. SMITH is former director of the Utah State Historical Society and the Idaho State Historical Society. "Faithful History/Secular Religion" first appeared in *Journal of the John Whitmer Historical Association* 4 (1984): 51-58.

MALCOLM R. THORP is professor of history at Brigham Young University in Provo, Utah. "Some Reflections on New Mormon

History and the Possibilities of a 'New' Traditional History" was first published in *Sunstone* 15 (Nov. 1991): 39-46.